Developmental Psychology

A STUDENT'S HANDBOOK

Developmental Psychology

A STUDENT'S HANDBOOK

Margaret Harris
Royal Holloway University of London, UK

George Butterworth
University of Sussex, UK

Psychology Press
Taylor & Francis Group

HOVE AND NEW YORK

Published in 2002 by Psychology Press Ltd
27 Church Road, Hove, East Sussex, BN3 2FA

Reprinted 2004

http://www.psypress.co.uk

Simultaneously published in the USA and Canada
by Taylor & Francis Inc
29 West 35th Street, New York, NY 10001

Psychology Press is part of the Taylor & Francis Group

British Library Cataloguing in Publication Data
A catalogue record for this book is available from the British Library

ISBN 1-84169-110-0 (hbk)
ISBN 1-84169-192-5 (pbk)

Cover design by Richard Massing, Hove, East Sussex

Cover illustration is Rembrandt's 'Teaching a child to walk'.
Copyright © The British Museum

Typeset in the UK by Facing Pages, Southwick, West Sussex

Printed and bound in Spain by BookPrint S.L.

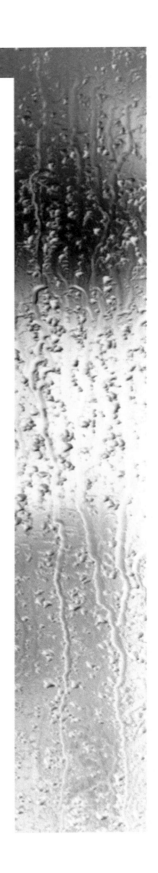

In memory of

George Esmond Butterworth

1946–2000

CONTENTS

About the authors

Margaret Harris was educated at Northampton School for Girls and Kettering High School. She gained her BSc in Psychology at Bedford College and her PhD at Birkbeck College, University of London. Margaret lectured at Birkbeck College and then became a Senior Lecturer and subsequently a Reader at Royal Holloway University of London. Her main research interests are in language development and reading, with an emphasis on the cognitive development of deaf children. Margaret is involved in several research projects investigating the early language development of children with severe/profound deafness. Her research has looked at the development of successful communication between deaf infants and their mothers and the implications of this for early sign and oral language development. She is particularly interested in the development of visual attention between deaf infants and their mothers and how this relates to early language development.

George Butterworth (1946–2000) completed a D.Phil at Oxford University after which he took up a teaching post at Southampton University. This was followed by a Chair in Psychology at Stirling University. He became a Professor at Sussex University in 1991. George was an authority on infant development and the origins of thought and perception in infants. His research interests were broad, encompassing topics as varied as the origins of self-awareness in human development and evolution, and children's understanding of geographical features of the Earth. George founded both the British Infancy Research Group and the journal *Developmental Science*. He was the first president of the European Society for Developmental Psychology and a former president of the British Psychological Society, Developmental Section. He was internationally respected for his scholarship and commitment to research.

Preface

Developmental psychology is an endlessly fascinating topic, not least because the 20th century saw such a radical transformation of our view of children. One hundred years ago nobody could have envisaged that babies are capable of learning before they are born or that, a few weeks after birth, they can do simple addition and subtraction. It would have been equally surprising to discover that four-year-olds can solve simple analogical reasoning problems. In this book we have tried to capture some of our own excitement about developmental psychology and the extraordinary achievement of human development.

There are many different ways to carve up development and whichever way one chooses is ultimately a compromise. In this book we have divided development both according to age and topic. Thus there are parts on prenatal development, infancy, the preschool years, and the school years; and chapters dealing with aspects of cognitive development and social development. In the school years part we also have separate chapters on the development of literacy and numeracy. Development does not, of course, divide up into these tidy packages, and many aspects of development could not be neatly fitted into our general plan. We had to consider two important issues.

The first issue concerns the division of development by age. Here there is a potential problem that, since development is a continuum, division according to age will be artificial. Also, there are important differences, both among children and within an individual child, in the course of development that make simple divisions according to age problematic. Children develop at different rates so children of similar ages may be at different levels in their social or cognitive functioning. Also, an individual child may be at one point in development for some abilities and at another point for other abilities. However, in spite of these problems, we wanted to emphasise that there are important features in common across development at particular ages, and we have tried to highlight these.

The second problem that we faced in planning this book was to describe the different facets of development. For the sake of simplicity, we chose to draw a broad distinction between social development and cognitive development. However, children typically develop their abilities within a social setting—at home, playgroup, or school—so that to think of cognition as separate from social development is an oversimplification. At the same time, the range and

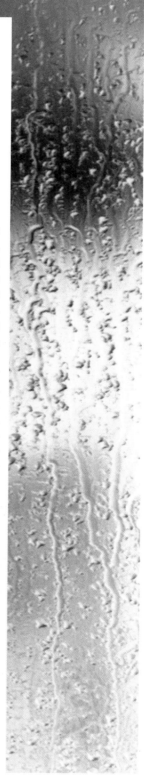

complexity of social interactions is, in part, determined by the children's cognitive level, so one could argue that understanding social development also requires some knowledge of developing cognitive skills.

This essential intertwining of social and cognitive development is reflected on the cover, which shows a drawing by Rembrandt of a young child being helped to walk by two adults. This drawing also depicts one of the adults pointing something out to the child. This simple act of pointing captures an important and unique aspect of human development—parents show their children things in the world. As far as we can tell, although the offspring of other species may learn from adults by watching their behaviour, it is only human beings who actively seek to teach their children and point out the delights of the world.

Margaret Harris
Oxford
October 2001

Part 1

A framework for developmental psychology

CHAPTER 1

CONTENTS

A brief history of developmental psychology

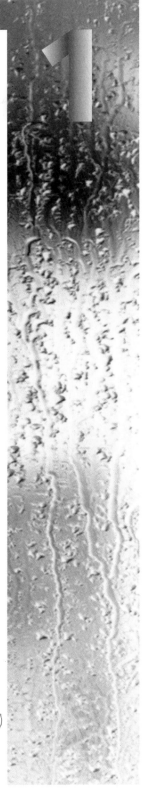

increase wealth
better hygiene
control of childhood disease

The scientific study of children's development began about 150 years ago. Until this comparatively recent period, Western societies did not study the childhood years—from the age of about seven to adolescence—even though early childhood had long been recognised as a distinct period in the life cycle. The coming of the industrial revolution in the 19th century provided an impetus for the systematic study of childhood since it brought with it an increasing need for basic literacy and numeracy in factory workers that was eventually met by the introduction of universal primary education. This, in turn, made it important to study the children's minds so that education itself could become more effective. Other social factors such as increased wealth, better hygiene, and the progressive control of childhood diseases meant that the chances of a baby surviving childhood and growing to adulthood were greatly increased. This increase in survival rates also contributed to a greater focus on understanding development throughout childhood.

The new-found wealth of Western society also extended the period of childhood. As the age at which children began work was gradually raised, the idea of adolescence—as a distinct stage interspersed between childhood and adulthood—became increasingly important. As the 20th century progressed, ever more sophisticated skills were required as technology advanced. This was reflected in a steep rise in the school leaving age. At the beginning of the century many children began work well before the age of 10 and a minimum school leaving age—15 years—was not introduced in the UK until 1944. By the end of the century this has increased to 16 years with many children continuing school education until they were 18. As the length and scope of education advanced, adolescence became an increasingly important area of study.

Although the age range covered by developmental psychology may have increased, the overarching aim of the subject has not fundamentally changed: This is to describe and explain the nature of developmental change from its starting point to its end point. As you will discover from this handbook, developmental psychology begins before birth with the growth of the foetus. It moves on to consider birth and infancy, passing through the preschool years and entry into school, and ending with the transitions from adolescence to adulthood. A fully rounded account of development will consider many inter-related aspects of developmental change including language and cognitive ability, motor skills, social and emotional development, and interaction with family members and peers.

Scientific explanations of development have one central principle: Developmental changes occur both as a result of growth and through the interaction of the child with the environment. Characterising the dynamic principles that underlie growth, self-organisation and increasing complexity are of fundamental importance in developmental explanation. Development involves changes that occur over time yet, despite change, there is also stability and continuity with the past as new aspects of self, behaviour, and knowledge are formed. How new ways of acting and new knowledge emerge from the interaction between elements of earlier levels of understanding and new experience is of central concern to many developmental theories.

Two major strands of influence can be discerned in developmental psychology. These reflect a concern with growth, on the one hand, and with the impact of environmental influences on the other. Concerns with developmental growth take some of their inspiration from the biology of growth and evolution, whereas other aspects of explanation—those concerned with the impact of the environment on the child—consider the ways in which different cultures and different patterns of childhood experience channel development. From this dual perspective we can see that the explanation of human development requires us not only to understand human nature—because development is a natural phenomenon—but also to consider the diverse effects that a particular society and a particular set of experiences have upon the developing child. Development is as much a matter of the child acquiring a culture as it is a process of biological growth. Contemporary theories of development make the connection between nature and culture, albeit with varying emphases and, of course, with various degrees of success.

In a recent review, Cairns (1998) argues that the biological roots of developmental psychology are the strongest. He identifies two core ideas in 19th-century biology that shaped the newly emerging science of developmental psychology. These are the developmental principle outlined by Karl Ernst von Baer (1792–1876) and the evolutionary theory of Charles Darwin (1809–1882).

The central principle of developmental psychology

Developmental change results from an interaction between biology ("nature") and experience ("nurture"). However, the interaction is a complex one because environmental factors can directly influence biological growth (e.g. brain growth) and genetic factors can influence the child's environment (e.g. a sociable child producing different reactions from others than an antisocial child).

The developmental principle

Von Baer, whose work is relatively unknown today to developmental psychologists, was a pioneer of comparative embryology. He was born in Estonia, where he began his career as a biologist. Later he moved to Russia before returning to Estonia at the end of his career.

Von Baer proposed that development proceeds in successive stages, from the more general to the more specific and from an initial state of relative homogeneity to one of increasing differentiation (Cairns, 1998). Von Baer's view of development was revolutionary when it was first advanced even though the notion of successive stages is widely accepted within modern developmental psychology. In order to understand the revolutionary nature of his views we need to understand the prevailing view of development that von Baer rejected.

When von Baer began his research, **preformationism** was part of the accepted view of development. In essence, preformationism claims that developmental transformations (such as those observed in the embryo) are illusory because the essential characteristics of an individual are fully predetermined at the outset of development. What changes is the size and inter-relation of parts within an organism but the essential properties are preset and predetermined. In other words, according to preformationism, development fails to bring about any new or novel properties. On this view, the course of development through childhood and into adulthood is fully specified at birth.

An alternative to preformationism in the 19th century was **recapitulationism**. The essential idea behind recapitulationism is that, in the embryonic period, organisms pass through the adult form of all species from which they have evolved (see Figure 1.1). Haeckel famously captured the essence of recapitulationism as "ontogeny recapitulates phylogeny", that is, the development of the individual re-enacts the development of the species. On this view, embryonic development could be seen as a "fast-forward replay of evolutionary history" (Cairns, 1998). Such a view inevitably leads to the conclusion that novel features can only be added in the terminal phase of development—what Haeckel (1874/1906) labelled the "biogenetic law".

Like evolution

Von Baer rejected both preformationism and recapitulationism. He showed, in his own research on embryological development in different species, that the embryos of related species are very similar to one another in their early stages of development as Haeckel had demonstrated (see Figure 1.1). However, von Baer found on closer observation that there were species-typical differences early in the course of development as well as in the final stages. (See Chapter 4, Development from Conception to Birth, for evidence about the early development of the human embryo.) Von Baer thus saw development as a continuing process of differentiation of organisation in which novel developments could occur at any point in development—on this basis he rejected Haeckel's biogenetic law.

Preformationism	Recapitulationism
• The essential characteristics of an organism are fully determined at the onset of development.	• The development of the individual re-enacts the development of the species.
• Observed developmental transformations are illusory.	• During the embryonic period organisms pass through the adult form of the species from which they evolved.
• The only real changes are the size and inter-relation of the parts within the organism.	• Novel features can only be added in the last phase of development.
• Development fails to bring about novel properties.	
• Development follows a predetermined course.	

FIG.1.1 Embryos of different species at three comparable stages of development.

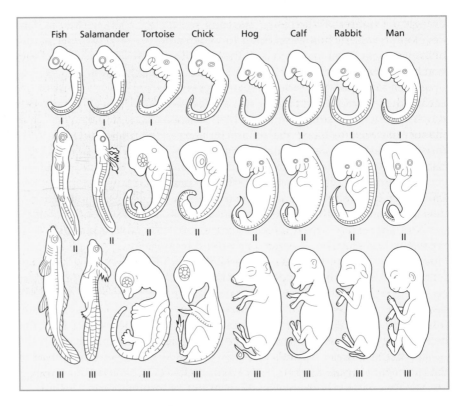

Von Baer's approach

• Rejected preformationism and recapitulationism.
• Development proceeds in successive stages.
• Development proceeds from the more general to the more specific.
• Development proceeds from relative homogeneity to increasing differentiation.
• Novel developments can occur at any point in development.

Although von Baer's work was not widely accepted in the 19th century—in part because he also espoused views of evolution that were counter to those of Darwin (see the next section, The Evolution of Development)—it did have a direct influence on developmental psychology in the following century. Von Baer's work was applauded by Herbert Spencer in his influential book, *A System of Synthetic Philosophy* (1886) and this, in turn, inspired the theorising of James Mark Baldwin. Baldwin's writing was an important influence on Jean Piaget (see The Emergence of Developmental Psychology, later in this chapter).

The evolution of development

Charles Darwin is often credited with establishing the scientific approach to developmental psychology. He was once described as having conquered developmental psychology in a single sweep. Darwin was particularly interested in the innate capacity for emotional expression and its subsequent early development. He closely observed the development of his own infant son, Doddy, who was born in 1840 (although Darwin did not publish his observations until 1877). Darwin studied emotions in Doddy between the second and fourth month of life and found definite evidence for anger, fear, surprise, and happiness. Darwin recorded some lovely observations. For example, he writes: "When about ten weeks old, he [Doddy] was given some rather cold milk and he kept a slight frown on his forehead all the time that he was sucking, so that he looked like a grown up person made cross." In another observation he says "When nearly four months old, and perhaps much earlier, there could be no doubt from the manner in which the blood gushed into his whole face and scalp, that he easily got into a violent passion."

Darwin and his son Doddy. Reprinted by permission of the Syndics of Cambridge University Library.

Darwin's observations on babies below two months of age are rather few but contemporary research suggests that newborn babies can perform seven facial expressions that are usually regarded as species specific and universal (happiness, sadness, surprise, interest, disgust, fear, and anger). It is nowadays claimed that these facial expressions can be reliably observed during standard hospital assessment procedures for newborns (Field, Healy, Goldstein, & Guthertz, 1990). (See Chapter 4, Development from Conception to Birth, for more information about the facial expressions of newborn babies.)

Darwin's studies of his infant son were intended to help him understand the evolution of innate forms of human communication. As we shall see, many basic developmental concepts, such as the idea that development can be understood as the progressive adaptation of the child to the environment, can be traced directly to Darwin and the influence of evolutionary theory. Another of Darwin's contributions was to introduce systematic methods to the study of development. The philosophical or anecdotal speculations of earlier theorists, such as Locke and Rousseau (see Fundamental Questions in Developmental Psychology, later in this chapter), were replaced by actual observations of developing children and this set the discipline on a scientific path.

The major biological foundations of developmental psychology were laid in the period between the publication of Darwin's theory of evolution in 1859 and the first decades of the 20th century. Darwin's theory of evolution located humans firmly in nature and made possible scientific questions about continuities and discontinuities between human beings and animals. Another effect of the Darwinian revolution was that people became curious about the biological origins of human nature. Evolutionary explanation led naturally to an emphasis on changes that occur as a function of time, both in the extremely long time scale of evolution and over the individual lifespan. Darwin's books on *The Origin of Species* (1859), *The Descent of Man* (1871), and *The Expression of Emotions in Men and Animals* (1872) raised questions about the origins of the human mind in the evolutionary past. They posed the challenging problem of the relation between individual development (**ontogeny**) and the evolution of the species (**phylogeny**).

Darwin's theory was vigorously popularised by the 19th-century embryologist, Ernst Haeckel, (1834–1919) who, as we have already noted, was impressed by the similar form taken by the embryos of many different species at certain times in their development. Somewhat paradoxically, given the major impact of Darwin on biology, the influence of Darwinism on the founding of

[handwritten margin note: ontogeny : ind dev Phylogeny : evolut of species]

developmental psychology has sometimes been interpreted as a negative factor (Charlesworth, 1992; Morss, 1990). Haeckel's principle of recapitulation encouraged the false idea that there exists a hierarchy of organisms in nature with humans at the top and other organisms arranged in strict sequence below—the so-called "scala naturae". This hierarchical view also encouraged the false idea that development (ontogeny) is a simple cumulative increase in capacities, rather than the complex, dynamic, and non-linear pattern of change that it has proved to be. It seems a little unfair to blame Darwin rather than Haeckel, however, since Darwin himself was never sure of the bases of heredity. In fact, when Darwin speculated on developmental questions he was characteristically cautious, insisting that his hypotheses were provisional but that they might be useful even if incomplete or wrong (Darwin, 1896/1967).

Today, it is no longer believed that "ontogeny recapitulates phylogeny" as Haeckel had argued. The more sophisticated view of the resemblance between different mammalian embryos is that the similarities reflect biological structures we still hold in common with our remote ancestors (Gould, 1977). Thus, there is no simple translation from the evolutionary past into present-day development. Nevertheless, clear stage-like changes in biological form led to the idea that other aspects of biological growth, such as cognitive and social development in humans, may also show distinct age-related stages in organisation.

The emergence of developmental psychology

The emergence of an independent developmental psychology is traditionally dated to 1882, with the publication of a book by the German physiologist, Wilhelm Preyer, entitled *The Mind of the Child* (1882/1888). This book was based on his observations of his own daughter and described her development from birth to two and a half years. Preyer insisted on proper scientific procedures, writing every observation down and noting the emergence of many abilities. He was particularly impressed by the importance of the extended period of curiosity evident in human infant development.

Wilhelm Preyer's work was translated into English in 1888, one of a burgeoning series of publications by then amounting to 48 full-scale empirical studies of children that had been carried out in Europe and the United States. The growing importance of developmental psychology as an independent discipline in the 1890s can be seen in the establishment of the first specialist scientific journals. *L'Annee Psychologique* was founded in 1894 by Binet and, in the USA, G. Stanley Hall (whose work we discuss later in this section) founded *Pedagogical Seminary* in 1891. In the same decade, the first research institutes devoted to the study of child development were set up at the Sorbonne and at Clark University. There was even a new term coined for this new field of study—paidoskopie. As Cairns (1998) points out, it is perhaps fortunate that this label did not survive even though the study of child development continued to go from strength to strength as the 20th century began.

Among other famous pioneers was Alfred Binet (1857–1911) who was working on experimental studies of thinking in young children in France. He is best known for developing the first intelligence test although, as Siegler

The French psychologist Alfred Binet (1857–1911).

(1992) has noted, "it is ironic that Binet's contribution should be so strongly associated with reducing intelligence to a single number, the IQ score, when the recurring theme of his research was the remarkable diversity of intelligence" (p. 175). As Cairns (1998) points out, the IQ test that Binet devised with Simon was primarily intended to provide a guide about how children might "learn to learn" rather than a system for classifying children according to intellectual level.

Binet had been critical of diagnoses of mental deficiency made by medical practitioners responsible for placing mentally retarded (learning disabled) children in special schools in Paris. The thrust of Binet's criticism was that no single sign of mental deficiency could reliably differentiate mentally retarded from normal children: In fact the same child might carry a different diagnosis, depending on which physician had made it. The urgent practical need for a valid and reliable test of intelligence led Binet to construct the **Binet–Simon scale**, which was published in 1905. Its main early application was to provide guidelines on the relative intellectual abilities and educational potential of mentally retarded children but his work was soon to find much wider application in education and training. Binet and Simon developed tests that were based on norms of performance for a given age and this soon led to the idea of a child's *mental age* as distinct from *chronological age* (see the box overleaf). Ten years later the idea of intelligence testing for children was well established outside France. In 1916, the now famous Stanford revision of Binet's test (known as the **Stanford–Binet test**) was published in the USA and, in Britain, Cyril Burt was developing a battery of reasoning tests for children that was inspired by Binet's techniques.

The importance of the Binet–Simon scale has rather overshadowed Binet's wider contribution to developmental psychology but he also made important advances in the study of children's cognition. Siegler (1992), in evaluating Binet's contribution to developmental psychology, suggests that he was an important pioneer in generating a unified theory of cognition and cognitive development. Binet's work was also very influential in making careful measurement a basic part of modern psychology. His intelligence scale laid the foundations for the extensive psychometric tests that are now widely used as a key aspect of assessment in education, clinical psychology, and other applied fields.

Among the most important, yet perhaps least well known, of the founders of present-day developmental psychology was the American, James Mark Baldwin (1861–1934). Baldwin made a major intellectual and administrative contribution to setting up scientific psychology. He was the founding editor of the first scientific psychology journal, *The Psychological Review* (1895), and was later editor of the important journal, *Psychological Bulletin*, and also one of the first presidents of the American Psychological Association (1897). He was influential in many ways in the new science of psychology, including establishing an international group of scholars who contributed to a four-volume *Dictionary of Philosophy and Psychology* (Baldwin, 1905). In 1903 a survey ranked Baldwin in the top five contributors to international research (Broughton & Freeman-Moir, 1982).

One of Baldwin's most important contributions to the founding of developmental psychology was made in the period from 1903 to 1908 when he was professor of philosophy and psychology at Johns Hopkins University. He

KEY TERMS
Binet–Simon scale: The first intelligence test developed by Alfred Binet, which contained a series of tasks of increasing difficulty. Performance on the scale could be compared with age norms to determine mental age.
Stanford–Binet test: The best-known US intelligence test. A revision of the Binet–Simon scale.

James Mark Baldwin
(1861–1934). Courtesy of
the Department of
Psychology, Indiana
University. Reprinted
with permission.

Mental age and IQ

The concept of mental age, which was first used by Binet, is best illustrated with some examples. Suppose that a child of exactly eight years of age is able to solve items in a test that are normally solved by children of the same age but is not able to solve items normally solved by older children. That child would be considered to have a mental age of eight years. However, if the same child consistently succeeded on test items normally solved by 10-year-olds, he or she would clearly be functioning intellectually at a mental age level that was above chronological age. In this case the child would be considered to have a mental age of 10 years. A child who is only able to solve items normally solved by younger children would have a mental age lower than chronological age.

The psychologist William Stern (1871–1938) devised the formula for calculating the **intelligence quotient** (IQ) which defines intelligence relative to age:

$$IQ = \frac{\text{Mental age}}{\text{Chronological age}} \times 100$$

In the example we have just considered, the eight-year-old with a mental age of 10 years would be credited with an IQ of: 10/8 x 100 = 125. Similarly a 12-year-old with a 15-year-old mental age would also have an IQ of 125 (15/12 x 100 = 125) because he or she would have the same relative standing in relation to age peers. A child who has a mental age that is the same as his/her chronological age is considered to be of average intelligence. This is because, on average, intellectual development in the population proceeds at the same rate as chronological age. Children of average intelligence have an IQ of 100.

published the first of a three-volume series entitled *Genetic Logic* (1915), a difficult work on the development of thinking in children. In this series Baldwin set out the foundations of a theory of the progressive development of knowledge in childhood. He proposed that development proceeds in a series of distinct stages that begin at birth, with innate motor reflexes, and progresses to the acquisition of language and logical thought. He proposed that moving through successive stages of development depends on feedback from the stimulating environment. In Baldwin's terminology the essential mechanisms for development were **assimilation** (incorporation of effects of the environment into the organism) leading to **accommodation** (plastic change) of the organism—concepts that form a central part of Piaget's theory of cognitive development (see Chapter 2, Developmental Psychology in the 20th Century). Baldwin emphasised that the child is as much a product of social experience as of biological growth.

From 1912 Baldwin lived in France, making periodic visits to the University of Geneva in Switzerland. He established a warm friendship with the child psychologist Edouard Claparede. Baldwin's books were translated into French and they became a major influence on a famous student of Claparede, Jean Piaget (1896–1980), whose theory of development will be considered in detail at various places in this book. Cairns (1992) offers a sympathetic review of Baldwin's many contributions to developmental psychology and its contemporary relevance; and Paul Harris (1997) discusses Piaget's relationship with Binet and Baldwin.

KEY TERMS
Intelligence quotient (IQ):
The ratio of mental age,
defined by an intelligence
test, to chronological age,
with a score of 100
representing "average IQ".
Assimilation: Process by
which new information is
"taken in" and incorporated
into existing schemas.
Accommodation: The
modification of a previous
scheme, or creation of a new
one, when required.

Across the Atlantic, G. Stanley Hall (1844–1924) played an important role in establishing the new science of psychology. There has been some debate about Hall's contribution to developmental psychology which has often been considered to be fundamentally flawed. Hall took up Haeckel's biogenetic law that "ontogeny recapitulates phylogeny", which supposed that the course of human development involves a repetition of the ancestral, evolutionary timetable (see The Developmental Principle, earlier in this chapter). This led, for example, to his thoroughly mistaken idea that children love to swing in trees because they recapitulate their monkey ancestry; or that the child has a primitive "savage" mind (or conversely, that the savage mind is childlike). He even argued that there is a scale of mental abilities with children (and women) at the bottom and men at the top!

> **Baldwin's approach**
>
> • Progressive development of knowledge in childhood.
> • Development proceeds in a series of distinct stages.
> • The stages begin at birth with innate motor reflexes.
> • The stages progress to the acquisition of language and logical thought.
> • Progress through successive stages depends on feedback from the environment.
> • Mechanisms for development involve incorporation of environmental effects (assimilation) and plastic change (accommodation).
> • A child is a product of both social experience and biological growth.

In other respects, if the recapitulationary aspect is overlooked, Hall's comparative observations are of interest. For example, his student Chamberlain noted that the period of growth to maturity in mammals, as measured by fusion of the skeletal structure, is relatively a much longer proportion of the lifespan in humans than in most other species. For example, the dormouse with a lifespan of four to five years reaches adulthood in about three months (5% of the lifespan), the rabbit with a lifespan of eight years reaches adulthood in eight to nine months (8.5% of the lifespan), whereas man with an average lifespan of 75 years reaches adulthood at 25 years (33% of the lifespan), in common with the elephant who lives to be 100 years and reaches adulthood at 33 years. Such a comparative perspective does provide an important framework for interpreting the transition from adolescence to adulthood in humans, where the physiological onset of puberty may occur as early as 10 or 11 years, but there is still quite a long developmental period before full physical maturity is reached.

It has been suggested that Hall lacked a systematic programme of thought, being loosely eclectic and borrowing from various methodological and intellectual traditions (Dixon, 1990). It is certainly possible that Hall's enthusiasm for recapitulation theory seriously undermined the potential positive contribution of the comparative method to developmental psychology. One of his severest critics at the time, Edward Lee Thorndike, pointed out that no one would mistake the human embryo at any stage for an adult fish. Rather, structures may sometimes be similar because they are necessarily formed in a particular way. For example, a four-chambered heart is most economically constructed by twice subdividing a single chamber.

Perhaps Hall's most important contribution to developmental psychology was as an importer and translator of research and theorising that was being carried out beyond the USA. He helped to bring Preyer's book, *The Mind of the Child* (1882/1888), to a wider audience in America and, as the President of Clark University in the USA, he was responsible for inviting Sigmund Freud to the United States in 1909 and thus promoted Freud's psychoanalytic ideas. The Freudian influence is perhaps most clearly seen in theories of social and

Hall / supports Darwin Recapitulationist

emotional development, especially in research concerning attachment between parent and child. We will be considering contemporary ideas influenced by Freudian theory, especially the work of John Bowlby, later in this handbook (see Chapter 2, Developmental Psychology in the 20th Century, and Chapter 6, Early Social Development).

Fundamental questions in developmental psychology

Throughout the period when developmental psychology was establishing itself as an independent discipline several fundamental questions emerged (Cairns. 1998). We have already discussed the relation between evolution and development which was a major issue for debate in this early period. Arguments for and against recapitulation continued until this view was discredited by Gould in 1977. Another topic with a long history but a less clear resolution is the nature–nurture problem.

It was Francis Galton who first labelled the "nature–nurture" problem. Galton, who was a cousin of Charles Darwin, was impressed by the fact that genius tended to run in families. This suggested to Galton that there was a strong inherited component in intellectual ability and he argued for this view in his book, *Hereditary Genius* (1869).

The essential debate between nature (inherited factors) and nurture (upbringing) concerns the extent to which a person's behaviour and characteristics are the product of inborn (genetically determined) potential or of experience. Historically, extreme views have been expressed on both sides of this debate. The 17th-century English philosopher, John Locke (1632–1704), thought the child was born a "tabula rasa" (blank slate), whose every characteristic would be moulded by experience. On this view, the newborn has no psychological structure and is extremely malleable to the effects of the environment (Bremner, 1994). Locke's environmentalist view tends to deny that

Francis Galton (labelled)
Nature vr Nurture

Left: The 17th-century English philosopher John Locke (1632–1704). Copyright © Popperfoto. Right: The 18th-century Swiss philosopher Jean-Jacques Rousseau (1712–1778). Copyright © Popperfoto.

innate factors make any important contribution to psychological development. Instead, Locke placed great emphasis on learning as a way of explaining how children's knowledge and understanding develop with age.

In sharp contrast to Locke, the views of the 18th-century Swiss philosopher, Jean-Jacques Rousseau (1712–1778), were more inclined to a "natural" theory of human development. In his famous book, *Emile* (1762/1974), Rousseau argued that children should be treated as children rather than as miniature adults. He divided development into discrete, sequential stages, beginning with an animalistic stage from birth to about five years, followed by a dawning self-consciousness in middle childhood, rationality at around twelve years, and social conscience arising at puberty. He considered that children are innately "good", requiring little by way of moral guidance or constraint for normal development, and that they grow according to "nature's plan". Rousseau's account emphasised the child's "natural" propensities and minimised the effects of upbringing or experience.

This kind of view of the inherent goodness of children famously found expression in Wordsworth's poem "Ode: Intimations of immortality" published in 1807. Wordsworth describes the newborn child as:

> …trailing clouds of glory do we come
> from God who is our home:
> Heaven lies about us in our infancy!

Wordsworth sees the effects of experience as largely bad:

> shades of the prison house begin to close
> upon the growing boy

Rousseau's influential views help to explain why the behaviour of so-called "feral children" attracted such great interest in the 18th and 19th centuries. It was thought that the behaviour of children, who had apparently been raised in the wild, might help to define the animalistic "natural" human stage and to explore the limits of socialisation of human nature. The box overleaf reviews a number of these anecdotal accounts of feral children. They provide a fascinating insight into changing views of development.

Rousseau's views were also an important inspiration in education. The most influential of his followers was Johann Pestalozzi whose views had worldwide impact on educational practice. Pestalozzi, who opened a school in 1799 where he was able to test his ideas about education, argued that teaching methods should be adapted to the natural development of the child. His school was attended by pupils from all over Europe and Friedrich Froebel, who founded kindergarten education, was a teacher there for four years and greatly inspired by Pestalozzi's ideas.

Very general views of "nurture" and "nature"—for example those of Locke and Rousseau—and anecdotal evidence about feral children set the stage for prolonged and misguided debates about the relative contributions of "nature and nurture" to development. Contemporary developmental psychologists prefer to avoid such dichotomous approaches to explanation in favour of "interactive" or "dialectical" accounts that attempt to capture more adequately the complex, dynamic interplay of factors contributing to development.

Feral children

The word "feral" is normally used to refer to animals that were once domesticated but who have returned to the wild. In the case of feral children, the term has come to refer to children who were discovered in the wild and brought back to civilisation. There have been many reports of feral children whose survival and upbringing has often been attributed to animals. Candland (1994) notes that the great naturalist and taxonomist, Linnaeus (1707–1778), listed nine cases that he classified under the taxonomic category "Primates, Man and Apes", as "Loco ferus": four-footed, non-speaking, and hairy. These include a wolf boy from Hesse (1344), a bear boy from Lithuania (1661), and a sheep boy from Ireland (1672). The study of such children was thought to have both political and educational significance for they might reveal the nature of the uncivilised mind and how best to educate and instruct children. It was assumed that the relative importance of nature and nurture in human development might thus be elucidated.

Among the most famous cases is that of Victor, the Wildboy. Victor was captured in 1799 as a boy when he was aged 11 or 12 years. He was found wandering naked in the woods near Aveyron, France. Victor was eventually taken to Paris, about a year later, where his presence aroused much interest among people expecting to have their first glimpse of a "wild and noble savage" just as described by Rousseau. Instead, what they found was a disturbed child, who was incapable of speech, of maintaining attention and who spent his time rocking backwards and forwards. Victor came into the care of Dr Jean-Marc-Gaspard Itard, a physician working at the asylum in Bicetre (near Paris) with Phillipe Pinel, the man who was among the first to advocate the humane treatment of the insane. Pinel considered Victor to be incurably mentally retarded. However, Itard thought that Victor may simply have been showing effects of lack of socialisation and set about to educate Victor over a period of five years. Itard attempted to teach Victor to speak but eventually had to acknowledge failure. Victor was able to speak only three words at the time he died at the age of 40 years.

In addition to Victor, Candland (1994) analyses four famous cases of feral children. "Wild Peter" was a boy aged about 12 years who was discovered in Hameln, Germany in 1724, living off raw vegetables and birds which he caught and dismembered. Peter eventually became a guest of King George I of England, to be studied as a scientific curiosity. "Kaspar Hauser" was discovered in Nuremberg, Germany in 1828 aged 16 years. It is reported that he was brought up in a cell with little opportunity for movement or the learning of speech. However, it was claimed that he eventually acquired language by learning from an adoptive sibling.

The "Wolf Children", Kamala and Amala, were discovered in 1920 by the Reverend J.A.L. Singh, in Midnapore, India. They were aged eight years and eighteen months respectively and were apparently living with wolves. Dr Singh and his wife, who brought up

Dr Itard and Victor. Reproduced from J.-M.-G. Itard (1932), *The wild boy of Aveyron*. Translated by G. Humphrey and M. Humphrey. New York: Century.

the girls in their orphanage, described them as typically moving around on all fours and eating food from a dish by mouth, like a dog. Sadly, Amala died a year after entering the orphanage but Kamala lived to the age of 17 years. Gesell (1941) describes how Kamala eventually came to walk upright, to talk in short sentences and to become socialised to the extent that, at the age of 15 years, she was able to pick out her own clothes from the wash, help care for the babies in the orphanage, and make appropriate use of the toilet facilities. Gesell estimated that her mental and language development at the time of her death was equivalent to that of a three and a half year-old child.

Candland (1994) comes to the conclusion that Rousseau's romantic idea of man's original animal nature receives little support from the study of feral children. Indeed, cases of feral children do not provide an answer to the question of how much of human nature is to be attributed to nature and how much to children's exposure to the social, educational, or political environment. Rather, what psychologists now realise is that many different factors contributed to the behaviour of feral children. These include both social factors—lack of normal parenting and contact with other humans—and inherent disabilities such as deafness, the inability to speak (dysarthria), and mental retardation that may have been responsible for "animal" behaviours, such as quadrupedal gait. These cases also cast doubt on the use of anecdotal evidence in developmental science. It is extremely difficult to prove that any of these "feral" children were actually raised by animals and not simply abandoned by their parents because they had disabilities apparent from an early age.

Kamala and Amala sleep overlapping one another. Reproduced with permission from J.A.L. Singh and R.M. Zingg (1939), *Wolf-children and feral man*. New York: Harper & Brothers Publishers. Courtesy of the Centennial Museum.

Another contemporary issue of concern that has its roots in the early days of developmental psychology concerns the timing and plasticity of development—an issue that also relates to the studies of feral children. By the beginning of the 19th century, when ideas about the importance of education were being developed by Pestalozzi, the prevailing view was that development was the product of both innate predispositions and experience. However, there remained considerable debate about *when* in development the effects of experience were most potent; and also about the related question of when development ends. G. Stanley Hall argued that the most important influences of experience occurred in adolescence. In his view, early experience had little effect since evolutionary forces laid down the path of development from birth until puberty. Freud took the opposite view, arguing that the most potent effects of experience were in infancy: Patterns of thought and behaviour that were laid down in infancy determined patterns of adult behaviour. Freud argued that these patterns were so resistant to change that psychoanalytic intervention was necessary to alter a maladaptive pattern. Baldwin's view differed from both Freud and Hall in that he argued for personality development as a continuing process throughout the lifespan. This view of continuing change from birth to adolescence came to be the dominant one in developmental psychology as Baldwin's ideas were expanded into a comprehensive theory of developmental change by Piaget.

Conclusion and summary

Developmental psychology is concerned with age-related changes in experience and behaviour. The aims of the discipline are to describe the changes that take place in children's abilities and to explain why they occur. Both of these are very difficult tasks, and the last 150 years have seen increasing sophistication both in the ways that developmental changes are observed and in the kinds of explanation that are offered to account for these changes.

Many of the fundamental questions in developmental psychology—such as the comparative contributions of genes and experience to individual differences in development—have their origins in philosophy, but the scientific study of children was founded upon the insights of evolutionary biology in the 19th century and in particular the work of Karl Ernst von Baer and Charles Darwin. Von Baer's work was concerned with the development of the embryo and his most important contribution was to discredit the recapitulationist view that, in embryonic development, organisms pass through the adult form of all the species that have been ancestral to them during their evolution. First, he demonstrated that the embryo of a higher animal is never like that of a lower animal, and second, that development is a continuous process of differentiation and organisation, with development proceeding in successive stages, from the more general to the more specific. Von Baer concluded that developmental processes demand rigorous study in their own right and cannot be derived from analogies to evolution. This view of embryological development was extrapolated to development after birth by James Mark Baldwin and his successors, including Jean Piaget.

Darwin's views on evolution also had an important influence on developmental psychology, especially his writings on the evolution of the emotions and intelligence. He also carried out pioneering observations of his own children. Cairns (1998) notes that Darwin's contribution to developmental psychology has been the subject of debate. He argues that an assessment of Darwin's contribution depends heavily on the particular aspects of development that are considered. Perhaps the most important general contribution of Darwin's writing was to emphasise the importance of a comparative approach in which the development of human infants is set within the wider context of development in other species. Comparisons between human development and abilities and those present in the great apes—especially chimpanzees—have become an important part of modern developmental psychology and we use comparative evidence at various points in this handbook in order to determine the unique aspects of human development.

By the end of the 19th century developmental psychology was well established as a scientific discipline in Europe and the United States. Cairns (1998) argues that developmental studies flourished despite the powerful influence of traditional psychological laboratories—such as that of Thorndike—which took a rather narrow view of learning and animal behaviour. Both in Europe and the United States a number of journals dedicated to developmental psychology were founded and specialist research institutes and professional organisations were established.

By the 1920s various distinct schools of developmental psychology had begun to emerge, each emphasising a different aspect of nature or nurture. The field had become fragmented and a synthesis was needed so that the complex interaction of biological and social factors could be more adequately understood. This work of synthesis was mainly accomplished by the "grand" theories of the middle 20th century that are described in the next chapter.

Further reading

- Cairns, R.B. (1998). The making of developmental psychology. In R.M. Lerner (Eds.), *Handbook of child psychology: Vol. 1. Theoretical models of human development* (W. Damon, Gen. Ed.; pp. 25–105). New York: Wiley. This chapter in the authoritative *Handbook of child psychology* provides a detailed account of the early influences on developmental psychology in the 19th century and traces the changes that have occurred through the 20th century.
- Candland, D.K. (1994). *Feral children and clever animals: Reflections on human nature.* Oxford, UK: Oxford University Press. This is a very readable book that gives detailed accounts of the studies of feral children that we describe briefly in this chapter.
- Harris, P.L. (1997). Piaget in Paris: From "autism" to logic. *Human Development, 40,* 109–123. This paper describes the development of Piaget's views about children's thinking. It is quite a difficult paper and is intended for advanced undergraduates.
- Parke, R.D., Ornstein, P.A., Reiser, J., & Zahn-Waxler, C. (Eds.). (1994). *A century of developmental psychology.* Washington DC: American Psychological Association. This edited book contains chapters written by active researchers in developmental psychology who reflect on the history of psychology and the influence that earlier research has had on the development of their own ideas.

CHAPTER 2

Developmental psychology in the 20th century

The empirical basis of modern developmental psychology was established in the early part of the 20th century. During this time there was still great concern with the nature–nurture debate (see Fundamental Questions in Developmental Psychology in Chapter 1), with theories tending to advocate one or the other factor as the over-riding influence on development. The period coincided with an intense interest in theories of learning based on the work of the Russian physiologist, Ivan Pavlov. Pavlov's now famous studies of learning in dogs established that some types of learning take place through the association of stimuli and responses, under conditions of reward and punishment. For example, in his studies of "classical conditioning" Pavlov showed that a hungry animal will readily learn that a signal, such as a bell, regularly predicts the arrival of food. As a result the dog will soon salivate in anticipation of food whenever the bell sounds. What has happened is that the dog has learned to associate the bell with food and the normal (unconditioned) response of salivation to food has become associated with (conditioned to) the sound of the bell.

Learning or maturation: The rise of opposing schools

This focus on the laws of learning led to the rise of a school of psychology known as **behaviourism**, whose major figure was John Watson (1878–1958). Watson had distinct ideas about child development based on "learning" theory. He was very interested, for example, in whether infants naturally showed fear of animals or whether such fears were learned (see the box on the next page). He concluded that these fears were learned.

Watson believed so strongly in the potential of children to learn through experience that he wrote:

> *Give me a dozen healthy infants, well formed and my own specified world to bring them up in and I'll guarantee to take any one at random and train him to become any type of specialist I might select—doctor, lawyer, artist, merchant-chief and yes, even beggar man and thief, regardless of his talents, penchants, tendencies, abilities, vocations and race of his ancestors.*
>
> *(Watson, 1930, p. 104)*

John Watson (1878–1958). Copyright © Archives of the History of American Psychology/The University of Akron.

Watson's studies of childhood fears

In his book, *Psychology from the Standpoint of a Behaviorist* (1919), Watson reported a study of three children who were introduced to novel birds and animals over a period of several days. In one case, Watson presented a six-month-old baby called Thorne with a black cat, a pigeon, a rabbit, and, later on, with a whole series of animals at the local zoo including a camel and a zebra. He studied Thorne's reaction to their presence in a number of different conditions and found that, even in the dark, she did not display fear on any occasion although she was very interested in all the animals and looked at them intently. She also reached out to touch the smaller animals.

Having shown that children did not have any innate fear of animals, Watson went on to study the acquisition of irrational fears through learning. He reports the case of a six-month-old baby who had a small dog tossed into her pram. (How this came about Watson does not reveal.) The baby became terrified and subsequently showed a fear reaction not only to dogs but also to rapidly moving toy animals. At 18 months the unfortunate baby was tested by having a tame white mouse placed on the floor near her. She responded by crying and rushing into her father's arms.

A similar—and more famous—study was carried out on the baby, "Little Albert", and reported by Watson and Raynor (1920). They showed that, after Albert was frightened while playing with a furry toy, he also learned to be afraid of other furry objects (such as a beard) and animals.

As this quotation vividly illustrates, "nature" took rather a back seat to "nurture" in Watson's explanation of the causes of development. He believed, for example, that whether a person is left handed or right handed was a function of early training rather than of genetic factors—a view that has now largely been discredited. Watson's views were partly based on inherent American optimism and partly on an extreme view of the extent of human plasticity. That is, the developing child was considered to be extremely malleable and highly susceptible to the effects of environmental influences.

Learning theory approaches to development continued to exercise great influence, especially in the USA, until quite recently. They still find useful application in dealing with some developmental problems, such as bed-wetting, or fears and phobias, where techniques based on the laws of conditioning first described by Pavlov, and developed by Watson, have been applied. However, the contemporary influence of learning theories on development is rather limited by comparison to other more recent schools of thought.

The diametric opposite to an extreme learning theory approach was the maturational school, led by Arnold Gesell (1880–1961). Gesell originally trained as a teacher and then pursued his doctoral studies under G. Stanley Hall (see The Emergence of Developmental Psychology, in Chapter 1) in developmental psychology. Then, while director of

---

Behaviourist approach (Watson)

- Studied the acquisition of irrational fears through learning.
- Believed strongly in the potential of the child to learn through experience.
- An environmentalist viewpoint; "nurture" rather than "nature".
- An extreme view of human plasticity.
- The developing child is extremely malleable and susceptible to the effects of environmental influences.

the Yale University Clinic of Child Development, he qualified in medicine. He made pioneering observational studies of infants and young children using 35 mm films in his photographic observation dome. Thelen (1984) says that Gesell shared Darwin's commitment to the naturalistic method of observation of children and that his theory was deeply rooted in biology. His main idea was that the time-locked processes of biological growth are particularly important for the appearance of various motor and perceptual abilities in early development.

Links with embryological theories can also be found in the pioneering research of Myrtle McGraw during the 1920s and 1930s. McGraw attempted to establish whether principles derived from animal embryology might also apply to the growth of human behaviour. She became famous for a study of motor development in identical twins, in which one of the pair received additional stimulation of various motor responses, while the other served as the normal developmental control. Despite additional practice, the rate of motor development in the pair remained closely correlated and this was widely believed at the time to support a maturationalist theory of development (Bergenn, Dalton, & Lipsitt, 1994).

> **Maturational approach (Gesell/McGraw)**
>
> • Used the naturalistic method of observation.
> • The approach is rooted in biology.
> • Time-locked processes of biological growth are particularly important for the appearance of motor and perceptual abilities (Gesell).
> • Studies with identical twins revealed that motor development rate was similar regardless of practice (McGraw).
> • Nativist viewpoint; emphasised "nature" rather than "nurture".

Contemporary evaluations of Gesell and McGraw acknowledge that their theories were not simply maturationalist but, unlike the environmentalists, such as Watson, and Gesell and McGraw, tended to emphasise "nature" at the expense of "nurture" as a cause of development. The rather nativist view of Gesell—and his insistence upon the importance of evolution in shaping the course of development—is illustrated by the following quotation which stands in stark contrast to the earlier quotation from Watson:

> *The child grows. The capacities and, to no small extent, the directions of growth*
> *are the end products of ages of evolution.*
>
> *(Gesell, Ilg, & Bullis, 1949, p. 44)*

As a comparison of the views of Watson and Gesell reveals, the middle period in the founding of developmental psychology produced a polarisation between extreme environmentalism—somewhat similar to Locke's view (see Fundamental Questions in Developmental Psychology, in Chapter 1) of the child as a "tabula rasa" on which experience would have a major effect—and an extreme maturationist view. The influence of **maturation** was most strongly espoused by those interested in such aspects of development as hand–eye co-ordination and the acquisition of motor skills, like walking, which seemed to proceed according to a strict biological timetable. (It should be noted, however, that Gesell recognised the significant individual variation in the age at which children reached particular developmental milestones.)

These sharply polarised views of nature versus nurture, although out of date now, were important because they led to distinct fashions in child rearing and education each based on the rival views. The environmentalists emphasised habit training as a means of teaching children, for example, in toilet

KEY TERM
Maturation: A sequence of physical growth characteristics, strongly influenced by genetic inheritance, that unfold as individuals grow older; common to all members of a species.

training or the acquisition of basic skills like reading and writing. Maturationalists emphasised the biological need for the child to be "ready" for particular types of experience before learning could occur.

The extreme maturationist or environmentalist accounts of development that dominated the early part of the 20th century were succeeded by theories that attempted a post-Darwinian synthesis of "nature" and "nurture". We will introduce the major themes and influences in mid-20th century developmental psychology by considering the work of three eminent developmental psychologists, Jean Piaget, Lev Vygotsky, and John Bowlby. All three offered very broad theories concerned respectively with intellectual, social, and emotional development. The similarities and differences between these theories illustrate many of the key issues of controversy within developmental psychology.

Jean Piaget (1896–1980)

Jean Piaget has had the most profound influence on our understanding of development. He lived such a long and productive life that he straddled the whole of the modern history of developmental psychology, almost from its foundations to the late 20th century. Piaget began his studies in Neuchatel—a Swiss canton—where he was studied philosophy (including logic) and scientific methodology at senior school. Even at this early age he was interested in biology and the way in which organisms adapted to their environment through experience. In 1907, at the precocious age of 11 years, Piaget published his first paper "On sighting an albino sparrow". The curator of the local natural history museum was so impressed by the paper that Piaget became his part-time and unpaid assistant, and, on Saturday afternoons, he collected and catalogued the molluscs of the Swiss lakes. At university, Piaget studied Biology and Philosophy and, in 1918, he was awarded a doctorate for his work on the special adaptations evolved by the molluscs in the shallow waters of the Swiss lakes.

The Swiss psychologist Jean Piaget (1896–1980). Copyright © Popperfoto.

In the same year, Piaget left Neuchatel for Zurich where he studied experimental psychology. He also attended lectures given by Jung and other psychoanalysts and he studied the writings of Sigmund Freud. In the following year, 1919, Piaget left for Paris where, as Paul Harris (1997) notes, he first came into contact with experimental studies of children: Although Binet had died in 1911, his influence was still strong and his approach to the study of children continued. Freud had also worked in Paris at the end of the previous century and, by the time that Piaget arrived, psychoanalytic theory was becoming accepted within the academic community. Another important figure, James Mark Baldwin, was in exile in Paris when Piaget arrived. Paul Harris (1997) has argued that the ideas of all three figures—Binet, Freud, and Baldwin—made important contributions to the development of Piaget's own theory about the way that children's thinking develops over time.

In Paris, Piaget continued with his study of logic and the philosophy of science as well as psychology. He also conducted clinical interviews with psychiatric patients. Piaget began his experimental study of children when Simon—Binet's collaborator (see The Emergence of Developmental Psychology, in Chapter 1)—invited him to make use of Binet's laboratory. Piaget's first task was to standardise Burt's tests of reasoning on a sample of French children (P.L. Harris, 1997). Piaget's approach was characteristic of the one that he adopted in much of his later research: He employed the clinical method (see Carrying Out Research in Developmental Psychology, in Chapter 3), using probing questions to uncover what the children understood. Piaget was especially interested in the errors that children made and the possibility that these could be explained as internally consistent rather than random. According to Harris, this search for a systematic pattern in the production of children's errors stemmed from Piaget's strong background in logic (see the following box for an example of Piaget's early research in Binet's laboratory, which illustrates his approach).

> **Initial work of Piaget**
>
> - Influenced by the work of Binet, Freud, and Baldwin.
> - Relied upon the clinical method, using probing questions to uncover what children understood.
> - Was interested in the errors children made and the possibility that these were not random.
> - Searched for a systematic pattern in the production of children's errors.
> - Worked towards a logical, internally consistent explanation of children's errors.

Piaget's early studies of children's thinking

Piaget's early search for a logical—internally consistent—explanation of children's errors is very evident in his investigation of Burt's transitive reasoning problems such as: *Edith is fairer than Suzanne. Edith is darker than Lily. Who is darkest, Edith, Suzanne, or Lily?* The correct answer is *Suzanne* but children cannot usually solve such problems until the age of 11. The younger children who Piaget tested often said "Lily" who is, of course, the fairest of the three.

Piaget was able to account for the children's apparently illogical conclusion that Lily was the darkest rather than the fairest by getting to the heart of the children's own logic. He realised that the children were treating the relational terms, "fairer" and "darker", as meaning "fair" and "dark", respectively (that is, they were treating the terms as categorical rather than relational). This meant that the children interpreted *Edith is fairer than Suzanne* to mean that both Edith and Suzanne were fair, whereas they interpreted *Edith is darker than Lily* to mean that both were dark. Thus, on this interpretation, Lily is the darkest because she is the only one who is completely dark and Suzanne is fairest because she is the only one who completely fair. Edith, who is both fair and dark, is seen as intermediate in complexion. Paradoxically, this interpretation leads to exactly the opposite conclusion to the correct one.

In 1921 Piaget returned to Switzerland—this time to the Institut Jean-Jacques Rousseau in Geneva where he was appointed as director of studies. By then Piaget had completed many hours of clinical interviews with children and he continued this practice in Geneva. Piaget remained in Geneva for the rest of his life, developing a theory of how knowledge is acquired, which he called

---

Developments of Piaget's initial work

- Studied how knowledge is acquired and developed the theory of "genetic epistemology".
- Studied thought and language in preschoolers and early school-age children.
- Believed that intelligence arises progressively in the baby's repetitive activities.
- Described how concepts of space, time, causes, and physical objects arise in development.
- Investigated the beginnings of fantasy and symbolism in infancy.
- Outlined a theory that states that the precursors of thinking and language lie in the elementary actions, perceptions, and imitations of babies.

"genetic epistemology". His first books were about thinking and language in preschool and early school-age children: *The Language and Thought of the Child* (1923/1926) and *Judgement and Reasoning in the Child* (1924/1926). These were widely influential and much to his surprise were acclaimed the world over.

In 1923 Piaget married Valentine Chatenay and in collaboration they studied the development from birth of their own three children, Jacqueline, Lucienne, and Laurent. Their observations on the origins of thought and language in infancy formed the basis for three of Piaget's most influential books: *The Origins of Intelligence in Children* (1936/1952), which describes how intelligence progressively arises in the baby's repetitive activities, *The Construction of Reality in the Child* (1937/1954), which describes how elementary concepts of space, time, causes, and physical objects arise in development, and *Play Dreams and Imitation in Childhood* (1945/1962) which describes the beginnings of fantasy and symbolism in infancy. In this trilogy Piaget outlined his theory that the precursors of thinking and language lie in the elementary actions, perceptions, and imitations of babies.

Many other influential books were to follow, especially those which had an impact on educational theory and practice in mathematics and science teaching, such as *The Child's Conception of Number* (1941/1952: with Szeminska) and *The Child's Conception of Geometry* (1948/1960: with Inhelder and Szeminska).

In some of his later works, such as *Biology and Knowledge* (1971), Piaget outlined his theory of the relation between evolution and the acquisition of knowledge as a biological process. Piaget is sometimes unjustly accused of recapitulationism (see The Evolution of Development, in Chapter 1) because he tried to draw parallels between evolution and developmental theory. He argued that acquiring knowledge can be thought of as an evolutionary process in the sense that knowledge is adaptive: More adequate knowledge allows children to deal with their environment more effectively. Piaget also argued

---

Later work of Piaget

- Outlined a theory of the relationship between evolution and the acquisition of knowledge as a biological process.
- Acquiring knowledge is an evolutionary process in the sense that knowledge is adaptive, and having more adequate knowledge allows children to deal more effectively with their environment.
- How children acquire knowledge may show parallels with the historic progress of science.
- Unjustly accused of recapitulationism because of drawing parallels between evolution and developmental theory.

---

that how children acquire knowledge, particularly scientific ideas, may show important parallels with the historic progress of science; but there is no suggestion that the sequence of stages in acquiring knowledge recapitulates the history of ideas (for an extensive discussion of recapitulationism and Piagetian theory see Butterworth, Rutkowska, & Scaife, 1985).

Piaget's technical vocabulary, which he adopted from James Mark Baldwin (see The Emergence of Developmental Psychology, in Chapter 1), is biological. Two key concepts are *assimilation* and *accommodation* (see page 10). Assimilation refers to the taking in of new information by the structures of the mind.

Previous experience is organised in schemas—a structured organisation of past experience—and new information is either assimilated to an existing schema or, if it is inconsistent in some way with an existing schema, accommodation ensues so that the schema is modified to incorporate the new information. Thus, equilibrium is achieved through accommodation, as the organism adapts to, or incorporates the effects of, the environment. The notion of **equilibration** is also based on the idea of achieving a natural balance between the individual and the world, just as there is a balance of the forces that sustain life in nature.

Piaget's model of development is of a self-regulating interaction—between the child and the physical and social environment—that gives rise to new forms of knowledge. His theory is analogous to the formation by natural selection of new species in evolution, where new forms of life arise from pre-existing ones under the influence of pressures from the environment. In evolution, only those species that can adapt to the new environment survive. By analogy, new forms of knowledge arise in development because they are better adapted to the demands of the environment than the forms they replace.

Piaget described four major stages of development (each with sub-stages) that extend from infancy to adulthood. These are the **sensorimotor**, the **preoperational**, the **concrete operational**, and the **formal operational stages** of intellectual development. The ages associated with each stage are averages and may vary considerably from child to child and from culture to culture but they occur in an invariant order. Piaget believed that the first three stages are universal, whereas he thought stage IV to be characteristic of some adult thinking only in advanced, technological societies. We discuss each of these four stages in detail later in this book

Piaget's ideas on the development of thinking have had a profound influence on 20th-century developmental psychology. Some idea of his impact can be gained from the fact that developmental researchers cite Piaget more frequently than any other psychologist, save Sigmund Freud. Piaget's description of the developing mental powers of the child has inspired many followers and has also provoked much constructive criticism with which we will become more closely acquainted in subsequent chapters. Even though he died in 1980, work in the Piagetian tradition continues and there is little doubt that Piaget's theory will exercise great influence for many years to come. (For a more extensive account of Piaget's influence on psychology, biology, philosophy, and cybernetics see Boden, 1994.)

Piaget's overall commitment to **genetic epistemology** continues to attract many followers, although many of the details of his theory have, by now, been quite heavily criticised. There are two main ways in which the general theory has changed under the pressure of modern evidence. First, much contemporary research has demonstrated that babies are much more competent than Piaget had assumed. In particular, babies are much more able to perceive reality than Piaget's own observations had led him to believe. This evidence alters the status of perception in the overall process of intellectual development (see Infants' Perception of Objects: An Alternative to Piaget, in Chapter 5). A second area of criticism concerns Piaget's idea that all knowledge, whatever its specific nature, can be fitted to one general stage theory. It has been argued that knowledge acquisition may be better understood as domain-specific, that is, pertaining to particular areas of knowledge, rather than as a process that operates regardless

KEY TERMS

Equilibration: Using the processes of accommodation and assimilation to produce a state of equilibrium between existing schemas and new experiences.

Sensorimotor stage: Piaget's first stage in the process of adaptation, from birth to about two years, in which infants co-ordinate sensory perceptions and motor abilities to acquire knowledge of the world.

Preoperational stage: Piaget's second stage of cognitive development involving internalisation of forms of actions that the infant has already mastered. The key feature of this stage, which lasts from two to six or seven years, is that the child is able to focus only on one salient feature of a problem at a time and is dominated by the immediate appearance of things.

Concrete operational stage: Piaget's third developmental stage in which children begin to use logical rules to solve problems. They can deal with more than one salient feature of a problem at a time and are no longer dominated by appearance. However, they are not yet able to deal with abstract problems. This stage lasts from the ages of six or seven to eleven or twelve.

Formal operational stage: The final stage in Piaget's theory, from 11 or 12 onwards, in which the child becomes able to consider all possible combinations in relation to the whole problem and to reason about an entirely hypothetical situation.

Genetic epistemology: The critical study of the validity, methods, and scope of genetics.

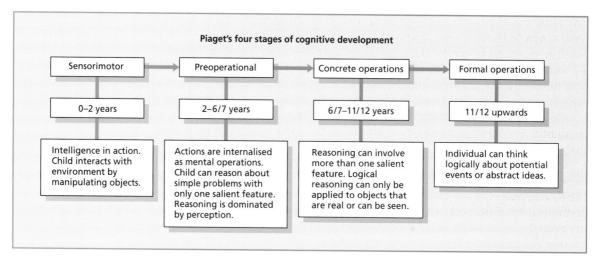

Piaget's four stages of cognitive development

Sensorimotor	Preoperational	Concrete operations	Formal operations
0–2 years	2–6/7 years	6/7–11/12 years	11/12 upwards
Intelligence in action. Child interacts with environment by manipulating objects.	Actions are internalised as mental operations. Child can reason about simple problems with only one salient feature. Reasoning is dominated by perception.	Reasoning can involve more than one salient feature. Logical reasoning can only be applied to objects that are real or can be seen.	Individual can think logically about potential events or abstract ideas.

of the content of what is to be known. (For a discussion of the difference between domain-specific and general approaches to the development of cognition see Karmiloff-Smith, 1992.)

Lev Semeonovich Vygotsky (1896–1934)

The Russian psychologist Lev Semeonovich Vygotsky (1896–1934).

Piaget was mainly concerned to explain the development of intelligence and reasoning in humans from its biological roots. Lev Semeonovich Vygotsky, by contrast, was most concerned to show how culture influences the course of development. Culture is used as a broad term to describe the customs of a particular people at a particular time and their collective intellectual, material, scientific, and artistic achievements over historical time.

Lev Vygotsky, a Russian Jew, was born in the same year as Piaget. Although less well known than Piaget, because he died at the early age of 38, years before his work was published in the West, he too has had great influence on the shaping of developmental psychology. Little is known of his early years except that he was the second of eight children, his father was a bank official, and that Vygotsky's home was at Gomel, a small town about 400 miles south-west of Moscow (Kozulin, 1990; Valsiner, 1988).

Vygotsky studied literature and cultural history at Moscow University where he graduated in 1917, the same year as the October Soviet Revolution. From 1917 he taught literature and psychology at the teacher training college in Gomel. He founded a literary journal and carried out literary research that was eventually published in his book, *The Psychology of Art* (Vygotsky, 1971). He was also working on ideas in psychology and presented a paper on the relation between Pavlovian conditioned reflexes and consciousness at the Psycho-Neurological Congress in Leningrad, in 1924. As a result of the impression these ideas made on his fellow psychologists, Vygotsky was invited to join the Institute of Psychology in Moscow in the same year.

In line with the prevailing Marxist theory of the time, Vygotsky saw culture and social organisation, and the historical forces that shape society, as having an important influence upon the development of the child's mind. Paradoxically, Vygotsky's revolutionary work fell foul of Stalin and his writings were suppressed in Russia. His early death from tuberculosis meant that he did not become well known, outside a close circle of students and colleagues, until 1962 when his major book, *Thought and Language,* was first translated into English (a second, much revised, edition was published in 1988). His student, Alexander Luria, a distinguished neuropsychologist, did much to keep the Vygotskian tradition alive in the former Soviet Union, especially in describing how language comes to regulate action, attention, and consciousness.

As his Marxist philosophy required, Vygotsky was particularly concerned to identify the historical and social aspects of human behaviour that render human nature unique. This is not to deny that biological processes contribute to development: It is rather to affirm that social and cultural factors make an important contribution to the development of human intelligence. For example, the development of the nervous system will be much influenced by genetic factors but the dialectical approach also insists that complex aspects of cognition are brought about by the requirements of social life.

For Vygotsky, speech has the pre-eminent role of carrying culture: Language both stores and carries the historical stock of social experience and it is a "tool" of thought. People also differ from animals because they use tools to create artefacts that change the conditions of life. Culture is constituted both symbolically, in language and materially, in the artificial environment.

One of the main differences between Piaget and Vygotsky concerns their views on the relationship between language and thought. Vygotsky placed much greater emphasis than did Piaget on the formative role of culture on development as it is transmitted both through social interaction and speech. Consequently, Vygotsky saw a much closer link between the acquisition of language and the development of thinking; and he also gave much greater prominence to the importance of social interaction in development, especially as it influenced language and thought. Given the important role of social factors in determining development, Vygotsky's approach is less committed to fixed stages in development. Instead, he describes "leading activities" typical of certain age periods around which intellectual development is organised—such as emotional contact in infancy, playing games in early childhood, learning in schools. Nevertheless, these periods correspond rather closely to the stages as classically defined because, Vygotsky (1962) argues, society has come to structure the social process of upbringing to correspond closely with the major biological periods of development.

Vygotsky's ideas were in fact rooted in Western psychology. He had read James Mark Baldwin's theory of development (which was available in French and had been translated into Russian in 1911), and, like many educated Russians, he was able to read French and so was acquainted with Binet's ideas about intelligence and Piaget's writings on language and thought in the child. Indeed, Vygotsky (1934/1987) wrote an important critique of some aspects of Piaget's reinterpretation of psychoanalytic ideas in developmental terms (P.L. Harris, 1997).

Vygotsky's approach

- Influenced by Baldwin and Binet.
- Concerned with the historical and social aspects of human behaviour that make human nature unique.
- Social and cultural factors are important in the development of intelligence.
- Speech carries culture in that it stores the history of social experience and is a "tool" for thought.
- People differ from animals because they use tools to create artefacts that change the conditions of life.
- There is a close link between the acquisition of language and the development of thinking.
- Gave prominence to the importance of social interaction in development as it influences language and thought.
- Does not deal with fixed stages of development but describes "leading activities" typical of certain age periods around which intellectual development is organised.

In some respects, then, Vygotsky's intellectual heritage was similar to Piaget's. However, Vygotsky was formulating his ideas during the revolutionary period in Russia when great emphasis was placed on the way in which the social organisation channels human potential. It is not surprising that Vygotsky emphasised the role that culture and social organisation has upon the development of the child's mind. These ideas can be seen very clearly in Vygotsky's theory of the **zone of proximal development**.

The "zone of proximal development", or ZPD, may be defined as the difference between what a child can achieve unaided in a particular situation—such as completing a puzzle or playing with toys—and what can be achieved with the help of adults, older children, or, even, with children of similar age. A simple illustration of the ZPD can be seen as the difference between how an 18-month-old child might attempt to stack a set of beakers when there is no older person there to assist and how he/she might attempt the same task with the assistance of a more experienced partner. Vygotsky's important contribution was to point out that the child's own knowledge develops through experience of adults guiding the child towards a more sophisticated solution to a task. In the case of the beaker play, for example, the adult might guide the child towards a systematic selection of beakers on the basis of size. The zone of proximal development therefore measures the "leading edge" of the developmental process, where teaching, instruction, and the peer group may exercise their greatest effect.

A recent illustration of the ZPD appears in a study by Linnell and Fluck (2001) who looked at the counting skills of preschool children. Children of this age find counting difficult (see Chapter 13, Learning to Do Mathematics) but it is an activity that they often carry out with a more experienced partner. Linnell and Fluck compared preschoolers counting in two conditions, one on their own and the other with the assistance of their mothers. They found that the children were more accurate both at counting out objects and selecting the correct number of objects when their mothers guided them through the task. The following extract illustrates the important role of maternal guidance in the challenging task of counting out three toys and placing them in a basket for a clown doll (called Billie) to play with. The child is 32 months old.

Mother:	*Right shall you give Billie some? You have to count them as you put them in.*
Child:	Yeah. (taking one item from the basket)
Mother:	*Now you count them.*
Child:	One (takes out another toy and holds one in each hand)
Mother:	*That's it.*
Child:	Put them in there? (Holding them over Billie's basket)
Mother:	Yeah. (Child drops toy into Billie's basket) *And Billie would like one more. One, two …*
Child:	Three. And this one (taking another toy out of the basket)
Mother:	*Go on then—give it to Billie.*
Child	(Picks up another toy so he again has one in each hand)
Mother:	*He only wants three.*
Child:	(Drops both toys into Billie's basket)
Mother:	*That's four.*

(*Linnell & Fluck, 2001, p. 215*)

KEY TERM
Zone of proximal development (ZPD): The gap between capacities that are being developed and those that are not as yet functioning fully.

Vygotsky saw play as related to the concept of the ZPD. Although play typically occurs in the absence of explicit instructions from the adult, it may make use of culturally provided artefacts to support it (such as toys) and it often involves trying out culturally defined roles (teacher, mother, father, doctor, bus driver). Vygotsky says "In play the child functions above his average age, above his usual everyday behaviour, in play he is head high above himself" (1933/1976, p. 552).

As we noted earlier, Vygotsky argued that there was a close link between language and thought. Initially, language—and the complex mental processes that go hand-in-hand with language—are something that only adults have access to. The earliest thought of the child is preverbal. Thus, when adults carefully explain something difficult to a young child, they give the child access to intellectual processes that are normally based on language. In this way, social relationships provide the child's initial contact with language-based intellectual processes and the context in which the child can learn to internalise these same processes that, with further development, will later operate autonomously as verbal thought.

Vygotsky called this pattern of development, in which intellectual processes move from being external—social—to internal, "the general, genetic law of cultural development". He describes it as follows:

> *All the basic forms of the adult's verbal social interaction with the child later become mental functions ... Any function in the child's cultural development appears twice, or on two planes. First it appears on the social plane and then on the psychological plane. First it appears between people, as an interpsychological category and then within the child, as an intra-psychological category. This is equally true with regard to voluntary attention, logical memory, the formation of concepts and the development of volition.*
> *(Vygotsky, 1981/1988, p. 73)*

Long after his death, Vygotsky's social approach to developmental psychology continues to be very influential. There is not really a modern Vygotskian school but his influence can be clearly discerned in the work of Jerome S. Bruner (b. 1915), an American developmental psychologist who was particularly influential in introducing Vygotsky to Western scholars. The influence of Vygotsky is also evident in the continuing exposition by writers such as Valsiner (1988) and Wertsch (1991).

The American psychologist Jerome S. Bruner (b.1915).

Bruner offers a synthesis of many features of Piagetian and Vygotskian psychology (Bruner, Olver, & Greenfield, 1966). He describes three forms of knowing: **enactive representation** (i.e. knowledge based in action or knowing how to do things), **iconic knowledge** based on representing knowledge through visual imagery, and **symbolic knowledge** based on language and transmitted through culture (i.e. knowledge expressed as a verbal proposition that something is the case). These forms of knowledge only partially overlap. For instance, in learning how to ski, enactive representation plays the most important role, and any amount of reading the instruction manual will not guarantee success. On the other hand, expert skiers may improve their performance both by visually imagining the downhill course and through verbal feedback on their performance: In consolidating skills, both iconic and symbolic modes can contribute.

> **Bruner's approach**
>
> - Involves the synthesis of many Piagetian and Vygotskian features.
> - Identified three types of knowledge that partially overlap.
> - Enactive representation is knowledge based on knowing how to do things.
> - Iconic knowledge is based on representation through visual imagery.
> - Symbolic knowledge is based on language and transmitted through culture.
> - Criticises the information-processing explanations of behaviour.
> - Emphasises how culture shapes knowledge of self, and children participate in culture through language.

Bruner was closely associated with the foundation of the cognitive revolution while a Professor at Harvard University in the 1960s. However, he has recently been critical of the reliance, within cognitive science, on the "computational metaphor" and other information-processing explanations for behaviour (see Chapter 3, Observing and Modelling Developmental Change). Instead, he claims that students of development need to take into account the ways in which culture shapes our knowledge of self (Bruner, 1990). All cultures, he argues, incorporate a folk psychology, or set of normative descriptions about what makes people "tick". Children learn the culture's folk psychology early on through the stories they hear, which helps them to organise their experiences. That is, cultures help the child construct meanings, especially through symbolic tools passed from generation to generation. Folk psychology is not primarily based on logical processes (much emphasised in Piagetian psychology) but on narrative and storytelling. Thus children come to participate in culture through language, especially though personal narratives that are culturally universal and which explicitly refer to the self, as children and their parents recreate remembered experiences from their own lives.

John Bowlby (1907–1990)

The British psychologist John Bowlby (1907–1990). Photograph by Martin Argles. Copyright © The Guardian.

Whereas Piaget's and Vygotsky's theories were mainly concerned with the child's intellectual development, John Bowlby was primarily concerned with emotional development and the formation of personality. His theory, although an eclectic mixture of ideas from various developmental disciplines, was ultimately based in the Freudian psychoanalytic tradition. It offers a critical synthesis of evidence from modern research in psychology and biology with some of the more traditional psychoanalytic concerns about development

Bowlby was born in London in 1907. He was the fourth of six children of a distinguished family. John Bowlby followed his father into medicine and took a first-class honours degree in preclinical sciences and psychology at Cambridge University (1929). Before going on to finish his medical studies, he worked in a school for maladjusted children where he became convinced that some of the problems of the severely disturbed, antisocial, young people might be explained as the result of faulty relationships between parents and children. He was particularly struck by disturbed adolescents, who seemed incapable of giving or receiving affection, a deficiency which he thought to be a consequence of prolonged lack of affection in early childhood. He subsequently trained as a psychoanalyst and qualified in medicine and psychiatry at the University of London in the early 1930s.

Bowlby became a child psychoanalyst and worked during the 1930s at the London Child Guidance Clinic. He was sympathetic to the analytic approach but rather critical of some of its more unscientific aspects. He developed a unique synthesis of method and theory drawn from the traditions of Freudian psychoanalysis, from observation and recording of natural history, from field studies of behaviour in the natural environment (especially the work of Konrad Lorenz and Nicholas Tinbergen in ethology), from comparative studies of attachment in non-human primates (especially the work of Harlow in the USA and Hinde in Britain), and from cognitive developmental psychology.

The lynchpin of Bowlby's theory was an attempt to explain the formation of the earliest attachment bonds between infant and mother along ethological principles reformulated in human terms. Early ethologists studied the innate mechanisms whereby young animals recognised and followed their mothers immediately after birth. Bowlby was interested in the existence of similar mechanisms in the formation of attachment between human infants and their caretakers—especially their mother. His original aim was to explain the consequences for personality development of severe disruption of the attachment bond between a mother and her child.

Bowlby's theory placed less emphasis on the traditional Freudian account of infantile sexuality, with its oral, anal, and phallic stages in the formation of personality. Instead, he argued for a primary emotional bond between the infant and her mother that was unrelated to infantile sexuality. (See Holmes, 1993 for a sympathetic account of Bowlby's life and work.) There was another important difference between Bowlby and Freudian psychoanalysts which lay in their respective methodologies. Freudian psychoanalysts employ a developmental method that is primarily retrospective and biographical: They obtain information about childhood through clinical interviews with adults who reflect on their childhood experiences. There is a strong emphasis on the importance of early experience for later development, especially in the concepts of fixation and regression to earlier stages and their role in psychopathology. Bowlby was influenced by some aspects of Freudian theory and method. However, one of his main contributions was to shift the focus from retrospection to the study of the actual formation of emotional relationships and their prospective consequences. Empirical work in Bowlby's tradition has been carried out by many scholars, most notably by Mary Ainsworth in the USA (e.g. Ainsworth, 1973) and by Robert Hinde in Britain (e.g. Hinde, 1982).

A key idea in Bowlby's theory is that the mother provides a secure base from which the developing infant can explore the world and periodically return in safety. The emotional attachment of the baby to the mother normally provides the infant with a sense of safety and security. The evolutionary function of such attachment behaviour is thought to be that, in the short term, it protects the child from predators and, in the longer term, it provides the model on which all other relationships are based. Thus a secure attachment in infancy will pave the way for secure and successful attachments in adulthood that will contribute to the reproductive success of the species in the long term.

Bowlby was much influenced by the work of Harlow (e.g. Harlow, McGaugh, & Thompson, 1971) who tested the psychoanalytic theory that the infant becomes attached to the mother because she satisfies the child's basic needs, such as hunger and thirst. In psychoanalytic theory these basic needs are known as primary drives. The assumption that the child learns to love the mother because she provides for these basic needs has been nicknamed the "cupboard love" theory. Harlow pointed out that mothers not only provide food but also comfort and warmth. He studied the effects of maternal deprivation on infant rhesus monkeys, reared in social isolation, and found that they grew up to be severely incapacitated in their social relationships and ultimately they became very poor, incapable parents (see the following box).

Harlow's research on maternal deprivation in monkeys

Harlow tested the primary drive theory in a study in which he gave baby rhesus monkeys the choice of clinging to a comfortable cloth-covered support which did not dispense food or to an uncomfortable wire support which dispensed milk. The monkeys would feed on the wire support but immediately returned to cling to the preferred cloth-covered support, which suggested that contact comfort was more important than simply being provided with food.

Contact comfort in the rhesus monkey. Reproduced with kind permission of Harlow Primate Laboratory, University of Wisconsin.

In further tests Harlow showed that, given the choice of a comfortable cloth-covered support that dispensed milk and an identical one that did not, the monkeys preferred the support that dispensed milk. However, during the first 20 days the infant monkeys actually preferred a heated wire support to a comfortable but cold cloth support, which suggests that warmth was also a factor. Thereafter, they preferred the cloth support, even though it did not provide food. These results led Harlow to argue that the Freudian "cupboard love" theory of attachment was inadequate. Instead, Harlow argued that a multifactorial theory of attachment in rhesus monkeys is required, which includes such species-specific factors as the desire in monkeys to cling, as well as the more general factors of contact comfort and motherly warmth.

In monkeys, the mother initially provides basic "organic affection" and attachment develops as the mother meets the physical and emotional needs of the infant. This, in turn, provides a sense of safety and security as the infant monkey becomes more mobile and ready for autonomy. The monkey's curiosity about the external environment has as its counterpart the sense of emotional security that provides the courage for exploration.

According to Harlow, the longer-term importance of the love of the mother for her offspring and, reciprocally, the attachment of the infant monkey for the mother, is that it establishes a sense of basic trust that is preparatory for social relationships between peers (people of the same age). These emotional relationships, in turn, lay the groundwork for heterosexual relationships and for eventual satisfactory parenting in a long-term cycle of species reproduction.

Bowlby applied some of Harlow's ideas to human development. He argued that the first attachment bond in humans is analogous to that in rhesus monkeys but it is based on species-specific human behaviours. In human infants clinging is poorly developed so crying and smiling serve the purpose of eliciting maternal caretaking in the early months. As the child becomes more autonomous the quality of attachment of the infant to the parent is an important factor in regulating the child's willingness to explore. Emotionally secure children use the mother as a base, to which they can periodically return as they explore the novelty of their surroundings, while keeping their mother clearly in view (see Chapter 6, Early Social Development, for more on the details of the formation of human attachment bonds).

A secure attachment relationship is thought to lead the child into a range of psychologically healthy developmental pathways. Bowlby argued that insecure patterns of attachment contribute to the formation of a neurotic personality because they take the child down psychologically unhealthy developmental pathways. That is, either the malformation or the forcible disruption of attachment bonds may progressively give rise to personality problems and mental ill health. One example, for which some evidence exists, concerns the relationship between disruption of attachment in young girls and the onset of depression in adulthood. Girls whose mothers die before their 12th birthday have a greatly increased risk of severe depression in adulthood (Brown & Harris, 1980). It is important to note, however, that such an outcome of disrupted attachment is not inevitable. Large-scale epidemiological studies, exploring the role of family experiences as antecedents of depression and anxiety disorders in later life, show that many factors can ameliorate the long-term effects even of the severe disruption caused by the death of a parent. These include good relationships with the surviving parent and other family members, friendships with peers, success in school, making a good supportive marriage, and being of resilient personality (Holmes, 1993).

An early, practical application of Bowlby's ideas arose in the changes he brought about in the hospitalisation of young children. As a result of his work on the separation occasioned when children had to go into hospital, from the 1950s onwards parents have been allowed to remain in hospital with their young children. A very great deal of research is now devoted to studying the formation and elaboration of patterns of attachment between parents and children in cultures as diverse as the United States, Britain, and Japan. Attachment theory has been extended to encompass not only the relation between parent and child but also transgenerational effects, such as the transmission of secure or insecure patterns of attachment through typical parenting behaviour from generation to generation (van Ijzendoorn, 1995a). Children who were insecurely attached to their own parents tend to become parents of insecure children. The relation between attachment,

---

Bowlby's approach

- Ideas derived from Freudian psychoanalytic tradition, with biological and psychological influences.
- Greatly influenced by Harlow's work with rhesus monkeys.
- Mainly concerned with emotional development and the formation of personality.
- Also concerned with maladjustment during childhood and its relation to faulty relationships between parents and children.
- Sympathetic to the analytic approach but critical of its unscientific aspects.
- Developed a unique synthesis of method and theory drawn from Freudian psychoanalysis, observation and recording of natural history, field studies of behaviour, comparative studies with primates, and cognitive development theory.
- Attempted to explain the formation of the earliest attachment bonds between infant and mother along ethological principles that were reformulated in human terms.
- Argued for a primary emotional bond between infant and mother/caretaker that was unrelated to the traditional beliefs of Freudian infant sexuality.
- Shifted the focus from retrospective psychoanalytical study to the study of the formation of emotional relationships and their consequences.
- The mother/caretaker provides a safe and secure base from which the infant can explore the world.
- Secure infant attachment paves the way for psychologically healthy developmental pathways.
- Insecure infant attachment leads to a neurotic personality and subsequent psychologically unhealthy developmental pathways.

temperament (i.e. factors such as sociability, anxiety), and personality development also offers an opportunity to unite biological, social, and cultural aspects of development within a single explanatory framework (Bretherton, 1994).

Conclusion and summary

In the first half of the 20th century the work of John Watson was very influential to the field of psychology. His ideas can be seen as part of a wider emphasis on theories of learning that concentrated on very specific types of animal behaviour that could be demonstrated under strictly controlled laboratory conditions. Watson extended the idea of conditioned behaviour in animals to the behaviour of children when he demonstrated that young children could be taught to fear certain kinds of animal if they associated these animals with negative experiences.

Watson's behaviourist account placed experience at the centre of development. He argued that, with the right kind of experience, children could be taught to achieve anything. Arnold Gesell, a contemporary of Watson, proposed a very different account of development that emphasised nature rather than nurture. In complete contrast to Watson, Gesell used naturalistic methods to study development—including a pioneering use of photography—and he considered a wide range of behaviours rather than the isolated behaviours that were examined by Watson. This difference in methodology between Watson, the behaviourist, and Gesell, the maturationalist, highlights the complex relationship that exists between theory and methodology. Clearly, the view of development that emerges from a particular study will be heavily influenced by the methodology that is chosen for that study. However, in many cases, the type of theory that a researcher holds will guide their choice of methodology.

As the 20th century moved on the sharply polarised theories of the earlier years gave way to accounts of development that emphasised the interaction of nature and nurture. This change in emphasis was accompanied by a broadening in the number of different methods that were used to collect data on developmental change. Notably, experimental procedures developed specifically for use with children were introduced.

We chose to focus on the work of three influential researchers: Jean Piaget, Lev Semeonovich Vygotsky, and John Bowlby. Much contemporary research in developmental psychology is based upon, or is a reaction to, the theories of these three men. Each of their theories shares the assumption that development occurs in stages, although they differ in their main focus. Piaget's theory is mostly concerned with the mechanisms of intellectual development and the acquisition of knowledge. Vygotsky's main contribution was to our understanding of the way in which culture influences development through language and the social and material structure of society. Bowlby was an eclectic thinker who drew on Freudian theory and many other sources in biology, psychology, and ethology to propound an original theory of interpersonal relationships and socio-emotional development. The theories of all three men will be evaluated in greater detail in subsequent chapters where we review contemporary findings on cognitive, social, and applied aspects of developmental psychology.

The stage-like general theories of development that Piaget, Vygotsky, and Bowlby expounded have been supplemented in recent years by approaches from dynamical systems theory and from connectionist computer models. These new approaches raise important questions about whether we should think of development as a progression from one stage to the next. We discuss these more recent approaches to the understanding of development in the next chapter where we consider alternative ways to conceive of developmental change.

Further reading

- Boden, M. (1994). *Piaget* (2nd ed.). Glasgow, UK: Collins Fontana. This is a good place to start if you want to find out more about Piaget and the development of his ideas. It is intended as an introduction to the subject.
- Harris, P.L. (1997). Piaget in Paris: From "autism" to logic. *Human Development*, *40*, 109–123. This paper describes the development in Piaget's views about children's thinking and his methods of data collection. It is quite a difficult paper and is intended for advanced undergraduates.
- Holmes, J. (1993). *John Bowlby and attachment theory*. London: Routledge. This authoritative book describes the origins and development of Bowlby's thinking about the nature and significance of attachment.
- Kozulin, A. (1990). *Vygotsky's psychology*. Hemel Hempstead, UK: Harvester. This book provides a detailed account of Vygotsky's ideas and examines their significance.
- Thompson, R.A. (1998). Early sociopersonality development. In N. Eisenberg (Ed.), *Handbook of child psychology: Vol. 3. Social, emotional, and personality development* (W. Damon, Gen. Ed.; pp. 25–105). New York: Wiley. This detailed chapter reviews studies of attachment and considers how attachment can be measured and how early attachments are related to later behaviour. It is a good place to find out about the complexities in defining and characterising infant attachment.

CHAPTER 3

Observing and modelling developmental change

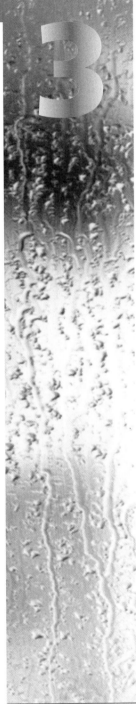

As we saw in Chapter 1, A Brief History of Developmental Psychology, development is fundamentally about change. In this chapter we consider various different ways of thinking about and modelling developmental change. One useful distinction is between two types of change, both of which are important in developmental psychology. These are **transformational change** and **variational change** (Overton, 1998). Transformational change refers to a change over time in form or ability. Children show a great deal of transformational change as they grow from infancy into childhood and adolescence as both their physical appearance and abilities undergo significant development. Variational change is a more subtle concept that refers to the degree that a change varies from an assumed standard. It can best be understood with an example. The ability to think undergoes the striking transformational change from infancy to adolescence that we chart in the chapters of this book. However, at any given developmental level of thinking, variational change is reflected in the different kinds of solutions to particular problems that are used at different times. The description and explanation of variational change is a particular strength of information-processing models of development such as that of Siegler (1998) that we discuss in Information-Processing Approaches, later in this chapter.

A great many abilities—both mental and physical—show variational change. For example, some children are much better at reading than others. Understanding how reading develops requires not only an explanation of transformational change, that is how the strategies involved in reading develop over time, but also an explanation of variational change, that is how the reading strategies of good readers differ from those of less good readers. Understanding variational change also requires us to determine what is within the normal range. Thus for reading we need to know, for any given language, what level of reading is age-appropriate: This requires information about the proportion of children who will read at different levels at a given age so that we can distinguish between good, average, and poor readers.

One theory that provides a useful starting point for thinking about both transformational and variational change is that of the evolutionary biologist, C.H. Waddington, who developed an influential model of the epigenetic landscape.

The epigenetic landscape

Waddington, who published *The Strategy of the Genes* in 1957, was concerned with the complex relationship between phenotype and genotype. The phenotype of an individual is the set of observable characteristics—how the individual looks and behaves—whereas the genotype is the genetic characteristics—the pattern of genes that the individual possesses. The genotype does not predict the phenotype in any simple way especially in more complex organisms: Individuals who appear very similar to each other may have phenotypes that are very different. The crucial point is that the phenotype is the result of an interaction between the genotype and the environment as Waddington's metaphor of the **epigenetic landscape** was intended to explain. He writes:

> *I envisage [development] as a set of branching valleys in a multidimensional space that includes a time dimension, along which the valleys may extend. The development of the phenotype of an individual proceeds along a valley bottom; variations of genotype, or of epigenetic environment, may push the course of development away from the valley floor, up the neighbouring hillside, but there will be a tendency for the process to find its way back.*
>
> (Waddington, 1957, p. 258)

FIG. 3.1 The epigenetic landscape (based on Waddington, 1957).

Figure 3.1 is a diagram of Waddington's epigenetic landscape. The ball represents the developing organism, while the layout of the hills and valleys, along which the ball may roll, represents possible pathways for development. The landscape imposes constraints on the movements of the rolling ball as it progresses downhill. For example, an environmental perturbation might knock the ball off course (i.e. away from the valley floor) but a much greater knock will be required to produce the same effect if the ball is in a deep valley rather than a shallow one. Put another way, the consequences of a particular environmental factor will be very different according to where and when in development it occurs. There will also be differences in the course of development according to the incline of the valley floor into which the ball descends. A valley with a steeply inclined floor will cause more rapid rolling downhill of the ball than one with a less steeply inclined floor. This difference can be seen as representing the relative rapidity of development at different points.

The diagram illustrates how one might think of the possible pathways that development could take. Some developmental processes, both before and after birth, are only affected by extreme environmental influences, whereas others are much more susceptible to such influences. Consider, for example, prenatal development—the development of the baby in the womb before birth—which we discuss in Chapter 4, Development from Conception to Birth. The development of arms and legs in the foetus is strongly determined by the genes—a process known as "canalisation"—and only extreme environmental effects during foetal development will stop this happening. (See Stages in Prenatal Development, in Chapter 4, for a discussion of how the taking of the drug, thalidomide, by pregnant women affected the development of arms and legs in their babies.) Other aspects of prenatal development—such as birthweight—are much more susceptible to environmental influences such as the smoking and drinking habits of the mother, which have direct effect on the foetus.

The location of junctions between the valleys in the epigenetic landscape model represents critical points in development, where further development may take one of several forms, depending on the prevailing environmental factors. The transition points between adjoining valleys can also represent movement between stages of development; and the slope of the valleys can represent the rate of a developmental process, with shallow valleys representing a relatively steady state and steep valleys, at choice points, representing rapid change and transition from one mode of organisation to another. At such transition points, crucial environmental influences may have important consequences even though exactly the same environmental circumstances would have no consequences at other points in the epigenetic landscape.

Perhaps the greatest significance of the model of the epigenetic landscape is that it alerts us to the possibility that development can proceed along many alternative pathways that end up at the same place. The principle of "**equifinality**"—as this is called—explains how development may be slower or quicker in different individuals because it has reached the same end state by different developmental routes. It also leads us to expect that there will be important individual differences in both the rate and course of development in spite of similar end points.

The precise workings of the genes and the environment in development have become much clearer since Waddington's original book in 1957. Behavioural genetics has made great progress in establishing the proportion of variability in behaviour that may be attributed to genetic or to environmental influences for many traits. One way to find out about the relative contribution of genes and the environment is through twin studies that compare genetically identical twins with fraternal twins. Genetically identical twins occur when a fertilised egg divides, whereas fraternal twins develop from different eggs and so have only half their genes in common (just like brothers and sisters). Twin studies have revealed an important role for genetic factors in many general traits, including intellectual ability, aspects of personality, and some forms of psychopathology, including autism.

Twin studies also provide important evidence about two kinds of environmental effects. Twins who are brought up together have a shared environment that may act to make their behaviour more similar. However, twins who are brought up in different environments—typically because they were separated at birth—have different experiences that may make them more dissimilar. However, the interaction between genes and environment is potentially even more complex than this because the presence of certain genes may predispose an individual to seek out a particular kind of environment. For example, Locke (1993) has argued that the neural structures of human infants impel them towards certain kinds of sensory and physical stimulation. In other words, babies seek out particular kinds of stimulation and activities and, in so doing, construct their own environment. It has also been suggested that

KEY TERM
Equifinality: The principle that variations in development route and speed nevertheless result in the same end.

identical twins, who are reared apart, often end up with rather similar environments because their similar genes lead them to seek out similar kinds of stimulation (Bouchard, Lykken, McGue, Segal, & Tellegen, 1990). Thus, even when it is known that strong genetic factors exist, an understanding of development still depends on identifying sources of environmental feedback that give rise to particular emergent properties of developing individuals (Pike & Plomin, 1999). As Plomin, Corley, De Fries, and Faulkner (1990) note, in a discussion of children's television watching:

> *It is critical to recognise that genetic effects on behavior are not deterministic in the sense of a puppeteer pulling strings. Genetic influences imply probabilistic propensities rather than hard-wired patterns of behavior. We can turn off the television as we please, but turning it off or leaving it on pleases individuals differently, in part due to genetic factors.*
>
> *(Plomin et al., 1990, cited in Locke, 1993)*

In view of the complex interaction between genes and environment, development can be thought of as a series of changes within a self-organising system. On this view, development is emergent: Its causes are non-linearly related to the outcome and often it is not obvious how earlier forms of organisation come to influence later ones. Changes in development may occur suddenly and it is not always clear what precise environmental effects have triggered such changes. Furthermore, small perturbations at the beginning of such a self-organising process can have large effects later on as the epigenetic landscape model illustrates. Two examples from the development of bird embryos illustrate this point.

Gottlieb (1992) found that Mallard duck embryos need to hear their own vocalisations if they are to respond appropriately, after hatching, to the mother Mallard duck's assembly call. Mallard embryos, who were deprived of hearing their own vocalisations or those of other Mallard chicks incubating in adjacent eggs, were relatively poor at recognising their own species after hatching. Wallman (1979) found that if domestic hen chicks were not permitted to see their toes in the first two days after hatching, they failed to peck at mealworms in the manner of normal chicks. In other words it was the sight of the chicks' own toes that triggered the pecking behaviours they subsequently used to feed on worms. These two examples show that quite small, non-obvious features of the auditory or visual environment may serve an important role in the emergence of species-typical behaviours with long-term consequences for subsequent behavioural organisation.

Stage theories of development

One of the fundamental questions about developmental pathways is whether the course of development is best understood as a continuous process of change or whether there are sharp discontinuities, or stages, in development. Note that the question of whether there are developmental stages is separate from the question of what gives rise to stages. Piaget, whose own thinking was very much influenced by Waddington's idea of the epigenetic landscape, introduced the concept of stages in his theory as a way of demarcating qualitatively distinct periods in development.

Within developmental psychology the term, stage, has a rather specific meaning. It is intended to convey the fact that there is a change in the quality or characteristics of the individual that has arisen as a function of development. The American psychologist, John Flavell (1963), has suggested the following criteria for a stage in development:

1. Stages are distinguished by **qualitative changes**. It is not a matter of simply being able to do more of something but it also involves doing it differently. For instance, babies usually move around first by crawling (or bottom shuffling) and only later by walking. These are qualitatively different types of locomotion and therefore this aspect of motor development has at least one of the characteristics of a developmental stage.
2. The transition from one stage to another is marked by *simultaneous* changes in a great many of the other aspects of a child's behaviour. For example, when children first learn to speak, which involves understanding the symbolic value of words, they also behave as if objects have symbolic properties in their play, when they pretend that a brick is a car, or a doll is a person. That is, there is a widespread effect of acquiring the capacity to treat the world in terms of symbol systems.
3. Stage transitions are typically rapid. A good example is the adolescent growth spurt where a child may, in a few months, gain several inches in height and several pounds in weight. Similar, rapid reorganisations can be observed in other areas, as when the child acquires language and there is an exponential increase in the number of words learned once the first 30 or so words has been acquired (although many stages are actually involved).

Although the major modern stage theory of development was that of Jean Piaget, many other theorists have used the notion of stages. Freud describes the oral, anal, and phallic stages of infancy and the Oedipal stage of early childhood, and Vygotsky characterised a series of stages that coincide with those of Piaget. Each of these authors was influenced by the evolutionary implications of Darwin's theory which explains why there is considerable resemblance between them. The table below compares the stages proposed by Piaget,

COMPARISON OF MAJOR STAGES OF DIFFERENT THEORISTS			
Period of development	**Piaget**	**Vygotsky**	**Freud**
Infancy 0–2 years	Sensorimotor	Affiliation	Oral Anal Phallic
Early childhood 2–7 years	Preoperational	Play	Oedipal
Middle childhood 7–12 years	Concrete operational	Learning	Latency
Adolescence 12–19 years	Formal operational	Peer	Genital activity
Adulthood	Formal operational	Work	
Adapted from Cole and Cole (2001).			

KEY TERM
Qualititative changes: Distinctions based on how degrees of change are expressed.

Vygotsky, and Freud. The detail of the stages need not concern us for the moment. What is important is that all three theories use the notion of stages that span essentially similar periods of development.

Bowlby, whose work we introduced in Chapter 2, did not subscribe strictly to the Freudian stage theory even though many of his ideas were influenced by Freudian theory. Bowlby denied that there was a strict linear succession of stages in development and adopted instead a stage theory derived from Waddington's epigenetic landscape. On this account, several lines of development were possible, the outcome depending on the particular organism–environment interaction.

There are more radical alternatives to traditional stage theories and we examine three of these in the next sections—the dynamic systems approach, connectionist modelling, and the information-processing approach.

The dynamic systems approach

Dynamic systems theory is the study of the ways in which systems that are open to the effects of the environment change over time. The aim is to produce a mathematical model that describes how *qualitative* changes in organisation come about through the accumulation of small-scale *quantitative* changes. In embryology, for example, irreversible changes in the form of the embryo occur as energy is absorbed by the developing system.

Dynamic systems theory attempts to model non-linear dynamics. There are two sorts of dynamics: *linear* and *non-linear*. **Linear dynamics** are based on Newton's laws of motion of which the third law is best known—for every action, there is an opposite and equal reaction. The theory of linear dynamics is most obviously applied to mechanical interactions, such as billiard ball

Dynamic systems theory

- Study of the ways that systems are affected by the environmental change over time.
- Describes how qualitative changes in organisation come about through the accumulation of quantitative changes.
- Models non-linear dynamics.
- Can be implemented on a computer.

Linear dynamics

- Based on Newton's laws of motion.
- Can be applied to mechanical interactions and physical systems.
- Result in proportional adjustments so that damage occurs in a smooth, continuous manner.

Non-linear dynamics

- More typical of biological systems.
- Change is sudden after passing through a marginal state between old and new forms.
- Can be discontinuous, or a "step" change, or U-shaped, or inverted U-shaped functions.

collisions. Such dynamic interactions with the environment result in proportional adjustments so that any change is performed in a smooth, continuous way. However, smooth change of this kind is not characteristic of the patterns of change that occur in development. For developmental change **non-linear dynamics** provide a more appropriate model and this is why it is this kind of change that dynamic systems theory attempts to model (Thelen & Smith, 1994; van Geert, 1993, 1998). The systems described by non-linear dynamics change suddenly after passing through a fluctuating, marginal state between old and new forms of stable organisation.

The difference between linear and non-linear dynamics is well illustrated by Muir (1999) who describes four different patterns of developmental change (see Figure 3.2). The four patterns are continuous, discontinuous, U-shaped, and inverted U-shaped developmental functions. The continuous developmental function is consistent with linear dynamics, whereas the discontinuous, step function, and the two U-shaped functions are consistent with non-linear dynamics. The example of continuous, linear change in Figure 3.2 might represent something like an increase in height that gradually levels off with development. This example is typical of the kind of continuous change that occurs in development because the degree of change levels off with age: Children grow fastest when they are very young and their rate of increase in height gradually tails off.

In the other three profiles depicted in Figure 3.2, the nature of change over time is rather different. In the case of discontinuous change, there is a sudden change in behaviour—sometimes called a "step" change. In the case of the inverted U-shaped function, an ability gradually improves and then declines with age; and in the case of the U-shaped function an ability may be present early in life, only to disappear and re-emerge later in development. Such U-shaped patterns have been observed for behaviours such as neonatal stepping movements that appear immediately after birth then disappear before

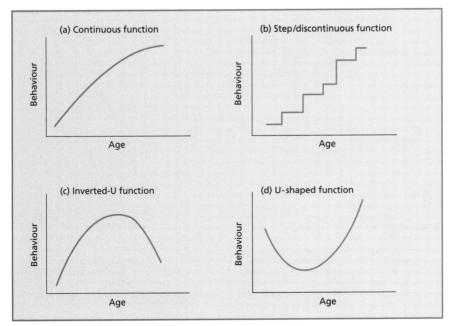

FIG. 3.2 Developmental functions showing change with age. The continuous function in (a) is linear, whereas the step, inverted-U, and U functions in (b), (c), and (d) respectively are non-linear.

KEY TERM
Non-linear dynamics:
Sudden change in a discontinuous step or U-shaped pattern.

reappearing when children start to walk (Butterworth, 1989). We discuss the relationship between neonatal stepping and later walking in Chapter 4, Development from Conception to Birth.

Van Geert's research provides a good illustration of the way that dynamic systems theory can model developmental change. One example (van Geert, 1993) concerns vocabulary development in a young child—a topic that we examine in detail in Chapter 7, The Beginnings of Language Development. Dynamic modelling begins by identifying a number of variables that are relevant to describing vocabulary development. In van Geert's model there were two variables—the growth rate (a measure of how quickly vocabulary size is increasing, r) and what van Geert describes as "feedback delay" (f). In simple terms, feedback delay is a measure of the impact of knowing a certain number of words on later learning. Both growth rate and feedback delay can be independently altered in the model. Van Geert has shown that, for the particular child whose acquisition he was attempting to model, a growth rate of 0.35 and a feedback delay of one week produced the best fit between the model and the data. The fit between the model and the data was very close (see Figure 3.3).

Van Geert (1998) suggests that dynamic systems theory can be used in three different ways. First, it can describe development as a process that occurs over real time. Second, it can be used as a method for fitting observed data to dynamic models and, reciprocally, for modelling change in a way that helps to make theories more explicit. Third, dynamic systems theory may be useful as a broad metaphor for explaining the rapid transitions typical of stage changes.

An important feature of the dynamic approach is the role that is afforded to chance in setting development along a particular trajectory. Chance or random (stochastic) variability has traditionally been considered as a source of error in psychology. It has no place in the workings of a fully determined system

FIG. 3.3 A well-fitting curve develops if the empirical curve is considered as a two-step process. The first step seems to be an initial growth period that stabilises at about 25 words in week 12. Then there is a secondary growth period that starts at this level and stabilises at about 350 words. Adapted from van Geert (1993).

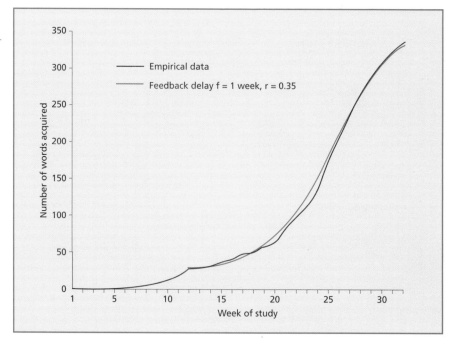

(i.e. where there is precise knowledge of the initial and final point of development). In modern dynamic approaches, however, it has been realised that chance may play a creative role in development, with rather different outcomes emerging from very similar initial conditions through the operation of random factors. Van Geert's (1993) computer simulations illustrate how small changes in outset conditions can give rise to large changes in outcome.

Examples of the creative contribution of chance can be found in the development of the brain and in the development of motor abilities. Initially, random processes give rise to variation in brain structures or in behaviour and this variation, in its turn, enables competition and selection between alternative developmental outcomes. This process is obviously reminiscent of the Darwinian principle of natural selection. In the formation of the brain there is competition in the growth of nerve axons for a limited number of target sites. An initially random process of exuberant growth is eventually stabilised as the network of neural connections becomes functional and particular nervous system pathways are selected for further development. At the behavioural level, similar principles apply to the early development of movements, such as reaching and grasping, where random variation in patterns of activity offers a basis for the eventual selection of effective forms of action.

The connectionist approach

Another way to model the non-linear change—and to account for rapid stage transitions—is to use **connectionist models** which, like those of dynamic systems theory, are implemented on a computer. They consist of a large number of highly interconnected nodes. Each node is connected to every

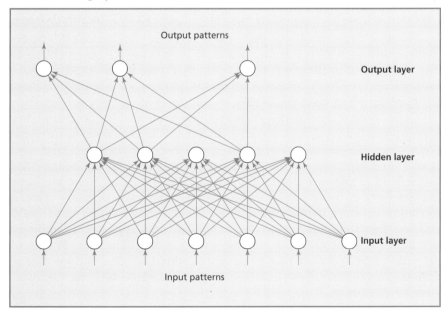

FIG. 3.4 A simple connectionist network, showing input, hidden, and output layers. As learning occurs, there is weight adjustment in the nodes between layers, working from the output layer back to the input layer. As each trial occurs, the weights of the nodes at the next level down are adjusted so they will produce the desired level of activation in each node at the higher level that has just been adjusted.

KEY TERM
Connectionist models:
Models of learning implemented on a computer in which there are many interconnected nodes.

Connectionist models

- Connectionist networks can be implemented on a computer.
- The models consist of a large number of interconnected nodes that are arranged at different levels.
- Learning occurs by altering the strength of the connections between nodes in the different layers, so some become stronger and others weaker.
- The network compares the pattern produced in the output layer with the correct response, and adjusts the weights of the connections of the different layers to ensure the most accurate relationship between patterns of input and patterns of output.

other node either directly or via connections to intervening nodes. Figure 3.4 shows one type of connectionist network that consists of three different layers, an input layer, an output layer, and a hidden layer. Each layer has a different number of nodes with the largest number in the input layer and successively fewer nodes in the hidden and output layers. Learning in a connectionist network (**c-net**) takes place by altering the strength of the connections between nodes in the different layers.

At the start of a study all the connections between the input, hidden, and output nodes are of equal strength but, as learning occurs, the strength (or "weight") of connections is altered so that some become stronger and others become weaker. The weights change because the c-net is able to compare the pattern being produced in the output layer with the correct response. There are various ways that this comparison between the current response of the network and the correct response can be achieved. One way is through **backpropagation**, often abbreviated to "backprop". The weights of connections leading directly to the output layer are adjusted after each trial to produce a more accurate response. Then the weights of the nodes at the next layer down are adjusted so that they will produce the desired level of activation in each node at the higher layer that has just been adjusted. This process continues until the weights connecting each layer down from the input layer have been altered. This process of weight adjustment, working backwards from the output layer to the input layer, occurs after every trial. At first, the weight of connections fluctuates considerably with each learning trial but, slowly, the weights stabilise as they move to a setting where, overall, they ensure the most accurate relationship between patterns of input and patterns of output. (For more technical details of how this occurs see Elman et al., 1996.)

C-nets were originally designed to demonstrate that learning can occur without rules but they have also shown that stage-like changes in learning can occur when the same kind of learning process is applied over and over again. An early connectionist model was developed by Rumelhart and McClelland (1986) in order to demonstrate how the past tense might be learned without using a rule. In English, the past tense of many verbs is formed by adding ED to the verb stem as in *hunt–hunted* and *talk–talked*. Verbs that take the ED ending are described as regular verbs. However, a significant number of English verbs do not take the ED ending. These are known as irregular verbs and their past tense can be formed in one of a number of different ways as in *sing–sang, swim–swam, fall–fell* (where the vowel changes), *have–had* or *go–went*.

The c-net used Rumelhart and McClelland (1986) was a relatively simple one in that it had only a single layer of connections (see Figure 3.5 for a diagram of a small section of the network) but there were 460 input unit and 460 output units with each input unit connected to every output unit. Rumelhart and McClelland presented 420 different word stems as the input and the task of the

KEY TERMS

C-net: Abbreviation of connectionist network.

Backpropagation: In a c-net, one method of altering the connections between nodes during the learning process. Achieved by adjusting the weights of connections backwards after each trial.

Overregularisation errors: The tendency to apply grammatical rules in situations that should be exceptions to those rules.

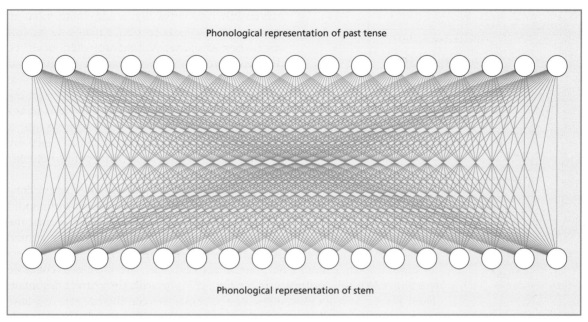

FIG. 3.5 The learning network in Rumelhart and McClelland's (1986) model of the acquisition of the English past tense. The input layer refers to the stem of the verb and the output layer refers to the equivalent past tense. Reproduced with permission from J.L. Elman, E.A. Bates, M.K. Johnson, A. Karmiloff-Smith, D. Parisi, and K. Plunkett (1996), *Rethinking innateness: A connectionist perspective on development.* Cambridge, MA: MIT Press.

network was to learn to produce the appropriate past tense for each stem. All the verbs were presented once in each set of training trials. At the end of training, the performance of the c-net was rather similar to that shown by children when they learn to produce past tense forms (see Figure 3.6) The learning curves were similar to those of children, regular and irregular verbs were treated differently, and, most strikingly, the c-net produced overregularisation errors just like children. **Overregularisation errors** occur where the ED ending is used incorrectly with an irregular verb as in *singed, falled,* or *goed.* (See Inside-out Theories in Chapter 8 for further discussions of c-net models of learning the past tense.)

One of the main claims about the strength of connectionist models made by Elman et al. (1996) in their book, *Rethinking Innateness,* is that they demonstrate how the same learning mechanism can give rise to different kinds of performance at different times. This raises the question of whether connectionist models can also account for stage transitions in development. In order to do this they have to show not just a steady increment in performance across time—or even a U-shaped

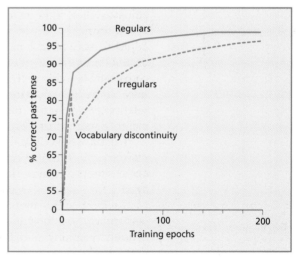

FIG. 3.6 Performance on regular and irregular verbs in the Rumelhart and McClelland (1986) model of the acquisition of the English past tense. The vocabulary discontinuity at the tenth training epoch indicates the onset of overregularisation errors in the network. Reproduced with permission from J.L. Elman, E.A. Bates, M.K. Johnson, A. Karmiloff-Smith, D. Parisi, and K. Plunkett (1996), *Rethinking innateness: A connectionist perspective on development.* Cambridge, MA: MIT Press.

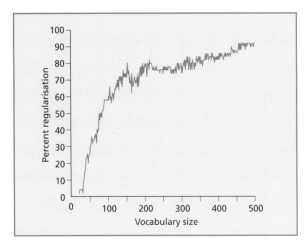

FIG. 3.7 Network performance on novel verbs in the Plunkett and Marchman (1993) simulations. The graph plots the tendency to add a suffix to a novel stem. Reproduced with permission from J.L. Elman, E.A. Bates, M.K. Johnson, A. Karmiloff-Smith, D. Parisi, and K. Plunkett (1996), *Rethinking innateness: A connectionist perspective on development.* Cambridge, MA: MIT Press.

curve—but substantial and rapid changes. There is compelling evidence that c-nets can exhibit stage-like transitions. For example, the model of vocabulary acquisition developed by Plunkett and Marchman (1993)—in which labels are matched to images—demonstrates the typical "spurt" in rate of learning new vocabulary that has been found in many studies of early language development. When children first start to talk they initially produce new words rather slowly but, once their vocabulary has reached 30 or so words, they show a marked increase in the rate at which they acquire new words. In the c-net, success at matching labels to images was rather low for the first 20 to 30 epochs of training but after that there was a dramatic increase in the success rate (see Figure 3.7).

Similar "stages" have been demonstrated in c-net modelling of the balance beam problem (see Figure 3.8a). Siegler (1981) found that when children are given a balance beam they show four clear stages in performance when they are asked to judge which end of the balance beam will go down (see Chapter 11, Cognitive Development in Middle Childhood). At stage 1 (age four years) children judge only on basis of weight (or mass) and so will say that the side with the heavier mass will go down. Then, at stage 2, children take distance into account if the masses on either side are equal. At stage 3 children are correct when either mass or distance differ but they can only guess when both differ. Finally, at around 12 years, children are able to take both weight and distance into account.

McClelland and Jenkins (1991) attempted to reproduce these four stages in the learning of a c-net. Weights were initially set at random so there was no systematic decision at first but the weights moved rapidly from their random state and systematic output patterns begin to emerge. Early on in the training, 85% of performance fell into stage 1 and involved only differences in mass. Then distance began to be taken into account if the mass on the balance were equal (stage 2) and then the network showed correct performance if there was no conflict between distance and mass (stage 3). The network did not, however, reach the correct solution demonstrated by children at stage 4.

At first sight there are some impressive similarities between the performance of children (as shown by Siegler) and the performance of the network over its training epochs. There were abrupt transitions from one stage to the next and the order of the stages was the same. However there are some important differences between the learning shown by children and that shown by the McClelland and Jenkins c-net. First, the training regime provided more information about mass or weight in the early part of training—which probably explains why the c-net initially gave priority to mass rather than to distance. Second, the design of the c-net explicitly separated out information about weight and distance. Finally, systematic feedback about accuracy was provided after every learning trial.

Where c-nets have been most useful is in demonstrating that stage-like learning can emerge from a single, underlying learning process. As we saw in the previous section, proponents of dynamic systems theory such as van Geert (1991) and Thelen and Smith (1994) have argued against the view that there are fundamental changes in the nature of children's representation of the kind proposed by Piaget. They have demonstrated that apparently striking examples of non-linear changes in development (such as the increasing number of words that a child can produce over the first two years of life) can be explained as non-linear functions. They argue that marked changes in behaviour—which can be taken as evidence of a child's transition from one stage of development to another—can be explained in terms of a single process operating over the entire course of development. C-nets offer this same possibility. By showing that marked changes in behaviour over time can be explained as emergent properties of a system that is functioning in the same way right from the start of learning, developmental psychologists must consider that stage transitions may arise from incremental changes in the same underlying capacity.

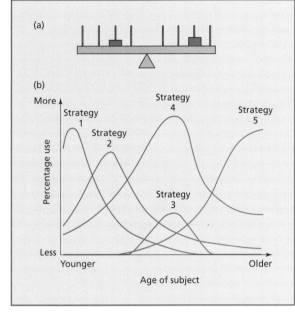

FIG. 3.8 (a) The balance beam. (b) Siegler's overlapping wave model of cognitive development. From R.S. Siegler (1996), *Emerging minds: The process of change in children's thinking.* Copyright © 1996 Oxford University Press, Inc. Reproduced with permission.

Information-processing approaches

The information-processing approach to explaining development was first advanced by Klahr and Wallace (1976) and Siegler (1998). This general approach emphasises the detailed analysis of the processes involved in individual tasks and their modelling in computer programs. The idea is to consider how children's ability to meet the processing demands of a particular task changes over time. For example, a task may require a certain number of items to be held in memory at the same time and so this aspect will prove problematic for young children who can only remember a small number of items. Similarly, a particular task may require a child to carry out a particular kind of reasoning, for example to deal with two dimensions that are changing independently but are inter-related. Again, young children will find it difficult when they have to take two variables into account simultaneously.

In order to explain the issues that are raised by an information-processing approach we will concentrate on Siegler's theory which is set out most recently in his book, *Children's Thinking* (1998). When we considered connectionism in the previous section, we discussed Siegler's study of children's performance on the balance beam problem. Siegler outlined four stages that children progress through in solving this problem. They begin by taking only the weights on either side of the balance beam into account when they predict whether one side will tip down or whether the beam will balance. At the next stage children can take account of distance if the weights on either side are equal. They then progress to a point where they are correct when either the weights or the distance from the fulcrum are the same and the other variable is different but, if both weight and distance, children resort to guessing. In the final stage, which does not develop until around 12 years, children are able to take both weight and distance into account. Interestingly, even in Western society, not all children reach this final level where they realise that the balance of the beam is determined by the product of weight and distance (e.g. weight x distance) on each side.

Siegler's analysis of children's thinking has explored the role of increasing cognitive abilities in memory and in the processes that are involved in the retrieval and manipulation of information in memory. There is now good evidence about the way that children's working memory develops with age. Working memory is used when people have to remember a set of items—such as an address or telephone number—for a short time. Older children can maintain considerably more information in working memory than younger children because they are able to make better use of rehearsal when they have to remember a number of items. Rehearsal is important because items fade rapidly from working memory and so to retain them it is necessary to repeat or rehearse them. It is easy to show how important rehearsal is in working memory by asking someone to recall a list of items while repeating aloud something like "double-double". This effectively blocks rehearsal and dramatically reduces the amount that can be remembered. Children become much more efficient at rehearsal as they grow older and, whereas a typical five-year-old can only remember between three and four items, eleven-year-olds can remember around five items (Hitch & Towse, 1995). Most adults can remember six or seven items when they use rehearsal.

Clearly, the amount of information that a child can remember will have a strong impact on the level of task complexity that they can manage. However, the amount that can be remembered is not the only thing that is important. Another important feature is the ability to encode information. Children often fail to encode the important features of objects and events simply because they have not realised what these are. Siegler has been interested in the way that efficient encoding develops over time. For example, in the balance beam task, children progress from encoding only weight to encoding both weight and distance.

Another central idea in Siegler's theory is that children have, at any one time, a number of different ways of thinking about many topics. These varied ways of thinking compete with each other so that, over time, the more advanced ways become increasingly prevalent. Children thus have alternative strategies for solving problems that compete with each other over time. With experience, some strategies are used less and less, while others—the ones that prove effective—are used more and more. At the same time, new strategies come in and others disappear completely. Figure 3.8b illustrates Siegler's model which he describes as an overlapping waves model.

Siegler has used his model to explain children's developing abilities across a range of tasks including arithmetic, telling the time, spelling, and problem solving as well as performance in memory tasks. One attractive feature of Siegler's model is that it is good at explaining variational change since his view is that several different strategies are available to children at particular points in

---

Information-processing approach

- Emphasises detailed analysis of the processes involved in individual tasks and their modelling in computer programs.
- Considers how a child's ability to meet the processing demands of a particular task changes over time.
- Children have alternative strategies for solving problems that compete with each other over time.
- With experience the successful strategies are used more and the less successful strategies are used less.

development. For example, most five-year-olds can use a variety of strategies for simple addition problems such as 3 + 4. Sometimes they count from 1 putting up one hand with three fingers, and the other hand with four fingers and counting the total from 1 to 7. At other times, the same children might use their fingers but recognise the total number of fingers without counting especially if the total number is small. On other occasions they might recall the answer without counting or using fingers. Siegler argues that all children use a range of strategies and that the same child, tested on different days, will use different strategies. We discuss children's use of strategies in Chapter 13, Learning to Do Mathematics.

Carrying out research in developmental psychology

Having discussed alternative theories about the nature of developmental change, we turn to the methods that have been adopted to study change. As we have seen, development takes place as a process over time; and it is influenced by many factors including nutrition, parenting, schooling, and biological growth. It is not possible to study all the factors that influence development at the same time and so it has been necessary to design research methods that allow sources of error in an investigation to be controlled.

Ethical issues in the assessment and testing of children

It is important to be aware that any study of development entails ethical considerations that will govern how the investigation is carried out, how it is reported, and the confidentiality of the information about participants. Professional organisations such as the American Psychological Association (APA) or the British Psychological Society (BPS) publish such ethical guidelines to which psychologists must adhere.

In Chapter 2, Developmental Psychology in the 20th Century, we mentioned a famous study that was carried out by Watson in 1919 to investigate childhood fears. The study involved deliberately subjecting a small child to a frightening situation. Such an experiment could not be carried out today as research in developmental psychology is now governed by a very strict code of ethics.

Probably the most detailed guidelines for the ethical treatment of children in psychological investigations is provided by the Society for Research in Child Development (SRCD). Full details of the guidelines can be read on the SRCD website at www.srcd.org. Two of the most important issues covered in the guidelines concern the kind of procedures that can be used with children and, equally importantly, the consent that must be obtained before any study can be carried out. Regarding the first issue, the guidelines state that:

The investigator should use no research procedure that may harm the child either physically or psychologically. The investigator is also obligated at all times to use the least stressful research procedure whenever possible.

It is clear that such a guideline would prohibit Watson's stressful procedure but care also has to be taken that children are not subject to less obvious stresses such as loss of self-esteem or embarrassment.

The second important principle concerns what is called "informed consent". This principle applies to all research in psychology in that any participant must fully understand what is involved in a study before giving agreement to take part. The problem is that young children may not be able to fully understand what they will be required to do and so they cannot give informed consent. In such a case the study can be explained to a suitable adult—such as a parent or teacher—who can then give consent on behalf of the child. Even when this has happened, however, it is still very important that children have a good understanding of what will happen in a study and they are also given an opportunity to agree or not to agree to take part. They should also be allowed to withdraw from a study part-way through. In the case of infant studies it is important that the investigator abandon a study if an infant shows signs of discomfort or prolonged distress.

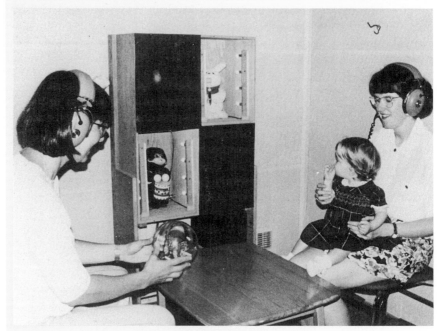

A child being tested in a laboratory setting.

KEY TERMS
Longitudinal studies:
A research design in which data are gathered from the same individuals over a period of time.
Cross-sectional studies:
A research design in which children of various ages are studied at the same time.

In order to observe the process of development it is necessary to make comparisons between people at different ages and this raises methodological complications because people differ along so many dimensions. The solution to these problems has been to sample the population very carefully in order to make controlled comparisons between selected groups. Developmental research is also constrained by time. Where developmental changes occur rapidly, as in infancy for example, it is often important to carry out **longitudinal studies** in which the same child is studied on successive occasions. However, where long-term developmental relations are of interest, it may only be feasible to carry out **cross-sectional studies** where groups of children of different ages are compared to obtain an understanding of the typical characteristics of

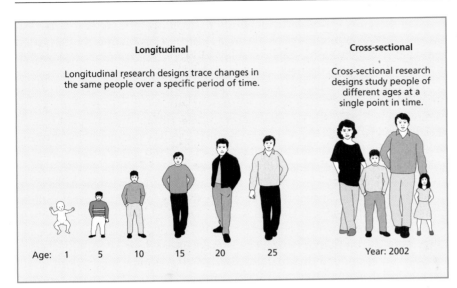

FIG. 3.9 Longitudinal and cross-sectional research designs.

children at any given age. Figure 3.9 illustrates the main differences between longitudinal and cross-sectional studies.

In a *longitudinal design* the developmental psychologist collects information about the same group of children at different ages. Thus, if a study involves the comparison of the behaviour of children at five, six and seven years a group of children would be tested when they were five years old and then they would be tested again, at the ages of six and seven years. Longitudinal studies have the advantage that they can clearly reveal the pattern of changes within the same individual over time. Obviously, this method may require a prolonged commitment from a researcher if changes occurring over several years are to be studied but a major advantage is that differences among individuals—an important aspect of variational change—will emerge clearly since it is possible to see whether, for example, there are relationships over time in particular aspects of behaviour.

The advantage of longitudinal designs for looking at change over time is well illustrated in a study by Bates, Bretherton, and Snyder (1988) of early language development. The researchers followed children from the time they were 10 months old until they were just over two years old. The main focus of the study was the relationship between very early language ability and later ability. Bates et al. found that there were important consistencies between children's language in the first year of life and their language several months later. They also found some important inconsistencies. For example, children's understanding of words before their first birthday was highly predictive of how well they could understand language at 16 months. However, early comprehension was not predictive of how well children were talking at 20 months. Looking at the relationship between earlier and later development in this way is only possible if the same children are studied over a period of time. Analysis of change within the individual is essential where there is large individual variation in development, as in the case of language.

It should perhaps be noted, however, that there are some potential problems with longitudinal designs. Perhaps the major one is that they take a considerable amount of time because researchers have to wait for the children to grow older.

Another difficulty is that participants often drop out of the study for practical reasons such as moving out of the area. A further problem is that repeated testing may not be appropriate if a child is likely to learn about a task and so behave differently on the next occasion of testing.

For a number of reasons it may be more appropriate to use a *cross-sectional* design that compares two or more different groups of children who are of different ages. Unlike the longitudinal design each group of participants is seen at only one age. Thus, if a researcher wished to study development between five and seven years, three different groups of children would be selected who were five, six, and seven years old respectively.

A cross-sectional design has the advantage that studies can be carried out much more quickly since it is not necessary to wait for an individual child to grow older. Cross-sectional studies will reveal the general way in which behaviour and ability change with age and they are often used when a wide age range is to be compared. However, cross-sectional designs will not always reveal as much about individual differences in development nor about subtle changes in behaviour over time. They are probably best used when it is expected that children will show a high degree of similarity in their development.

Because they are less time consuming to carry out, the majority of studies in developmental psychology employ cross-sectional designs. This prevalence is reflected in this book where we describe many cross-sectional studies. One such study was carried out by Hughes and reported by Donaldson (1978). This experiment was concerned with the developing ability of children between the ages of three and a half to five years to understand what another person can see from a particular viewpoint. In order to test this a group of children was selected so as to span the age range. They were all given the same task in which they were required to play a game of hiding a boy doll out of sight of a policeman doll. The hiding game was played with a model that could be varied in complexity so that it was increasingly difficult to tell whether the policeman could see the boy doll.

The results showed that the youngest children could almost always tell whether the policeman could see the doll providing that the layout of the model was very simple. However, as the task was made more difficult by increasing the complexity of the model, the younger children became less accurate. The oldest children in the study could perform accurately even with the most complex layout.

In a cross-sectional design, such as the one we have just described, it is very important that the children who are compared differ only in age and do not differ in any other respect that might affect the outcome of the experiment. For example, it is generally important that the children at the different age levels have similar levels of ability. Sometimes researchers use **intelligence tests** to select children of similar ability levels for the different age groups. Other factors that may be relevant include gender (male or female), socio-economic status of parents, birth order (only child, first born, second born, etc.), handedness (left or right handed), and whether children live in an urban area or in the country. Of course, not all of these factors will be relevant in every study. It will depend on what aspect of development is being investigated.

Some factors about the selection of participants are also of concern in longitudinal designs. In both cross-sectional and longitudinal research designs, it is essential to allow for effects of the **cohort** being studied.

KEY TERMS
Intelligence tests: Measures of intellectual ability, such as the IQ, Binet–Simon, or Stanford–Binet tests.
Cohort: A statistical term for a group of people with something in common, usually having been born in the same year, in which case their development can be said to have occurred under similar social and historical conditions, with shared experiences.

People born in the same era may share environments that are not held in common with people born in a different era; and the long-term effects of such environmental differences may confound our investigations. For example, nutritional standards have significantly changed over the last 50 years in Western Europe and the quality and quantity of food available to children born in 1940 was significantly different to that available in 2000. Education has also changed and a wider range of subjects is taught at school. Children also stay at school longer and many more progress to tertiary education. These historical changes will have repercussions on many aspects of physical and mental development.

A study by Schaie (1990) illustrates the importance of cohort effects. Schaie was interested in whether people's mathematical and reasoning abilities had changed over time. He tested a large sample of adults born between 1889 and 1959 and found that reasoning skills had consistently increased: Adults born in the 1950s had the best reasoning skills and adults born in the 1890s had the worst. However, the pattern for mathematical ability was not one of simple improvement with time. There was an increase in number skills among adults born between 1889 and 1910 followed by a period of stability until 1924. Between 1924 and 1959, however, there was a consistent decline in ability. These findings are important for studying the effects of ageing because they show that intellectual functioning is not only a function of age but also of the year in which someone was born.

Methods of data collection

In addition to the choice between a longitudinal and cross-sectional research design, developmental psychologists also have a variety of different methods of data collection available to them. Many studies continue to use **observation** of naturalistic behaviour. Methods of observation include simple diary records, of which Darwin's study of his son Doddy is an early example (see The Evolution of Development, in Chapter 1), and observations made in natural settings such as the home or nursery. There are also standardised laboratory observations such as when mother–child interaction is observed under standardised conditions with an identical environment containing identical toys.

In recent years the opportunity for observation has been greatly extended by the use of videotaping, which allows behaviour to be analysed in much greater detail. In particular, the use of slow motion allows the observer to record subtle aspects of behaviour that cannot be reliably recorded from live observation. Video analysis allows the temporal sequence of related behaviours such as looking, pointing, and vocalising to be precisely determined. It also allows the same segment of behaviour to be viewed over and over again to check out the accuracy of observation both within and between observers.

Other ways of studying development are through the use of **clinical methods** such as interviews—famously used by Piaget—and by standardised tests of general abilities such as intelligence and of more specific abilities such as language, reading, and mathematics. Probably the most common method of data collection in developmental psychology is to carry out an experiment and collect appropriate measures of children's behaviour. A huge range of different experimental methodologies are in common use and the one that a researcher selects will depend both on the age of the participants and the hypothesis that

KEY TERMS
Observation: A naturalistic method of data collection, using diary records and observation in the natural environment, or standardised conditions in a laboratory.
Clinical methods: A research method in which questions are tailored to the individual, with each question depending on the answer to the previous one. Often used to assess mentally ill patients.

Naturalistic observation of mother–child interaction in a home setting.

is under investigation. The greatest range of possibilities for gathering data occurs with older children who can often take part in studies that are rather similar to those carried out with adults. The greatest challenges come with studies of infants and young children. The chapters on infant development in the next section of the book, Part 2: Early Development, describe some of the ingenious ways that have been developed for collecting reliable data from young babies who have a very limited repertoire of responses.

Experimental studies of children's development offer the greatest precision in testing hypotheses because they allow very tight control of key variables. This explains their popularity among researchers. However, other ways of gathering data are also important. Observational methods can provide the opportunity to look at behaviour in a natural setting. They are also invaluable for reflecting the enormous richness and complexity of children's behaviour especially in social situations. What is evident from this book is that, from its inception, developmental psychology has benefited enormously from the wide range of methods of data collection that are used.

Assessing children's abilities

Many studies in developmental psychology require the selection and matching of children on particular abilities. Often children are selected on the basis of IQ— a measure of their general level of intellectual functioning (see The Developmental Principle, in Chapter 1). IQ is assessed by giving children a range of different subtests that assess different aspects of their overall ability. Then scores are averaged across the subtests to produce an overall IQ score. For example, in the British Ability Scales (Elliot, 1996), which are often used to assess the IQ of preschool and school-age children in the UK, there are subtests to measure verbal reasoning, short-term memory for numbers and pictures, non-verbal skills (e.g. the ability to construct a pattern using a set of blocks), as well as spoken and written language and numbers skills.

The particular subtests that are chosen for use with a given child will depend on a number of factors including the age of the child and the particular aspects of ability that are important. For example, if an educational psychologist suspects that a child has a particular kind of learning difficulty, a wide range of subsets will be used. These will reveal which skills are problematic for a child and which ones are not. This information can then be used in deciding what kind of educational provision will be most suitable for the child in question.

In other cases, particularly where children are being recruited for a research study, only specific abilities will be measured. For example, it may be important to match children on the basis of non-verbal abilities, in which case one or more non-verbal subtests would be used. In other cases, an experimental design might require children to be selected on the basis of their reading or mathematical ability. Here, specialist tests designed to measure the relevant skill will be used.

Conclusion and summary

The prevailing view of development in the mid- to late 20th century was one of stages. However, as the last century drew to a close, some radical alternatives to stage theories were proposed. Two of these, dynamic systems theory and connectionism, make use of computer simulation to model development. Both approaches have been able to show that stage-like changes in behaviour can result from an accumulation of tiny changes within an homogeneous system. In other words, a step change in children's ability need not be explained as a qualitative change. A third approach, information processing, has emphasised the importance for development of changes in cognitive capacities such as working memory and increasing control over the selection of strategies.

Research in developmental psychology encompasses a wide range of methodologies including observation, interview, and experimentation. Both longitudinal and cross-sectional designs are used extensively although we have noted that the latter approach often minimises individual differences among children. Whatever the methodology, all developmental psychologists are bound by a strict ethical code that guides their approach.

Further reading

- Elman, J.L., Bates, E.A., Johnson, M.H., Karmiloff-Smith, A., Parisi, D., & Plunkett, K. (1996). *Rethinking innateness: A connectionist perspective on development*. Cambridge, MA: MIT Press. This book provides an excellent introduction to connectionist modelling of development.
- Harris, M. (1998). Can connectionism model developmental change? *Mind and Language, 13*, 442–447. This paper explains some of the strengths and limitations of connectionist modelling of developmental processes.
- Klahr, D., & MacWhinney, B. (1998). Information processing. In D. Kuhn & R.S. Siegler (Eds.), *Handbook of child psychology: Vol. 2. Cognition, perception, and language* (W. Damon, Gen. Ed.). New York: Wiley. This is an authoritative account of different information approaches to conceptualising development.
- Siegler, R. (1998). *Children's thinking* (3rd ed.). Upper Saddle River, NJ: Prentice-Hall. Siegler has produced the most extensive information processing account of development and in this book he examines information-processing accounts of many areas of development. The book is suitable for first- and second-year undergraduates.
- Thelen, E., & Smith, L. (1998). Dynamic systems theories. In R.M. Lerner (Ed.), *Handbook of child psychology: Vol. 1. Theoretical models of human development* (W. Damon, Gen. Ed.; pp. 563–634). New York: Wiley. This chapter provides an authoritative introduction to dynamic systems theory and its use in the modelling of development.

Part 2

Early development

CHAPTER 4

CONTENTS

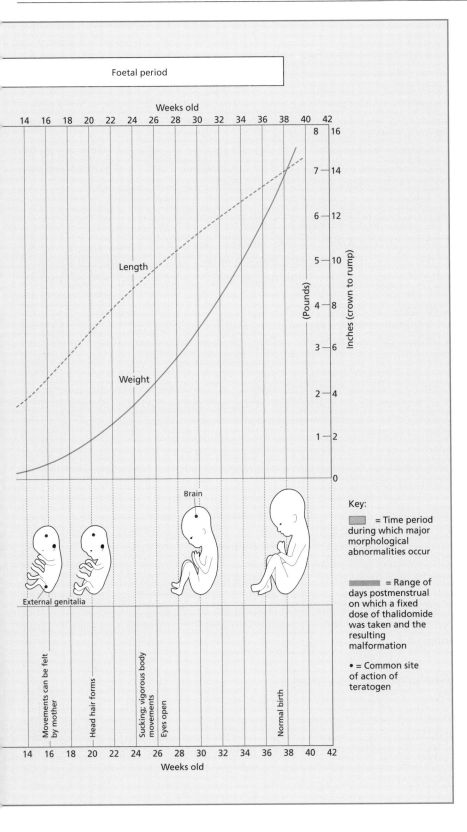

Foetal period

Weeks old

Length

Weight

Brain

External genitalia

Movements can be felt by mother

Head hair forms

Sucking; vigorous body movements

Eyes open

Normal birth

Weeks old

Key:

= Time period during which major morphological abnormalities occur

= Range of days postmenstrual on which a fixed dose of thalidomide was taken and the resulting malformation

• = Common site of action of teratogen

the main stages of prenatal development and Figure 4.2 shows the sensitive periods when the developing embryo is particularly susceptible to teratogens (foreign substances). These risk factors reveal in their own way that prenatal development depends on the interaction of the developing foetus with the environment, as the epigenetic landscape model would predict (see The Epigenetic Landscape, in Chapter 3). The concept of developmental stages is also readily apparent in prenatal development where there are clear distinctions between the various forms of the embryo and foetus that develop.

Human gestation takes 40 weeks between conception and birth. As we noted earlier, the prenatal period has traditionally been divided into three sub-stages: the germinal, embryonic, and foetal stages.

The germinal stage: From conception to 14 days

At conception, when the sperm penetrates the egg, a new type of cell is formed, called the zygote. This fertilised egg contains 23 pairs of chromosomes, of which half are derived from the mother and half from the father. Since the chromosomes are paired randomly during meiosis (the process of genetic recombination which occurs during fertilisation of the egg) the zygote contains a unique genetic code that will result in an individual whose inheritance combines aspects of both parents. The genes contained in the 23 pairs of chromosomes make up an individual's **genotype**. In the case of identical twins the genotype is the same (since they develop out of a single fertilised egg) but their **phenotype** (the observable characteristics of the individual) will differ since the interaction between heredity and environment will not be exactly the same for both twins. In the cases of non-identical twins and singletons, both the genotype and the phenotype will differ between individuals since they result from the separate fertilisation of different eggs under varying environmental circumstances.

The first two weeks after conception are primarily a period in which the fertilised egg (zygote) undergoes repeated division into identical copies. Cleavage occurs by the rapid division of the zygote to form a hollow ball of identical cells (the blastula) which becomes implanted in the wall of the uterus. The blastula eventually collapses in on itself to form the gastrula which is a hollow, egg-shaped structure. The gastrula has three layers of cells called the ectoderm, mesoderm, and endoderm. The formation of the gastrula thus marks a transition in cellular organisation from the earliest stage, where the individual cells are potentially able to participate in forming any tissue, to a differentiated state.

The embryonic stage: From 14 days to the 7th week

KEY TERMS
Genotype: The pattern of genes that an individual possesses.
Phenotype: The set of an individual's observable characteristics.

The three layers of the gastrula eventually become the basis for all bodily structures as the process of cell differentiation continues during the embryonic stage. Eventually 350 different cell types are formed. The ectoderm cells eventually form the skin, the lungs, and the nervous system; the endoderm cells form the lining of the digestive tract, the liver, and associated digestive organs; the medosderm gives rise to other organs such as the heart and kidneys, blood cells, bones, muscles, and tendons. These cells migrate to new locations to give rise to the structural organisation of the individual. There is rapid differentiation with formation of limbs, fingers, and major sensory organs. By eight weeks, the embryo is about 2 cm long, limb buds have appeared, and eyes and eyelids have begun to form.

All changes in the early embryonic form reflect changing patterns of cell contacts and the choreographed folding and unfolding of sheets of cells to achieve the species-typical shape of the organism. Specifically how the typical form of the organism emerges is not fully understood. Not only do genetic factors have a role, but also biochemical gradients of mutual influence between the cells, local interactions between groups of cells and the position of the cells in the blastula can all have an effect on differentiation and cell migration (see Michel & Moore, 1995).

The embryonic period is the danger period for German measles (rubella). Babies are at risk of being born blind and brain damaged if the virus is contracted during the first month (up to 47% of babies with rubella), second month (22% of babies with rubella), or third month of pregnancy (7% of babies with rubella). Girls in Western societies are often immunised against rubella during adolescence to avoid problems caused by catching German measles when they reach reproductive age and become pregnant. As a result, the incidence of both deafness and blindness has fallen, since maternal rubella was a major cause of both disabilities.

The importance of the prenatal environment for the normal development of the embryo is starkly illustrated by the thalidomide tragedy. In the 1970s, pregnant women who had taken the drug thalidomide during early pregnancy, to alleviate morning sickness, gave birth to infants with various malformations. The site of malformation depended on the exact time after conception that the drug crossed the placenta to the developing embryo. At different points in development, the same dose of thalidomide resulted in different deformities, either to the legs, arms, or ears (as shown in Figure 4.3).

One lesson from the thalidomide tragedy and the effects of rubella is that the interacting systems of the mother's intra-uterine environment and the developing embryo are extremely finely balanced. Development only seems inevitable when everything goes to plan. Where abnormal environmental (or genetic) conditions obtain, the developing embryo may be forced down abnormal pathways at choice points in the epigenetic landscape, with resulting atypical development. The orderly development of the embryo is the outcome of the interaction of many variables that regulate the sequence of development, the chemical reactions, and the intra-uterine environment. The resulting form of the embryo is a well-organised whole, yet it arises from many discontinuous, changing processes. Dynamic systems theory offers a useful framework for understanding how such complex causal

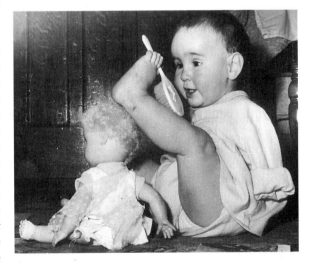

FIG. 4.3 In the early 1960s, the use of thalidomide as a morning sickness drug caused many children to be born without arms and/or legs. A generation of children had to learn how to operate artificial limbs or be unusually dextrous to earn the independence taken for granted by other children. Copyright © Popperfoto.

interactions nevertheless result in rather typical, discontinuous changes in form, which are at first buffered through canalisation and then enhanced as the embryo enters a new epigenetic pathway.

The foetal stage: From 8th to 38th week (before birth)

The foetal stage coincides with major developments of the nervous system. The foetus rapidly takes on distinctively human characteristics so that by 12 weeks it is easily recognisable. By 16 weeks it is 15–17 cm long but it cannot survive outside the mother's body because the lungs are immature.

The foetus continues to develop for the normal gestational term of 40 weeks. Like all biological phenomena there is natural variation in the time of onset of birth and in the duration of the birth process itself. For a first-born child, a natural labour may last 13–14 hours, or even longer.

Prematurity used to be defined as birth before 266 days but some babies who are born early are of normal weight and health. Nowadays, fairly complicated measures of size in relation to date of conception are used and a birth weight of less than 2500 g (5½ pounds) is used to define prematurity. Being born extremely prematurely (less than 25 weeks gestation) puts the infant at considerable risk of subsequent mental retardation. Wolke and Meyer (1999) have found that approximately 30% of such extremely premature babies have IQs below 70 at age eight years.

The normal baby at birth, around 40 weeks, weighs about 3150 g (7 pounds) and is about 53 cm (21 inches) long. The head, which has grown fastest in utero, is disproportionately larger than the body. Head and neck take up about 30% of the total body volume by comparison to 15% at six years and only 10% in adults. It is worth remembering that the changing proportions of the body pose particular problems in gaining motor control—a point to which we will be returning in Chapter 5, Cognitive Development in Infancy. Changes in body proportions also illustrate the epigenetic principle that different parts of the whole child may develop at different rates. In utero, the head grows fastest but, later in development, the proportions of the body change as hands and feet, shoulders, trunk, arms, and legs have separate growth spurts (Sinclair, 1978).

In Western societies, where babies are usually born in hospital, the newborn is assessed for birth condition using simple standardised measures of physical well-being, such as the **Apgar scale**, which gives a score based on measures such as skin colour, heart rate, muscle tone, and respiratory effort. Recently, more psychological tests, such as the **Brazleton scale**, have been devised to measure variables like ease of calming the newborn, irritability, and other temperamental characteristics. Characteristic reflexes, such as sucking, the rooting reflex (where the baby will turn toward stimulation of the cheek), and the stepping reflex (where the baby makes alternating movements of the legs when held with the feet touching a surface) may also be measured. These innate reflexes are culturally universal (Eibl-Eibesfeldt, 1989).

Behaviour in the foetus

Until recently it was not possible to study the behaviour of the normally developing foetus except under very unusual circumstances. As a consequence, not very much was known about foetal behaviour before birth. Some of the most detailed and fascinating accounts have become available in recent years from developmental biologists and developmental neurologists. These reveal that the foetus is constantly active. It has been suggested that the continuous activity of the foetus may feed back into growth processes and give rise to the innate behaviours that can be observed in the newborn. Some of these innate behaviours may, in turn, be related to subsequent developments after birth.

The very first detectable movements of the embryo are the heartbeats that appear when the embryo is only three weeks old and ½ cm long. In fact, the beating of the heart occurs before there is any nervous system at all and the heartbeat is really a biochemical phenomenon since muscle tissues "beat" when placed in saline solution. Soon, a regular rhythm is established and, by five weeks, the whole embryo is dominated by the rhythm of the heart.

Only after the heart starts beating does the nervous system begin to form. In an early study carried out in the 1930s, Hooker (1939) observed foetuses aged eight weeks and only 2 cm long. He showed that lightly touching a foetus with a hair, in the area of the mouth, led to mouth opening. Stimulation also tended to produce movements of the limbs and trunk. By 16 weeks, however, the foetal response to external touch is localised to the area of contact.

These early studies presupposed foetal responses to be the result of reflexes to external stimulation. Little was known about spontaneous foetal movement patterns. Although pregnant women often note feeling foetal movements at about 16 weeks gestation, they are only aware of the most gross movements. In fact, depending on the measuring technique, up to 20,000 movements per day can be recorded in the foetus of less than 16 weeks gestational age.

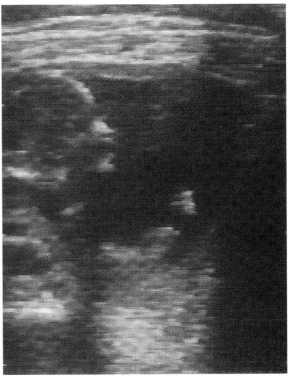

FIG. 4.4 Ultrasound image of a foetus at 15 weeks.

The advent of real time ultrasonic scanning in the 1970s has offered a safe means of imaging foetal movements in utero. Using this technique, ultra high frequency sound (outside the audible range) is transmitted into the pregnant woman's abdomen. The echoes of the sound are picked up electronically and converted to a visual image which provides a view of the foetus as it moves. Skilled observers can interpret these images to obtain information about foetal behaviours. Figure 4.4 shows an ultrasound picture of a foetus.

De Vries, Visser, and Prechtl (1984) have described 15 different movement patterns in the 15-week foetus (see the box later in this section). They observed foetal breathing movements, where the amniotic fluid is regularly inhaled and exhaled, stretching movements and turning movements. Later in foetal development, they observed thumb sucking. Under the relatively weightless conditions of the foetal environment, these movement patterns are well co-ordinated. Some of the behaviours show a pre-adaptive organisation that will be essential for postnatal life. Foetal breathing movements may be an example.

At about 17 or 18 weeks the amount of foetal activity drops and a stage transition occurs which lasts to the 24th week. It has been suggested that this relatively quiescent period coincides with the formation of the higher regions of the brain that will modulate the behaviours until now controlled by mid-brain centres. After the 24th week, finer degrees of movement control are observed, including expressive facial movements. Foetal activity resumes, in the increasingly cramped living quarters, and is now subject to sleep–wake cycles. A 40-minute cycle of activity can be observed, which is endogenously generated and continues after birth, and a 96-minute cycle, which drops out after birth and which is linked to the mother's sleep cycle. By 30 weeks gestational age, rapid eye movement sleep (REM) can be observed in the foetus. This is a phase in the sleep–wake cycle which, in adults, is associated with dreaming but which, in the foetus, is more likely to be related to the cycles of biochemical activity of the brain. At 32 weeks about 70–80% of the time is spent in REM sleep, associated with the foetal "breathing" movements mentioned earlier.

The first postural reflex, to be observed at 28 weeks, is the **tonic neck reflex** (TNR). In this movement pattern the arm and leg, on the side to which the head is turned, extend and the opposite arm and leg are flexed. This "fencer posture" continues to the eighth postnatal month and it is thought to have the effect, once the baby is born, of bringing the baby's hand into the visual field. The grasp reflex is also present by 28 weeks.

The spontaneous movement patterns of the foetus may serve not only to exercise the developing system but also to provide the system with feedback. Some evidence comes from a condition known as **foetal alcohol syndrome** in which the babies of alcoholic mothers suffer from malformed joints. Among other symptoms, the articulation of the limbs is abnormal and this is thought to arise because the alcohol passing across the placenta anaesthetises the foetus. This prevents the normal patterns of movements that assist the growing joints to take their correct shape. Experiments in chicks have shown that as little as two days of restricted leg movements during the sensitive period for formation of the joints is sufficient to result in abnormalities. Another possible function of prenatal activity is that it provides a high level of input to the developing ears, eyes and other sensory receptors. The cutaneous (skin) taste and olfactory (smell) receptors in the vestibular and auditory systems are all functional by the 24th gestational week. The visual system is functional by the 26th week. Finally, the continuous rotation and "crawling" movements of the young foetus may prevent adhesion to the uterine wall. The implication is that foetal behaviour contributes to normal development; it is not simply a question of automatic maturation, nor is the foetus simply a reflexive responder. We return to this issue when we discuss foetal brain development later in this chapter, in Evolution and Development of the Brain.

Spontaneous foetal movement patterns

In ultrasonic scanning, sound at frequencies well above the normal range of human hearing is harmlessly transmitted through the abdomen of the pregnant woman. The sound is reflected from the foetus (and other internal structures in the mother) and these "echoes" are turned into moving pictures by a computer.

This allows the spontaneous behaviour of the foetus to be observed. The technique has revealed a wide variety of patterns of movement, many of which are similar to the behaviour that will be observed later in postnatal life. The table below summarises the developing pattern of foetal movements. (These observations are summarised from De Vries et al., 1984, p. 50–53.)

It seems likely that these movements are, from the outset, internally driven patterns of activity and not merely reflexive responses. In fact, between 11 and 20 weeks the foetus is in almost continuous movement with static periods lasting only three to six minutes. The frequency of movements varies on a diurnal cycle, with maxima around midnight and minima first thing in the morning. What might be the significance of movement for the developing embryo? There are four major hypotheses:

1. The activity may serve no developmental role but merely accompanies the development of the nervous system.
2. The activity may feed back into the development of the nervous system.
3. The activity serves no role at the time but is important in anticipating patterns of behaviour that will be required postnatally.
4. The activity may be adaptive in the foetal environment and may serve no purpose thereafter.

DEVELOPING MOVEMENT PATTERNS IN THE FOETUS

Week		Week	
7	**Just discernible movements**—Between 7 and 8.5 weeks a small and slow shifting of the foetal contours can be seen. Small size of the foetus (about 2 cm) and limit of resolution of scanning equipment restricts detailed analysis.		tongue movements, or the head may rotate from side to side around the midline. Forward displacement of the head may be accompanied by hand–face contact when sucking may be observed.
8	**Startle**—A quick generalised movement, lasting about one second, always initiated in the limbs and sometimes spreading to neck and trunk.	10	**Hand–face contact**—Hand slowly touches face and fingers frequently extend and flex.
8	**General movements**—The whole body moves but no distinctive pattern or sequence of body parts can be observed. These movements may cause the foetus to shift in position. The movements are graceful in character.	10	**Rotation of foetus**—The foetus can rapidly change position by a complex rotation either of the head in relation to the trunk (somersault type of movement) or by alternating stepping movements of the legs which result in rotation around the hips.
9	**Hiccup**—Jerky contraction and abrupt displacement of the diaphragm, lasting about one second and occurring in rapid succession.	10–11	**Stretch and yawn**—This pattern of behaviour strongly resembles the species-typical yawning pattern, with elevation and rotation of the arms and prolonged wide opening of the jaws followed by rapid closure of the mouth.
10	**Breathing movements**—Foetal breathing movements obviously do not involve inhalation of air. A regular pattern of movement of diaphragm, thorax, and abdomen can be observed, sometimes in combination with jaw opening and swallowing of amniotic fluid.	12	**Finger movements**—The fingers can move independently of each other.
		14	**Rotation of the hand**—The hand moves at the wrist, independently of movement of the fingers.
9	**Isolated arm or leg movements**—Rapid or slow extension and flexion movements of the arm or leg, can be accompanied by rotation of the limb without involvement of other body parts.	16	**Global extension**—Feet and head thrust against opposite uterine walls.
		18	**Eye movements**—Well-controlled, endogenously generated, lateral scanning movements of the eyes can be observed, although the foetus cannot be seeing anything as there is insufficient light in the womb.
9–10	**Retroflexion, anteroflexion, and rotation of the head**—The head is slowly displaced backwards, sometimes with jaw opening and	24	**Thumb sucking**—The hand is brought to the mouth and repetitive jaw movements can be observed.

The limits of resolution of the ultrasound scanning system are such that not much can be observed before about seven weeks and so we cannot be sure whether activity *per se* is contributing to the formation of the nervous system in its very earliest days. We do know that a nervous system is not necessary for activity since muscle, when placed in saline solution, automatically acquires rhythmic twitching movements. In addition, the heart, which is one of the earliest organs to form, shows spontaneous beating before the nervous system has begun to develop. Observations such as these suggest that the question is how the developing nervous system comes to gain control over spontaneous rhythmic movement.

De Vries, Visser, and Prechtl (1984) have suggested that foetal movements may serve both anticipatory and ontogenetic adaptation. Some movements may be specific adaptations to the prenatal environment: For example, stepping serves to avoid adhesion to the uterine wall and to exercise the limbs and it may anticipate the pattern used for locomotion. Other foetal behaviours anticipate birth: Foetal breathing movements aid the formation of the lungs and will be necessary for breathing air after birth. Movements may also provide the important input to developing sensory systems. For example, the visual system is fully formed by the 26th gestational week. Eye movements will provide proprioceptive feedback, even though there are no visual consequences. The auditory system has, in some respects, attained an adult level of organisation by the 24th week. The intra-uterine auditory environment may therefore contribute to the formation of the auditory nervous system (although this has not been demonstrated). Research on foetal hearing does show that the characteristic intonation pattern of the mother's voice is readily audible and that the foetus is responsive to it (De Casper & Fifer, 1980).

Very little is known about the neuromuscular basis of foetal movements. Nerve cells are present in the embryo by three weeks postmenstrual age and at this time the nervous system has already begun to differentiate. At this age, the major structural features such as the spinal cord, are not yet formed.

Neuromuscular development in the foetus		
Age	*Movement*	*Neuromuscular development*
3 weeks	None.	Nerve cells present; nervous system begins to differentiate but spinal cord is not yet formed.
8 weeks	General writhing movements.	Spinal cord present with primary afferent nerves and interneurones, but the two systems are still separate.
10 weeks	Increase in spontaneous movements.	Connections between sensory fibres and interneurones are established.
11 weeks onwards	Appearance of isolated movements and general, global movements.	Eightfold increase in the number of motor neurone synapses.
13–15 weeks	Clearly defined movement patterns.	Threefold increase in neurones connected to the major segments of the body; nerve fibres become myelinated.

By eight weeks, the spinal cord contains motor neurones that will innervate the developing motor system, primary afferent nerves that bring information from the periphery and interneurones that will connect the two systems, although they are not yet interconnected. The movements observable in the embryo at this time are general writhing motions.

At 10 weeks the connections between the sensory fibres and the interneurones are established to close the spinal reflex arc and an increase in spontaneous movement is observed in the foetus. From 11 weeks there is an eightfold increase in the number of synapses on the motor neurones, which coincides with the appearance of isolated movements observed by De Vries et al. (1984) and a great increase in the number of general, global movements. From 13 to 15 weeks there is a threefold increase in the neurones connected to the major segments of the body. The process of myelinisation of the nerve fibres begins at 12 weeks in the ventral part of the spinal cord and coincides with the clear differentiation between various movement patterns that appear in the 12th to 15th week.

Of course, it is possible that changes in foetal behaviour and changes in the formation of the central nervous system (CNS) may be purely coincidental, so caution must be exercised in interpreting this evidence. It is possible however, that neurone and synaptic density is sufficient by eight weeks to generate the spontaneous movement patterns of the embryo. These spontaneous patterns may set up feedback processes that contribute to the further differentiation of the emerging CNS. Movement is increasingly well co-ordinated, with intra-joint co-ordination appearing first, then inter-joint co-ordination within limbs, followed by co-ordination between limbs. Co-ordination across the body midline between the arms, as is also the case for the legs, occurs before co-ordinated movement of the arm and leg on the same side of the body. Limb movements are co-ordinated with head and torso movements. Michel and Moore (1995) suggest that the neural circuitry involved is being constructed as the behaviours develop. Given the very early appearance of these co-ordinated movements it is apparent that much foetal behaviour must be regulated by systems within the spinal cord and lower brain stem. In the quiescent period leading up to birth, the inhibition of foetal activity which typically occurs may be effected by later developing systems located higher in the brain.

Evolution and development of the brain

In the line of proto-hominids leading to humans we can see a steady increase in the size of the brain over the last four million years (see Figure 4.5). Even allowing for the changes in brain to body weight ratios, there has been an absolute increase in brain size over human evolution although the process is not as simple as the diagram suggests because brain to body size ratio in Neanderthal man was actually *greater* than in modern man. Neanderthal man and modern man co-existed about 100,000 years ago until Neanderthal man became extinct. So, not only is the absolute cranial capacity important but the organisation of the brain appears to be important in differentiating modern humans in the course of evolution.

FIG. 4.5 The evolution of brain and skull size.

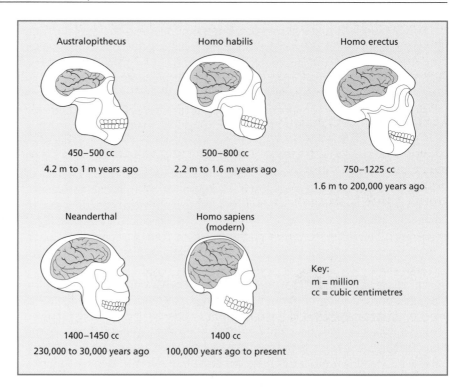

As the amount of brain tissue increased, so did the need to bring oxygen to the brain and fossil remains show major changes in the surface distribution of the veins and arteries carrying blood to and from the brain. Holloway and La Coste-Larey Mondie (1982) suggest, after examining casts taken from fossilised skulls, that not only has brain size increased but the relative proportions of the brain devoted to different functions have also changed. Thus, for example, the proportion of the brain devoted to primary visual analysis (primary striate cortex) is actually *less* in humans than in our hominid ancestors or in chimps. These changes began as long as three to four million years ago.

The reorganisation of the frontal lobes to give rise to Broca's area, implicated in speech production, began between 2.5 and 1.8 million years ago. This suggests that a greater priority in allocation of brain tissue to different functions may have been accorded to processes such as social communication through speech and language in *Homo erectus*. Nevertheless, the human brain does have the structures **Wernicke's** and **Broca's areas**, that are specific to the control and comprehension of speech. Cerebral asymmetries are also typical of the human brain with consequent patterns of lateral dominance, including handedness and these became noticeably marked around 1.5 million years ago.

The average weight of the brain in the newborn baby is 450 g and by adulthood the average weight is 1400 g. Thus, at 25% adult size, the brain of the human newborn is already relatively large by comparison both with remote human ancestors and living primates—the newborn human brain is about 75% the size of an adult chimpanzee. However, there is still a great deal of growth to come and, although the fastest rates of growth are in infancy and early childhood, brain growth continues to adulthood. Growth shows a stage-like

KEY TERMS
Wernicke's area: The region of the cerebral cortex concerned with speech comprehension. Named after Carl Wernicke.
Broca's area: The region of the cerebral cortex concerned with speech production. Named after Paul Broca.

sequence with major spurts and quiescent periods that may correspond to developmental stages (Fischer & Rose, 1994).

The relatively large size of the head at birth accounts for the top-heavy appearance of the newborn, with the head occupying about 25% of the total body length. At three years, brain growth has attained approximately 75% of adult weight and by six years, 90% of the adult weight has been attained. Figure 4.6 illustrates the proportion changes from birth to adulthood.

Purves (1994) estimates that the fully developed adult brain contains 100 billion neurones and that to achieve such numbers, assuming that once formed the neurones do not further subdivide, the foetal brain must add 250,000 neurones per minute in early development. This is really a phenomenal rate of growth. Figure 4.7 shows the gross aspects of this development.

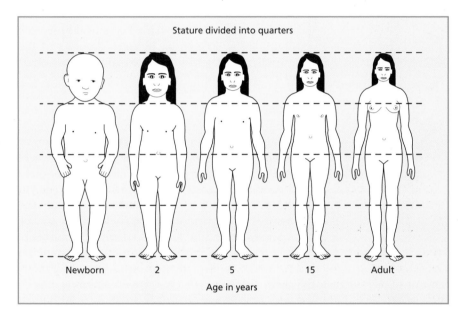

FIG. 4.6 Changes in body proportion with age. Adapted from Sinclair (1978).

By the first nine weeks of foetal development the brain has already taken on its adult shape, with the typical convolutions of the cortex that allow the brain cells to proliferate yet occupy the minimal brain volume. Shatz (1992) contrasts two models of how such a massive set of neural linkages might form. One, a non-developmental, preformationist view, might be that the circuitry is prespecified, perhaps by the genes, analogous to the wiring diagram of a computer. At some point in development the whole brain is switched on and begins to function. The alternative—developmental—view is that the neural connections elaborate themselves from a basic wiring pattern that is determined, but not fully specified, by the biochemical activity of the genes, and which is elaborated as a result of electrochemical activity. This is rather a modified

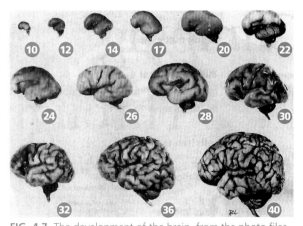

FIG. 4.7 The development of the brain, from the photo files of Jeanne-Claudie Larroche. The numbers indicate the foetal age, in weeks. Reproduced from R. Kunzig (1998), Climbing through the brain. *Discover Magazine*, August 1998.

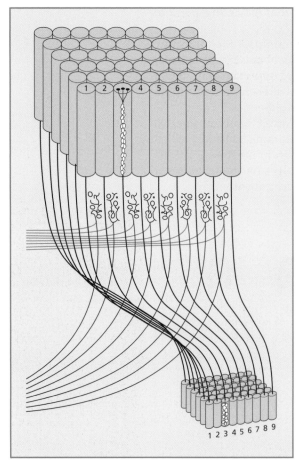

A simplified version of Rakic's (1987) radial unit model in which cells migrate from a proliferative zone beneath the eventual cortical layer to form a typical columnar organisation of the cortex. Adapted from Rakic (1987).

or partial, preformationist hypothesis (see The Developmental Principle, in Chapter 1) since the basic framework of connectivity is presupposed but its elaboration is left unspecified so that there is a role for feedback through experience.

In some cases, such as the embryonic visual system, basic visual pathways are laid down before there is any possibility of visual feedback since the retina has not yet formed. Similarly, the parietal and temporal lobes of the 24-week foetus are already asymmetric, which suggests that the foetal brain is pre-adapted with structures important to the acquisition of language. Such observations suggest that some of the basic aspects of brain architecture must be specified genetically, but this is not the whole story. Modern theories of the growth of the nervous system suggest that other principles, based on neuronal activity and the timing of events in brain growth, also govern brain connectivity. For example, Rakic (1995) has proposed a radial unit model for the development of the cerebral cortex in which cells migrate from a proliferative zone beneath the eventual cortical layer, to form the typical columnar organisation of the cortex. A change in the timing of cell division in the proliferative zone impacts greatly on the number of cortical columns that will form. For example, an additional round of cell division at the time of cell proliferation will double the number of cortical columns; two additional rounds will quadruple the number of columns. Johnson (1998) suggests that such differences in developmental timing may be sufficient to account for the very large range of surface areas of cortex, which can vary by a factor of 100, in mammalian species

The developing nerve cells have a "growth cone" at their tip. This has the function of sensing biochemically the appropriate molecular pathway along which to grow so that the developing cell can establish a connection with the appropriate target cell. Finding the correct address, however, remains somewhat haphazard and it seems that incorrectly connected nerves are eliminated as a result of feedback, at a later stage in development.

Of course, the nervous system operates by the transmission of electrical signals. The connectivity of the system is not determined solely by molecular biochemistry but also by the patterns of firing of nerve cells and as Shatz (1992) says: "cells that fire together, wire together" (p. 238). Correlated patterns of firing across the synaptic connections between nerve cells strengthen their linkages and this can result in long-lasting changes to the patterns of transmission of electrical activity within the CNS. This process is reminiscent of the processes that occur in the learning of connectionist systems (see The Connectionist Approach, in Chapter 3).

The patterns of firing at the synapses may be dependent on feedback from activity, both in sensory and motor systems. Activity may simply amount to the firing of cells within the appropriate circuits, which has the effect of strengthening the connections in the wiring and eliminating false linkages, or it may be dependent on feedback from the actual physical activity of the sensory and motor systems. The advantage of, so-called, "activity-dependent" brain modelling is that the CNS can be fine-tuned by experience and thereby enable adaptability. Activity dependent modelling of the nervous system also requires far less genetic specification, since only major circuits need to be encoded in the genes, with the fine detail being left to experience to establish.

An evolutionary perspective on development

Studies of hominid evolution provide a useful background for understanding several aspects of development in humans as do comparative studies with chimpanzees, our nearest primate relative.

Humans and chimpanzees descended from a common ancestor, *Ramapithecus* (also known as *Sivapithecus*) who lived between 12 and 7 million years ago. This animal closely resembled the living Asian orangutan. In the period between twelve and seven million years before the present time, the hominoid apes (chimpanzees and gorillas) diversified. The origin of hominids is generally taken to be about four million years ago, with *Australopithecus* who walked upright rather than on all fours. It is often argued that the importance of bipedal locomotion lay in freeing up the hands, for tool use, for carrying, and for communication by means of gestures.

Evidence for this change to bipedalism comes from the discovery of a trail of footprints of two adults and a juvenile *Australopithecine* that were made in volcanic ash about four million years ago (Leakey, 1979). Figure 4.8 shows the footprints which proved to be very similar to those of modern man on a variety of biomechanical measures and very different from those of chimpanzees who have rather similar hands and feet.

Upright locomotion has had several consequences. One of the major effects of bipedalism is to alter the distribution of weight over the ground, necessitating a lateral spread of the pelvic girdle. In chimpanzees and *Australopithecines*, the birth canal outlet of the pelvic girdle is almost circular and there is no need for the foetus to twist its head to emerge. In modern humans, however, by the time of birth the head is so large that it is necessary for it to rotate to one side to enable passage through the birth canal. Babies are born with the ATNR (asymmetric tonic neck reflex), which arises just prior to birth and persists for about three months afterwards. Nine out of ten babies spontaneously turn to the right and extend the right hand in the same direction. One in ten babies turns to the left, with left hand extension into the visual field. These asymmetric patterns predict the child's eventual handedness. Interestingly, the mother's uterus is usually twisted to the right, thus providing a neat complement to the foetus' own tendency to orient rightwards in the final stages of pregnancy.

Other developmental evidence for deep seated right-hand preference comes from recent ultrasonic scanning studies that show foetuses from about 15 weeks engage in predominantly right-handed thumb sucking (Hepper, Shahidullah, & White, 1991). Research on hand–mouth co-ordination in newborn babies also shows that it is predominantly the right hand that makes contact with the mouth

FIG. 4.8 This 70-metre trail of hominid footprints fossilised in volcanic ash was discovered by Mary Leakey during her expedition to Laetoli, Tanzania in 1978. Copyright © John Reader/ Science Photo Library.

(Butterworth & Hopkins, 1988). Taking the evidence as a whole, the main selection pressure for development of handedness in human evolution may, therefore, have been the process of birth.

Another effect of maternal bipedalism on the infant during pregnancy is that the infant is carried vertically so that, toward the end of gestation, one ear faces inwards (normally the left ear) and the other faces the abdominal wall. It has been suggested by Previc (1994) that this differential intra-uterine exposure to the pattern of the mother's speech (so-called eavesdropping) may contribute to left hemispherical specialisation for sound, which is also correlated with species-typical right handedness. This intra-uterine experience may in turn contribute to the development of speech (see Chapter 7, The Beginnings of Language Development).

Sitting, standing, and walking

In the weeks and months after birth the baby progressively gains locomotor control in a typical sequence which was first described by McGraw (1943). Babies lift their head first, then they become able to raise head and chest, then to lift their head and trunk by raising themselves on arms and hands and, eventually, on all four limbs. By nine months babies usually crawl, although some babies get around by bottom shuffling. Soon they will pull themselves to stand upright and, by 12 months, most babies take their first steps in walking. The table below summarises the major milestones in motor development, although the indicated months are only approximate and will vary considerably from child to child.

The hand print of an adult male chimp (grey) compared to that of a three-year-old female child (blue).

Many theorists assumed a purely maturational basis for the development of gross motor skills as these are known. However, studies have shown that cultural factors, which allow differential experience, may enter into motor development. An early study by Dennis and Dennis (1940) studied the Hopi Indians of New Mexico who, at that time, were only partly Westernised. It was traditional to strap the infant securely to a cradle board (Figure 4.9) which the

MOTOR DEVELOPMENT IN THE FIRST TWO YEARS			
Months	**Behaviour**	**Months**	**Behaviour**
1	Lifts chin when prone; holds head erect for a few seconds	11	Pulls self up by holding onto furniture
2	Lifts head up when prone	12	Crawls on hands and knees; sidesteps around furniture
3	Rolls from side to back	13	Stands alone
4	Lifts head and chest when prone; holds head erect	14	Walks alone
5	Rolls from side to side	15	Climbs stairs
6	Sits with slight support	16	Trots about well
7	Can roll from back to stomach, stepping reactions	17	Climbs on a low chair, stoops
8	Tries vigorously to crawl, sits alone for short time	18	Can walk backwards
9	Can turn around when left on floor, makes some progress crawling	19	Climbs stairs up and down
10	Stands when held up	20	Jumps, runs

Adapted from Griffiths (1954).

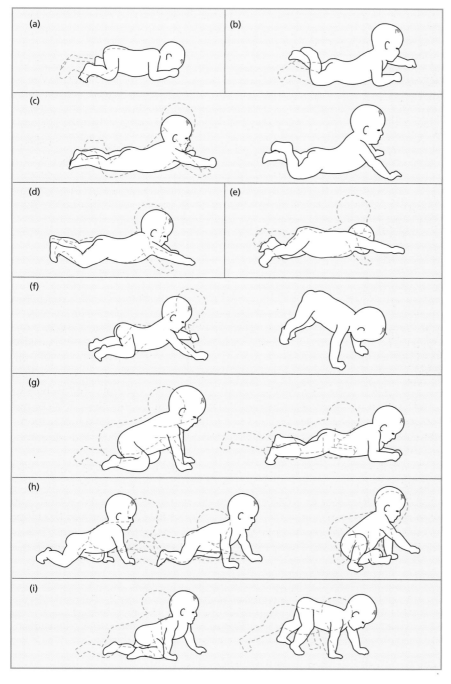

(a) to (i) shows the sequence of infant neuromuscular development in the achievement of an integrated crawling pattern. Adapted from McGraw (1941).

mother carried on her back while engaged in her work. The cradle board limited the opportunity of the infant to engage in unrestricted motor activity. Despite this, the traditionally reared Hopi babies learned to walk at the same age as the Westernised Hopi (who were not strapped to cradle boards).

At first sight, it seemed that the restriction of the opportunity to practise movements did not affect the age of walking. However, on closer examination, it emerged that the babies were not strapped to the boards for more than six

The sequence of infant neuromuscular development in the achievement of walking. (a) newborn or reflex stepping; (b) inception of cortical inhibition; (c) transition to cortical control; (d) inception of deliberate stepping; (e) inception of independent walking; (f) heel-to-toe progression; (g) an integrated gait. Adapted from McGraw (1940).

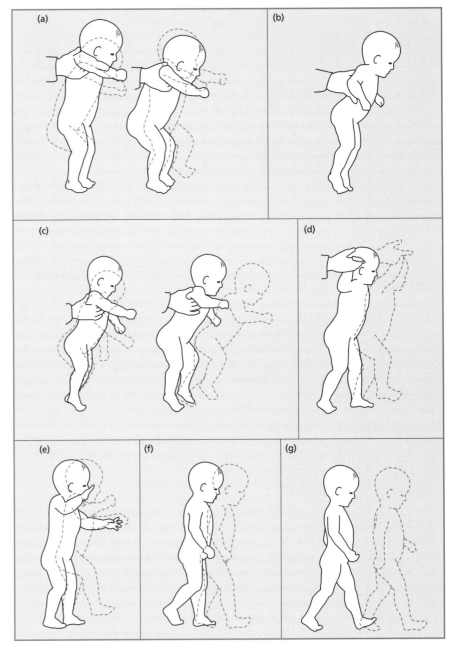

hours a day, and so it cannot be assumed that they did not have the opportunity for walking practice when they were not strapped to the board.

Dennis and Najarian (1957) studied severely deprived infants in an orphanage in Teheran. They found that children as old as two years had still not acquired even the most elementary motor skills of sitting or standing. They attributed the delay to the almost total lack of social stimulation in the orphanage. This finding nicely illustrates Vygotsky's point that the social structure enters into development at the zone of proximal development (see Chapter 2, Developmental Psychology in the 20th Century). When the baby is learning to walk, the "scaffolding" of the social environment, as Bruner called it, usually passes unobserved. However, it is easy to see the social contribution when the child takes her first faltering steps with the protection and support of the parent. There is also evidence from some African tribes who give practice to infant postures, such as the Kipsigi of Nigeria, that control of sitting can be accelerated by up to five weeks (Super, 1976).

Further evidence for an effect of experience on motor development comes from studies of the continuity between the newborn stepping reflex and later crawling and walking movements. Zelaso, Zelaso, and Kolb (1972) showed that practising the innate stepping reflex prevented it from disappearing in development and this resulted in marginally earlier walking than in a control group of babies who did not practise the stepping movements. More recently, Zelaso and colleagues (Zelaso, Zelaso, Cohen, & Zelaso, 1993) have extended this research on the effects of practice to another neonatal behaviour, the so-called neuromotor sitting position. To elicit this behaviour, the adult must support the newborn beneath the thighs, while allowing the baby to rest her back against the examiner's chest. When the baby seems secure, the support to the infant's back is briefly removed which results in the baby attempting momentarily to straighten the back. Zelaso et al. (1993) showed that effects of training were specific to the posture being trained. Babies who were trained in sitting improved in the control of that posture but not in stepping. Conversely, babies who were trained in stepping improved in stepping but not in sitting. Control babies who were observed weekly, but not trained, did not show a comparable improvement in sitting or stepping in the first 10 weeks of life.

The most recent evidence for effects of early child-rearing practices on gross motor development comes from a recent change in the sleeping position of young babies. In many countries, concerns about cot death led to a well-publicised campaign to place babies on their back, rather than their stomach, when they were put in their cots to sleep. This change produced a gratifying reduction in the incidence of cot death but an unpublished study in Holland showed that this change in early sleeping position delayed the age at which babies pushed up with their arms when placed on their stomachs. Babies who were placed on their stomachs to sleep had plenty of opportunity to push their arms against the mattress and so raise their heads. However, babies placed on their backs had much less opportunity to practise this manoeuvre.

We have seen that a range of complex movements occur in the foetus. The question that arises is whether there is any relation between prenatal movement patterns and postnatal behaviour. The transition from womb to world involves the possibility of new types of action in which new, more extensive movements become possible and vision can be used to control activity. However, the change from a liquid to an air environment means that babies are faced, for the first time, with managing the additional weight of their own bodies.

It is very likely that there is a continuous relationship between some foetal movement patterns and later forms of behaviour, across the transition brought about by birth. For example, De Vries et al. (1984) describe a stretch and yawn pattern at 10 weeks foetal age (see the box on page 69). With such an obvious

FIG. 4.9 Native American Indian cradle that restricts the infant's movement. Copyright © Mary Evans Picture Library.

and universal behaviour we are tempted to suppose continuity in the organisation of yawning and stretching movements throughout the lifespan.

A complex motor pattern, always at a slow speed, consists of forceful extension of the back, retroflexion of the head, external rotation and elevation of the arms. The yawn is similar to the yawn observed after birth, prolonged wide opening of the jaws followed by quick closure, often with retroflexion of the head and sometimes elevation of the arms.

(De Vries et al., 1984, p. 53)

It has been known for some time that newborn babies will make the so-called "stepping reflex". If the newborn baby is supported in an upright posture, so that there is some pressure on the sole of the foot, this will elicit a cyclic stepping movement, as the legs alternate in walking movements. Such motor patterns have generally been considered to be reflexes, which disappear as the baby matures (although as we noted the stepping reflex can be sustained with appropriate practice).

A variety of explanations for the disappearance of the stepping reflex have been put forward. For example, it has been argued that development of the cerebral cortex (the outer layer of the brain), results in the inhibition of these motor patterns. An important recent insight has been that babies put on weight so fast after birth—especially in the upper legs where fat is deposited to act as insulation—that the legs become too heavy to lift. The reflexive stepping movement actually re-emerges when the baby is held so that the legs are under water and their weight is thereby reduced. Thelen (1984) has argued that the disappearance of stepping is illusory, and that there is a relationship between stepping and later crawling and walking. She suggests that the patterning of walking movements is innate but that the baby must gain sufficient strength to support its own weight before upright locomotion becomes possible. So, the argument here is that there may be continuity between the stepping movements observed as the foetus rotates in the womb, the crawling movements of the six-month old baby, and the typical alternating walking movements of upright locomotion.

Of course, there may also be a discontinuity between neonatal stepping movements and walking at the end of the first year. Other aspects of development are also proceeding in parallel during the first year. In particular, babies are developing sophisticated intentions and some theorists have argued that humans walk when they do, typically at the end of the first year of life, because the general change in intellectual development enables the baby to use the motor system as a means to an end. That is, babies walk when they do in order to fulfil their intentions to explore. The behaviour of walking, typically seen at the end of the first year, emerges perhaps as a combination of an innate motor pattern, which is continuous with the behaviour seen in the womb, and intellectual processes that arise later in development and which bring walking under voluntary control (Zelaso, 1984).

The sensory capacities of the neonate

In the early period after birth, the baby's senses are already well developed, although vision will continue to develop over the first months of life.

Vision

Relative to adult standards, visual acuity in the newborn is poor. However, we need to beware of falling into the trap of supposing that it is therefore inadequate for the infant's purposes. Although the finest spatial detail that a newborn can see is very much less than an adult, it is perfectly adequate for the large social objects, such as faces, that the very young infant will frequently encounter. Neonates can discriminate between stationary black and white stripes an eighth of an inch wide and a uniform grey surface. By three months the stripes can be as narrow as a 64th of an inch wide. Moving the cards, so that the stripes attract visual following movements, gives a finer measure of visual discrimination.

At birth, the lens of the eye, which brings the visual image to a sharp focus at the retina by a series of muscles that change its shape, is not yet fully functional. This means that the eyes of the neonate have a fixed focal length. Only objects that are 21 cm from the eyes of the newborn will be perceived in sharp focus. The fixed focal length arises because, until the infant is about three months old, the lens does not accommodate by changing the curvature of its surface in order to bring objects at different distances into focus (see Figure 4.10).

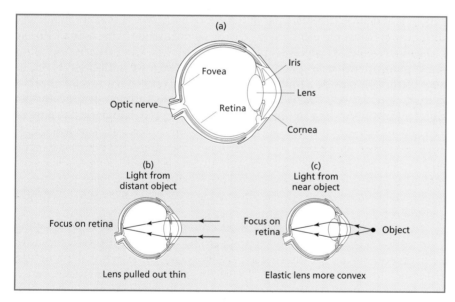

FIG. 4.10   The process of accommodation. (a) shows the main parts of the eye; (b) shows how the lens becomes thinner to focus on the retina when looking at a distant object; (c) shows how the lens becomes thicker to focus on the retina when looking at a near object.

Interestingly enough, the fixed focal length of 21 cm coincides with the average distance of the mother's face from the baby, when the infant is held in the mother's arms. So, even though distant objects will be blurred, important social objects can be seen from birth. Furthermore, since the eye is functioning at a fixed focus, the depth of field (i.e. the range over which an object can move without the retinal image becoming blurred) may well be sufficient to keep track of large moving objects, with the important limitations on perception being set by the inexperience of the visual system of the brain.

It is also known that babies younger than four months of age see colour in the same way as normal (i.e. non-colour-blind) adults. Bornstein, Kessen, and Weiskopf (1976) showed that babies divide the physical spectrum of light into the four main colour categories: blue, green, yellow, and red. Babies respond to transitions across the boundaries between colours as a change in the stimulus. Thus, at wavelengths between 480 and 510 nm, where adults perceive the colour as changing from blue to green, infants will also respond as though there are two different colours. (This change is shown using a habituation paradigm described in the box on pages 107–108.) However, a change of the same magnitude within a colour category, e.g. from 480 to 450 nm, is treated by the infant as another instance of the colour blue in a habituation test. Thus, long before the beginning of language or any formal tuition, babies group the visible wavelengths of light into categories of colour much like those of adults in many different cultures. Such findings of universal colour categories in early perception have important implications for they suggest that structures available at the level of perception may have primacy in the processes of cognitive development.

Stereoscopic vision depends on the fact that the eyes, being horizontally separated, have a slightly different image from each other. The corresponding points of the image on each eye are slightly further apart for near objects than for far ones (see Figure 4.11) and the brain makes use of this retinal disparity to read depth from the fused images of the two eyes.

Although there is depth perception by other means, such as the relative size of objects and through motion parallax at the retina (if two objects are at different distances the nearer one undergoes greater lateral motion at the retina with eye or head movements), stereoscopic binocular vision—particularly useful for depth perception in near space—does not start to develop until about 13 weeks after birth. This may be a function of poor control over the convergence of the eyes since, when we focus both eyes on the same object, the eyes must converge differentially according to the distance of the object. Changes in the axes of

FIG. 4.11 As the eyes are set a short distance apart, each eye receives a slightly different image from the same scene. The difference in the retinal images, at identical places on each eye, is called binocular disparity. The brain makes use of these slight differences as one way of registering spatial depth. This is the principle of the stereoscope, where photographs taken from slightly different angles, corresponding to the position of each eye, appear to the viewer to fuse as a single three-dimensional image.

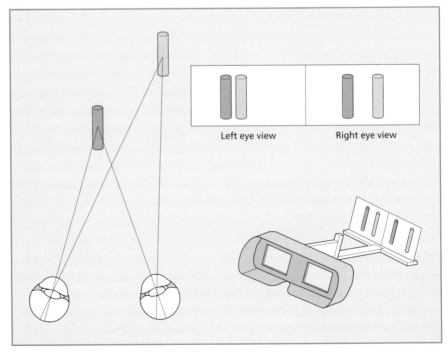

alignment of the eyes in the early weeks of life and "tuning" the visual cortex of the brain, so that the neural cells responsible for binocular vision receive the same information from both eyes, may be responsible for stereoscopic vision. The box below summarises research on brain plasticity as illustrated by the tuning of binocular vision through experience.

Brain plasticity and experience

Modern neurophysiological studies suggest that brain development depends upon systems whose structures anticipate species-typical experiences (i.e. experience-expectant systems) and also on systems which are constructed through experience (i.e. experience-dependent systems). Changes in the organisation of the brain as a result of experience-expectant mechanisms may occur during sensitive periods that are of restricted duration, whereas experience-dependent brain changes may occur through the lifespan.

A classic example of experience-expectant development of the visual system arises in the case of total visual deprivation from congenital cataract, where a person is born blind and may have had no visual experience until adulthood, when sight is restored. Typically such patients have difficulty in recognising the shapes of simple objects, although they immediately see in colour. It is often argued that their difficulty stems from a lack of education of the visual system in early development and it has proved difficult to train such people when the operation to restore sight is carried out in adulthood (Gregory & Wallace, 1963). However, such cases are actually highly ambiguous because an adult whose sight is restored has had a long time to learn to depend on other senses, such as touch, to make discriminations. Sight-restored adults may therefore be unable to recognise objects, or to name them, on the basis of visual information alone, precisely because they depend on other modalities to identify objects.

Difficulties in knowing whether such long-term effects of visual deprivation actually reflect underlying differences in the nervous system are overcome by carefully controlled studies carried out with animals. These have shown, beyond reasonable doubt, that cells in the visual cortex of the brain are experience expectant. In general, the connectivity of the cortex is less complex in animals that have been visually deprived than in normal animals. This suggests that the sensory input is somehow implicated in organising the connections between neurones at various levels of the nervous system.

Greenough, Black, and Wallace (1987) suggest that experience-expectant processes can explain neuronal selection within the nervous system. The argument is that the developing brain takes advantage of the evolutionarily expectable properties of the visual environment by an initial period of cell proliferation, which is then followed by cell pruning on the basis of the actual properties of the visual environment encountered. The description below is of the development of ocular dominance columns in binocular vision in mammals. However, the principle of cell proliferation followed by selection can also apply to muscle innervation in the foetus as well as to sensory feedback in the auditory system.

In mammals with binocular vision, the visual field of the eyes overlaps in the centre, as shown in Figure 4.12. The axons to the cortex from each eye will there-fore overlap in their field of view. In normal development, the responsibility of

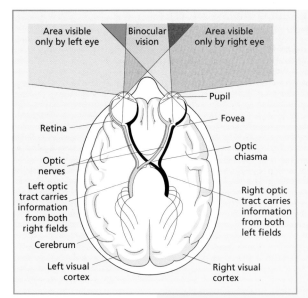

FIG. 4.12 The route of visual signals. Note that all light from the fields left of centre of both eyes (blue) falls on the right sides of the two retinas; and information about these fields goes to the right visual cortex. Information about the right fields of vision (grey) goes to the left cortex. Data about the binocular vision go to both cortices.

each eye for a particular region of visual space is initially not strictly segregated. However, eventually the cortical cells responsible for the binocular area of the visual field become organised in strictly demarcated columns. In animals where one eye has been closed, the open eye takes over much of the territory normally shared between axons. Thus, axon proliferation, followed by competition and eventual axon absorption, gives rise to the final, highly organised structure of the visual cortex responsible for binocular vision. In the normal development of kittens for example, the process is complete in about two months and deprivation thereafter does not result in changes in organisation. Kittens reared in the dark remain sensitive to deprivation until about eight months. This is evidence for a sensitive period for cortical organisation based on experience, which is normally completed quite soon after birth.

It is important to remember that selective effects may apply to motor development as well as to perceptual development. As was noted earlier, some experience-expectant processes may require the organism to provide its own experiences. Thus, foetal movement patterns may have a highly selective effect on the precise pattern of innervation of the motor system. There is evidence that constraining the legs or anaesthetising the limbs in the foetus, as in foetal alcohol syndrome, results in grossly abnormal structure and function of the limbs. These abnormalities might give rise to repercussions on the organisation of the relevant parts of the nervous system, but this remains to be proved.

Individual development, of course, depends upon individual experience. Changes in the organisation of the brain as a function of individual experience are difficult to demonstrate. However, Greenough et al. (1987) report that rats reared in so-called enriched environments actually show increased interconnectivity of the synapses of the brain. Brain morphology differs whether the rats are reared in environmentally complex conditions (groups of 12 housed in cages filled with objects that animals are free to explore), social conditions (housed in pairs without toys), or social isolation. The synapses of the environmentally enriched rats exceeded those of the rats reared in social isolation by 25%.

In summary, in the formation of the nervous system, experience-expectant factors operate by cell proliferation followed by pruning or selection. In the experience-dependent case, which continues into adulthood, synapses form in response to the particular properties of the experience to be stored. Caution is needed though in supposing that such processes are uniformly spread through the brain. While the process of brain development as measured by thickness of the cortex in visual, parietal, and temporal cortex reaches a maximum at about 20 months, frontal lobe enlargement continues to about six years. This asynchrony between different brain systems in humans may correspond to sequential dependencies in the time course of brain development in different regions.

Extensive research on binocular vision indicates very strongly that binocular aspects of visual functioning depend on early visual experience during a "sensitive" period. The concept of a sensitive period is derived from ethology, it designates a period of susceptibility for a particular kind of learning. It is related to the concept of plasticity that may be defined as the capacity of the nervous system to undergo transformations as a result of experience. The period of maximum sensitivity is up to two years and declines thereafter. There are important implications for the treatment of squint, where the axes of the eyes are not parallel (this condition is also known as **strabismus**).

In a child with a squint, the binocular cells in the visual nervous system do not receive the same input from equivalent regions of the two eyes. For this reason it is important to realign the squinting eye by surgery if vision is not to be adversely affected. Children who have received corrective surgery after the sensitive period of two years do not regain stereopsis, whereas infants who had strabismus corrected during the sensitive period show some evidence of regaining binocular vision (see Aslin, 1985 for an extended discussion).

Newborn infant eye movements are very similar to those of adults in their dynamics. Successive shifts of visual fixation from object to object are known as saccades. Smooth tracking movements of the eyes develop at about two months, whereas younger infants follow moving objects by making a series of saccadic jumps in their eye movements (further information about newborn infant vision is available in Atkinson & Braddick, 1989). Infants make eye movements both in utero and in the dark, which shows that the scanning pattern must be internally generated and not simply a reaction to visual stimulation. The newborn is thus born prepared to explore the visual environment.

Haith (1980) has suggested that the looking patterns of the newborn infant may be governed by the following four rules:

1. If awake and alert and light not too bright, open eyes.
2. If in darkness, maintain a controlled detailed search.
3. If in light with no form, search for edges by relatively broad, jerky sweeps of the (visual) field.
4. If an edge is found, terminate the broad scan and stay in the general vicinity of the edge.

Newborns are particularly prone to picking out the external edges of visual objects, although they will shift their gaze to the interior of the object if it has internal movement. So, babies are scanning for salient features of objects. They do not simply search at random, even though their ability to scan improves over the first three months.

Hearing

The auditory system begins to function well before birth. Physically, the inner ear has grown to its adult size by the 20th gestational week and the middle ear, with its complex structure of bones and membranes, is functional by the 37th week of pregnancy, although it continues to change shape and size into adulthood. The shape of the external ear is adultlike by the 20th gestational week although it will continue to grow in size until the child is about nine years old (Rubel, 1985).

KEY TERM
Strabismus: Another name for squint; caused by paralysis of an eye muscle.

Infants are attentive to sounds from before birth but, since the middle ear of the foetus is filled with amniotic fluid, the conduction of sound will be quite different than postnatally. The foetus will only be able to hear loud external sounds that are transmitted through the mother's abdominal wall and which penetrate a fairly high level of background noise. Mothers report feeling their baby startle to such loud sounds at about 32 weeks gestational age. The mother's speech, transmitted downwards through the diaphragm, is the most likely source of sound to be heard by the baby. Most perceptible are the patterns of onset and offset at the higher frequencies that are not masked by the mother's heart beat and the rushing noise of her blood circulation.

Studies have shown that newborns can distinguish their mother's voice from the voice of another female, suggesting that aspects of the mother's voice may become familiar to the child in utero. De Casper and Fifer (1980) carried out an ingenious study to demonstrate this. Mothers read aloud during the last trimester of their pregnancy from a story book so that the same story was "heard" by the foetus many times. Then, on the first day after birth, babies listened with earphones to either the mother's voice or that of a stranger reading the same story. As they listened they sucked on a dummy and they learned to adjust their pattern of sucking in order to hear their mother's voice rather than the stranger's. It therefore seems very likely that this preference for the mother's voice has its origins prenatally. Newborn babies generally prefer voices in the female range (average frequency 260 cycles per second) to the male range (on average one octave lower at 130 cycles per second). Adults and children use a higher pitched tone of voice when they talk to babies, as if this is a particularly effective way of speech "getting through" (Snow, 1977).

Smell and taste

Newborns show aversion to a sour taste just as do adults. They will pucker up their lips and show a "disgusted" expression. They can also discriminate sweetness in liquids and show contented emotional expressions. Newborn babies show a similar range of expressions when presented with smells that are unpleasant (rotten eggs), or pleasant (a milky smell, honey, chocolate). The babies in this study (Steiner, 1979) were tested in the first few hours of life, before they had been fed, so they had had no oral experience of food.

Neonates recognise the smell of their own mother's breast milk within the first six days of life. MacFarlane (1975) placed a pad, which the mothers had previously worn to catch seeping breast milk, on one side of the infant's head and a pad from another nursing mother on the other side. Babies turned their heads toward the side of their mother's pad. They preferred the familiar smell, which they must have learned rapidly to recognise in the first few days of life.

Intersensory perception: Auditory–visual co-ordination

Wertheimer (1961) was one of the first to ask whether there may be innate relationships between the senses. Immediately his daughter was born, when she was only eight minutes old, he made a random series of soft "clicking" noises to her left and right ear. He noticed that her eyes moved towards the sound on 18 out of the 24 occasions of testing (and away from the sound on six trials).

Statistically speaking, the baby looked to the sound significantly more often than would have been expected by chance. If the infant was unaware of the spatial direction of the sound then we would expect half her eye movements to be towards and half away from the sound (i.e. 12 towards and 12 away). Wertheimer therefore concluded that there is an innate co-ordination between seeing and hearing, such that when the baby hears a sound, the eyes will be reoriented as if to discover the visual object at its source.

These results have subsequently been replicated and clarified by several investigators. Butterworth and Castillo (1976) found that newborn babies made sound-contingent eye movements but, in their study, the neonates looked away from the source, presumably because it was too loud. In another study by Castillo and Butterworth (1981) newborn babies were shown identical pairs of red dots on the left or right of the field of view. These were either at the same place as the sound source or opposite the sound source. Babies looked more frequently at the dot that was on the same side as the sound source.

This study showed that newborns would look to a distinctive visual feature of the environment for the source of a sound, even when the sound actually came from the other location which was not visually marked. This example of "visual capture" corresponds to the phenomenon an adult experiences at the cinema, where the sound is attributed to the figures on the screen, even though it actually emerges from loudspeakers at the side of the hall. This is good evidence that vision and audition interact in sound localisation from birth, with vision assisting audition to localise sounds.

In a rather convincing study by Muir and Field (1979), two rattles were set into identical motion on either side of the baby. Only one of the rattles made a sound, since the granules inside had been removed from the other rattle. Newborn babies preferred to look toward the sounding rattle. This again suggests that auditory and visual systems of the neonate function are mutually supportive and co-ordinated systems from birth.

Childbirth

Childbirth in humans offers a fascinating insight into the ways in which biological and cultural processes combine in human reproduction. Foetal pituitary and adrenal systems initiate the birth process, releasing hormones which disinhibit uterine contractions in the mother. The foetus' head pressing into the mother's cervix triggers nerve impulses that pass up the mother's spinal cord to the hypothalamus. Signals pass from the hypothalamus to the pituitary gland, resulting in the reflexive release of the hormone oxytocin which, in turn, stimulates cervical contractions in the uterus, and this in turn stimulates more oxytocin release (see Figure 4.13). The hormone prostoglandin is also released in the uterine wall and this too stimulates contractions in a positive feedforward loop eventually resulting in the expulsion of the baby. The process of going into labour may be preceded by a period of less sharply defined uterine contractions that occur over several nights before delivery. The onset of labour in humans is often at dusk, which suggests that light-sensitive processes may be involved in triggering contractions. Birth in humans is often at night, whereas in some nocturnal species, such as the rat, birth usually occurs in daylight, during the afternoon. It is tempting to speculate that birth is

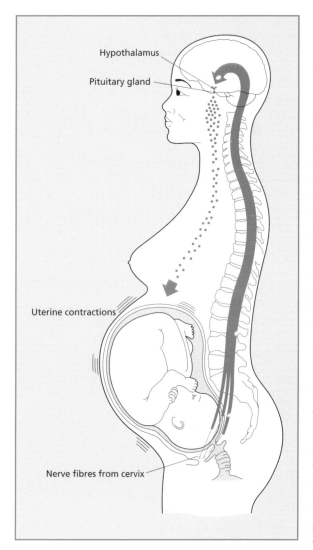

Hypothalamus

Pituitary gland

Uterine contractions

Nerve fibres from cervix

FIG. 4.13 The reflexive release of oxytocin. Nerve fibres from the cervix carry messages to the mother's brain to stimulate the release of oxytocin, which in turn stimulates uterine contraction. Adapted from Nathanielsz (1992).

timed to take place when the mother is safely in the confines of the nest (Nathanielsz, 1992).

These biological processes are themselves embedded in social practices. The anthropologists Rosenberg and Trevathan (1996) make the point that humans, of all primates, are the only species where the female needs assistance to give birth. This is because the pelvic girdle, which is adapted for the upright, walking posture, is wider than it is deep and the infant must rotate the head to emerge from the birth canal. The effect of the rotation is that babies are usually born facing away from the mother, out of her reach and with the back of the head emerging first (see Figure 4.14). Rosenberg and Trevathan suggest that it is this specific evolutionary adaptation for bipedalism that created the necessity for the midwife. Virtually all societies assist women with birth and, of course, there are wide variations in such cultural practices.

Significant cultural variations surround even the universal biological aspects of reproduction. Family planning practices vary widely from society to society with contraceptive pills being widespread in some cultures while remaining banned in other advanced cultures, such as Japan. Family planning is a matter of cultural and political concern. Fogel (1991) points out that, in countries with high population growth, such as India, the population would double every 25 years without family planning. India passed a law in 1970 (which was repealed in 1977) requiring sterilisation of all parents of two or more children who wished to continue to receive social welfare payments. China too has checked the rate of population growth by restricting families to one child. There are, however, other societies that forbid contraception on religious grounds and where families of seven children may be common. In advanced technological societies couples, who would otherwise remain childless through infertility, may now have children through artificial insemination and even by surrogate parenting. Personal and cultural values are clearly an important aspect of the process of reproduction.

Similarly, there is great cultural variation in the practices surrounding birth itself. In advanced technological societies, drugs may be used to relieve pain and most births take place under sterile conditions in hospitals. In other societies pain relief may come through the use of music in labour, as among Laotians, or by applying heat to the abdomen of the mother, as in the Comanche tribe of North America (Fogel, 1991). There are also cultural variations in the position for giving birth, from sitting in special birthing stools, to kneeling, to lying with support to the back.

Fogel (1991) reports that, in traditional Japanese society, a number of community rituals surround pregnancy and birth. From the fifth month of pregnancy, women wear a special belt beneath the kimono to symbolise the child's tie to the community. After birth, the umbilical cord is dried and saved in an ornamental box to remind the mother and child of their originally close physical bond. On the day of birth and on the third and seventh day of life, feasts are celebrated among the relatives to ensure good health for the baby, and a naming ceremony is performed on the seventh day. This example shows clearly how intimately linked are the biological and cultural aspects of childbirth. These examples show the mutual dependence of biology and culture in the processes of reproduction and birth. Biology and culture function as mutually embedded systems, with both having an important part to play in the very origins of development.

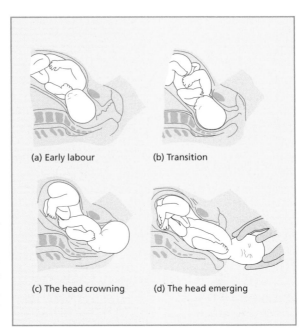

(a) Early labour   (b) Transition

(c) The head crowning   (d) The head emerging

FIG. 4.14 The rotation of a baby's head during birth means that humans are the only species that need midwife assistance with birth. Adapted from Clarke-Stewart and Koch (1983).

Conclusion and summary

We began this chapter by charting the stages of prenatal development from conception to birth. In the embryonic period, especially during the first trimester, the foetus is very vulnerable and damage often results if the mother contracts rubella, or the foetus is exposed to certain drugs, excessive quantities of alcohol or tobacco, or to environmental contaminants. Abnormalities in foetal development show that the model of the "epigenetic landscape", which we introduced in Chapter 3, provides a useful framework for thinking about development. Where there are non-optimal conditions during the foetal stage the development of an individual may be forced down many abnormal pathways that result in atypical development.

The reader may ask whether development is a process of continuous change or a series of discontinuous transitions from one type of organisation to another. Most contemporary theorists would argue that a full understanding of the process of development requires both continuous and discontinuous aspects of developmental change to be taken into account. The recent exciting evidence from prenatal development research gives us some idea about the initial state of the developing system. For example, in the case of walking, we find evidence in the foetus for movement patterns that are analogous to crawling and walking but which will not be fully developed until several months later.

Birth marks a transition to a new environment, one that will offer new opportunities, especially for vision and action. However, once again, we must expect continuities as well as discontinuities with the earlier stages of development. As far as the development of perception is concerned, the evidence suggests that all the basic sensory systems are functional from birth or before. This is not to say that the process of perception is fully developed. On the contrary, much development is still to come. However, even newborns will show preferences in what they attend to in vision, in hearing, in taste, and in smell. This implies that they are not passive recipients of stimulation, nor are they simply captured by sensory stimulation. The same questions about continuity and discontinuity need to be asked. If the neonate has the ability for basic perception of reality, how does this initial state enter into the subsequent course of development? This is an issue that we return to in the next chapter.

Recent research into neural development has also raised important questions about early development after birth. Some of the major features of brain development in phylogeny and ontogeny were reviewed in this chapter. Modern man has the largest brain and the longest period of brain growth of all primates. A comparison between rhesus monkeys and humans shows that whereas the monkeys achieve maximum synapse density (i.e. the greatest number of nerve cell interconnections) at the age of two to four months this point is not reached until seven to twelve months in the human infant. Another important aspect of brain development is that different areas and different layers of the cerebral cortex develop at different rates. Recent research (see Johnson, 1988, for a review) shows that deeper layers of the cortex mature before more superficial layers. Thus, at birth, in layer 5 of the primary visual cortex around 60% of dendritic growth has already taken place, whereas in layer 3 (which is closer to the surface) only about 30% of dendritic growth has taken place. There are also differences in timing between the different areas of the cortex. For example, the frontal cortex matures several months later than the primary visual cortex. Such differential development across cortical areas has not been reported in other species.

We saw that, while the basic architecture of the brain may be genetically determined and species specific, the major changes that occur in brain development concern the connectivity of the nervous system. The connectivity of the system is partly inflexible—experience expectant—and determined by genetic factors in interaction with experience to give rise to a species-typical brain architecture. It is also partly flexible—experience dependent—and driven by the electrochemical activity of the individual neurones. Furthermore, it is possible that the electrical activity of the neurones is itself driven by motor and sensory feedback processes derived from activity and from the perceived environment. We reviewed some evidence from foetal development that implicates both emergent motor patterns and sensory feedback in the development of the brain. Brain development depends in part on the characteristics of the environment and partly on individual experience; and, importantly, relations between brain development and experience are bidirectional. Such plasticity is highly economical because it enables the nervous system to develop appropriately to the demands of the environment, without the detailed characteristics of a particular environment having to be specified by genetics.

With birth comes even greater opportunity for experiential factors to enter into development processes as the effects of culture come into play. There are variations in the process of giving birth and in the ways in which different societies welcome the newborn. There are differences in the amount of time that newborns spend with their mothers, in the places that they go to sleep, and the positions in which they are placed for sleep. There are variations in the amount of time spent in face-to-face contact and in the opportunities that are provided for physical activity. From the moment of birth, then, we can see that human development is simultaneously determined by both biology and culture.

Further reading

- Corbalis, M.C. (1991). *The lopsided ape*. Oxford, UK: Oxford University Press. This readable book discusses the unique relationship between brain and behaviour in humans from a comparative perspective.
- Johnson, M. (1998). The neural basis of cognitive development. In D. Kuhn & R.S. Siegler (Eds.), *Handbook of child psychology: Vol. 2. Cognition, perception, and language* (W. Damon, Gen. Ed.; pp. 1–50). New York: Wiley. This is a detailed chapter that provides an up-to-date review of studies of brain development before and after birth. It is suitable for advanced undergraduates.
- Michel, G., & Moore, C.L. (1995). *Developmental psychobiology: An interdisciplinary science*. Cambridge, MA: MIT Press (Chapter 6). This chapter provides a detailed account of embryological development. It is intended for advanced undergraduates and assumes some prior knowledge of the structure and organisation of the brain.
- Van der Molen, M.W., & Ridderinkof, K.R. (1998). The growing and aging brain: Life-span changes in brain and cognitive functioning. In A. Demetriou, W. Doise, & C.F.M. van Lieshout (Eds.), *Life-span developmental psychology* (pp. 35–99). Chichester, UK: John Wiley. This chapter provides an introductory account of the development of the human brain during the prenatal period and early childhood. The chapter begins by taking the reader through the basic structure of the brain, so it is good place to start to find out more about this highly technical area.

CHAPTER 5

CONTENTS

Cognitive development in infancy

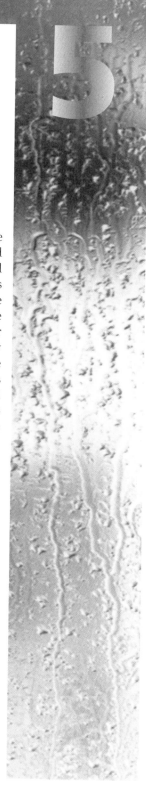

The newborn baby (or neonate) was for a very long time thought to be little more than a helpless, reflexive organism with immature motor skills and capable of seeing or hearing very little. The 19th-century philosopher and psychologist, William James, famously described the world of the newborn as a "buzzing, blooming confusion, where the infant is seized by eyes, ears, nose and entrails all once" (1890). This vivid phrase conveys an image of a passive infant, inundated by meaningless sensations, with little awareness of self or external reality. One of the major achievements in developmental psychology of recent years has been to show that William James' preconception of the perceptual world of the newborn was fundamentally mistaken. The infant has proved to be much more competent in perception, and so in cognition, than had been assumed. This late 20th-century view of the "competent infant" has also suggested that the influential view of infancy espoused by Jean Piaget is also incorrect in some essentials.

Piaget's theory of infant cognition

Piaget's own view of infancy was essentially one of increasing competence from birth, starting from a point of incompetence. He argued that infants have to *construct* knowledge about the environment through their own actions and that their perception is inadequate to provide information about the world. In Piaget's account, perception develops though patterns of activity. As we shall see, it is difficult to sustain this aspect of Piaget's argument in the light of contemporary evidence on perception in young babies. We begin this chapter with an overview of Piaget's own account of infancy. This is followed by a review of some contemporary evidence that is incompatible with Piaget's theoretical assumptions concerning the relationship between the baby's actions and perception of reality. We attempt to reconcile these conflicting views.

Piaget wished to explain how knowledge is acquired from the earliest beginnings. He argued that knowledge is constructed through the motor activities that link the baby to reality and which give rise to regular sensory consequences. Piaget called infancy the stage of sensorimotor development to capture his view about the formation of links between sensation and action. He identified six developmental stages in the sensorimotor period beginning, at birth, with reflexes and ending in the second year of life with symbolic representation (see the table below).

PIAGET'S HIERARCHICAL THEORY OF SENSORIMOTOR DEVELOPMENT

Stage I: Reflexes
Age: Birth to 6 weeks
e.g. sucking

Stage II: Primary circular reactions
Age: 6 weeks to 4 months
First acquired habits, e.g. thumb sucking

Stage III: Secondary circular reactions
Age: 4 to 8 months
Goal-directed behaviour, e.g. visually guided reaching to objects

Stage IV: Co-ordinated secondary circular reactions
Age: 9 to 12 months
Differentiation of means and ends in intentional acts, e.g. searching for a hidden object

Stage V: Tertiary circular reactions
Age: 12 to 18 months
Application of established means to new ends, e.g. in the bath, baby squeezes water from a sponge, pours water from a can, holds water carefully in a basin, and studies the water falling under different conditions

Stage VI: Symbolic representation
Age: From 18 months
Mental combinations of means and ends
Insightful discovery of new means through active experiment, e.g. toddler pulls an object through playpen bars using a stick. Toddler has concepts of object, space, time, and causes

---

Sub-stage I: Reflexes

The initial connection of the infant with the environment is elementary and through simple reflexes. The reflexes, while pre-adapted for rather specific stimuli, are soon applied to a wide variety of new objects. For example, the sucking reflex was evolved for feeding but it is soon applied to many things, including the baby's own hand. In Piaget's terminology, the reflex assimilates new objects and in turn accommodates to the new properties of objects encountered. This means that the baby sucks her own hand, and even though this does not provide any food, she discovers new information about her hand through sucking. Thus, sucking has allowed assimilation of information about the hand, and in turn, sucking has been changed or accommodated to allow for exploration of non-food objects.

Sub-stage II: Primary circular reactions

Once the reflex has become co-ordinated with another action pattern, it is called a primary circular reaction. This terminology is taken from James Mark Baldwin (see The Emergence of Developmental Psychology, in Chapter 1), who first described these repetitive patterns of activity in babies. A circular reaction is purposeful and not simply reflexive. It has a goal, which once reached, terminates the action and sets in motion a new cycle of activity. For example, the baby may bring her hand to her mouth, touch the mouth, and then remove it. The mouth is the goal of the activity and, once attained, the sequence is typically repeated over and again.

The sub-stage of primary circular reactions lasts from approximately six weeks to four months. The baby repeats activities for the simple pleasure of doing so and, in the course of the actions, discovers her own body. She discovers that she has eyes that can see, ears that can hear, and arms that can reach. She discovers that objects can simultaneously be looked at and listened to, or that they can be simultaneously touched and felt. These aspects of self-awareness are constructed in the course of activity and as a result of the baby's assimilation and accommodation to real things.

Sub-stage III: Secondary circular reactions

In the next sub-stage, from four to eight months, the primary circular reactions become co-ordinated. That is, there is a hierarchical integration of the action patterns so far developed. The infant's interest also shifts from repeating actions for their own sake to studying the consequences of the actions. The baby may initially note some accidental consequence of her movement but will then repeat the movement to make the interesting event happen again, as for example when she shakes her legs and the hood of her pram moves, or when she pulls on a cloth and manages to drag a toy towards her. As in the previous sub-stages the circular reactions are terminated by the achievement of the goal.

Sub-stage IV:
Co-ordinated secondary circular reactions

When secondary circular reactions become hierarchically integrated among themselves they are known as co-ordinated secondary circular reactions. This sub-stage lasts from nine to twelve months. The baby is now able to organise sequences of actions as a means to an end and is no longer restricted to dealing with the consequences of only one action at a time. For example, she can co-ordinate the action of reaching and grasping a cloth covering an object with

A six-month-old using a cloth to retrieve an object: (a) he first puts the cloth in his mouth; (b) next he grasps the toy as it comes into reach. The infant does not appear to pull the cloth with the intention of retrieving the toy. From P. Willatts (1985), Development of problem-solving in infancy. In A. Slater and G. Bremner (Eds.), *Infant development*. Hove, UK: Psychology Press. Photographs by Peter Willatts, reproduced with permission.

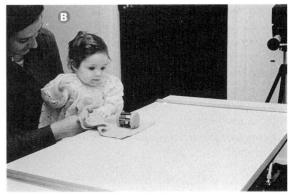

An eight-month-old showing efficient use of a cloth as a means of retrieving an out-of-reach object: (a) the toy is presented, this time in the far condition; (b) and (c) the infant pulls the cloth in a single, uninterrupted movement; (d) when presented with the toy in the near position, the infant was equally successful and adapted her pull to the changed distance of the object. From P. Willatts (1985), Development of problem-solving in infancy. In A. Slater and G. Bremner (Eds.), *Infant development*. Hove, UK: Psychology Press. Photographs by Peter Willatts, reproduced with permission.

a subsequent action of reaching and grasping the object thus revealed. The action pattern is not only terminated (a feedback process) by reaching the goal, as in earlier sub-stages, but it is also goal directed since a remote goal is specified from the outset (a feedforward process) and a sequence of co-ordinated actions is produced.

Sub-stage V: Tertiary circular reactions

The next main change is that infants can deliberately vary their patterns of activity in an effort at trial and error experimentation. They are not concerned simply to make an interesting event last longer but to vary the event itself in order to arrive at a better understanding. A typical behaviour at this stage is throwing things out of the pram. This allows the baby both to investigate object trajectories and discover something of gravity—and also the limits of their parent's patience with the game!

Sub-stage VI: Symbolic representation

Infancy ends with the capacity for representation. Piaget uses the word in a specific sense to mean presenting reality to oneself mentally—hence, *re-presenting* reality. Evidence for representation includes deferred imitation—imitating an event some time after it has happened—pretend play (see Play, in Chapter 6) and the beginnings of language (see Chapter 7, The Beginnings of Language Development). Symbolic representation arises as a consequence of the ability to represent reality. Symbols are arbitrarily related to their referents; the symbol stands for an object and serves to represent it. Symbols arise in play, when one object "stands for" another, and also in language, where speech and gestures serve to represent objects.

Representation marks the end of the sensorimotor period. Now babies are not only able to act directly on reality but they also become able to plan actions in relation to imagined realities. The acquisition of the "symbolic function", as Piaget called it, marks a qualitative change to a new stage of development in which symbol systems will play a major part in the development of thinking.

One important idea that runs through Piaget's account of sensorimotor development is that "touch tutors vision". The idea is that babies have to learn to perceive the world by correlating touch with vision during the early months of life. The assumption has been that, even though the visual system is functional at birth, the visual sensations received by the baby are initially meaningless. As Morss (1990) has pointed out, this starting assumption about infant perception leaves the newborn a "prisoner of the senses". Even though vision is functional at birth (see Chapter 4, Development from Conception to Birth), if the senses are not connected then the baby's experience would not be of reality as adults know it— it could only be a world of meaningless sensations. This is why James argued that early experience would be a buzzing, blooming confusion.

The effect of importing these assumptions into developmental psychology is that it is necessary to explain how the infant can organise experience in order to progress in understanding the visual world beyond such chaotic beginnings. Piaget suggested that the visual world of the newborn is two dimensional and lacking in depth. Perception of shape and size develops only slowly, during the first six months of life. Piaget assumed that the senses are initially separate and become co-ordinated through the child's own activities. In the first three months seeing and hearing become co-ordinated but remain separate from touching and looking. Then, between three and six months, a new, multisensory co-ordination develops which incorporates touch, vision, and hearing. Only when this has happened does the infant become capable of knowing that the same physical object can simultaneously give rise to tactile, visual, and auditory sensations.

Piaget (1937/1954) argued that the baby gradually comes to know about the properties of objects through her own activities. A very important aspect of his theory concerns the acquisition of the "object concept". The object concept is defined by Piaget as a belief that physical objects are:

> *Permanent, substantial, external to the self and firm in existence even though they do not directly affect perception and to conceive of them as retaining their identity whatever the changes in position.*
>
> *(Piaget, 1937/1954, pp. 5 and 7)*

A radical alternative to the traditional view of visual perception that Piaget adopted was the one developed by James Gibson (1966). Gibson stressed that space is not empty, but full of textured objects and surfaces. He argued that perception of visual space occurs because terrestrial space is filled with structures that are perceived in relation to the surfaces of the earth. These textured surfaces reflect light to the eye and the pattern of texture is preserved in the image that falls on the retina, the light sensitive surface of the eye. The relative distance of objects from the observer is preserved in the retinal image because the pattern or texture of the retinal image becomes more fine grained as the distance from the observer increases. These patterns of texture are called **texture gradients** (see Figure 5.1).

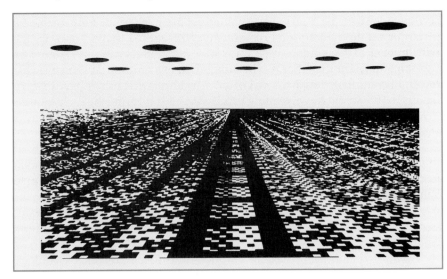

FIG. 5.1 Depth specified by texture. Reproduced with permission from W. Schiff (1986), *Perception: An applied approach*. Acton, MA: Copley.

The implication of Gibson's theory for infancy is that perceptual systems have evolved to put the infant in direct contact with the real world from the outset. The theoretical implication is that babies may be able to perceive the world visually before they can act upon it. Thus, far from Piaget's view that babies perceive the world by acting upon it, Gibson's view would suggest that babies can learn about the world through perception itself (see Butterworth, 1994 for a detailed account of this argument).

Empirical studies of perception in infancy not only tell us about infant perception but they also enable us to choose between rival theories as to the status of perception in early development. If very young babies can perceive the shape and size of an object, this would imply that they visually perceive the real world of objects from the outset, without any need for prolonged learning. Furthermore, if babies can inter-relate information obtained through different senses *before* they have extensive capabilities for movement, then this would allow them a prolonged period of learning through the distance senses (vision and audition) before they have precise control over action.

One invaluable source of information about young babies' perception of the world is to study their reaction to objects. Piaget's own view was that babies have to learn about the properties of objects. He argued that the object concept stands at the foundations of thought, calling it the "first invariant" of thinking. Unlike Gibson, Piaget assumed that direct perception of the properties of objects was not possible and so babies must build up, or construct, understanding through the successive co-ordinations of sensorimotor activity. He was of the opinion that, until the child is about 18 months old, appearances and disappearances of objects are not understood as the movements of single objects in space.

Piaget's account of the development of the object concept

Following from his general account of the sub-stages of infancy, Piaget (1937/1954) proposed that six sub-stages could be observed in the development of the baby's understanding of object disappearance. Each sub-stage in Piaget's account of what is usually described as **object permanence** corresponds to the general level of sensorimotor organisation appropriate to that sub-stage. As with the stages of sensorimotor development, the ages are approximate but the sub-stages were said by Piaget to be universal and always to occur in the same order. Piaget illustrated each of his sub-stages with observations from the development of his own three children.

Sub-stage I: Reflex action (0–1.5 months)

In the first weeks of life infants do not search for an object that disappears. Instead, the baby simply repeats a reflex or stares at the place where an object has disappeared. Piaget argues that these actions do not require an understanding of object permanence; rather, the child simply repeats the action pattern that is effective in locating the nipple, or stares at the place of disappearance:

> *Lacking prehension, the child could search with his eyes, change his perspective etc. But that is precisely what he does not know how to do, for the vanished object is not yet for him a permanent object which has been moved; it is a mere image which reenters the void as soon as it vanishes, and emerges from it for no objective reason.*
>
> *(Piaget, 1937/1954, p. 11)*

Sub-stage II: Primary circular reactions (1.5–4 months)

Repetition of reflex actions slowly leads to a new level of co-ordination (called a primary circular reaction) as the baby explores the objects in the environment. These primary circular reactions are most simply conceived of as habits and, through them, babies first discover the properties of their own body. They "discover" their eyes, arms, hands, and feet in the course of acting on objects. Objects also offer particular types of resistance to actions and so the baby must modify action patterns (accommodate them) to take these object properties into account; but the infant is still not aware that objects exist independently of the habitual pattern of activity.

Sub-stage III: Secondary circular reactions (4–8 months)

A new level of co-ordination is achieved at about four months as the primary circular reactions become mutually assimilated and the infant gains simultaneous control over different sensorimotor subsystems. This level of co-ordination is called a secondary circular reaction. The baby makes discoveries

> **KEY TERM**
> **Object permanence**: The understanding that objects have substance, maintain their identities when they change location, and ordinarily continue to exist when out of sight.

by accident and then repeats the activity as if to find out what caused the particular event of interest. The focus of action shifts to external objects as babies repeatedly explore objects in their environment. Typical actions are repetitive kicking or hand movements, rattle shaking, and exploration of sheets and duvets. Repetition implies a kind of recognition through action and the beginnings of memory but the baby still lacks awareness of object permanence outside the patterns of activity themselves.

Piaget's observation of Laurent at 5 months 24 days illustrates this sub-stage:

> Laurent's reaction to falling objects still seems to be non-existent: he does not follow with his eyes any of the objects which I drop in front of him. At 0.5 26 on the other hand, Laurent searches in front of him for a paper ball which I drop above his coverlet. He immediately looks at the coverlet after the third attempt but only in front of him, that is where he has just grasped the ball. When I drop the object outside the bassinet Laurent does not look for it (except around my empty hand while it remains in the air).
>
> (Piaget, 1937/1954, p. 14)

Piaget says that a greater degree of permanence is attributed to vanished images, since the baby will look for things that fall and will retrieve a partially hidden object. However, permanence remains exclusively connected with the action in progress:

> The child's universe is still only a totality of pictures emerging from nothingness at the moment of the action, to return to nothingness when the action is finished.
>
> (Piaget, 1937/1954, p. 43)

Piaget argues that the primary reason for failure to search is because the baby does not understand that the hidden object continues to exist. Figure 5.2 illustrates the baby's problem in searching for a hidden object.

Sub-stage IV: Co-ordinated secondary circular reactions (9–12 months)

The essential advance of this sub-stage is that infants, for the first time, become able to co-ordinate means and ends. Babies can now remove covers and search for a hidden object because they can separate the action (the means) from the object to which it is applied (the ends).

Piaget's observation of Laurent at 8 months 29 days illustrates means–ends co-ordination:

> Laurent plays with a tin box. I take it from him and place it under his pillow; whereas four days previously the child did not react in similar circumstances, this time he grasps the pillow and perceives the box of which he immediately takes possession.
>   ... At 9 months and 20 days he searches for a little duck under his pillow, under a spread cloth etc. The behaviour pattern has now been acquired and is accompanied by a growing interest.
>
> (Piaget, 1937/1954, p. 45)

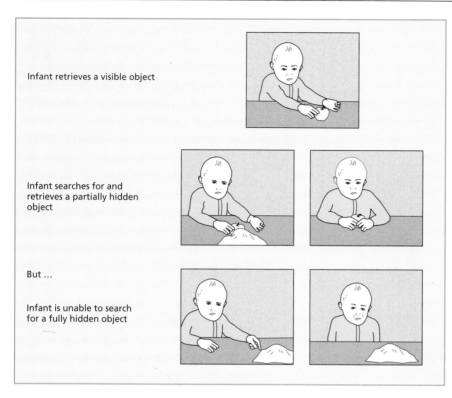

FIG. 5.2 Stage III infants have a problem when they attempt to search for a hidden object. This six-month-old infant successfully retrieves a partially hidden object, but cannot retrieve an object that is completely hidden. Adapted from Bower (1982).

In spite of these important advances, object permanence is still not fully acquired since babies make curious errors when they first become able to search. These errors are variously known as "stage IV" errors, "perseverative" errors, or "A not B" errors. An object is hidden at a point A; the child searches for it and finds it. Next the object is placed at a new position B, and it is covered while the baby watches. The baby searches for it at the original position A, even though she has just seen the thing disappear at B (see Figure 5.3).

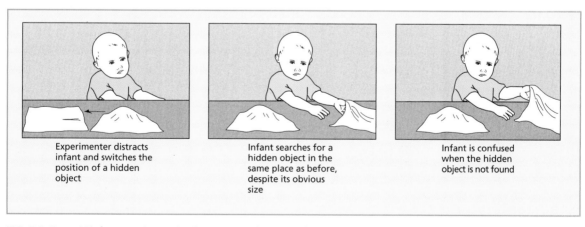

FIG. 5.3 Stage IV infants tend to make the perseverative error. This nine-month-old infant thinks that an object that has been hidden in a particular place will always be in that same place, despite the obvious size of the hidden object. The infant is confused when the hidden object is not found in the previous location. Adapted from Bower (1982).

Piaget argued that perseverative errors demonstrate that the baby perceives the object to be an extension of action. According to Piaget, babies have learned a pragmatic procedure for making vanished objects reappear. They do not understand that objects are unique and therefore can only be in one place at one time. Instead, they are under the impression that their own actions made the object reappear.

Sub-stage V: Tertiary circular reactions (12–18 months)

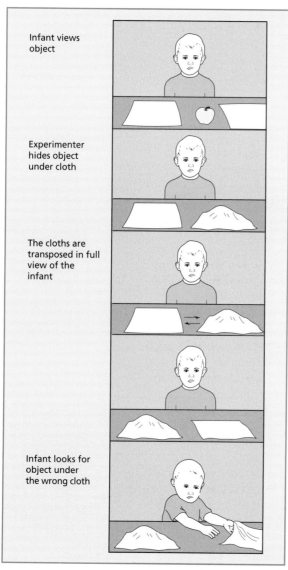

Infant views object

Experimenter hides object under cloth

The cloths are transposed in full view of the infant

Infant looks for object under the wrong cloth

FIG. 5.4 Stage V infants tend to make the invisible displacement error, and cannot yet cope with an object's location being switched while it is concealed by a cloth. This 14-month-old infant is not aware that the hidden object has been moved, despite watching the experimenter switching the cloths over. Adapted from Bower (1982).

The essential progress over the previous stage is that the baby will actively experiment to discover new means to an end in problem solving. By a process of trial and error babies discover that, in order to find a hidden object that has been moved from A to B, they should search where they last saw the object rather than where they first found it. In spite of this advance, the babies' knowledge of the object still rests in action as they continue to make errors in a slightly more difficult search task—the stage V errors—where the baby has to imagine the movement of an object between A and B. In this more difficult task, the baby initially searches for an object at one location (A) and then the object is moved to a new location (B) out of sight of the baby. In a test situation this so-called "invisible displacement" is achieved by moving the object to a new location while it is under a cloth (see Figure 5.4).

The stage V error is demonstrated by Piaget's observation of his daughter, Jacqueline, at one year six months. She had been playing with a potato, putting it in and taking it out of a box:

> *Jacqueline is sitting on a green rug and playing with a potato which interests her very much … I then take the potato and put it into the box while Jacqueline watches. Then I place the box under the rug and turn it upside down thus leaving the object hidden by the rug … and I bring out the empty box … she searches for the object in the box, looks at the rug etc., but it does not occur to her to raise the rug in order to find the potato underneath.*
>
> (Piaget, 1937/1954, p. 68)

Piaget argues that babies at stage V understand object permanence only to the extent that they can keep track of the movements of a visible object. This is why invisible displacement is still a problem.

Sub-stage VI:
Representation (from 18 months)

The final stage in constructing the object concept consists in "representing" the object. In Piaget's terminology, this means that the baby must be able to imagine the object and be able to retrieve this information from memory. He describes his daughter Jacqueline at 1 year 7 months and 20 days:

> *Jacqueline watches me when I put a coin in my hand, then put my hand under a coverlet. I withdraw my hand closed. Jacqueline opens it then searches under the coverlet until she finds the object. I then take back the coin at once, put it in my hand, and then slip my closed hand under a cushion situated at the other side (on her left and no longer on her right); Jacqueline immediately searches for the object under the cushion. I complicate the test as follows: I place the coin in my hand, then my hand under the cushion, I bring it forth closed and immediately hide it under the coverlet. Finally I withdraw it and hold it out, closed to Jacqueline. Jacqueline then pushes my hand aside without opening it (she guesses that there is nothing in it, which is new), she looks under the cushion, then directly under the coverlet where she finds the object.*
> (Piaget, 1937/1954, p. 79)

Piaget says the object is now definitively freed from action and perception alike. The baby conceives of the object as permanent and as retaining its identity independently of any action the infant may carry out.

Infants' perception of objects:
An alternative to Piaget

Piaget's theory of the sensorimotor stage and of the development of object permanence rests heavily on the assumption that perception is insufficient to inform the developing child about the physical world. This is why there is so much emphasis on action in his theory. Piaget considered that extensive touching and grasping of objects, as well as looking, was necessary for gradually piecing together knowledge about object properties. One important source of evidence against Piaget's theory came from infants born without arms or legs following the thalidomide tragedy (see Stages in Prenatal Development, in Chapter 4).

These babies often showed normal intellectual development, despite the fact that they lacked the opportunity for extensive physical interaction with objects (DeCarie, 1969). In particular, they lacked the opportunity to hold things and look at them simultaneously, a condition Piaget considered essential to tutor the visual system about the solidity of objects.

Other evidence against the Piagetian theory that "touch tutors vision" came from ingenious experiments which have demonstrated that infants have a precocious understanding of essential object properties such as solidity. An early study by Bower (1971) suggested that babies perceived a "virtual object" as solid. He produced a virtual object by projecting a polarised light shadow of a stationary cube, which infants viewed using polarising goggles. They were surprised—as measured by a change in heart rate—when their hand passed through the object as they swiped at it. Bower (1971) also showed that three-month-old babies were "surprised" when an object that had been seen to pass behind a screen failed to reappear when the screen moved on (see Figure 5.5). In another experiment, Bower presented babies with an object that was made to disappear instantaneously, as if "annihilated", by using a series of mirrors that could be rapidly moved so that the reflected image of the object suddenly could no longer be seen. Babies who had been trained to suck on a nipple in the presence of the object stopped sucking, as if the conditioned stimulus no longer existed.

FIG. 5.5 A "virtual" object created by polarised light. An intangible visible object is produced by casting a shadow with polarised light onto a rear projection screen. When the shadow is viewed through polarising goggles, the object appears to be solid and situated in front of the screen. Infants are surprised when they reach out, and their hand passes through an apparently solid object. Adapted from Bower (1971).

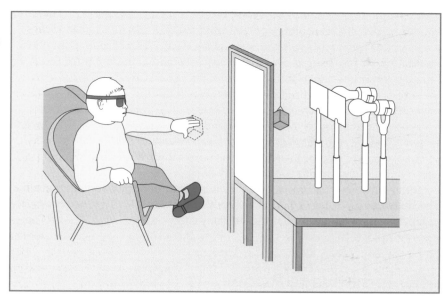

Another important early study demonstrated that very young babies can also extract basic visual information about objects that they have touched but not seen. Meltzoff and Borton (1979) tested babies aged 29 days in a task where the baby was given a pacifier of a particular shape to suck. Some babies received a smooth dummy, others received a knobbly dummy but, in both cases, the dummy was placed in the baby's mouth without being seen by the baby (see

FIG. 5.6 Dummies used in Meltzoff and Borton's (1979) study.

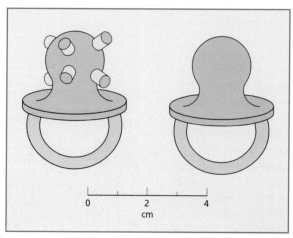

Figure 5.6). The baby actively explored the dummy with lips and tongue. Then large-scale models of both dummies (measuring 6.4 cm across) were placed to the left and right in the baby's visual field. Babies preferred to fixate the shape that they had explored orally. They looked at the model that was the same shape as the dummy they had been sucking for approximately 70% of their total visual fixation time.

The Meltzoff and Borton experiment shows that active oral exploration conveys something to the baby of what the object looked like. Of course, this could be as simple as "knobbly" versus "smooth" but the important point is that tactile exploration through oral touch is linked to vision even at one month of age. The infant data suggests that infants can recognise the equivalence of information picked up by different sensory modalities.

Over a number of years Baillargeon (1999) has systematically measured infants' perception of physical objects. Her studies involve repeated presentation of a visual display using the **habituation method** (see the box on pages 107–108). Changes in looking patterns, when a new object or event is presented, reveal which combinations of physical events babies perceive as possible or impossible. Babies often show renewed interest in a familiar display when an impossible event happens while they are watching.

In an early study Baillargeon (1991) used a display that appeared to violate the principle that a solid object cannot move through the space occupied by another object. A screen, in the form of a drawbridge, seen end on by the infant, was rotated repeatedly in a 180-degree arc (see Figure 5.7). Once the infant was habituated to this display, a large box was placed behind the screen and the infant was shown one of two test events. In one condition—the possible event— the screen stopped rotating when it was obstructed by the box. In a second, impossible event, the screen continued to rotate through a full 180 degrees, as if the box were no longer behind it. Babies of three and a half months looked longer at the impossible event than at the possible event. This suggests that infants perceived the continued existence of the hidden box and that they also perceived that the screen could not rotate through it.

In subsequent experiments, Baillargeon (1991) went on to demonstrate that, by six and a half months, babies not only understand that the screen should stop when there is a box behind it, but also that the screen will stop at different positions depending on the height of the box, or depending on whether the object behind the screen can be compressed or not. That is, the baby appropriately perceives occlusion and the possible physical interactions between rigid and elastic objects, and finds it unusual (to say the least) when the experimenter presents visual events that violate basic physical laws.

Another source of evidence about infants' object perception comes from their reaction to the light being turned off. If visual contact is so essential for

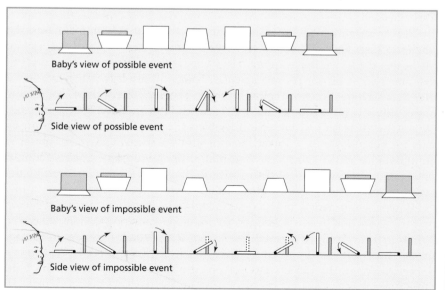

FIG. 5.7 Baillargeon's drawbridge study. Adapted from Baillargeon, Spelke, and Wasserman (1985).

Baby's view of possible event

Side view of possible event

Baby's view of impossible event

Side view of impossible event

KEY TERM
Habituation method:
Method used to assess abilities of infants in which a stimulus is presented repeatedly until the infant's attention decreases significantly. Then a novel stimulus is presented and the increase in attention is measured.

object permanence then loss of visual contact should result in the ending of object search as it does when an object is covered. Bower and Wishart (1972) also demonstrated that babies, who will not search under a cloth for a hidden object, will reach for an object made invisible by turning off the light. Bower's finding was initially treated with some disbelief because it ran counter to Piaget's claims, but Hood and Willatts (1986) were able to show that babies' ability to reach for objects once the lights were turned out was reliable and that they reached to the right if the object had appeared on their right, and to the left if an object had appeared in that position (see Figure 5.8). Thus, out of sight is not out of mind, as the simple theory of object permanence in babies might propose.

FIG. 5.8 A five-month-old infant reaching in the dark. The infant (a) looks at the object; (b) looks away when the light goes out; (c) reaches to the object's remembered position. From B. Hood and P. Willatts (1986), Reaching in the dark to an object's remembered position in 5-month-old infants. *British Journal of Developmental Psychology, 4,* 62. Copyright © The British Psychological Society. Reprinted with permission.

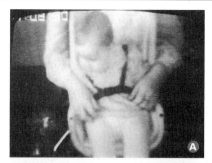

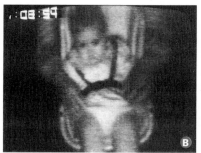

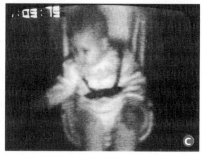

Bower's argument, which is based on the work of the Belgian psychologist Michotte (see Thines, Costall, & Butterworth, 1990, for a full account of Michotte's theory), is that continued existence and annihilation (i.e. permanent disappearance) of objects are specified quite differently when an object undergoes a transition from being "in sight" to being "out of sight". When one object moves behind another, the way texture in the occluded object is deleted (wiped) by the texture of the occluding object specifies that one object is simply moving behind another. In the case of impermanence, when an object is annihilated it either "implodes" so that all its texture disappears without deletion, or it slowly loses texture around the edges (and is replaced by the textured ground) as it disappears. An example would be a puddle evaporating.

Bower's argument is that babies' perceptual systems are capable of picking up this distinction between temporary occlusion and annihilation. When the lights are turned off, we perceive the light as going "out of existence" and not the objects that it was illuminating. Reciprocally, when a light is turned on in a darkened room, the objects are perceived as pre-existing before the light illuminates them.

Methods of studying infant perception

Even young babies show spontaneous visual preference, preferring to look at one thing rather than another. This means that it is possible to study what the infant chooses to look at. The pioneer of the visual preference method was Robert Fantz (1965). The infant, who may be lying down, or who can be specially supported, is presented with a pair of visual targets, one to the left and the other to the right of the midline. The investigator notes the direction of the baby's first eye movement and the total amount of time that the infant fixates the target. On succeeding trials, the targets are alternated from left to right, so that any bias a baby may have for looking to one side or the other cancels out.

In the early studies using the preference technique, babies were presented with simple choices between patterned or plain two-dimensional targets. It was established that babies prefer to look at patterns rather than plain surfaces. In one of Fantz's studies, a face-like mask was compared with a bullseye pattern and it was found that newborns showed a preference for the face-like stimulus (see Figure 5.9). Similar methods were used to demonstrate that babies discriminate different colours and to measure their visual acuity. Visual acuity is a measure of how fine is the detail that the eye can discriminate. This is shown for babies by their preference for finer and finer graded black and white stripes over a uniformly grey surface.

A variation of the Fantz technique involves presenting babies with the same stimuli repeatedly. This is called the *habituation method*, since it involves accustoming the baby to the visual object, so that it becomes progressively less interesting. Then, once the infant's attention has declined to some criterion value (usually 50% of the time spent fixating the target on the first trial), a new object is presented and any recovery of interest by the baby is measured. Providing that babies do not naturally prefer one stimulus over another, this method creates the potential for discriminating between a

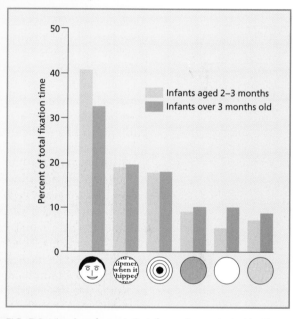

FIG. 5.9 Visual preferences in infancy demonstrated by Fantz (1961). Even young babies prefer to look at patterned rather than plain objects. Newborns show a strong preference for the face-like stimulus. From R.L. Fantz (1961), The origins of form perception. *Scientific American, 204*, 66–72. Reproduced with permission.

The habituation technique involves showing the baby a habituating stimulus, such as the cross on its own, until it looks away for two seconds or more. The next trial begins when the baby starts looking at the stimulus again, and trials continue this way until the total of any three consecutive trials from the fourth trial on is 50% or less than the total of the first three trials. At this point the baby is said to be habituated to the initial stimulus (the cross), and looking at the novel stimulus (the triangle) can then be measured and assessed. From A. Slater (1985), Visual memory and perception in early infancy. In A. Slater and G. Bremner (Eds.), *Infant development*. Hove, UK: Psychology Press. Photograph by Alan Slater, reproduced with permission.

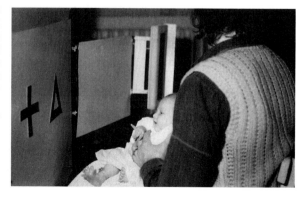

familiar stimulus and a new one, once again revealing what the baby perceives. Furthermore, the success of this method also implies that the baby remembers something of the stimulus, since the procedure relies on the test material becoming increasingly familiar. Many contemporary studies of infant perception use variations of the visual preference and habituation methods to tease out what babies may be capable of perceiving.

Baillargeon (1991) has studied the ability of five and a half month-old infants to comprehend occlusion using a habituation paradigm (see the previous box). Two groups of babies first saw several repetitions in which either a tall rabbit or a short rabbit moved behind one edge of a horizontal screen to reappear at the far end. Then, a central portion of the screen was removed and a test sequence was shown to both groups of babies, where the tall or short rabbit disappeared and reappeared without becoming visible in the intervening window (see Figure 5.10a). Babies attended longer to the impossible event (i.e. where the tall rabbit failed to appear in the window) than to the possible event (i.e. where the short rabbit would have remained occluded beneath the window). This shows that babies perceive not only that the rabbit continues to exist but that it retains its physical size when occluded. For good measure, Baillargeon has replicated this experiment with babies of three and a half months, using tall and short carrots, and obtained essentially the same results.

Baillargeon (1999) has reviewed her programme of research on infants' comprehension of occlusion using the habituation paradigm. She argues that babies look longer at events that violate basic principles of object permanence than at events which are consistent with the principles. As early as two and a half months babies understand that one object is either behind an occluding object or it is visible. This "all or none" initial concept rapidly becomes modified as babies become more experienced with different types of occlusion event. Thus, by three months, they detect violation of partial occlusion events and expect to see the object become visible if the lower edge of the occluder is discontinuous with the surface of support, for example above the supporting surface. By three and a half months, babies attend to the height of the object and expect tall objects to become visible when they pass behind short occluders (see Figure 5.10b)

Babies of four and a half months were tested in a study in which they saw an arm lowering an object into or behind a short or tall container (Hespos & Baillargeon, 2001). They were surprised when a tall object disappeared *behind* a short container but not when the same object disappeared *inside* the short container. It was not until five and a half months that babies detected the violation of containment (see Figure 5.10c).

FIG. 5.10 (a) Schematic drawing of the familiarisation and test events used by Baillargeon and Graber (1987—region of attention adapted from Bogartz et al., 1997). (b) Schematic description of the development of the infants' knowledge about occlusion events. (c) The test events used in the container and occluder conditions (Hespos & Baillargeon, 1999). (d) Schematic description of the development of infants' knowledge about support events. Reproduced with permission from R. Baillargeon (1999), Young infants' expectations about hidden objects: A reply to three challenges. *Developmental Science*, 2(2), 115–163. Copyright © Blackwell Publishers Ltd.

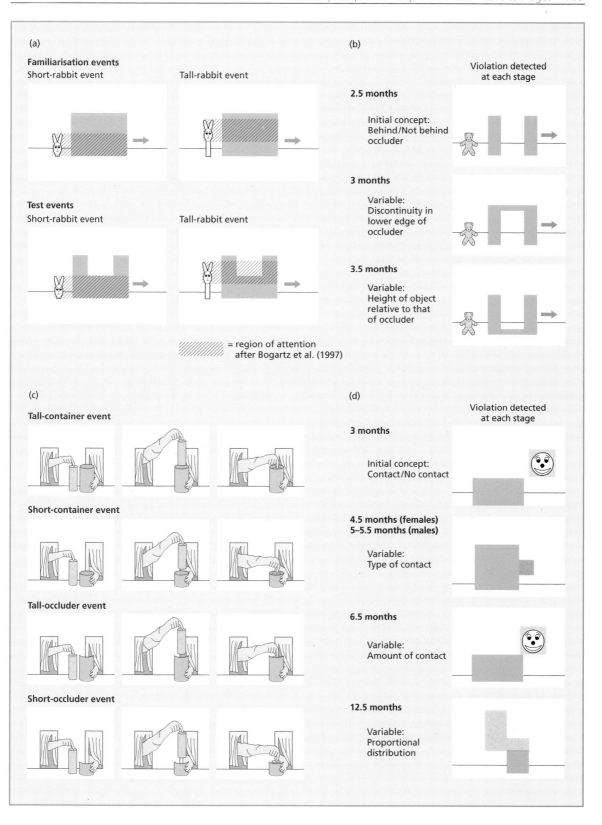

(a)

Familiarisation events
Short-rabbit event   Tall-rabbit event

Test events
Short-rabbit event   Tall-rabbit event

///// = region of attention
after Bogartz et al. (1997)

(b)

Violation detected
at each stage

2.5 months

Initial concept:
Behind/Not behind
occluder

3 months

Variable:
Discontinuity in
lower edge of
occluder

3.5 months

Variable:
Height of object
relative to that
of occluder

(c)

Tall-container event

Short-container event

Tall-occluder event

Short-occluder event

(d)

Violation detected
at each stage

3 months

Initial concept:
Contact/No contact

4.5 months (females)
5–5.5 months (males)

Variable:
Type of contact

6.5 months

Variable:
Amount of contact

12.5 months

Variable:
Proportional
distribution

With other physical concepts, such as support relations between objects, Baillargeon has detected a similar developmental progression. Very young babies have an initial all or nothing concept of support, if objects are in contact this is sufficient. By four and a half months the surfaces in contact must be consistent with the direction of gravity and babies are surprised if an object released in contact with the side of another object does not fall. It is not until twelve and a half months that babies expect the surfaces to be in contact, in the vertical plane and that such an arrangement is only stable if the proportionate distribution of the supported object which lies on the support is adequate for stability (Figure 5.10d).

These studies have raised considerable controversy not least because they seem to suggest that babies may have innate knowledge of object permanence—a nativist theory—and yet it is clear that babies' expectations, as revealed by habituation studies, are actually changing with age—a finding consistent with an empiricist theory. Can the baby be a nativist and an empiricist at the same time? Are developmental psychologists simply resurrecting an 18th-century debate that should have been laid to rest?

Smith (1999) takes Baillargeon to task for preformationism (see The Developmental Principle, in Chapter 1). She argues that it makes no more sense from a developmental point of view to claim that fingers and toes are innate than to argue that aspects of knowledge of physical objects are innate. She stresses instead that a dynamic, epigenetic approach to development will be sufficient to resolve the apparent nativist–empiricist conflict. However, Spelke (1999) points out that, in embryology, to say that something is not preformed does not mean that it is learned. Fingers and toes are not preformed in the fertilised egg but nor are they learned. Rather, such anatomical structures emerge in advance of their functions. Similarly, she suggests that basic knowledge structures may be present as an aspect of the functioning of perceptual systems. This is precisely what theorists of perception such as Michotte (1963) and Gibson (1966) would have argued. Gestalt psychologists, such as Koffka (1935), were interested in the principles of perceptual organisation that may act as initial constraints on infant perception. Koffka asked why we are constrained to perceive objects rather than the gaps between them and perhaps Baillargeon's initial "all or none" concepts serve to define these constraints. On the other hand, perceptual constraints may not yet amount to concepts or knowledge of object permanence in the sense intended by Piaget.

What about the developmental changes that Baillargeon observed? Such changes would be highly consistent with the description of perceptual discrimination learning given by Gibson and Spelke (1983). In discrimination learning, perceptual systems become attuned to the information that discriminates one event from another. An analysis of the dynamic figure–ground relationships in the various experiments described by Baillargeon (1999) may reveal rather different transformations of the object–background relations under different types of disappearance. Thus, when an object disappears behind a flat screen, it simultaneously occludes the background. Once the object vanishes behind the screen the background remains visible on either side of the screen throughout the event. This double relation of object to screen (which occludes background) and object to background specifies that one thing slid behind another. In monitoring such an event the baby may actually make use of visual skills for keeping track of moving objects relative to the background. When an object is swallowed up by a container, however, the moment of disappearance is specified relative to the boundary walls of the container and visual tracking is now insufficient. Such an explanation would emphasise the perceptual aspects of the task. One can imagine other situations in which stationary objects are occluded by moving containers or by moving screens. The whole set of systematic comparisons between moving objects, moving screens, and moving containers needs to be carried out under controlled conditions to find out the answer.

If babies are able to perceive that hidden objects continue to exist—as the literature seems to suggest—we might ask why babies make errors on object search tasks. Piaget's observations on failures in manual search have been replicated on many occasions so there can be no doubt that his meticulous observations about the various stages that babies go through in object search are correct. What we need to ask is why do babies fail to search if they perceive object permanence? Why does it take them so long before they can use their information about objects in order to get their hands on objects that have been hidden? Why is there this disjunction between perceiving the physical properties of objects and using the information to retrieve them?

Memory in infancy

One problem is that babies have difficulty co-ordinating actions with memory. Given a limited ability to hold things in mind, the nine-month-old baby may be able to retrieve hidden objects but complicating the task may put considerable strain on the baby's ability to hold in mind that she had set out to retrieve the object from a particular place. This may explain, at least in part, why babies fail to search or why they make errors.

The stage IV error has been extensively studied and it has been shown that errors are not inevitable, as would be required if the baby truly believes that the object exists only as an extension of her action. Diamond (1988) has shown that a delay of about three seconds is necessary between hiding the object and allowing retrieval for babies at eight months to make the perseverative error of searching at the initial location (A) when the object was seen to disappear at a new place (B). The time needed to generate errors increases by about two seconds per month, so that 12-month-old babies only make search errors when the delay exceeds 12 seconds.

There are many other factors which influence the probability of error in babies at stage IV, including the number of alternative locations, whether the object is hidden or simply placed under a transparent container, whether the task is administered in the vertical plane or the horizontal plane, and whether there are distinctive "landmarks" in the field of view. Errors are reduced, for example, when there are distinctively different covers at locations A and B (Butterworth, Jarrett, & Hicks, 1982; see Figure 5.11).

Wellman, Cross, and Bartsch (1986) analysed the results of more than 70 studies of the stage IV error and came to the conclusion that there are two main factors leading babies to the typical perseverative error. These are the length of the delay between hiding the object and allowing the baby to retrieve it; and the number of alternative locations from which the baby must choose.

The significance of the delay between hiding the object and allowing the baby to search for it can be explained by the developing memory abilities of

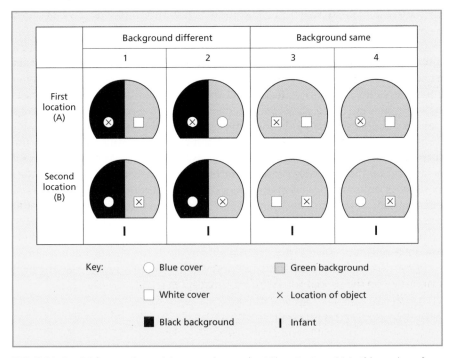

FIG. 5.11 Spatial factors determining error in search at Piaget's stage IV. In this version of Piaget's stage IV search task, an object X is hidden on a small table at successive locations to the baby's left and right side. The visual-spatial position of the object is defined relative to the colour of the table surface and relative to the colour of the hiding covers. Babies aged between 8 and 12 months can make use of visual-spatial information to overcome the tendency to make perseverative errors. In fact, errors are eliminated in condition 4, where distinctively different covers rest on a continuous background. It is likely that the visual-spatial cues act as landmarks in the small-scale space that help the baby to keep track of the object's movements from A to B. Adapted from Butterworth et al. (1982).

babies that increase rapidly over the first year of life. Rovee-Collier (e.g. Hartshorn & Rovee-Collier, 1997; Hartshorn et al., 1998) and her colleagues have conducted a series of studies to show this using an ingenious paradigm in which babies learn to kick vigorously in order to move a mobile that is attached to their legs. Then, after an interval, they are put back in the same situation to see whether they remember what they learned before. The results showed a clear developmental trend. Two-month-old babies, who were retested after 24 hours, began to kick immediately showing that they remembered their earlier experience. However, when three days had elapsed, the babies showed no sign of remembering what they had learned and took as long to start kicking as they had on their first exposure to the situation. Three-month-old babies showed signs of remembering for eight days, but by the thirteenth day they had forgotten what they had learned earlier. Six-month-olds showed signs of remembering at 14 days but not at 21 days.

Hartshorn et al. (1998) carried out a similar study with older infants using a task that involved learning to press a lever in order to make a model train move. (This task is, of course, much more suitable for older infants than the leg-kicking task.) The results of the train task showed an increasing length of memory with age, with nine-month-olds remembering their previous learning for six weeks and eighteen-month-olds remembering for as long as fourteen weeks.

Another approach to assessing the role of memory in object search has been through connectionist modelling. Munakata (1998) developed a connectionist model of the stage IV error. She noted that, in the typical object search task, infants have more opportunity to build up expectations about where an object is hidden through vision than they do through action. This is because the baby can watch an object being hidden even when it is out of reach. Munakata designed a connectionist network (see Figure 5.12) in which the input units corresponded to three locations, A, B, and C, two types of cover, and two types of object. There were two groups of output units that represented the differential experience of the visual and manual system during the task and there was one intermediate "hidden layer" connecting the input and output layers in the network. The initial network structure included a bias to respond appropriately to location information but the network was not given initial preferences with respect to object or cover types.

Munakata (1998) ran 10 versions of the object search task on the simulation, varying parameters such as the number of locations, whether the covers over the objects were distinctive or not and the length of delay between hiding the object and the start of the search. All of these are factors that have been shown to affect the performance of babies in the search task. Munakata found that, under some regimes, the gaze output units were significantly more accurate at keeping track of the object at B (new location) than the reaching output units. In other words, the tendency to perseverate at A, the old location) was restricted to the reaching units which had had less experience of retrieving the object from location B than the gaze units had had of observing it being hidden at B. She interprets this difference in tendency to perseverate as a function of differential memory strength for location within the gaze and reaching systems. Interestingly enough, similar results have been obtained with human infants who also show a dissociation between looking and reaching in Piaget's stage IV task at certain points in development (Ahmed & Ruffman, 1998).

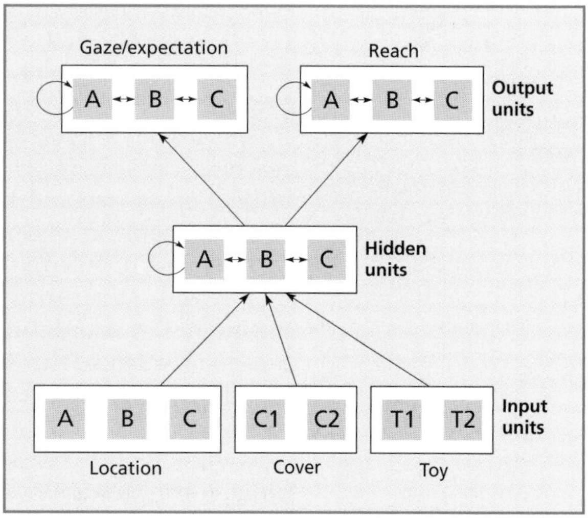

Although this connectionist model does not explain why babies make search errors—since many parameters other than memory were not included— it does suggest ways in which biologically plausible explanations for perseveration may be developed. If the network architecture can be made to simulate more accurately the brain systems responsible for co-ordinating intended actions with visual memory it might prove possible to relate babies' behaviour in the stage IV task to developments in frontal lobe functions that are typical of babies at this age (Diamond, 1988).

FIG. 5.12 Munakata's (1998) A$\bar{B}$ network. Reproduced with permission from Y. Munakata (1998), Infant perseveration and implications for object permanence theories: A PDP model of the A$\bar{B}$ task. *Developmental Science, 1*(2), 161–184. Copyright © Blackwell Publishers Ltd.

Reaching and grasping

Another important aspect of development in infancy that may affect the object search task is fine motor skill, that is, reaching and grasping. How do babies gain control of their hand? Visual perception has a particularly important part to play in the control of action because it provides feedback about the success of actions and enables errors to be corrected.

Piaget (1945/1962) thought that hand movements and vision are initially independent. He noticed that three-month-old babies spend a lot of time looking at their own hands and he argued that this period of "hand regard" enables infants to acquire visual control of the hand. His theory was supported by some extensive investigations made by White, Castle, and Held (1964), who noted that the onset of reaching could be slightly accelerated by equipping the baby with brightly coloured mittens.

Bower (1982), however, noted that congenitally blind infants also seem to go through a period of "hand regard" where their unseeing eyes follow the hand as it moves although no visual feedback can occur. Thus, it appears that the mechanisms controlling eye tracking and hand movement may already be coupled and this linkage is not established by visual feedback. Blind infants are delayed in reaching and grasping, despite the link between eye and hand, because they cannot see a target towards which to reach. In fact, Fraiberg (1974) suggests that reaching in blind babies depends on substituting audition for vision, with blind babies eventually reaching for objects they can hear.

This type of evidence led Bruner (1983) to argue that learning skilled reaching consists in gaining voluntary control over a pre-established co-ordination of eye and hand. He noted that two-month-old babies, when presented with an object in the visual field, made grasping movements with their hands but failed to extend their arms toward the object. At other times, they extended their arms but failed to grasp. He suggested that the problem for the infant lies in ordering the constituent actions into the appropriate goal-directed sequence. That is, part of the difficulty for infants lies in establishing the correct serial order between acts to fulfil the goal of reaching and grasping the object.

Contemporary research tends to favour the view that basic eye–hand co-ordination is innate. Bower (1982) and Von Hofsten (1983) have independently demonstrated that newborns will attempt to make gross "swiping" movements of the hand and arm in the vicinity of an attractive object that is suspended within reach. In a rather spectacular demonstration, Amiel-Tison and Grenier (1985) showed that if the weight of the baby's head is supported, 17-day-old infants will swipe at an interesting object, which may be interpreted as evidence for an ability to reach that is masked by the biomechanical constraints imposed by the weight of the head (illustrated in Figure 5.13). Another way to characterise this early form of reaching is to distinguish an innate transportation component of reaching that is eventually co-ordinated with a manipulation component guided by the visual properties of the object to be grasped (Jeannerod, 1984).

In early reaching, babies will swipe rather ineffectively at an interesting object, with only occasional contact and although these movements are goal directed they do not result in the baby grasping the object. These swiping movements are called **"visually elicited"** reaching, since they seem to be preprogrammed movements that are triggered by the sight of the interesting object. As the baby's aim gets better, contacts become more frequent and by about four months, the baby sometimes succeeds in grasping the object after

KEY TERM
Visually elicited reaching:
An infant's preprogrammed reaching towards an interesting object.

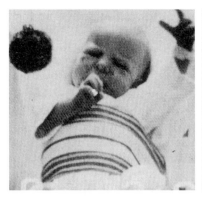

FIG. 5.13 A two-month-old swiping at an object. Reproduced with permission from L. Ronqvist and C. Van Hoften (1994), Neonatal finger and arm movement as determined by a social and an object context. *Early Development and Parenting, 3,* 81–94. Copyright © John Wiley & Sons Limited.

contacting it. That is, reaching is visually elicited and the action of grasping is triggered by touching the object. As the actions of visually elicited reaching and tactually elicited grasping become co-ordinated the baby increasingly becomes able to anticipate the arrival of the hand at the object. By about five months the so-called "top level reach" emerges, where both reaching and grasping are coming under visual guidance. The action of reaching is guided and the fingers close onto the object as contact occurs.

Von Hofsten (1980) showed that, when babies of six months are presented with a distant object that begins to move rapidly into their reaching space, they aim for a future position along the object's trajectory where their hand will make contact with the object. Their visual tracking also shows that they are co-ordinating their action with the visually specified future position of the object. Spelke, Vishton, and Von Hofsten (1995) found that such predictive behaviour was most successful if the object moved at constant speed along a linear or slightly curved path. However, if the path of motion was occluded by a screen, babies of six months soon learned to predict the point of emergence as revealed by their visual tracking. Furthermore, they could learn with comparative ease whether the object was moving along a linear trajectory connected on either side of the intervening screen and, with more difficulty, they could even learn that the object made a sudden turn behind the screen to re-emerge in a different direction.

Von Hofsten, Feng, and Spelke (2000) suggest that Gestalt principles based on perceptual similarity and good continuation of linear motion may constitute innate constraints on infant perception of motion. Thus babies readily extrapolate linear motion along unobstructed pathways and downward motion in the absence of a support. These properties of motion may be of very general applicability even in the absence of specific knowledge.

The detailed observations of reaching in babies are important because they once again show that the amount of pre-adaptive structure available in early development is greater than traditional theories would suppose. However, the baby only slowly gains the skills required to put the co-ordination to use. Contemporary theorists of motor development emphasise the extent to which such processes are self-organising. Development begins from pre-adapted systems that become inter-coordinated into more complex systems, themselves stable within certain dynamic limits. Reaching behaviour, as one example of this general process, becomes more stable and less likely to be perturbed by unexpected events as it becomes more skilled. Ineffective behaviours drop out of the repertoire as the effective ones are selected and integrated to form a new level of self-organisation (Thelen, 1989).

In fact, developments in the grips of babies can be observed well into the second year of life, as the infant becomes able to grasp objects and then gains finer and finer control over the fingers. Babies first grasp by pressing all the fingers against the object in the palm of the hand. These palm grips give way to more precise finger grips, so that by the end of the first year, the baby is able to pick up rather small objects in a "pincer grip" between the very end of the index finger and the extreme tip of the thumb. This precision grip is species-specific to humans. It involves full opposition of the fingers and thumb, so that they may be brought into contact for very skilled tool use, as for example in later development when sewing or writing.

Butterworth, Verweij, and Hopkins (1997) made a detailed examination of the emergence of different grips in babies using a graded series of cubes and spheres as standardised stimuli. These objects varied in size from 0.5 cm diameter (or edge) to 2 cm. Babies were filmed reaching and grasping the objects. The grips were in two major classes: power grips in which the object is grasped by pressing it against the palm with the fingers, and precision grips that involve holding the object between the thumb and one or more fingers. Figure 5.14 shows the four types each of power and precision grips.

The general developmental trend was for power grips to decrease in frequency and precision grips to increase between six and fourteen months. Note, however, that both power and precision grips were in the repertoire at six months. The switch from a predominance of power grips to a predominance of precision grips occurred at around 11 to 12 months, with power grips which involved no thumb opposition being eliminated. Two of the precision grips are of particular interest, the pincer, in which the tips of thumb and index finger are used to hold small objects, and the inferior forefinger grip, a less precise grip in which the thumb is abducted against the side of the knuckle joint of

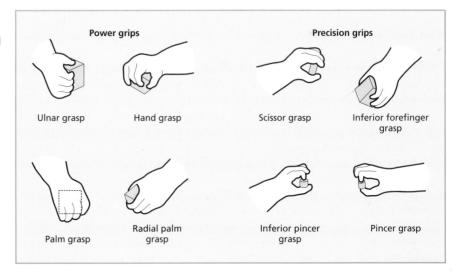

FIG. 5.14 Range of power and precision grips in the first year of life. Reproduced with permission from G. Butterworth and M. Harris (1994), *Principles of developmental psychology*. Hove, UK: Psychology Press.

Power grips

Ulnar grasp　　Hand grasp

Palm grasp　　Radial palm grasp

Precision grips

Scissor grasp　　Inferior forefinger grasp

Inferior pincer grasp　　Pincer grasp

the index finger. Both these grips are rather frequently used by the time that infants are 14 months old, in roughly equal proportions. The developmental process may therefore involve the selective retention of precision grips and selective elimination of power grips that do not make use of thumb opposition.

A comparison of the grips used by chimpanzees and human infants

Butterworth and Itakura (1998) compared the grips used by human babies and chimpanzees, using a graded series of cubes of apple as stimuli. Chimpanzees showed a transition from a predominance of power grips to more precise grips involving index finger and thumb—similar to that shown by infants—but this development did not occur until the animals were eight years old and approaching maturity. Furthermore, they never became as precise as human infants in picking up the smallest cubes between thumb tip and index finger. Chimpanzees very much preferred to use the inferior forefinger grip for small cubes (they were 36 times more likely to use the inferior forefinger grip than the pincer grip). It seems, therefore, that despite a similar developmental transition from power to precision in chimpanzees and humans, the capacity for very precise finger movements is significantly greater in humans than in chimpanzees and it develops very much earlier in humans. Thus, one important difference between humans and chimpanzees lies in the developmental timing of transitions in the fine motor control of grasping movements.

A chimpanzee picking up a bowl using index finger and thumb. From *Social learning in animals* by C. Heyes and B.G. Galef, copyright © 1996 by Academic Press, reproduced by permission of the publisher.

Reaching and grasping continue to develop in a variety of ways during the first year of life in babies. For example, once reaching and grasping have been mastered, the baby must learn to co-ordinate the actions of the two hands with each other. Bruner (1974) showed that six-month-old babies will reach and grasp a proffered object but, if the infant is then offered a second object, she drops the first one because she only has sufficient control over the action pattern to cope with one object at a time.

From about six months, the baby begins to get the idea of transferring the object from one hand to another but, if a third object is then offered, the baby will drop the second one. It is not until eight or nine months that the baby develops a storage routine. Now, the third and subsequent objects are deposited in a safe place following transfer from hand to hand. This sequence illustrates nicely how the action of visually guided reaching must be co-ordinated with memory to expand the range of application of the motor skill. The co-ordination of memory with reaching and grasping is known as **hierarchical integration**. The complementary use of the two hands also depends in part on the handedness of the baby (see the next box).

> **KEY TERM**
> **Hierarchical integration:**
> The use of memory to deal with three objects at a time, one in each hand, and one "stored" elsewhere.

The origins of handedness

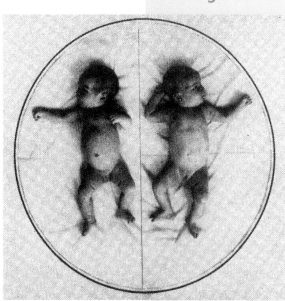

FIG. 5.15 A contrast in laterality trends. Reproduced with permission from A. Gesell, F.L. Ilg, and G.E. Bullis (1949), *Vision: Its development in infant and child*. New York: Paul B. Heober.

Research on development of the skilled control of reaching is informative about the origins of handedness. Approximately 88% of adults in Britain are right handed and the remainder are left handed. It is clear that spontaneous hand preferences can be modified through training as has been the case, at various times in history and in different cultures, when left handedness has been suppressed and children have been taught to use their right hand. However, hand preferences are not simply a matter of learning. It is now thought that handedness can be predicted from the spontaneous preference of the infant to lie with the head and arm to the right (or left) in the tonic neck reflex posture which can be observed in the foetus and continues to about eight months postnatally.

Figure 5.15 shows a newborn infant with a spontaneous left-facing preference and another with a spontaneous right-facing preference. If the theory is correct, then one baby should have grown up left handed and the other right handed (Butterworth & Hopkins, 1993). Consistent hand preferences begin to be noticeable by about eight months and they can reliably be observed by the middle of the second year of life (Ramsay, 1980).

Conclusion and summary

We began this chapter by reviewing Piaget's account of infant development. We have seen that many studies have now established that the infant's understanding of the visual world, especially the properties and behaviour of objects, is established much earlier than Piaget proposed. We have argued against the view that "touch tutors vision". At the same time we have noted the essential accuracy of Piaget's original observations of the developmental stages evident in the standard object search task where an object is hidden first at one location and then at another. We have suggested that a number of different skills are required to carry out the object search task successfully.

Babies need many months of practice to master the skills of reaching and grasping a visible object and they show evidence of difficulties in integrating vision, action, and memory that could contribute to failures in search. Reaching for an object in the dark does not give the baby the same problem as reaching for an object hidden under a cloth. Yet the demands of both tasks on the infant's memory, at least in terms of time "out of sight", may be quite comparable.

It therefore seems possible that an aspect of Piaget's explanation may still be viable; namely that babies at stage IV become able to co-ordinate two sequences of actions, as a means to an end, when they can search for an object hidden behind a cover. Babies must hold the goal in mind (i.e. the object) but first they must reach, grasp, and remove the cover and then reach, grasp, and remove the object in a hierarchically integrated sequence. The difficulty in searching for a hidden object is analogous to the hierarchical integration of action and memory in dealing with visible, multiple objects, described by Bruner (1974). This difficulty in sequencing actions need not be indicative of failure to perceive permanence and identity. Reaching for an object in the dark does not require the infant to co-ordinate a sequence of two separate actions—it requires only a single reaching and grasping movement—and babies can already carry out such actions successfully.

Once search is established, the evidence suggests that, although perseverative errors occur, they do not always take the form described by Piaget. It seems unlikely that the baby really experiences the object as an extension of action, as Piaget argued. But his argument here is mainly a consequence of his theory of the status of perception in early development. If infants do perceive reality appropriately, there may still be circumstances where their fragile ability to hold things in mind leads to error and conflict. This happens to absent-minded adults too but we do not necessarily suppose their whole structure of experience to be different as a consequence.

Further reading

- Bremner, G. (1997). From perception to cognition. In J.G. Bremner, A. Slater, & G.E. Butterworth (Eds.), *Infant development: Recent advances* (pp. 55–74). Hove, UK: Psychology Press. This chapter provides a good overview of cognitive development in infancy that is intended for undergraduates.
- Gopnik, A., Meltzoff, A., & Kuhl, P. (1999). *How babies think*. London: Weidenfeld & Nicolson. This very readable book provides an excellent introduction to the development of infant cognition. It is written for non-psychologists by three experts in the field.
- Slater, A. (1997). Visual perception and its organisation in early infancy. In J.G. Bremner, A. Slater, & G.E. Butterworth (Eds.), *Infant development: Recent advances* (pp. 31–54). Hove, UK: Psychology Press. This chapter, in a book written for undergraduates, provides a good summary of research in infant perception.

CHAPTER 6

CONTENTS

Early social development

In this chapter we consider infants' developing abilities to interact with other people. We consider the importance of these interactions for socio-emotional development and the formation of attachment bonds towards particular individuals who have a special significance for the baby.

Recognising oneself

Young babies, like almost all animal species, do not recognise themselves when they look in a mirror. Being able to recognise oneself in a mirror is seen as an important advance because it is taken as evidence of possessing a concept of self. One problem is assessing mirror recognition in young babies is that they cannot explain what they can see. This problem has been overcome by the invention of a "rouge removal" task—a simple but effective way to see whether someone recognises their own reflection. The idea is that if someone looks at their reflection and sees a strange mark on their face, they will reach up to remove it. However, if they do not recognise the face in the mirror as their own they will not attempt to do this.

In the rouge removal task, a small amount of rouge is surreptitiously placed on a child's face. Then the child is allowed to look in a mirror. Some infants as young as 15 months notice the strange mark on their face in their reflected image and reach up to remove it; and by the age of 24 months all normally developing children will respond in this way. Of course rouge removal is a tricky task and younger children, who do not yet attempt to remove the rouge, may respond to their own mirror image. For example, Bertenthal and Fischer (1978) found that babies from the age of 10 months would reach up to grasp a hat lowered just above their head but would not attempt to remove the rouge.

The fact that rouge removal occurs rather late in infant development suggests that there is a substantial cognitive component in mirror self-recognition. It has been found that mentally retarded Down's syndrome children are delayed on the rouge removal task until the age of three or four years (Mans, Cicchetti, & Sroufe, 1978). Chimpanzees (at about eight years) and orangutans (age unknown) can also perform the rouge removal task (Gallup, 1977) but this ability is not present in any other species. The task probably requires a combination of perceptual and cognitive abilities that include detection of the contingent nature of the mirror image, monitoring the position

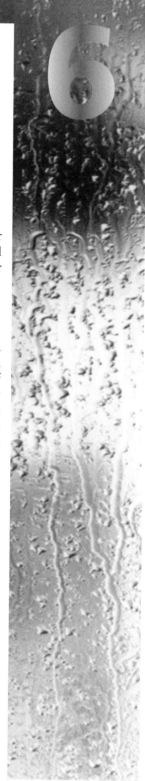

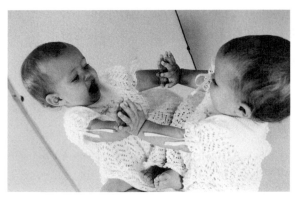

Copyright © Lupe Cunha.

of the hand and fingers in relation to the rouge mark, as well as recognising oneself. However, even though the rouge removal task may overestimate the age at which children first recognise images of themselves, evidence from recognition of photographs also suggests that self-recognition does not reliably appear until around the middle of the second year. Interestingly, infants often recognise other familiar people (such as parents and siblings) in photographs and videos before they recognise themselves in the same images.

Recognising other people

We saw in Chapter 4, Development from Conception to Birth, that very young babies have highly developed abilities to recognise familiar voices and smells. Both voice and smell are important in the early recognition of familiar people, usually the baby's mother and other members of the family. In real life, babies normally have information from all their senses to help in identification. Nevertheless, many studies have asked whether babies can also recognise their mother from her face alone.

Bushnell, Sai, and Mullin (1989) tested this hypothesis in a very carefully controlled study of five-day-old babies. The baby was seated facing a large white screen into which had been cut, at head height, two apertures separated by 12 cm on either side of the infant's midline. The mother and a female stranger, of similar hair length and hair colour, were seated behind the screen so that their heads were visible through the apertures. The screen itself was liberally sprayed with an air freshener to eliminate any olfactory clues and the mother and stranger exchanged seats from trial to trial to eliminate any possible side bias of the infant's looking. The mothers were silent during the experiment so that the babies could not use her voice as a cue.

The infant was supported upright, at 30 cm from the screen, and an observer measured the duration of the baby's fixation to each face over the 20 seconds following the appearance of the two faces. It was found that the neonates preferred to look at their own mother approximately 61% of the time. However, this preference was eliminated when mother and stranger wore identical wigs, which suggests that something about the mother's hairline may be distinctive for visually recognising the mother in the very early days.

This research begins to demonstrate the possibility of a developmental progression. Could an innate co-ordination between hearing and seeing help the baby rapidly discover what her mother looks like? Prenatal familiarity with the mother's voice, coupled with an innate tendency to look where a sound is heard, may be sufficient for the baby to learn the distinctive aspects of the mother's appearance very rapidly. There is good evidence that babies can link voices with faces. In one study by Spelke and Owsley (1979), the baby heard a tape recording of the mother's voice played over a loudspeaker placed exactly between the mother and father. The parents sat without talking or moving the mouth, so there was no information in visual synchrony with the sound. Babies from three months looked towards their mother when they heard her voice and towards their father when the recording of his voice was played. This suggests that correlated aspects of auditory and visual information, characteristic of each parent, must be remembered by three months.

Kuhl and Meltzoff (1982) examined another aspect of auditory visual co-ordination in four-month-old babies who were presented with two video-recorded faces of strangers to left and right of the midline. One face was shown repeating the vowel "i" while the other repeated the vowel "a". However, the baby heard only one sound track, to correspond with one of the visually presented sounds. Babies preferred to look at the face that corresponded with the sound track. This suggests that the babies must detect a correspondence between the auditory and visual information for the vowel sound. This ability might be very useful in acquiring language since it means that visual and auditory information for speech are to some extent overlapping (or redundant). An elementary level of lip reading may also help the young infant in producing appropriate speech sounds, as well as to perceive them. Further evidence in support of this hypothesis comes from difficulties that blind children have in learning to produce certain sounds (Mills, 1987).

It is an interesting question whether babies' knowledge of persons has different developmental roots than their knowledge of physical objects. People are a particular kind of physical object, albeit with social and animate qualities. According to Piaget, the various stages of object permanence apply also to the child's concept of a person and indeed, various studies have been carried out in which the baby has to search for her mother, who disappears behind a screen (or behind successive screens in an animated version of the stage IV task). Much the same results are obtained as for object search: Babies below eight or nine months fail to search for their mother when she hides behind a screen. From nine to twelve months they will search at the wrong place for their mother if she hides successively at two locations A and B. Thus they behave in just the same way as in the manual search task for an inanimate object. There is some evidence that person permanence develops slightly in advance of object permanence but, for the most part, Piagetian tasks yield broadly equivalent results whether the object hidden is a person or a thing (Bell, 1970).

Our earlier discussion of Piaget's search tasks suggested, however, that failures and errors in search may not reflect incomprehension of the principles of permanence and identity. Such problems may rather reflect the difficulty the child has in organising actions on the basis of information recalled from memory. It seems likely that a similar explanation may apply to the baby's developing understanding of persons. That is, early social interactions may be direct and not much influenced by specific memories. Then, as the baby gains sufficient experience with a particular caregiver, typical information about that person may be stored in memory and form the basis for recognition of the adult (certainly by three months; Spelke & Cortelyou, 1981). Thereafter, the infant may gradually become able to recall information from memory and this will give rise to new social phenomena, such as wariness or fear of strangers, which may indicate that a rather specific memory has formed with respect to familiar adults and which is responsible for wariness of the unfamiliar and fear of strangers, typical of the nine-month-old baby.

The reason for stating this is that so much information has accumulated about babies' special sensitivity to people that it is difficult to reconcile the new evidence with the view that babies have no awareness of the permanence and identity of significant persons in the natural environment before eight or nine months. There is clear evidence that babies are attracted to faces. A pioneering study by Fantz (1961) showed that newborn babies prefer to look at a face-like pattern rather than the same configuration of features arranged in a random pattern (see the box on pages 107–108). That is, faces seem to be of special significance, even to the newborn.

Of course, faces are complex, bilaterally symmetrical patterns and some investigators have argued that it is to attribute too much to the baby to suppose that their preference is for faces *per se* and not for some constituent of the facial pattern, such as its symmetry or complexity, or its dynamic animate qualities. Bremner (1994) reviews the literature on face perception in very young babies and concludes that none of these simpler explanations really accounts for the accumulated experimental data adequately. In fact, most studies have used artificial, two-dimensional pictures of face-like patterns to test the baby, and these are not stimuli the infant is likely to encounter in the natural environment.

In recent years investigators have turned to the study of real faces, in particular, the mother's face, in an attempt to gain greater ecological validity. We have already reviewed evidence (see Childbirth, in Chapter 4) showing that the focal length of the eye of the newborn is at 21 cm, approximately the distance between the mother's face and the infant when held in the natural position for breast feeding. In addition, we know that babies can recognise their mother's voice from birth (see Chapter 7, The Beginnings of Language Development); and that there is an innate co-ordination between seeing and hearing, such that the baby will look for the visual object at the source of the sound. It does not require a great leap of the imagination to suggest that babies may rapidly learn what their mother looks like from the already acquired knowledge of what she sounds like. Bushnell (1998) estimates that 11–12 hours experience is sufficient for the newborn baby to develop a preference for looking at the mother's face. This amount of experience is readily achieved by most infants by the time they are 49 hours old, even though they spend a great deal of their early life asleep. In Bushnell's view, there is no need to postulate a specific, innate mechanism that is specialised for faces. He argues that the salience of the face, with its dynamic properties, is sufficiently attention compelling to be attractive to babies without any specific face mechanism being required. This view is that face perception is just one aspect of a general process of perceiving and categorising objects, of which faces are a particularly common class. This general process account is rather different to the theory of Johnson and Morton (1991) summarised in the following box, who suggest that face perception requires an innate, species-specific face recognition system in newborns.

Are faces processed in a special way?

There has been a great deal of research on face perception in babies and opinion is divided on whether it is necessary to postulate an innate mechanism specialised for face perception. Lorenz (1961) argued that the face schema serves the purpose of species recognition. Modern proponents of the view that there is an innate face-processing system, Johnson and Morton (1991), suggest that the human visual system may have "prewired" sensitivities to specific physical parameters of faces. They suggest that infants are born with some information about the structure of faces (the CONSPEC mechanism), which may serve to underpin learning about the particular facial characteristics of significant other persons (through a CONLEARN mechanism). The **Conspec mechanism** specifies a minimal facial configuration comprising eyes, nose, and mouth within an external contour. It is a separate system, or module of the brain, dedicated to face perception. Johnson and Morton (1991) suggest that Conspec is a subcortical mechanism (possibly located in the superior colliculus of the brain) which passes on information to the cortex—to circuits specialised for face processing that develop at around two months.

Conspec is sufficient to allow the baby to attend specifically to faces but it contains little by way of detailed information about the face. Nevertheless, it is sufficient to fulfil the purpose of directing the infant's gaze to any face like object that comes into view.

Recent studies of newborn preference for schematic faces support the hypothesis that there is an innate basis for face perception. However, there is still some disagreement on whether the developmental process involves a transition between subcortical and cortical mechanisms. Although immature, newborns do have some cortical visual functions that may supplement mid-brain systems that perhaps simply orient the gaze in the direction of the interesting object (Simion, Valenza, & Umiltà, 1997). Furthermore, research on facial imitation in newborn babies suggests in fact that babies can reproduce a wide repertoire of facial gestures, which suggests that much may depend on whether the face is defined as simply a visual pattern, or as a dynamic entity capable of movement and expression.

Smiling and social recognition

Another body of literature, relevant to our understanding of infants' early social relations, exists in the ethological approach to human development. **Ethology** is the scientific study of behaviour as it occurs under natural conditions (Archer, 1993; Hinde, 1982). Ethologists are concerned with the causes, development, and the survival value of naturally occurring behaviour with special reference to the implications for evolutionary biology. Ethologists, following Darwin's (1872) work on the expression of emotions in men and animals, have made a particular contribution in the area of infant non-verbal communication and mother–infant attachment.

Smiling in the newborn period was long dismissed as an effect of wind, rather in keeping with the traditional attitude that saw the young infant as an incompetent participant in the social environment. Freedman (1974) went to the trouble to compare the infant's pained facial expression, when actually suffering from wind, with the smile of the newborn. He found many distinct differences between the facial expressions in the two cases such as in the tendency for frown lines in the forehead and red facial coloration when the baby is windy. So newborn smiling is definitely not wind, even though the smile is not obviously directed specifically to people.

It seems most likely that smiling, like other emotional expressions, is one of the species-typical human means of communication, which is at first internally generated and in a sense, presupposes an appropriate recipient, whether or not anyone is there to "receive" it. Smiling may be considered as a part of the system that serves to establish a bond between the parent and the child. Furthermore, under normal conditions, the parent will often see the baby smile and sooner or later, will perceive it as a social message.

Smiles are not restricted to visual stimuli. By six weeks, babies smile to voices, particularly their mother's familiar voice. Nevertheless, the sight of the face becomes a particularly strong stimulus for smiles. It has been argued by the ethologist, Ahrens (1954), that the eyes are a prepotent releaser of smiles. In ethology, a releaser is a specific stimulus responsible for triggering a particular behaviour pattern. Releasing stimuli are simplified configurations which serve in the animal kingdom as minimally sufficient to elicit complex sequences of behaviour in conspecifics. For instance, adult herring gulls regurgitate food for their young when the chick pecks on a red dot on the beak of the adult. The red dot is a sufficient stimulus to release the complex interaction involved in feeding. Ahrens assumed that smiling in babies operates to the configuration of the eyes, as minimal stimuli, in much the same way

Ahrens found that a pair of red dots painted on a white oval of card was sufficient to elicit smiling. Six dots scattered across the same area of card elicited even more smiling. His ethological approach suggests that smiling in babies is triggered by the eyes as "releasing stimuli". However congenitally blind babies will smile at the sound of their mother's voice or when touched, although they are often delayed in the development of smiling, so perhaps the eyes are only part of the complex to which the infant responds (Fraiberg, 1974). It seems likely that smiling may at first be internally generated but it soon becomes linked to familiar social stimuli and eventually, through social interaction, is most readily elicited by specific people. From about three months, smiling is truly social and reciprocal in that the baby's smile is now synchronised with the smiles of the caretaker, much to the gratification of the parents who begin to see their offspring as a lively social companion as a result of this new-found reciprocity. The baby discriminates between familiar and unfamiliar persons, although the infant shows no fear of strangers at this age.

So, it can be argued that social smiling, of the kind observed around three months, is a measure of the baby's recognition of the familiar adult, contrary to the more parsimonious view that the infant's smile is relatively indiscriminate and not particularly social. Smiling, once established as a reciprocal phenomenon with the parent, might suggest that the child has a memory, or mental model, of a particular significant person. Even if this is not the case, the multiple sources of information available to the baby about the mother and other familiar people (smell, visual appearance, characteristic manner of interacting, typical intonation patterns) would ensure that the same unique individual is recognised by the baby on each encounter.

Imitating other people

Imitation may be defined as establishing a correspondence between one's own behaviour and that of another person (Butterworth, 1999). Although there has been a recent interest in early imitation, the phenomenon was described by Baldwin (1894) who argued that imitation begins in the repetitive activities of babies. The basic mechanism of imitation, he argued, was the circular reaction, a repetitive cycle of activity in which achieving the goal of an act initiates a new cycle of activity of the same type. On this argument imitation begins by imitation of self—for example as the baby repeatedly sucks her own hand—before it becomes possible for the baby to imitate the actions of another person.

Piaget (1945/1962) shared Baldwin's view that imitation only slowly becomes a social act. He argued that for the infant to comprehend the relationship between her own behaviours and those of another person it is necessary to be able to represent the self in memory. He described a series of achievements culminating in representation whereby the baby infers the correspondence between self and other. For example, the infant at six months may see the mother move her hand and imitate the movement. Piaget argued that, because the infant can see that her own hand resembles her mother's hand, the visual information allows her to place her own actions into correspondence. Piaget considered that the imitation of facial movements was a much more advanced achievement, possible only from the age of about one year. This is because, on his view, the ability to imitate facial movements required mental representation (a mental model) of the appearance of the face. Piaget describes a baby from about eight months touching her mother's face and then touching her own, as if to establish the correspondence between invisible parts of her own body and visible parts of the mother's face. On these traditional theories imitation of facial expressions develops late because the infant must first establish, through inference, the relationship between another person's visible movements and their own invisible movements.

However, there have been other accounts of facial imitation in young babies For example, McDougall (1931) and Preyer (1882/1914) described babies imitating tongue and mouth movements at three to four months but their anecdotal observations did not carry much weight. It might seem that babies are actually imitating when they had merely learned to respond in a particular way to a particular cue. With the discovery of the perceptual abilities of babies the possibility that young infants may indeed be able to imitate facial expressions has received particularly careful study in the last 25 years.

Maratos (1998) studied imitation of finger movements (visible movement) and tongue protrusion (invisible movement) in newborn babies. She reported that babies can imitate both the visible and invisible movements. Meltzoff and Moore (1977) made carefully controlled studies of imitation of tongue protrusion, mouth opening, and lip pursing in newborn babies. Babies systematically imitated these stimuli and there was little possibility of explaining the ability away as a learned response (see Figure 6.1). Since these early and controversial demonstrations of neonatal imitation were made there have been several replications of newborn imitation of mouth, tongue, and facial movements. Evidence for imitation of tongue protrusion in newborns is particularly well established and it has now been observed in newborn infants in cultures as diverse as North America, Greece, Switzerland, Sweden, and a nomadic tribe in Nepal (Kugiumutzakis, 1999; Reissland, 1988; Vinter, 1986) There is also evidence for innate imitation of emotional expressions (Field, Woodson, Greenberg, & Cohen, 1982) and for auditory imitation of vowel sounds (Kugiumutzakis, 1999).

Although some researchers have been sceptical that the ability to imitate is innate (Anisfeld, 1991; Hayes & Watson, 1981; Kaitz, Meschulach-Sarfaty, & Auerbach, 1988), the balance of the evidence now suggests that babies can

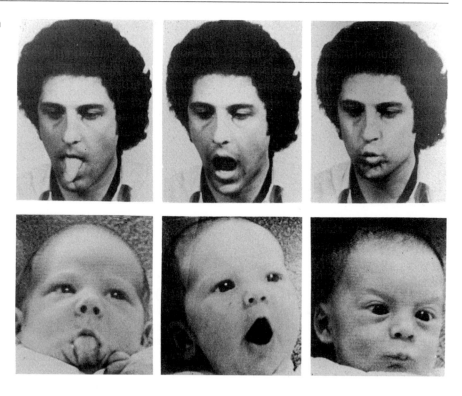

imitate facial movements from birth where the studies are carried out with sufficient sensitivity to the highly interpersonal nature of the task.

In the early attempts to explain the mechanism of imitation it was suggested that perhaps the imitative response was elicited—or "released"—rather automatically by some critical aspect of the stimulus. For example any moving object (not specifically a tongue) might be sufficient to elicit tongue protrusion in the newborn. Such general stimuli are called releasers by ethologists who have examples where minimal stimulus input is sufficient to elicit complex behaviour in the young. Meltzoff and Moore (1977) addressed this possibility and showed that tongue protrusion in the newborn is more likely to occur when the stimulus object is a real tongue rather than when it is a moving but inanimate object. Other aspects of the imitation of oral behaviour have now been carefully studied. For example, the baby often takes some time to respond to the stimulus and appears to make "searching" movements for the tongue (see Figure 6.2), which suggest that the imitative response is rather effortful and not automatically released (Meltzoff & Moore, 1994, 1997, 1999).

A second type of explanation stresses the perceptual abilities of the baby. This argument hinges on how we choose to explain perception and on how babies perceive the equivalence of different types of information obtained through different perceptual channels. Meltzoff and Moore (1999) argued that this problem is logically equivalent to matching information across sensory modalities and have proposed the **active intermodal matching hypothesis** (AIM) to explain newborn imitation. Active matching of the visual input to the proprioceptive properties of the motor output is required.

Further progress with this type of explanation has come from Vinter (1986), who showed that newborn babies imitate tongue protrusion only if they first

FIG. 6.2 Three infants imitating a large tongue-protrusion-to-the-side gesture. Meltzoff and Moore (1997) found that six-week-old infants imitated this novel act by correcting their behaviour so that it gradually matched the adult target. Reproduced with permission from A.N. Meltzoff and M.K Moore (1997), Explaining facial imitation: A theoretical model. *Early Development and Parenting*, 6, 179–192. Copyright © John Wiley & Sons Limited.

see the model tongue in motion. That is, information from the dynamics of the movement seems to be necessary for imitation. As in many other newborn behaviours, a U-shaped developmental function was found, with imitation of hand movements dropping out at about seven weeks and tongue and mouth imitation dropping out at about three months. The abilities reappeared at seven months and twelve months respectively. Kugiumutzakis (1999) has shown that newborns will imitate the repetitive vowel sound "a" and that the baby pays very close attention to the visual and auditory dynamics of the display. These demonstrations also show that it is necessary to take into account rather subtle interpersonal aspects of the testing situation and this may explain why some investigators have failed to replicate newborn imitation (Abranavel & Sigafoos, 1984).

There is therefore evidence that the mechanisms underlying newborn facial imitation may involve matching the dynamic patterns perceptible in the input to the proprioceptive output channel. This matching occurs whether the "translation" is from vision or from audition to the action of the mouth and tongue. The long-held distinction between visible and invisible movements proves to have been a red herring since the dynamic patterns of stimulation are not specific to the visual modality.

A further argument has been made that imitation is an expression of an inherent predisposition to recognise the actions and emotions of others as importantly similar to the self (Trevarthen, Kokkinaki, & Fiamenghi Jr., 1999). This raises the important question of *why* infants imitate. Kugiumutzakis (1999) suggests that the ultimate motive is a deep-seated need to communicate. Some of the specific imitative phenomena of newborns, such as mouth or tongue movements, emotional expressions, and hand movements, may be understood as the fundamental components of the vocal, gestural, and emotional systems characteristic of human communication.

With development in the first year the capacity for imitation undergoes further changes. Babies can now reproduce a response having seen only the end result. They can imitate after a significant delay since observing the stimulus and imitation can even take on symbolic properties. For example, Vinter (1986) showed that a static protruded tongue is sufficient to elicit imitation at 12 months. Piaget (1945/1962) himself observed that imitation at 12 months can take on a symbolic aspect. He described his daughter Jacqueline trying to work out how the drawer of a matchbox operates by systematically sliding her tongue in and out of her mouth. There is also evidence that the capacity for deferred imitation emerges after the ability to imitate immediately. Meltzoff and Moore (1999) showed that imitation 24 hours after first seeing the model is possible in babies of six weeks. This is significantly earlier than had previously been thought possible and it suggests that the infant is representing the stimulus imitated in memory.

Play

Babies begin to play with objects in the first year of life. Their ability becomes increasingly sophisticated as motor skills develop but until the age of 18 months or so play remains physical. Objects are picked up, sucked, banged together, or piled on top of each other. At around 18 months, however, there is a significant change in the way that young children play with objects. Belsky and Most (1981) observed babies playing in a room with toys. They found that, somewhere between 12 and18 months, the babies begin to play with objects in a symbolic way by pretending that they represent something else.

Early symbolic play involves the child as agent. For example, 18-month-old children might pretend to drink tea from a beaker—often to the accompaniment of vigorous drinking sounds—or they might pretend to comb their hair with a pencil. By the age of two children are able to move on from using themselves as an agent to using toys as agents. Watson and Fischer (1977) found that more than half of 14-month-old babies they studied could pretend to sleep by putting their head on a pillow but it was not until the age of two years that the children could treat a doll as an active agent and make her carry out various actions.

Vygotsky (1933/1976) provides an interesting account of how physical objects come to act as props for the early symbolic play of children. For example, when a child uses a stick as a hobby horse, the stick temporarily loses its own identity and gains aspects of the identity of the horse. That is, the customary identity of the object is replaced by a meaning that has been designated by the child and the signifier is differentiated from what is signified. The meaning of "horse" is what gives the stick its new significance. Vygotsky argues that, in object play, meaning is predominant over the physical characteristics of objects and the characteristics of the pretend object will guide the child's play. The hobby horse must be ridden and not used for other purposes.

Initially, the distance between the imaginary and the real is not very great and the gap is bridged by physical props, such as the stick. The stick, in its early use as a symbolic prop, serves as an index that physically represents a real horse in the child's play. Similarly, the beaker that is used for tea drinking is rather like a cup. Eventually, however, almost anything can be made to stand for anything else and play becomes increasingly internalised as pure symbolism.

Leslie (1988) argues that when young children pretend that one object is something else they suspend belief in order to consider the real and symbolic properties of objects at the same time. When a child pretends that a banana is a telephone—to use one of Leslie's examples—she is representing the situation as one that contains both a banana and a banana that is a pretend telephone. In other words the child has "decoupled" the properties of the real object from its mental representation so that the object can take on pretend properties.

Piaget saw play as the opposite of imitation. In imitation accommodation predominates over assimilation but, in play, assimilation predominates over accommodation as children adapt themselves to fit the demands of reality. That is, children assimilate the world to their own ego in play, rather than changing their own ideas to meet the demands of reality.

It is clear from these examples that symbolic play, like language, does not emerge in an all or nothing fashion. Both Vygotsky and Piaget agree that the child represents an imaginary reality initially through actions with the assistance of objects that serve as props. Such objects have the status of indices that assist the child to differentiate signifier and signified in the transition to purely symbolic play. With development, symbolic action becomes separated from gesture and bodily activity.

The development of play can often be assisted by interacting with a more experienced partner such as an older sibling or a familiar adult as Vygotsky argued in his account of the zone of proximal development (see the section on him in Chapter 2, Developmental Psychology in the 20th Century). Slade (1987) observed toddlers playing at home both on their own and with their mother. Both the level and complexity of play increased when the mother joined in, although this effect varied as a function of the mother's participation. The greatest change occurred when the mother actively joined in the child's activity and provided encouragement through explicit suggestions. When the mother merely commented on what the child was doing this was not nearly so effective in raising the level of play.

It is also important that adults make appropriate suggestions for extending play. O'Connell and Bretherton (1984) compared children's responses to mothers' suggestions during play at 20 and 28 months. At the younger age the presence of the mother served to foster physical and functional play whereas at the older age it was symbolic play that was facilitated. However, at both ages the mothers made suggestions about all three types of play so it was the child's current level of play that determined which suggestions were acted upon. This finding is not exclusive to play. The extension or "scaffolding" of cognitive, linguistic and social behaviours is most effective within the zone of proximal development.

The development of attachment

Although Bowlby (1969) was very much influenced by psychoanalytic ideas, he actually elaborated his theory of attachment as an alternative to the Freudian view that the love of the child for her mother arises as an effect of meeting the baby's primary needs. The Freudian view had been that attachment of the child to the mother arises through parental gratification of the child's basic needs such as hunger and thirst (the so-called primary drives). Bowlby, by contrast, stressed the security and sense of safety provided by the parent as being at the roots of emotional attachment.

Bowlby was particularly influenced by ethological theory, which stressed the importance of imprinting in the formation of attachments in many species of birds. Imprinting is a particularly rapid form of learning in which the specific characteristics of the mother hen are learned in a few hours after hatching by the baby chick. Newly hatched chicks will follow the mother hen and maintain proximity with her. This early experience of following is sufficient for them to learn the specific visual characteristics of the mother (although some of her auditory characteristics may actually have been learned before hatching just as human infants have prenatal experience of the mother's voice). The evolutionary significance of rapid imprinting is thought to lie in protection of the offspring from predation. In the longer term, imprinting is thought also to exercise an effect in the selection of partners for mating who may be chosen to resemble, to some optimal degree, the imprinted parent. The box below reviews further evidence on the biological bases of **attachment**.

Biological basis of attachment in primates

Harlow et al. (1971) made one of the main contributions to understanding the biological basis of attachment in primates. Harlow argued that the study of attachment is the objective study of love. He called this "affectional objectivism", and argued that there are five basic kinds of affectional feelings for others, each having different functions in the transition to adult heterosexual love and parental responsibilities.

The first two are the love of a mother for her child and love of the infant for the mother. Harlow argued that these are preparatory for peer experiences and lead to a basic sense of trust and security with others. The third kind of love identified by Harlow was peer (or age mate) love, which, he argued, is preparatory for both heterosexual love and paternal love.

Harlow carried out his main studies of the origins and long-term consequences of attachment with rhesus monkeys, in the 1950s and 1960s. He was influenced by Freud's assumption that the mother–child relationship is all important for development of personality. This assumption has been questioned in recent years and relationships are extended to include the development of children with other caretakers than the mother. The specific mother–child relationship nowadays tends to be seen as part of a network of relationships, rather than the exclusive link that it used to be considered. Nevertheless, the question Harlow was investigating was "which aspects of the mother–infant relationship are important for normal development?"

Freud had argued that the mother satisfies the infant's primary needs, especially for food but also for elimination. The so-called primary drive theory would predict that the attachment relationship would develop out of the satisfaction by the mother of the child's bodily needs, especially hunger. Harlow argued however that caretakers satisfy a hierarchy of needs only some of which correspond to the primary drives of classical Freudian theory. Rhesus monkey mothers provide warmth and contact comfort and in turn receive contact from their offspring who are innately predisposed to cling to them. This is an aspect of a reciprocal system, which applies only to animals within the same species. Contact comfort does not result in attachment, for example, if the baby monkey is reared with a kitten as a companion. In blind or brain-damaged monkeys, clinging can be disturbed and rhesus monkey mothers develop ambivalent bonds with them. Mothers also protect the baby rhesus monkey against external threat, although presumably this is not entirely a maternal function but may also involve the male.

KEY TERM
Attachment: The forming of a close emotional bond, particularly between mother and baby.

Harlow's famous experiments were carried out to establish the relative contributions of feeding and contact comfort in the formation of attachment bonds. He compared the behaviours of baby rhesus monkeys reared with a "surrogate" mother made of wire which offered different opportunities for contact comfort or feeding. (These studies were briefly summarised in Chapter 2, Developmental Psychology in the 20th Century). Body contact seemed to be the main factor motivating the infant rhesus monkey.

According to Harlow the stages in attachment development in the monkey are:

1. Organic affection in which the mother provides the basic bodily needs for contact, food, and cleanliness.
2. Comfort and attachment, which develop as the mother meets these physical and emotional needs.
3. Solace and security as the infant becomes more mobile and starts to explore the world.

By about six months the rhesus infant monkey is securely attached to the mother and the process of development of autonomy begins. The primary factor here is the balance between the infant monkey's healthy curiosity and its emotional security, which the infant needs to provide the courage to explore and satisfy the powerful motive of curiosity. Curiosity eventually leads to relative autonomy, and disattachment from the mother, an infant-governed process that will prepare the monkey for the next phase of development, which involves interaction with age mates.

Mother-governed processes also contribute to the development of detachment. Interestingly, maternal punishment proved to be almost non-existent during the monkey's first three months of life. Rejection of the offspring begins at about three months, increases to a peak at about five months and declines thereafter, by about nine months. The monkey becomes completely independent in locomotion between the second and third month and the mother will start to fend it off from clinging, unless there is danger. Harlow argued that the infant monkey goes through three stages from security of attachment, to ambivalence toward the mother, and finally to independence. In monkey mothers, the normal reproductive cycle may play an important part in this process of detachment, which often heralds the arrival of a new baby.

Detachment is a process of transition in which the strong physical tie to the mother is broken. It involves changes in the infant's responsiveness to mothers, changes in the mother's responsiveness to infants, and changes in responsiveness to the outside world. It is worth noting that Harlow's account of the development of attachment is actually rather different from that of the other major theory put forward by Konrad Lorenz, who described imprinting of the chick to the parent greylag goose (see Figure 6.3). Imprinting is a rapid process of learning the characteristic appearance and sound of the parent bird, which information the chick uses to maintain proximity with the mother. Lorenz's account may explain how the attachment bond is formed in birds but it doesn't explain how it is subsequently broken to allow the animal to acquire autonomy.

FIG. 6.3 Lorenz hatched some goslings and arranged it so that he would be the first thing they saw. From then on they followed him everywhere and showed no recognition of their actual mother. The goslings formed a picture (imprint) of the object they were to follow. Copyright © Science Photo Library.

Bowlby was well aware that attachment relationships may form in different ways in different species. He argued that the first attachment relationship is based on unlearned, species-specific behaviours. In monkeys clinging and following are early developing response systems by which the infant keeps the mother in proximity. In humans, where motor development is less advanced than in other primates, other response systems may be used as signalling devices to keep the infant in touch with the mother. Crying and smiling are particularly important in eliciting maternal caregiving. Bowlby's account of attachment in humans is essentially a spatial theory in which the formation of attachment bonds is mediated by looking, listening, and holding the infant.

To feel attached, on Bowlby's theory, is to feel safe and secure in the particular relationship. Insecure attachment involves mixed feelings—feelings of dependency and a fear of rejection. Although Bowlby broadly based his ideas in a psychoanalytic framework, he rejected the primary drive theory on a number of grounds. From ethology and the research of Lorenz, he noted that geese show bonding without feeding being involved. In fact, the reciprocal relationship can also be found since rhesus monkeys show feeding behaviour, as in Harlow's studies, without bonding being involved.

Bowlby argued instead that the biological basis for attachment in humans is protection from predators and an "innate need for companionship which is the infant's only way of self preservation" (1969). Attachment behaviour is, according to Bowlby, any action that results in a person attaining or retaining proximity to the preferred individual. It is triggered by separation or by the threat of separation and it is terminated by proximity, whether established visually or by physical contact. With development, the child is said to acquire a working model that represents the self in relation to others. The model is based on the primary relationship, with the mother.

Attachment has three key features.

1. *Proximity seeking to a preferred figure*. In primates this may develop more slowly than does imprinting in birds. The customary primary attachment figure is the mother but nothing precludes fathers or others serving the same function.
2. *The secure base*. The attachment figure provides a secure base from which the child can explore the world. The toddler seems tied to the mother as if by an invisible string which allows exploration only within a radius of security of the mother.
3. *Separation protest*, such as crying, screaming, or biting, which may be the primary, unlearned response following separation from the attachment figure.

The infant's perceptual abilities set the stage for early social responsiveness and the cycle of interaction between infant and caretaker at the root of the attachment process. Infants of less than two months old show signs of distress when the mother interrupts a social interaction, as revealed by the pattern of blood flow in the face (Mizukami, Kobayashi, Ishii, & Iwaka, 1990).

The onset of the smiling response is often taken as a significant marker in the process of attachment formation. Early smiling may be endogenously generated but it soon comes to be elicited by the caretaker and, by three months, is usually well established. Some analytically inclined theorists, such as

Winnicot (1971), maintain that contact comfort is also important for babies and Klaus and Kennel (1976) went so far as to argue that skin-to-skin contact between a mother and her newborn is important for bonding. However, subsequent studies have cast doubt on their findings.

Early processes of attachment formation provide the basic knowledge of the primary attachment figure that allows the baby to recognise him/her. From about eight months babies characteristically begin to show fear of strangers, at first only in the presence of the familiar figure with whom the stranger is closely compared. Soon, however, most babies show general fear of strangers and great wariness of novel objects, as if the infant can compare mentally the familiar with the strange. These changes mark the beginning of the ability to recall information from memory, or as Bowlby calls it "the internal working model".

From about three years language increasingly enters into the formation of personal relationships and the complexity of the system increases. As the child makes new relationships with peers it is argued that the security of attachment in them depends upon the quality of the primary relationship. Patterns of relationship established in childhood transfer through to adult life, with attachment and dependency remaining a feature of relationships throughout the life cycle (van Ijzendoorn, 1995a).

Attachment in babies is measured in the **strange situation test** devised by Mary Ainsworth (Ainsworth & Bell, 1970). This comprises a 12-minute session in which mother and one-year-old infant are put into a room, with the experimenter, with three-minute cycles of separation and reunion, so that the child's behaviour can be observed. The mother leaves the room for three minutes, leaving the baby alone with the experimenter. Mother returns and the infant's behaviour on reunion with her is observed. Finally both the mother and experimenter leave the room and the baby's behaviour on reunion is observed.

Three major patterns of behaviour were observed in the original study by Ainsworth and Bell (1970). The majority of infants (66%) were classified as secure (type B). Babies are distressed by the separation and, on reunion, they greet their mother, receive comfort, and happily return to play. Type A, 20% of babies, were classified as insecure, anxious avoidant. These babies give few overt signs of distress on separation and ignore the mother on her return. The smallest group (12%) were classified as insecure–resistant (type C). They are highly distressed by the separation but, unlike securely attached babies, they are not easily pacified on reunion. They seek contact but then resist and show anger. A small group, type D, has more recently been demarcated as insecure and disorganised. These babies show confused behaviour including freezing or stereotyped movements on reunion with the mother.

These patterns of attachment are thought to develop as a function of styles of mothering in relation to the temperamental characteristics of the child. Mothers of secure one-year-olds are said to be responsive and attentive to their babies at three months. Mothers of the insecurely attached tended to be inconsistent in their responses, and less attuned to the infant at three months. Sensitive mothers alter their rhythm of activity to suit the infant, with matching of actions, mutual attention, and entrainment of activity at three months. This is what the psychoanalyst, Daniel Stern (1985), has called "affect attunement".

Grossman (1988) has argued that the classification of infants at one year was 87% successful in predicting the classification of children at six years. Children who had been classified as secure showed greater concentration and played for

KEY TERM
Strange situation test: Used in attachment studies. The child is observed first with the mother, next with a stranger, then alone, and finally when reunited with stranger and mother.

Results of the strange situation study

Attachments

Type A (20%) Insecure–anxious/avoidant	Type B (66%) Secure	Type C (12%) Insecure–anxious/resistant	Type D (2%) Insecure–disorganised
• children are indifferent to where their mothers are sitting • may not cry when mother leaves and will allow stranger to comfort them • indifferent to the return of the mother	• children play comfortably and react positively to a stranger when mother present • become upset when mother leaves and are unlikely to be consoled by a stranger • happy again when mother reappears	• children stay close to mother and appear anxious even when mothers are near • become upset when mother leaves • not comforted by the mother's return and simultaneously seek renewed contact but also resist efforts to comfort them	• children seem to lack any coherent, organised method for dealing with the stress • disorganisation expresses itself in various ways, from acting dazed in their mother's presence to crying loudly whilst trying to climb onto mother's lap
Carer who is rejecting	Carer who is available, sensitive, and supportive	Carer who is inconsistent	Carer who is inconsistent and may abuse the child

longer at six years, thought to reflect greater ego control and resiliency. Children who had been rated as anxious–avoidant were considered by their teachers at six years to be overcontrolled, and the ambivalent children were considered undercontrolled. Thus, the argument is that infants who are one half of a competent parent/infant pair become resourceful children; and this developmental process is not explained by correlated factors such as the similar IQ of parent and child.

Infants with secure attachment histories are more popular with their peer group both at preschool and at primary school. They also have more secure friendships. Park and Waters (1989) observed four-year-old best friends together. Where both children were securely attached, the interaction was more harmonious and more responsive and less controlling than in cases where one member of the friendship pair was insecurely attached.

In recent years Mary Main and her colleagues in the USA have developed the adult attachment interview as a tool for assessing the "working model" of the parent. The adult has to choose five adjectives that best describe the relationship with their own parent during childhood. Parents are classified as autonomous or secure when their discourse is coherent, as dismissing where they are internally inconsistent, or as preoccupied when they are confused, angry, or preoccupied with a particular parent. The hypothesis here is that how adults evaluate their own childhood experiences is a relatively stable state of mind which influences their parental style and how they interpret the attachment signals of their own children. That is, the hypothesis is that attachment styles may be transgenerationally transmitted. Van Ijzendoorn (1995a,b) carried out a meta-analysis of 18 studies with 854 subjects which showed that parental mental representation of attachment as secure or insecure corresponded 75% with an independent classification of the infant.

Nevertheless, there is still a transmission gap which leaves unexplained the discrepant 25%. Autonomous parents tend to marry each other but there is still a mismatch between many parents, which might contribute if the hypothesis of transgenerational transmission is correct (van Ijzendoorn, 1995a,b).

There are problems, however, in supposing that what is being measured in infant or adult attachment is a fixed attribute of the person. The infant test tends to ignore contextual determinants of the response and the adult test relies entirely on autobiographical memory. Lability of the infant's response in the strange situation has been revealed quite clearly in cross-cultural studies. Miyake, Chen, and Campos (1985) in Japan found that these babies are disproportionately classified as insecure compared with the classification of babies in the USA. However, in Japanese culture babies are rarely left alone by their mothers and hence the test shows a huge effect of separation. In contrast, Grossman, Grossman, Spangler, Suess, and Unzner (1985) found that German babies are disproportionately classified as secure, relative to babies in the USA. This can be explained by the fact that, in Germany, the norm is to socialise infants for autonomy.

It is also important to note that the attachment classification may change depending on which parent accompanies the child during the test; and the retest reliability of the classification may vary as a function of the time interval between tests or whether it is carried out at home or in the laboratory. The mother's own reaction to being separated may also vary and influence the test outcome. Hinde (1995) has argued that it is important to remember that what is being measured is a relationship, rather than a property of the child. Thus, the same baby may fall into different categories depending on the particular relationship, although the consistency of classification over time is quite strong.

Fox (1995) has outlined problems with the adult attachment interview (AAI). He argues that the coherence of an adult's discourse about their own upbringing need not depend on the quality of the primary relationship with the mother but may be a more general function of an individual's life experiences and temperamental characteristics. These issues remain to be resolved.

It is also important to recognise that babies form attachments not only to their mothers but also to their fathers and to other siblings, especially when the brothers or sisters are involved in infant care, as happens in some societies. Societal values concerning infant upbringing also influence the patterns of attachment observed in strange situation tests. For example, German babies may be socialised for independence, whereas Japanese mothers rarely leave their baby in the care of another person. Consequently, German and Japanese babies are likely to have rather different degrees of experience at being left alone with a stranger and this, naturally, will influence how the infant is classified on Ainsworth's system. It does not mean that Japanese babies are more anxious than German ones. Attachment is a dynamic concept which must be understood in the appropriate socio-cultural context. It should not be thought of as a stereotyped fixed pattern. (For a comprehensive overview of the attachment literature see Bretherton & Waters, 1990.)

The practical importance of attachment research has already been briefly mentioned in Chapter 2, Developmental Psychology in the 20th Century. Hospitalisation and other brief separations of mother and infant are now treated more sensitively than in the past to avoid the distress experienced by babies over nine months when separated from their parent. Mothers are allowed to stay in hospital with their babies and young children. An important contemporary concern is with provision of day care for the young children of working mothers. Research suggests that brief separations of mother and baby, in an otherwise secure family situation may not disrupt a healthy attachment bond. On the other hand insecure attachment and separation where the family is already under stress may result in various "knock on" consequences. For example, in early schooling, the male child may be much less secure and compliant and may affiliate aggressively with other children, whereas the insecurely attached female child may show marked dependency (Turner, 1991).

Longer term consequences of disrupted attachment are more difficult to establish and, since the attachment system is rather flexible, they may in any event be reversible. For example, children brought up in orphanages, where there is limited scope for forming specific attachments, nevertheless can become securely attached to their adoptive parents even when adoption is as late as eight years (Tizard & Hodges, 1978). Theorists nowadays emphasise more the cumulative effects of successive risk factors in making the child vulnerable to disrupted attachment. A British study by Brown and Harris (1980) showed that girls from socially disadvantaged families, whose mothers died before their 13th birthday, were found to be at risk for psychiatric depression in their early 30s. These women had contracted early, unsatisfactory marriages and the onset of their depression often coincided with further extreme stressors, such as the death of the remaining parent. By contrast, women of similar backgrounds, who had made satisfactory marriages with supportive families and partners, were more resilient under similar conditions of bereavement and less at risk for psychiatric depression. This kind of transactional model (whereby psychological problems may be exacerbated or ameliorated by the sequence of life events) has been shown to have utility in explaining vulnerability to severe psychiatric illnesses in a wide variety of studies.

Responses to emotions

One important aspect of interaction with other people involves responses to their emotions. Newborns can imitate emotional expressions (Field et al., 1982) and they also cry in response to the prolonged crying of other babies (Hay, Pedersen, & Nash, 1982).

Towards the end of the first year, infants start to use adults' expressions as a guide to their own actions—a process known as **social referencing** (Campos & Stenberg, 1981). Social referencing can most easily be observed when infants are in an unfamiliar situation in which they are not sure how to proceed. They will look to their mother to check her reaction before carrying on with an activity. For example, when babies who can crawl are placed on a "visual cliff"— a clear, rigid plexiglass surface that goes over the top of what appears to be a steep drop—they behave differently according to their mother's expression. Babies pause when they reach the apparent drop but will continue crawling if their mother looks happy or interested. However, if mothers look sad or angry, most infants do not venture over the drop. Those who did (mainly when mothers looked sad) showed signs of ambivalence (Campos, Bertenthal, & Kermoian, 1981). Similarly, babies' reactions to a potentially frightening toy— such as a jack-in-the-box—are strongly affected by their mothers' reactions (Hornik, Risenhoover, & Gunnar, 1987).

Social referencing is not only to the mother. Babies who spend a lot of time with other caretakers will also use their emotional reactions as a guide (Camras & Sachs, 1991). Clearly, the use of an experienced adult as a point of reference is very useful since it means that babies do not have to deal with new situations on a trial and error basis.

Are babies aware of each other?

Early researchers on young children's reactions to their peers considered that babies were oblivious of each other's presence (Buhler, 1935). More recent research has suggested that babies are aware of each other from an early age. At two months, infants are aroused by the presence of other infants and engage in mutual gaze (Eckerman, 1979). By six–nine months infants look, babble, and smile at each other (Hay et al.,1982). Towards the end of the first year infants pay increasing attention to each other and engage in sustained interactions in which the smiles, vocalisations, and pointing of one infant provoke a matching response in the other.

Differences in interaction with boys and girls

So far we have not said anything about whether baby boys and baby girls are treated in the same way by their parents. Clearly the gender of a new baby is seen as important. When a new arrival is announced, the first question that most people ask is whether the baby is a boy or a girl. Shops that sell baby clothes and toys also tend to divide them into those for girls and those for boys.

Research shows that parents interact differently with boys and girls even when they are still babies. Yarrow, Rubenstein, and Pedersen (1975) found that girls experienced greater consistency and stability in interactions with caregivers, whereas boys received more varied and more intense stimulation. An experimental study by Will, Self, and Datan (1976) showed that adults behave in a different way with the same baby depending on whether they think the baby is male or female. Will et al. dressed a six-month-old baby boy in one of two identical outfits. One was blue and the other pink. When the baby was dressed in blue he was introduced to the adults as "Adam"; when he was dressed in pink he was introduced as "Beth". There were three toys to play with: a train (typical boy toy), a doll (typical girl toy), and a fish (neutral toy). The doll was handed to "Beth" significantly more often than it was handed to "Adam" and "Beth" was also smiled at more often than "Adam".

In a later study, using a wider range of toys, Smith and Lloyd (1978) found that mothers of babies between the ages of six and eight months were most likely to hand an unfamiliar six-month-old "boy" baby a hammer, whereas a "girl" baby was, again, more likely to be given a doll to play with. This pattern was entirely determined by the perceived gender of the baby and not the biological sex, which was carefully counterbalanced in the study. Smith and Lloyd also found that the mothers tended to encourage gross motor activity in "boy" babies and responded to such activity with further motor stimulation. In contrast, identical motor activity in a baby who was seen as a "girl" elicited soothing and calming behaviour.

The significant feature of these two studies is that the adults were behaving in different ways to identical behaviours from the infant—so it cannot be the case that they were merely responding to early differences in the behaviour of boys and girls. It is important to note, however, that parents may adopt a more gender-stereotypic response to an unfamiliar infant than to their own child. Lloyd and Duveen (1990) found that mothers responded to gross motor activity in their own 13-month-old infants in the same way regardless of gender. However, in the same study, the infants' own behaviour became more gender-differentiated when playing with their mother than with a stranger. Boys engaged in more gross motor activity and girls engaged in more object manipulation (though this latter increase was not significant). Lewis, Scully, and Condor (1992) have also found that there are complex interactions between the perceived gender of the baby and the actual behaviour of the baby and adult expectations about gender-appropriate behaviours. The same study also revealed the intriguing finding that adults' own gender perceptions were altered by playing with either a boy or a girl. Playing with a girl made adults feel more dominant and competitive (male traits), whereas playing with a boy produced higher scores on feminine traits (gullible, shy, and responsive to flattery).

Conclusion and summary

Babies are born with an ability to rapidly develop recognition of familiar adults using their hearing, smell, and vision. Very early on they also produce responses—notably smiling and imitation—that provoke positive responses from people around them. As the first year progresses the social interactions between infant and adult become increasingly complex and they reinforce the attachment bonds that are formed in the first weeks of life.

Early attachment has been seen as central to the psychological well-being of children. It paves the way for the many relationships that the child will form throughout life and secure attachment also provides a secure base from which to explore the world. The contemporary view of attachment has moved away somewhat from Bowlby's original characterisation and there is now emphasis on the multiple and dynamic nature of attachments. Nevertheless, Bowlby's essential view of the importance of attachment has remained.

What is clear is that babies are social creatures and that successful development in both the social and cognitive domains relies on interaction with other people. Social play provides an important vehicle for development as babies extend the boundaries of their ability; and social referencing allows babies to encounter new experiences with a useful guide to appropriate behaviour. Early social interactions may also serve to reinforce gender differences in early behaviour, especially the choice of toys. They are also important for the development of language, as we explain in the next chapter.

Further reading

- Butterworth, G.E. (1999). Neonatal imitation: Existence, mechanisms and motives. In J. Nadel & G.E. Butterworth (Eds.), *Imitation in infancy* (pp. 63–88). Cambridge, UK: Cambridge University Press. This chapter provides a detailed and up-to-date review of studies of imitation in neonates. It is intended for advanced undergraduates.
- Hay, D.F., & Demetriou, H. (199?) developmental origins of social understanding. In ~~~~~~ SULLIVAN ncer (Eds.), *The social child*. Hove, UK: ~~~~~~ book aimed at first- and second-year ~~~~~~ teractions between infants and

~~~~~~ ality development. In N. Eisenberg ~~~~ 3. *Social, emotional, and* ~~~~ Ed.; pp. 25–105). New York: ~~~~ of attachment and considers ~~~~ early attachments are related to ~~~~ er considers factors that affect ~~~~ al understanding.

CONTENTS

The beginnings of language development

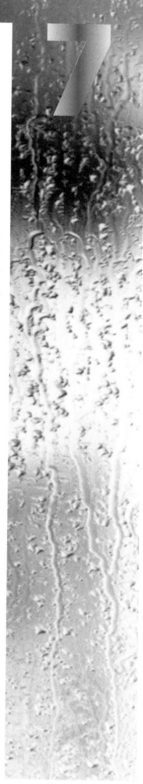

So far in the book we have considered cognitive and social development as rather separate processes. However, the development of cognitive skills takes place, for the most part, in a social setting. Adults and older children play an essential role both in providing models of behaviour and in guiding and expanding children's emerging abilities. We can view the development of language as the foremost illustration of the way that development is a process in which emerging cognitive skills are honed and sustained within a social environment.

It is impossible to exaggerate the significance of language as a human activity. Only humans have the extraordinary abilities that enable children to become fluent speakers and listeners. We will see in this chapter that it takes several years for children to become fully competent at speaking and understanding a language and many of the more complex aspects of sentence structure, as well as the meanings of many uncommon words, are not fully mastered until children are in primary school. However, the initial stages of learning to produce and understand language begin even before children are born.

The perception of speech sounds

There has been considerable speculation about how much babies are able to hear before they are born. Until recently, it was thought that the sound of the mother's voice was masked by the strong sounds of her heartbeat and other internal organs. However, it is now well established that that external speech sounds, including the mother's voice, can be heard clearly inside the womb (Richards, Frentzen, Gerhardt, McCann, & Abrams, 1992). In the late stages of pregnancy babies learn to recognise familiar sounds, as De Casper and Spence (1986) demonstrated in a seminal study which showed that babies could recognise a story that their mother had read to them before they were born.

In the De Casper and Spence study, 12 pregnant women were asked to read one particular passage from *The Cat in the Hat*—a rhyming children's story—twice a day for the last six weeks before their babies were due. (This meant that babies who were born on the due date were exposed to a total of three and a half hours of *The Cat in the Hat*.) Two or three days after birth, the babies were tested with a special dummy that was wired up to record sucking intensity. The babies sucked for two minutes so that the researchers could get a baseline for each baby—since babies vary in the amount that they suck—and then they were played either *The Cat in the Hat* passage or another passage that they had not heard before. Changes in the babies' rate of sucking turned a tape recorder on and off. The babies who were presented with the familiar passage altered their rate of sucking in order to hear it, whereas babies who heard an unfamiliar passage did not alter their sucking rate. Significantly, this difference in response to the two passages was found even when babies heard the passage being read by another woman, rather than their mother. This shows that the babies' prenatal experience with the passage itself, rather than with their mother's voice, made it appear "familiar" in some way.

A subsequent study by De Casper, Lecanuet, Busnel, Granier-Deferre, and Maugeais (1994) tested the response of babies while still in utero. A group of French-speaking women, who were in the 35th week of their pregnancy, recited a rhyme three times in succession every day for four weeks. Half the mothers recited a rhyme called *La Poulette*, while the other half recited a rhyme called *Le Petit Crapaud*. After four weeks the foetuses were presented with recordings of both rhymes spoken by an unfamiliar female voice. The recordings were presented using a speaker placed 20 cm above the mother's abdomen so that it was level with the foetus' head. In order to make sure that the mothers did not react differently to the two passages—and so have an effect on the foetus—they listened to music through headphones while the testing was carried out.

Foetal reaction to the two passages was measured by monitoring foetal heartbeat and comparing baseline heartrate with heartrate while the recordings of each rhyme were being played. There was a clear difference in foetal response to the familiar and unfamiliar rhyme with the former being significantly greater than the latter. While the unfamiliar rhyme was being played there was no significant change in heartrate from the baseline but, when foetuses heard the familiar rhyme, there was a significant decrease in heartrate showing that they could distinguish between the rhyme that their mother had recited to them and another rhyme that they had not heard before. As in the De Casper and Spence study, this discrimination did not depend on familiarity with the mother's voice.

Newborn babies show a general preference for familiar speech sounds. They prefer the human voice to other sounds and, at a few days old, will suck on an artificial nipple to hear a recorded human voice but will not suck so readily to hear music or a rhythmic non-speech sound (De Casper & Fifer, 1980). This preference for voices soon becomes more specific and, by four weeks, infants prefer their own mother's voice to that of another female (Mehler & Dupoux, 1994).

Babies also rapidly develop a preference for the language spoken around them compared to other languages that they have not heard before. Mehler, Jusczyk, Dehaene-Lambertz, Dupoux, and Nazzi (1994) have shown that four-day-old French infants can discriminate between French and Russian and they also show a preference for French. A recent study by Christophe and Morton (1998) suggests that, in the early weeks, babies are particularly sensitive to prosodic or rhythmical properties and this is the basis on which they make comparisons among languages. Thus two-month-old English babies were able to distinguish between English and Japanese, two languages that have different rhythmical properties, but they did not distinguish between English and Dutch, which are more similar in prosodic structure. Prosodic structure continues to be an important aspect of speech perception as babies develop and become increasingly familiar with the patterns that characterise their mother tongue. Jusczyk, Cutler, and Redanz (1993) have shown that nine-month-old English infants prefer to listen to words that follow the stress pattern occurring most frequently in English.

These findings all point towards the existence of innate abilities for perceiving speech. A study by Bertoncini, Bijeljac, McAdams, Peretz, and Mehler (1989) showed that babies process speech sounds more in one hemisphere than the other. Infants less than four days old were given a dichotic listening task in which sounds were presented in both ears. The infants responded more to a syllable change presented to the right ear than to the left ear but they showed an opposite pattern when they heard musical notes. A change in note produced more response when presented to the left ear than to the right. This suggests that, from birth, babies make more use of their right hemisphere for processing speech sounds than their left.

This very early specialisation for the perception of speech is further demonstrated by the ability of neonates to discriminate between speech sounds or **phonemes**. In a pioneering study, using the sucking paradigm described earlier, Eimas and his colleagues (Eimas, Siqueland, Jusczyk, & Vogorito, 1971) presented babies aged from one to four months with the single sound /pa/. At first the babies increased their rate of sucking in order to hear this new sound. Then, as it became familiar, their sucking rate settled back to the baseline. Once the babies were familiar with /pa/, a new but similar sound was played. For half the babies the new sound was a different phoneme, /ba/. The other babies heard a sound that differed acoustically from the original by an equal amount but did not cross the phoneme boundary. (In other words it would still be heard as /pa/ by an adult.) The babies in the first group, who heard /ba/, started to suck rapidly again in order to hear the new sound but the second group did not increase their rate of sucking suggesting that, just like an adult, they heard the "new" sound as similar to the original one.

Many subsequent studies went on to show that infants of one month or less are able to discriminate phonemes on the basis of many different kinds of phonetic contrast. For example, Eimas (1974) contrasted place of articulation (/p/, /t/, /k/) and Miller and Eimas compared phonemes that different in manner of articulation such as /d/ and /n/ and /d/ and /l/ (Eimas & Miller, 1980; Miller & Eimas, 1983). Trehub (1976) showed that infants could also discriminate between vowel pairs such as /a/ and /i/ or /i/ and /u/.

This accumulation of experimental evidence leads to the conclusion that newborn babies have the potential to make any phonemic discrimination. However, adults do not have this same ability. They are excellent at discriminating phonemes in their native language (or languages) but they are often unable to hear phonemic distinctions that occur in other languages but not their own. This is especially true if a phoneme boundary in a new language is incompatible with that of a phoneme boundary in the mother tongue. For example, in English, /r/ and /l/ are two different phonemes but, in Japanese, both sounds are variants of a single phoneme, which is why Japanese people, who learn English as adults, typically have great difficulty in hearing the difference between these two sounds. The reason why speakers of a particular language are not aware of phonetic contrasts that occur within a particular

KEY TERM
Phonemes: The smallest sound categories in speech in any given language that serve to distinguish one word from another.

phoneme boundary is that there is very wide acoustic variation in the way in which different speakers pronounce particular phonemes. There is also variation within an individual speaker. Thus, in order to identify a phoneme correctly, infants have to learn to disregard phonetic contrasts that are not phonemically significant in the language of their speech community. They have to engage in a process of "learning by forgetting", as Mehler and Dupoux (1994) describe it.

Research on infant abilities to perceive speech now suggests that selective sensitivity to the particular phonemes present in the language of the speech community—and loss of sensitivity to contrasts that do not distinguish phonemes—develops over the first year of life. Werker and Tees (1984), who compared groups of babies from three different monolingual speech communities, first demonstrated this development. The languages spoken in the three communities were English, Hindi (Indian), and Salish (North American Indian). Werker and Tees found that six-month-old babies who had heard only English could distinguish equally well between phoneme pairs in each of the three languages. However, slightly older babies of eight months showed less ability to discriminate phonemic contrasts that occurred either in Hindi or Salish but not in English. One-year-old babies who had heard only English were also completely accurate in distinguishing between English phoneme pairs but were only at chance level in discriminating phonemes that were specific to the other two languages. By contrast, one-year-old babies who had heard only Salish were completely accurate with Salish phonemes, and babies who had heard only Hindi were completely accurate with Hindi phonemes. This pattern of results was replicated in a longitudinal study with monolingual English babies (Werker, Gilbert, Humphreys, & Tees, 1981), which showed that, by 12 months of age, the babies' ability to discriminate non-English phonemes had declined to adult level.

A study by Kuhl, Williams, Laard, Stevens, and Lindblom (1992) suggests that the age at which the ability to discriminate phonemes first becomes language specific is even earlier than the eight months suggested by the Werker et al. studies. Kuhl et al. compared the ability of Swedish and American infants to discriminate vowel pairs. The vowels of Swedish and English are not identical and six-month-old babies proved to be more sensitive to vowel contrasts in their native language than those in the unfamiliar language.

The loss of ability to detect phonetic contrasts that do not cross phoneme boundaries in the language of the infant's speech community arises when these contrasts overlap with those of the native language. Babies and adults retain the ability to distinguish contrasts that do not overlap, as Best, McRoberts, and Sithole (1988) showed in a study using the "clicks" that occur in the tribal language of Zulus. These clicks do not involve the same phonetic contrasts as English and so there is no possible source of interference between the perception of clicks and the perception of English phonemic boundaries. Thus they continue to be discriminated by monolingual English speakers of all ages.

Interestingly, the ability to make phoneme distinctions is not uniquely human, as chinchillas can also discriminate between synthetic phonemes (Kuhl & Miller, 1978), suggesting that the ability to perceive speech may have developed from some more basic auditory perceptual ability. The important difference between chinchillas and human infants, however, lies not in the initial ability to distinguish phonemes but in the way that perception becomes language specific as particular phonemic contrasts take on communicative significance.

The development of babbling

Although infants rapidly become familiar with the phonemes of the language they hear being used around them, it takes several years before they can accurately produce all these different phonemes. Over the first year of life important developments take place as babies gain increasing control over the sounds that they are able to produce.

The development of infant vocal productions—**babbling**—is usually divided into stages. The two best-known stage classifications are those of Oller (1980) and Stark (1980) which are very similar to each other except in the names that are given to the various stages. The stages are summarised in the table below.

Stage 1, which covers the period from birth to two months, is known as reflexive vocalisation. At this very early stage the infant makes sounds to express discomfort and distress as well as vegetative sounds that relate to physical activity or essential bodily functions. Speech-like sounds are rare.

By stage 2 (two to four months), babies begin to use sounds for more directly communicative purposes. They coo and laugh when people are talking to them or smiling. These cooing and laughing sounds are initially produced singly but may then appear in sequence. Sustained laughter emerges around four months. As babies progress through this second stage, the primitive vegetative sounds gradually disappear and the frequency of crying falls. Vowel sounds become more varied.

Even at this early stage babies are capable of imitating aspects of adult vocalisations. Papousek and Papousek (1989) analysed the interactions between mothers and infants aged between two and five months. They compared successive mother and child vocalisations on a variety of parameters including pitch, duration, and rhythm. The proportion of infant vocalisations that matched immediately preceding maternal vocalisations increased across the age range from 27% at two months to 43% at five months. The most common basis for matching was pitch but babies also became increasingly likely to match falling or rising–falling patterns (pitch contours) in mothers' vocalisations.

Vocal play begins in stage 3 which covers the period from four to seven months. During this time babies begin to gain increasing control of the articulation of the larynx and the mouth. They experiment with both the

> **KEY TERM**
> **Babbling**: The meaningless vocalising of babies; includes speech-like vowel and consonant sounds.

INFANT PHONETIC DEVELOPMENT IN THE FIRST YEAR OF LIFE												
Age (months)	**0**	**1**	**2**	**3**	**4**	**5**	**6**	**7**	**8**	**9**	**10**	**11**	**12**
Stark (1980)		Reflexive crying and vegetative sounds		Cooing and laughter						Reduplicated babble			
								Vocal play			Non-reduplicated babble and expressive jargon		
Oller (1980)		Phonation		GOO stage		Expansion		Canonical babble			Variegated babble		

loudness and pitch of their vocalisations and the position of their tongue. This gradually allows the production of adult-like vowels and some of the features of adult-like consonants.

In order to understand why babies' vocalisations sound distinctively different from those of an adult, we need to look at differences between the vocal tract of infants and that of adults. Evidence from fossil remains shows that the evolution of the adult vocal tract has been an essential part of the development of modern humans (see the box on page 149).

The baby's vocal tract is not simply a miniature version of the adult tract. Indeed, up to the age of three months, the infant vocal tract resembles the vocal tract of a primate—and of prehumans—more closely than that of an adult human (see Figure 7.1). The larynx (voice box) is high up so that the epiglottis nearly touches the soft palate at the back of the mouth. The baby's tongue is large is relation to the size the mouth, nearly filling the oral cavity, while the pharyngeal cavity is very short compared to that of an adult, allowing little room for the back portion of the tongue to be manipulated. The reason for these

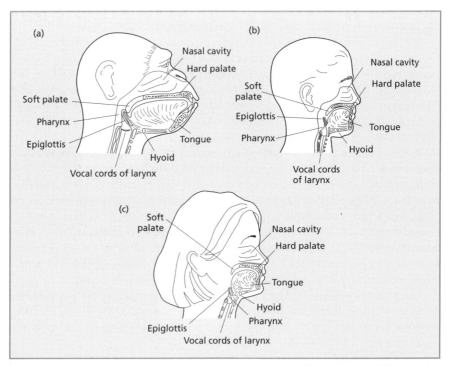

FIG. 7.1 Cross-section of the heads of (a) an adult chimpanzee, (b) an infant, and (c) an adult human. The chimpanzee's tongue forms the lower boundary of the mouth; the high position of the larynx allows it to lock into the nasal cavity during respiration. By contrast, more than half the human tongue is below the mouth where it forms the front boundary of the pharynx. The right-angled bend in the human airway where the mouth cavity and pharynx meet, and the proportions of the human tongue, make it possible to produce vowels such as [i] and [u] as well as the velar consonants [g] and [k]. In contrast to the chimpanzee's airway, the human's soft palate can seal off the nasal cavity from the rest of the airway during speech production. The vocal tract of a human infant resembles a chimpanzee's. Reproduced with permission from P. Liebermann (1992), Human speech and language. In S. Jones, R. Martin, & D. Pilbeam (Eds), *The Cambridge encyclopaedia of human evolution*. Cambridge, UK: Cambridge University Press.

special characteristics becomes clear when we realise that the infant's tongue at birth is designed to make the strong piston-like movements essential for sucking, rather than the range of complex tongue movement required for speech.

The evolution of the human vocal tract

The adult human vocal apparatus differs from that of other primate species in that the larynx is set further down in the neck. This creates a space above the voice box, known as the pharynx, which is much larger than that of chimpanzees and allows humans to utter the typical vowel sounds a, i, and u which are thought to be universal in all languages. The size of the pharynx depends on the point of articulation of the head with the spinal cord, which is revealed in fossils by the position of the foramen magnum, a hole in the base of the skull through which the spine connects with the brain stem. In *Australopithecus* the position of the foramen magnum is very similar to that of the modern chimpanzee. It lies toward the back of the skull implying that this hominid ancestor could produce only a limited range of sounds, comparable to those of a chimpanzee. In *Homo erectus* there is evidence for partial descent of the larynx with associated changes in breathing and swallowing patterns, a greater range of sound production but still less than modern humans. Archaic *Homo sapiens*, with a brain size of about 1100–1300 cc, first appeared about 0.5 million years ago and evidence for a modern respiratory tract appeared some time between 400,000 and 200,000 years ago.

From the age of four months the anatomy of the vocal tract gradually changes towards the adult form. There is also important neural maturation between three and nine months that allows the baby to develop increasing control over the fine motor movements essential for production of the full range of speech sounds. These neuro-anatomical changes over the first year go a considerable way to explaining why infants gradually develop an increasing mastery over their speech production. This is evident in the increasing range of sounds that are produced from the age of four months when vocal play first begins.

Around six months, an important change occurs when babies first begin to produce recognisable syllables, composed of a consonant sound and a vowel. Very early sounds include /da/ and /ba/. Oller (1980) describes this stage as canonical babbling and it appears quite suddenly. A little later, at around eight months, babies begin to produce reduplicated babbling in which the same sound is repeated, as in "da-da" and "ba-ba". Around 11 months there is another change as babies become capable of what Oller calls variegated babbling and Stark describes as non-reduplicated babbling. As these names suggest, at this final stage of babbling, babies begin to follow one sound with another sound that differs from it in some way. For example, babies may produce such combinations as "ba-da" or "da-de".

One question that is often asked about babies' early speech sounds is whether they correspond to the speech sounds that the baby hears in particular language communities. We have already seen that, over the first year of life, babies develop increasing sensitivity to the phonemes present in the speech of their language community so we might expect that their own production of speech sounds would be affected by the experience of listening to a particular language being spoken. However, Vihman (1992) analysed the types of syllables produced by children in the later babbling period who were growing up in different language communities. She paid particular attention to syllables that were "practised" in the sense of being used very frequently. Vihman found that the six most frequently occurring syllables (in order of frequency) were "da", "ba", "wa", "de", "ha", and "he". These syllables were largely independent of the phonology of the language spoken by the parents. For example, French babies produced the /ha/ syllable, even though French does not contain the /h/ phoneme. Similar results were reported in an earlier study by Locke (1983). He argues that there is a strong biological influence on phonological development. However, children's exposure to speech does seem to be important at one level because Oller and Eilers (1988) have found that children who are born with profound hearing loss do not develop canonical babbling within the first year of life, whereas, in normally developing hearing babies, this will have reliably developed by 10 months. Also, Oller and Eilers (1988) have found that, when the appearance of canonical babbling is delayed beyond 10 months, this provides a strong indication that a child will go on to have language difficulties.

Other aspects of speech production are clearly affected by the language environment of the infant. We have already seen that even young babies are able to imitate the prosodic contour and pitch of their mothers' vocalisations, so it comes as no surprise to find that babies babble with different prosodic patterns according to their language community. De Boysson-Bardies, Halle, Sagart, and Durand (1989) asked adults (all of whom were native speakers of French) to listen to 15-second samples of vocalisations from eight- to ten-month-old infants exposed to French, Cantonese, and Arabic. The adults were asked to decide which babies were growing up in a French-speaking community. They found it easier to make this decision for the younger than for the older babies and it was also easier to discriminate between babies exposed to Arabic or French than Cantonese or French. The investigators concluded that the adults were able to pick out distinctive prosodic features of the babbling. These were most evident in the eight-month-olds. For example, babies exposed to Arabic produced sounds while breathing both in and out, whereas the French babies produced sounds only when breathing out. Another study, by Whalen, Levitt, and Wang (1991), found that both American and English babies (exposed to English) produced mainly two- and three-syllable vocalisations with falling pitch, whereas French babies produced vocalisations with both rising and falling pitch.

Learning to say words

The sounds that children produce towards the end of the first year, such as "ba" and "da", feature in their first words. Inevitably, children's early attempts at words are phonetic simplifications of adult forms since, when children first start to say words, they are only able to produce a very limited number of phonemes. Processes of simplification continue right through the preschool years and, even by the age of five, many children will still have difficulty with some phonemes and especially with certain phoneme combinations.

The most frequent kinds of phonetic simplification include substitution of stop consonants for fricatives (as in "ti" for see), voicing of initial voiceless stop consonants (as in "doe" for toe), reduction of consonant clusters to a single consonant (as in "soo" for shoe or "sip" for ship), deletion of initial "h", and deletion of initial and middle unstressed syllables (as in "na" or "nana" for banana). Another process of simplification is called consonant harmony. Here the child will alter the production of one sound so that it is produced in a way that is more similar to another sound in the same word. Examples of consonant harmony are "gock" for sock—in which the "s" is replaced by "g", which is produced in a similar part of the mouth to the "ck" ending—and "means" for beans—where the "b" is replaced by "m" which is a nasal sound like the final "ns".

Some months before children first start to say words they begin to show signs of understanding them. This usually occurs when they are around seven or eight months old and the first words to be understood are typically the child's own name and the name of other family members—notably "mummy" and "daddy" and often the family pet—and familiar objects such as "clock", "drink", and "teddy" (Harris, Yeeles, Chasin, & Oakley, 1995).

Much of the evidence about developments in the number of words that children can understand comes from parental reports. The reliability of parental reports can be considerably improved if parents are given a structured questionnaire containing a checklist of the words that a young child might understand. Two widely used checklists make up the MacArthur Communicative Development Inventories (Fenson et al., 1990) or **CDI** as it is more commonly known. The checklists have been used extensively to gather data about early language development from 8 months to 28 months initially in English and now in a steadily increasing number of other languages. The period between 8 and 28 months normally spans the phase from children's first understanding of words through to the point where their ability to put words together begins to develop rapidly.

The CDI has two scales. The infant scale covers the period from 8 to 16 months. The toddler scale goes from 16 to 28 months. The infant scale asks parents to record communicative gestures that their child makes as well as words that the child can understand and words that he/she can produce. The toddler scale focuses only on production since, by 16 months, it becomes difficult to keep up with all the new words that their child understands. The norms for the CDI were derived from a sample of over 1700 children living in three different places in the United States and so they provide good evidence about normal language development.

Figure 7.2 shows the average number of words understood by boys and girls between 8 and 16 months. The number of words shown as being understood between 8 and 10 months may well be an overestimate since it is often difficult to decide whether a young child really understands a word or expression or is merely responding to a whole situation. However, two patterns in the development of early comprehension vocabulary are clear. First, girls were generally ahead of boys in the number of words they could understand and they showed a small but statistically significant advantage over boys. Second, both boys and girls showed a similar pattern of development with the number of words understood growing fairly slowly up to about 12 months at which point there was a sudden increase in vocabulary size.

KEY TERM

CDI: Communicative development inventories, developed by MacArthur, and comprising the infant and toddler scales.

This increase in vocabulary size has been noted in many other studies and a similar increase in the rate of development appears in production vocabulary as well. The increase is usually described as a "vocabulary explosion" or "vocabulary spurt". There are several different theories about why this spurt appears. One theory (e.g. Dore, 1978; McShane, 1979) is that it reflects the development of a "naming insight", that is, the child's sudden insight that all objects have a name. However, this theory does not stand up to inspection because children use object names right from the outset of production and very early on in comprehension (see the box on page 154). Another possible explanation is that the vocabulary spurt is a sign of a more general change in cognitive development. Again there seems to be a problem with this explanation for two reasons. First, by no means all normally developing children show a spurt. Second, spurts in comprehension and production do not usually occur together: The comprehension spurts typically occurs before the production spurt. This tends to suggest that the spurt is a function of the emergence of some kind of primitive lexical structure that takes place independently for comprehension and production.

Figure 7.3 shows how production vocabulary develops up from 10 to 16 months. Parents can usually provide very reliable information about the new words that their children are producing, providing that they are given clear instructions about what counts as a word. For example, as we saw earlier, children often simplify and shorten long words (e.g. saying "nana" for banana). The CDI data show that most children said their first word at around 10 months and gradually said more words over the next few months. Again there was a sudden increase in the rate of learning new words around 13 months. As for comprehension, girls were significantly ahead of boys in the number of words they were able to produce although the difference was fairly small.

A comparison of the graphs for comprehension and production over the same period shows that the number of words produced tends to be smaller than

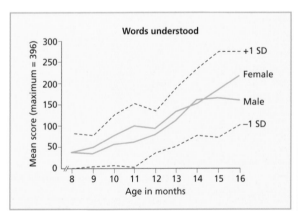

FIG. 7.2 The blue lines mark the mean number of words on the infant form reported to be comprehended by females and males at each month. The dotted lines indicate the range at each month for +/–1 SD for the sexes combined. Reproduced with permission from L. Fenson, P. Dale, S. Resnick, E. Bates, D. Thal, and S.J. Pethick (1994), Variability in early communicative development. *Monographs of the Society for Research in Child Development, 59*(5), 73.

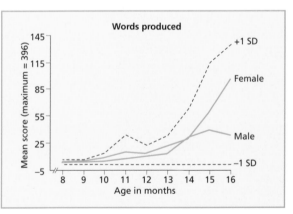

FIG. 7.3 The blue lines mark the mean number of words on the infant form reported to be produced by females and males, at each month. The dotted lines indicate the range at each month for +/–1 SD for the sexes combined. Reproduced with permission from L. Fenson, P. Dale, S. Resnick, E. Bates, D. Thal, and S.J. Pethick (1994), Variability in early communicative development. *Monographs of the Society for Research in Child Development, 59*(5), 74.

the number comprehended. The overall correlation between comprehension and production in the MCDI study was .45 when age was removed from the analysis (in order to account for the fact that the size of both comprehension and production vocabularies increases with age). Although the correlation of .45 was highly significant with such a large sample, it accounts for only 20% of the total variability. This reflects the fact that the relationship between comprehension and production is not the same for all children.

Although comprehension tends to follow behind production fairly consistently for the majority of children, the CDI data showed there was a clearly identifiable subgroup who had a comprehension vocabulary of more than 150 words but were saying few if any words. Children like this, who acquire a very large comprehension vocabulary before they say their first word, have also been described by Bates et al. (1988). There also seems to be a third, less frequent, pattern. In a longitudinal study of six children, Harris, Yeeles, et al. (1995) found two children (Ben and Katy) who understood only one or two words before they said their first word. They also showed a lag of less than one month from the time when they first understood a word to the time that they first said one. This compares to a more usual lag of around three months.

Children vary not only in the rate with which they understand and use new words but also in the proportion of different kinds of words that make up their vocabulary. Most children have more object names in their early production vocabulary than any other kinds of words but some children have a greater proportion of object names than others do. Katherine Nelson (1973) identified two distinctive styles in early language development—the **expressive style** and the **referential style.** Children who adopted the referential style had a large proportion of object names in their first 50 words, whereas expressive children had fewer object names but more action words and people's names.

Nelson suggested that the kind of words that children produce is related to their rate of language development. This suggestion was confirmed by Bates et al. (1988), who found that the children who acquire a greater proportion of object names tend to build up a vocabulary more quickly than children who have fewer object names in their early vocabulary (up to the age of about 18 months). However, data collected using the CDI (Bates, Dale, & Thal, 1994) have shown that this apparent association between the use of more object names and faster vocabulary is more complex than Nelson suggested. Bates et al. found that, for vocabulary sizes between 20 and 50 words, the proportion of object names varied between 12% and 100%. For children in the bottom 10th percentile, the proportion of object names was under 24%, whereas, for those in the top 10th percentile, the corresponding proportion was 62% or greater. These two most extreme groups were clearly very different and could unambiguously be classified as having "expressive" and "referential" styles, respectively, according to Nelson's original classification. However, close analysis showed that the children with a more referential style were actually *older* than children with a less referential style, which did not support the view that children who produced a large proportion of object names had more precocious language development. Bates et al. (1994) did, however, confirm that girls tended to have more object names in their early vocabulary than boys.

KEY TERMS
Expressive style: Style of early language development—more action words and people's names in early vocabulary.
Referential style: Style of early language development—more object names in early vocabulary.

The meaning of children's first words

The prevailing view in the mid-1980s was that the first words children produce are not the names of objects or actions. Rather, it was argued, first words are **context-bound** in that they are produced only in one specific situation or context (Barrett, 1986; Bates, Benigni, Bretherton, Camaloni, & Volterra, 1979; Dore, 1985; Nelson & Lucariello,1985). Some examples of context-bound word use are reported by Harris, Barrett, Jones, and Brookes (1988). James, one of the children they were studying, initially used "mummy" only when he was handing a toy to his mother and "there" only when pointing up to a picture on a frieze. Another child, Jenny, initially used "bye-bye" only when she was waving goodbye.

There is, however, increasing evidence that not all early words are used in only a single context. Bates et al. (1979) report some early words being **contextually flexible**, that is, they are used in more than one behavioural context (see, for example, Barrett, Harris, & Chasin, 1991; Bates et al., 1979; Dromi, 1987; Goldfield & Reznick, 1990; Harris et al., 1988; Lucariello, 1987). For example, in Harris et al. (1988), James used "teddy" to refer to one particular teddy in a variety of different contexts (for example, when sitting on teddy and when pointing to teddy's reflection in a mirror). This use, although restricted to a single referent (one particular teddy), is contextually flexible and it contrasts with James' use of "mummy". Another child, a little girl called Madeleine, first used the word "shoes" in a range of situations including looking at pictures of shoes in a book, pointing at her own shoes and also when holding her doll's shoes. Both "teddy" and "shoes" were being used as the name of the object to which they referred. In the Harris et al. (1988) study of the first 10 words produced by four children, out of the total of 40 words, 14 were initially used as object names.

Some authors (notably Dore, 1978 and McShane, 1979) have argued that young children's first use of object names comes about because they develop an insight that words can be used to name things. The development of such an insight has been thought to underpin the "vocabulary spurt", the point at which the rate of learning new words suddenly increases. However, the finding that children have both context-bound and contextually flexible word uses when they first start to talk suggests that there is no sudden development of a naming insight. Data from Goldfield and Reznick (1990) support this view. They studied 24 children from the age of just over one year and found that, as vocabulary size increased, there was an increasing proportion of object names. However, even before the vocabulary spurt occurred, almost half of the words used by the children were object names.

KEY TERMS
Context-bound words: Mid-1980s view that first words are only produced in one specific situation or context.
Contextually flexible words: More recent view that first words are used in more than one behavioural context.

The social context of early language development

The social-interactional context in which children hear people talking has an important role to play in the way that young children first begin to understand and use language. Day after day children play games such as "peekaboo" and "give-and-take" (in which objects are handed back and forth from child to parent) and they take part in the same caretaking routines (such as eating, having a bath, nappy changing) in which identical actions occur. Words and phrases used by the adult become a consistent part of these games and routines.

The importance of such games and routines for early language development was first highlighted by Jerome Bruner (1975), who argued that babies encounter language in a highly familiar social context because people talk to them about familiar events and objects. Their growing social competence allows them to remember and predict the familiar social events or routines—nappy changing, bath time, meal times, games of peekaboo—that occur day after day, According to Bruner, this developing knowledge of the social repertoire allows babies to build up insights into the meaning of the language that adults use as part of these routines.

There are two, rather different, versions of Bruner's theory. In the earlier version (Bruner, 1975), he proposed that there was a very close link indeed between the form of social routines and the form of language. However, in the later version, Bruner (1983) argued that there was *not* a direct correspondence between the structure of language and that of social routines. The reason for this change in Bruner's theory was the recognition that there is an important distinction between two aspects of language development. Social routines are important because they provide young children with a context for learning the meaning of words. However, they do not provide a context for learning the morphology and syntax of language since these aspects are not mirrored in social routines.

Morphology is the part of language concerned with the modification of individual words. For example, morphological rules determine how singular nouns are made plural (e.g. ship–ships; man–men) and how the tense of verbs is modified (e.g. I run, I am running, I ran). **Syntax** is concerned with the way in which individual words are combined into phrases and clauses. Bruner was correct in arguing that the way syntactic and morphological rules operate in language is not at all related to the structure of social interaction or other non-linguistic information. For example, there is nothing about the *meaning* of a noun that determines whether it will have regular plural (shoe–shoes) or an irregular plural (mouse–mice). So, looking for non-linguistic regularities in the real world will not help the child at all in learning how to form noun plurals correctly.

Bruner does not give many specific examples of exactly how familiarity with the social context might help young children to understand what adults are saying to them. The example in the box overleaf describes how Francesca slowly began to understand "Are you ready?" when it was said in the context of a highly familiar nappy changing routine.

The close relationship between parental speech and children's activity was demonstrated in a study by Harris, Jones, and Grant (1983, 1984–5). At 16 months of age, 78% of maternal utterances concerned objects on which the child was currently focusing attention. This proportion was considerably lower (49%) for a group of children who had delayed language development at two years of age (Harris, Jones, Brookes, & Grant, 1986).

There are two possible explanations for this finding. One is that the differences in the mothers' speech in the two groups arose *because* of differences in the language ability of the two groups. In other words, the two groups of mothers might have been talking differently because the two groups of children

KEY TERMS
Morphology: The form and structure of words in a language, especially the consistent patterns that may be observed and classified.
Syntax: The grammatical arrangement of words or morphemes in the sentences of a language.

Language and social routines: An example

An example of the way that a baby's familiarity with a social routine can pave the way for the very beginning of language understanding comes from Harris (1996) who reports the following extract from her diary of Francesca's early development.

Francesca always lay on a changing-table in her bedroom while her nappy was changed. From about three months of age, when Francesca had her new nappy on and her clothes re-fastened, her mother would take her by the hands and ask "Are you ready?" Then she would gently pull Francesca up into a sitting position. When Francesca was four months old, her mother noticed that she would start to lift her head from the changing-table when her mother asked "Are you ready?" What was striking was that Francesca did not try to lift her head as soon as her mother took hold of her hands but actually waited for the crucial question. At first, Francesca would try to lift her head only when her mother asked the question in the specific context of nappy changing. However, one month later, Francesca's understanding had increased so that she responded both when her father asked the question and in other situations. Indeed the whole routine had developed into a game in which Francesca lay on her back while her mother or father held her hands. She would look intently up at her parent's face and then attempt to pull herself up as soon as she heard "Are you ready?" This game was repeated several times on each occasion to the mutual delight of Francesca and her parents.

It is clear from this example that Francesca's understanding of "Are you ready?" grew directly out of the routine that took place with her mother at the end of a nappy changing session. By the time that Francesca was four months old she had become sufficiently familiar with the routine to be able to predict what came next. She was then able to associate the question "Are you ready?" with being raised into a sitting position and so to anticipate this event by raising her own head from the changing-table when she heard her mother ask the familiar question.

were talking differently. The other explanation is that these differences in maternal speech were responsible, at least in part, for the differences in the children's language ability.

There is good reason for preferring the second of these explanations because, when the speech of the two groups of mothers was sampled, all of the children, who were then 16 months old, appeared very similar. All of the children were at the preword stage and they were not producing any recognisable words. Evidence of differences among the children did not appear until several months later. At two years of age, the slower developers were still producing single words but the normal developers were producing utterances that were several words long. The two groups also differed in their vocabulary size with the normal developers saying more words than the slower developers. Because these differences between the two groups did not emerge until several months after the mothers' speech was sampled, it is unlikely that the mothers' speech styles were being influenced by the speech of their children. These findings can, therefore, be seen as evidence that the close tying of maternal speech to the current social context is an important factor in early language development.

Other aspects of the developing patterns of communication between mothers and children would appear to be important for the development of language. Most notable among these are establishment of **joint attention** between mother and child and the child's understanding of **reference**.

Collis (1977) and Collis and Schaffer (1975) have shown that joint visual attention is common in the first year of life; mothers and babies tend to look at the same objects. Their argument is that joint attention in the first year of life occurs because mothers tend to follow their children's line of regard although, by the second year, infants pay increasing attention to where their mother is looking. Butterworth (1998a; Butterworth & Jarrett, 1991) has shown, however, that the looking behaviour of young infants is rather more sophisticated than the findings of Collis and Schaffer suggest. Babies as young as six months are successfully able to follow their mother's line of regard providing that the object of regard is in front of the infant and it is the first one that the baby encounters when turning to look. By 12 months babies are still unable to locate a target that is behind them but they can locate a target even when it is not the first one that is encountered in turning to look. By 18 months babies can successfully locate objects behind them although they are still easily distracted if there is already something in their field of view.

A significant development for the establishment of joint reference occurs towards the end of the first year when infants show signs of understanding pointing and look in the appropriate direction when someone else points (Leung & Rheingold, 1981; Schaffer, 1984). Pointing is crucial to arguments about the development of referential communication because this gesture provides an important non-verbal procedure for picking out an object in the environment both for the benefit of another person and for oneself. The ability to point is uniquely human. Even chimpanzees are incapable of using an outstretched arm and index finger to indicate (Butterworth, 1994) and this difference between the chimp and the child appears to have implications for differences in their vocabulary development.

Babies begin to point at around one year and, soon after doing so, they use pointing to direct attention. Infants typically check that mothers are attending to the object of interest: They point and then turn to check that the mother is looking in the direction of the point (see Figure 7.4). Butterworth and Franco (1990) found that pointing and checking were invariably accompanied by vocalisation which supports the view that pointing is communicative. They also found that, by 15 months, infants would first check to see whether the mother was looking at them and only then point in order to redirect attention.

There is a relationship between the child's production of pointing and language development. Bates et al. (1979) showed that both giving and communicative pointing (pointing followed by checking) were predictive of early vocabulary development; and Folven, Bonvillian, and Orlansky (1984–85)

FIG. 7.4 Human infant pointing and checking. Reproduced with permission from G. Butterworth (1998b), What is special about pointing in babies? In F. Simion and G. Butterworth (Eds.), *The development of sensory, motor, and cognitive capacities in infancy*. Hove, UK: Psychology Press.

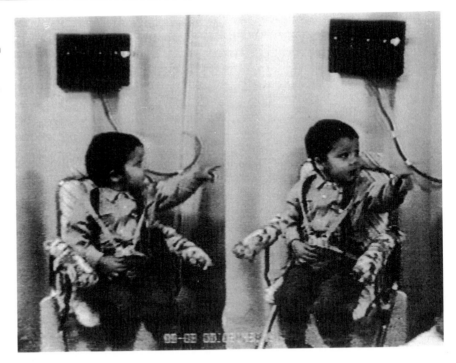

found that the frequency with which children produced communicative pointing between 9 and 12.5 months was positively correlated with the size of both spoken and signed lexicons during the second year of life.

Harris, Barlow-Brown, and Chasin (1995) showed that the development of pointing was related to the development of language in a very specific way. In a longitudinal study they followed both the emergence of pointing and the early understanding of words in a group of children. The age at which children first pointed was highly correlated with the age at which they first showed signs of understanding the names of objects. For example, the first object name that Francesca understood was "nose". She began by touching the nose on a toy koala when asked and then, the following day, she was asked "Where's mummy's nose?" and "Where's daddy's nose?" Francesca reached out and touched her parents' noses. This first occurred when she was just over nine months old. The same day she pointed at a plant in the conservatory. This was the first time that she pointed. This suggests that referring to objects in the world by pointing at them and understanding that they have names are very closely interlinked processes that may well have a common origin.

Pointing tends to elicit very specific responses from adults. Masur (1982) investigated maternal responses to children's first pointing gestures and found that these produced a very high rate of response. Significantly, most maternal responses involved labelling the object at which the child was pointing. Baldwin and Markman (1989) have explored the significance of pointing in the child's acquisition of new vocabulary. They have shown that children as young as 10 months of age spend significantly longer looking at novel objects when they are pointed at than when they are merely presented to the child without pointing. When an object is labelled, as well as being pointed to, the amount of looking is even greater suggesting that the young child is most predisposed to look at objects which are singled out both through pointing and through the use of an accompanying verbal label.

Recent studies of joint attention in autistic children have shown major differences between autistic children and control groups in abilities thought to be basic to communication. Autistic children have difficulty interpreting and producing pointing as a signal of something interesting for others to see (Curcio, 1978). This difficulty gives rise to other specific problems with language for autistic children. Hobson (1993) notes that those autistic children who acquire speech have particular difficulties with personal pronouns (I, you) and with relative terms for time and space (here, there, come, go). Such "deictic terms" are relative to who is speaker or listener in a conversation. The use of the correct deictic terminology in conversation depends on the role (speaker, listener) and the spatial frame of reference (near or far from or towards or away from some landmark known to the speaker and listener).

What can we learn from the language development of blind children?

Studying the early language of blind children can show how children's perceptual experience can affect their language development. Landau and Gleitman (1985) followed the language development of two children called Kelli and Carlo who were blind from birth. Both children took a long time to say their first word—Kelli was 23 months old and Carlo 26 months—and Landau and Gleitman conclude that "relatively late onset of speech is characteristic for blind children" (p. 27). However, the first words of blind children were similar to those of sighted children.

There were interesting differences for some words that are concerned with seeing. Landau and Gleitman tested Kelli's understanding of the verbs "look" and "touch". When asked to "look" at an object, Kelli would explore it with her hands but when asked to "touch but not look", Kelli touched, banged, or stroked an object, but did not manually explore it. Landau and Gleitman conclude from this that there is a common basis for the meaning ascribed to "look" by blind and sighted children. For the sighted child, "looking" involves exploration with the eyes. For the blind child "looking" also involves exploring with the dominant modality used for object perception, in this case, touch.

Mills (1987) studied a blind girl called Lisa to discover how she understood the word "see". She found that Lisa used "see" to refer to the auditory modality. On one occasion, having complained that she could not "see" the noise being made by a tape recorder, Lisa moved into a better position to hear it. This example is similar to Kelli's interpretation of "look" in that it involves the substitution of a modality that is salient to a blind child for one that is not. The two studies suggest, however, that blind children may vary in the modality that they choose as an alternative to vision.

Dunlea (1989) also concludes that blind children make use of information about touch and sound in lieu of visual information but she sees the lack of visual information as having much more extensive consequences. She presents a detailed account of the acquisition of the first 100 words by three blind children. Although blind children can hear what is being said to them, their opportunities for observing the social context in which words occur are severely limited.

Dunlea's study shows that this limitation has some important implications for early language development.

Dunlea found that blind children acquired new words at roughly the same rate as sighted children but they did not show the same pattern of development. In comparison to sighted children (see the box on page 154), blind children used words in a rigid way and were generally very unwilling to extend their initial use of words either beyond the scope of their own action or to unfamiliar objects. This makes them very different from sighted children who very rapidly extend their use of individual words. Indeed, one of the most striking features of the early vocabulary of sighted children is that many words are used in a contextually flexible way right from the outset. Another feature of the lexical development of the blind children studied by Dunlea was that they showed a very steady rate of vocabulary development. There was no sign of the typical burst in rate of acquisition that occurs after the first 30 or so words. Dunlea's contention is that, even by the end of the single-word period, blind children have not yet learned about the general relationships between words and objects and actions. This suggests that visual experience has an important role in guiding the development of the conceptual processes that underpin young children's early vocabulary development.

Dunlea also found that, in spite of differences in early vocabulary, the blind children progressed to multi-word utterances at much the same point as sighted children. Once they had a vocabulary of around 100 words, they began to combine words even though, at this stage, much of their vocabulary was still highly restricted. Dunlea concludes that, for the blind child, the stimulus to begin combining words appears to be independent of their state of lexical knowledge. Thus the language of blind children provides further evidence that some aspects of language development, notably syntactic development, occur as the result of language-specific processes that are not affected by social experience or more general cognitive development.

Conclusion and summary

Babies are born with very good speech perception abilities that allow them to begin to gain experience of spoken language even while they are still in utero. Over the first year of life their speech perception abilities become increasingly language specific and babies gradually lose their ability to distinguish among speech sounds that do occur in the language or languages of their speech community. During the first year of life babies also develop their ability to produce speech sounds and, by the age of six months, most babies are beginning to produce canonical babbling and by eight months they are producing reduplicated babbling as in "da-da" and "ba-ba". Failure to produce canonical babbling at this age is often a sign that a child either has a hearing problem or a specific difficulty with language that will become evident later on.

Children's early language development is the result of a complex interaction between innate abilities and experience. The development of early vocabulary is very closely linked to young children's experience of hearing familiar adults use words in familiar contexts; but, as children gain in competence, they become more and more capable of learning new words on the basis of very little experience—a process that is referred to as "fast mapping". By the time children reach the preschool years they commonly learn between 10 and 20 new words every day.

The data on language development collected using the CDI have shown how much individual children vary in the size of their vocabulary at different ages, and in their ability to combine words. For the majority of children the ability to produce words follows a little behind the ability to comprehend, but a significant number of children can understand more than 150 words before they first start to talk, whereas other children may begin to use words as soon as they can understand them. Children also vary in the proportion of different kinds of words in their early vocabularies.

Evidence from blind children suggests that early vocabulary learning is firmly grounded in visual as well as social experience. However, learning about syntactic rules seems to be a process that is much less rooted in social and visual experience and hearing children, blind children, and deaf children acquiring sign language show much greater similarity in syntactic development.

There is no single route to the mastery of language and children, especially in early childhood, show a large range of individual variation both in their speed of development and in the strategies that they employ. Their progress through early language might be thought of as a journey through an epigenetic landscape rather than a passage through a linear succession of stages. It is perhaps for this reason that there have been a number of attempts to produce connectionist models of language development (see Chapter 3, Observing and Modelling Developmental Change).

Further reading

- Barrett, M. (1999). *The development of language*. Hove, UK: Psychology Press. This edited book provides chapters on different aspects of language development. The chapters are written for undergraduates.
- Harris, M. (1992). *Language experience and early language development: From input to uptake*. Hove, UK: Lawrence Erlbaum Associates Ltd. This book reviews evidence about the relationship between children's early language development and the language that people around them use. It is written for undergraduates.
- Hirsch-Pasek, K., & Golinkoff, R.M. (1996). *The origins of grammar*. Cambridge, MA: MIT Press. The first part of this book provides a useful framework for comparing theories about language development. The second part describes a series of fascinating studies that use preferential looking to examine the language abilities of very young children.
- Locke, J.L. (1993). *The child's path to spoken language*. Cambridge, MA: Harvard University Press. This fascinating book considers the many different strands that come together when children acquire language. It is a good place to find out about the wide range of competencies that develop during infancy. It is intended for advanced undergraduates.
- Messer, D.J. (1994). *The development of communication*. Chichester, UK: Wiley. This book, which is suitable for first- and second-year undergraduates, provides a detailed account of early communication and language.

Part 3

The preschool years

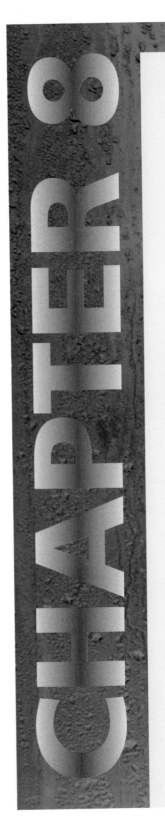

CHAPTER 8

CONTENTS

Language development in the preschool years

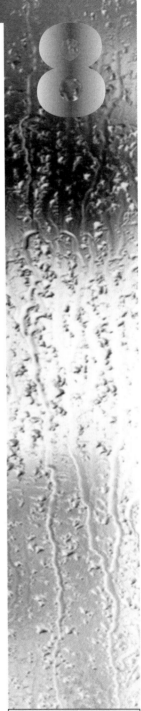

In this chapter we consider how children move on from their first production of words to the beginning of word combinations and the acquisition of morphology. Two main types of explanation—inside-out and outside-in theories—of the origins of developing morphological and syntactic abilities are discussed. In the final part of the chapter we review some recent experimental evidence about the development of grammatical understanding and we see how the performance of a two-year-old child in a test of sentence comprehension compares with that of a talented chimpanzee.

Combining words

Most children are combining words into simple utterances by the time that they are two years old. The length of children's utterances is measured by MLU or **mean length of utterance**. This measure is calculated by taking a sample of 100 or so utterances and working out their average length in morphemes. One word may also be one morpheme but, where a child produces a word that is not in its stem (or basic) form, this counts as more than one morpheme. So *Baby cry* is two words and also two morphemes but *Baby cried* is three morphemes because the stem form "cry" has been modified to the past tense form by adding the ED morpheme.

Data from the Bristol Language Project (Ellis & Wells, 1980) show that children vary considerably in the age at which they first combine words and in the time that it takes them to move from an MLU of one and a half to an MLU of three and a half. This progression in MLU is very important from the point of view of mastering syntactic rules because, by the time children are combining three, four, or five words, they have begun to develop an awareness of simple syntactic regularities.

A measure of the longest sentence that a child can produce is sometimes more revealing than a measure of MLU. Figure 8.1 shows the maximum length of sentences produced by children aged between 16 and 30 months in the Fenson, Dale, Resnick, Bates, et al. (1994) study using the Communicative Development Inventory (CDI). (See Inside-out Theories, later in this chapter.) Average maximum sentence length rose from just under two morphemes at 16 months to around 8 morphemes at 30 months. Girls were slightly ahead of boys but this difference was not significant.

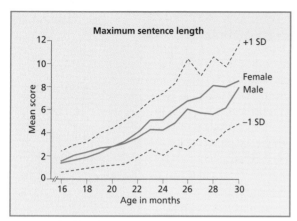

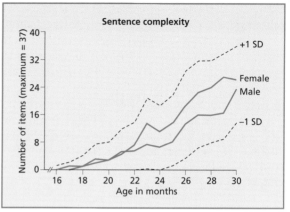

FIG. 8.1 The blue lines mark the mean scores for maximum sentence length on the toddler form reported to be produced by females and males at each month. The dotted lines indicate the range at each month for +/−1 SD for the sexes combined. Reproduced with permission from L. Fenson, P. Dale, S. Resnick, E. Bates, D. Thal, and S.J. Pethick (1994), Variability in early communicative development. *Monographs of the Society for Research in Child Development, 59*(5), 82.

FIG. 8.2 The blue lines mark for females and males the mean number of sentence pairs on the toddler form for which the parent selected the more complex option as typical of their speech. The dotted lines indicate the range at each month for +/−1 SD for the sexes combined. Reproduced with permission from L. Fenson, P. Dale, S. Resnick, E. Bates, D. Thal, and S.J. Pethick (1994), Variability in early communicative development. *Monographs of the Society for Research in Child Development, 59*(5), 82.

As the utterances that children produce become longer they tend to become more complex. One of the sections in the CDI toddler scale asks parents about the length and complexity of their children's utterances. Rather than asking parents to report actual utterances that their children had produced, they are given choices between pairs of sentences and asked to indicate which one is more like the kind of utterances that their child is currently saying. The sentence pairs are graded from very simple sentences to increasingly complex ones. At the simplest end of the scale, parents are asked to decide whether their child says sentences like *two shoe* or *two shoes*. At the most complex end of the scale they have to decide between *I sing song* and *I sing song for you* and between *Baby crying* and *Baby crying cuz she's sad*. You can see that in all cases, the second option is the more complex utterance. There are 37 sentence pairs in all and a child scores between 0 and 37 according to the number of second options that are chosen by the parents.

Figure 8.2 shows the average sentence complexity score from the CDI study. The score is around 0 at 16 months and has risen to around 24 by 30 months. The sharpest increase in sentence complexity occurs after 24 months indicating that this is the age at which most children begin to show rapid syntactic development. You will also see from Figure 8.2 that girls produced more complex sentences than boys of the same age. This difference was significant.

Morphological development

Two factors contribute to sentence complexity. One is the number of words that children can combine in a single utterance and the other is the number of morphological endings (grammatical morphemes) that they use. For example, *two shoes* is considered to be more complex than *two shoe* because the former includes the plural *s* morpheme on the noun. Again the CDI data can tell us about children's developing ability to use grammatical morphemes.

The CDI concentrates on four morphemes that children tend to acquire early on. Two are used to modify nouns—the regular noun plural (S) and the possessive (S)—and two are used to modify verbs—the progressive (ING) and the past tense (ED). The CDI data show that, at 16 months, few children were able to use any of these grammatical morphemes. By the age of two, most children were using two of them and by two and a half most children were able to use all four. The majority of children used the two noun morphemes before they used the two verb morphemes and the *ed* ending proved to be the most difficult of all. This finding is in line with a pioneering study carried out by Roger Brown in 1973.

Not all nouns are made plural by the addition of the *s* morpheme and not all past tenses of verbs end in ED. However, once children start to use these two morphemes, they sometimes incorrectly apply them to words that have an irregular pattern. For example a child might say *mouses* or *teeths* (instead of "mice" and "teeth") and *blowed* and *comed* (instead of "blew" and "came"). These kinds of errors are known as *overregularisations*.

The CDI toddler scale contains a list of common overregularisation errors (14 noun overregularisations and 31 past tense verb overregularisations) and parents are asked to indicate which of these their child has produced. Children generally make very few of these overregularisation errors before their second birthday. By two and a half, about 25% of the children in the sample were reported as using eight or more of the overregularisations but the majority of children used fewer than five out of the total of forty-five items. This finding is consistent with other recent studies (notably Marcus et al., 1992) showing that children make overregularisation errors much less often than was originally thought.

Overregularisation errors have been seen as theoretically important in child language development because they provide evidence that children are developing an awareness of morphological rules. It has often been argued that children apply newly derived morphological rules very strictly to all nouns and verbs even if they are irregular. However, it now seems that, as with other aspects of language development, there is considerable individual variation and by no means all children go through a stage of overregularisation. Recently, new insights into this problem have been provided by connectionist models of the learning of the past tense. We describe these later in this chapter.

Inside-out theories

One useful way of characterising theories about language development is to divide them into inside-out and outside-in theories as proposed by Hirsh-Pasek and Golinkoff (1996). Inside-out theorists claim that children acquire language according to the innate linguistic constraints of a "language faculty". According to such theorists, children's own experience of hearing language plays a very minor role in language development. By contrast, outside-in theorists place a much greater emphasis on the role of experience and they also argue that the mechanisms underpinning language learning are general purpose rather than language specific. The main differences between the inside-out and outside-in approaches are summarised in the table that follows.

A COMPARISON OF INSIDE-OUT AND OUTSIDE-IN THEORIES OF LANGUAGE DEVELOPMENT		
	Inside-out theories	**Outside-in theories**
Initial structure	Linguistic	Social or cognitive
Mechanism of language development	Domain-specific	Domain-general
Source of structure	Innate	Learning procedure
Key theories	Chomsky (1981, 1986)	Bates & MacWhinney (1989)
	Hyams (1986)	Bruner (1975, 1983)
	Landau & Gleitman (1985)	Nelson (1977)
	Pinker (1989)	Snow (1989)
Adapted from Hirsch-Pasek and Golinkoff (1996).		

The first, and most famous, inside-out theorist was Noam Chomsky. Since Chomsky first published his influential critique of Skinner's "Verbal Behavior" in 1959, he has amplified his views on the nature of language acquisition in a series of influential monographs culminating in "Knowledge of Language" (Chomsky, 1986). Although these developments mark an important change in Chomsky's thinking, the essence of his fundamental view of the nature of language acquisition has remained unchanged. Chomsky's claim is that:

> *Language is only in the most marginal sense taught and that teaching is in no sense essential to the acquisition of language. In a certain sense I think we might even go on and say that language is not even learned ... It seems to me that, if we want a reasonable metaphor, we should talk about growth. Language seems to me to grow in the mind rather as familiar physical systems of the body grow. We begin our interchange with the world with our minds in a particular genetically determined state. Through interaction with experience—with everything around us—this state changes until it reaches a mature state we call a state of knowledge of language ... this series of changes seems to me analogous to the growth of organs.*
> *(Chomsky in conversation with Brian McGee, 1979)*

This quotation encapsulates one key tenet of the inside-out view—experience and the language environment have only a minimal influence on the innately driven processes of language development in the child. In the quotation Chomsky talks of "interaction with experience" but this is only in the sense that children need exposure to the particular language used in the part of the world where they are growing up. This minimal contribution for language experience is necessary even in Chomsky's theory in order to explain why a child, who grows up surrounded by people speaking English, will learn to speak English rather than, say, French, Italian, or Japanese.

The other main tenet of the inside-out view is that the processes involved in language acquisition are language specific and thus distinct from those involved in other aspects of cognitive development. The main reason why Chomsky argues for this uniqueness of language processes is that, for him, acquiring a language involves the acquisition of a body of language-specific knowledge. In Chomsky's early theory (Chomsky, 1965), this knowledge was characterised as a set of syntactic rules but, in his more recent theorising, Chomsky (1986) has argued for a set of principles and parameters. One aim of this theory is to explain how the many different languages of the world can be acquired from a common starting point. Each language parameter has various settings that vary from one language to another. For example, one of the most widely discussed parameters, called "pro-drop", has two possible settings. One setting is for languages like Italian, where sentences without a grammatical subject are allowed and the pronoun can be omitted (—hence "pro-drop") and the other setting is for languages, like English, where sentences without subjects are not permissible. This difference between languages that allow subjectless sentences and those that do not can be seen in an English sentence such as "*It's raining*" which is translated into Italian simply as the verb "*Piove*". In Chomsky's theory, exposure to a few sentences of Italian would produce one setting of the pro-drop parameter and exposure to a few sentences of English the other. Chomsky makes it clear that, in his theory, parameter settings are "triggered" by exposure to a particular language rather than being learned.

As a linguist, Chomsky has been concerned with the general mechanism by which children acquire language rather than with the detail. However, a number of psychologists have developed their own inside-out theories which share Chomsky's claim that innate, language-specific processes underpin language development. Like Chomsky, both Gleitman (1990) and Pinker (1984) have argued that children have a great detail of language-specific knowledge at their disposal before they begin to acquire a particular language. For Pinker this knowledge concerns the existence of grammatical word classes, like noun and verb, and syntactic categories such as subject and object. Where the views of Pinker and Gleitman differ from those of Chomsky is in the role of language experience or input. As we have noted, Chomsky argues that hearing a language merely "triggers" a particular parameter setting, whereas Pinker and Gleitman both see language input as having a more extensive role. This can be seen in Pinker's argument that children use a process called "semantic bootstrapping" in order to divide the words they hear into their correct classes.

The idea behind "semantic bootstrapping" is that children are able to link certain semantic categories such as "person" or "thing" to their corresponding grammatical word class and syntactic categories by a series of "linking rules". The linking rules described by Pinker (1989) are complex and outside the scope of this book but a simple example will serve to illustrate the general idea. Suppose that a child hears the following sentence while, at the same time, seeing her pet cat playing: "Fluffy is chasing the ball". It will be clear from the context that Fluffy is the actor (i.e. carrying out the action), that "chasing" refers to an action and "ball" to an object or thing. Thus, through linking rules, "Fluffy" and "ball" can both be interpreted as nouns and "chasing" as a verb. Additionally "Fluffy" can also be identified as the subject of the sentence and "ball" the object.

The use of linking rules together with innate knowledge of word categories would only get children so far in discovering syntactic rules so, in Pinker's theory, there is another kind of bootstrapping called "syntactic bootstrapping". This involves inferring information about the syntactic properties of words from their position in the sentence and extending these inferences to new cases which occur in similar syntactic positions. For example, if a particular verb always has a noun occurring both before and after it, as would be the case for a transitive verb like "chases", it would be treated differently from an intransitive verb, like "run", which always occurs with a preceding noun but never has a following noun.

Pinker has shown that children are able to generalise morpho-syntactic information in a way that suggests they are capable of syntactic bootstrapping. In a well-known study by Pinker, Lebeaux, and Frost (1987), four-year-old children were taught nonsense verbs that described unusual actions. For example, children were given two contrasting sentences, "The pig is *pilking* the horse" and "I'm *mooping* a ball to the mouse". The critical difference between these sentences lies in the type of verb that they contain. The first sentence uses a verb—like "brush" or "rub"—in which one animal (the pig) does something to another animal (the horse). The verb in the second sentence is different because it is performed on an inanimate object (a ball). This kind of verb functions in the same way as "roll" or "throw".

Children were asked to explain what had happened in the pictures—a technique that was designed to see whether they could form a past tense for the nonsense verbs. If they understood the distinction between the two types of verb they should produce different responses for the two pictures. This was what happened. The children produced descriptions such as "The horse is being pilked by the pig" and "I mooped the mouse a ball" but not, for example, "The mouse is being mooped by the ball". This latter form would not be correct.

Pinker et al.'s (1987) study shows that, by four years of age, children have already developed a good understanding of the difference between verb classes. The question is whether this understanding grows out of innate knowledge or whether it emerges from children's experience with language.

Certainly the ability to use morphemes productively is widespread. Preschool children can add morphemes to real words in order to create (or "coin") novel words. Clark (1995) has described a large number of examples including cases where a child coins a verb from a noun (*Is Anna going to babysitter me?*) or an adjective from a verb (*Try to be more rememberful, mom.*) Such example show that preschool children are aware of some of the rules of word formation, for examples how to form a verb infinitive using an ER ending or an adjective using the common FUL ending as in "careful". However the fact that children can respect word class distinctions—and use them in novel ways—does not tell us anything about the source of their ability to do this. They could be using a language-specific ability underpinned by innate knowledge (as Pinker proposes) or they could using a more general kind of distributional analysis in which they separate out word classes on the basis of their particular patterns of occurrence within different sentence types.

Outside-in theories

In Chapter 7, The Beginnings of Language Development, we considered Bruner's theory about the way that the child's experience of social interaction provided a springboard into language. This theory is one example of an outside-in theory, which emphasises the role of experience and argues for general-purpose rather than language-specific processes in language learning.

Another, rather different, outside-in explanation comes from Bates and MacWhinney (1989) in their **competition model**. Rather than seeing the origins of linguistic knowledge as social, they argue for general cognitive mechanisms being involved in language development. The basic idea behind the competition model is that children note distributional evidence in the language

KEY TERM
Competition model: Bates and MacWhinney's explanation of language development as originating from general cognitive mechanisms rather than from social interaction.

input and, from this, deduce linguistic rules. Details of this approach have recently been developed in connectionist models of language development.

Connectionist modelling was introduced in Chapter 3, Observing and Modelling Developmental Change (see The Dynamic Systems Approach) where we saw that c-nets can model stage-like transitions in learning. Many connectionist models, beginning with the early model of past tense learning of Rumelhart and McClelland (1986), have been concerned with aspects of language learning. The Rumelhart and McClelland model used verb stems as input and their past tense form as output. When Rumelhart and McClelland first published their results there was a great deal of interest in the apparent similarity of children's learning of the past tense and the learning of the c-net, notably in the production of overregularisation errors in which the regular ED ending was applied to irregular verbs (see Morphological Development, earlier in this chapter). However, close examination of the training procedure used by Rumelhart and McClelland revealed that this similarity arose from certain characteristics of the training regime (see Plunkett & Marchman, 1993). Most notably, the overregularisation errors were produced by a change in the training set. Initially, Rumelhart and McClelland had presented only 10 stems (8 regular and 2 irregular) and had allowed rote learning of their past tense. Only then was the training set increased to 420, most of which were regular verbs. Since the majority of verbs—especially those in the first 10—were regular, this inevitably meant that the use of the ED ending would be the most strongly represented output in the c-net and so its use would predominate.

Plunkett and Marchman (1993) carried out their own study of past tense learning using a somewhat different type of c-net. Unlike Rumelhart and McClelland they used a multi-layer c-net with what are called hidden units that serve to groups various units from lower levels (see Figure 8.3). This kind of c-net with hidden units is the most commonly used in modelling because, unlike a single-layer c-net, it allows the grouping of units from spatially separated parts of the network (see Elman et al., 1996 for a discussion of this issue). The aim of the Plunkett and Marchman study was to show, like Rumelhart and McClelland, that a c-net could model children's learning of the past tense without recourse to a rule but, unlike Rumelhart and McClelland, they aimed to do this while using the same training set throughout. This consisted of 500 verb stems that were mainly regular, reflecting the fact that regular verb forms are considerably more common in English than irregular. However, each irregular verb was presented more often than each regular verb.

The performance of the Plunkett and Marchman c-net was very similar to that shown by young children (see Figure 8.4). As learning occurred, the network produced an error for an individual verb, then the correct response, then an incorrect response, and so on. This pattern of error, recovery from error, reoccurrence of the error also

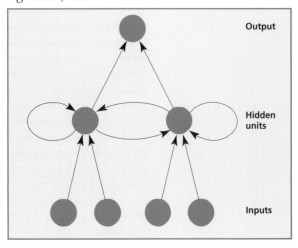

FIG. 8.3 A recurrent network. The network has fully interconnected hidden units; each hidden unit activates itself and the other hidden unit. As a result, the current state (activation) of a hidden unit reflects not only new input from the input units, but the hidden units' prior activation states. Reproduced with permission from J.L. Elman, E.A. Bates, M.K. Johnson, A. Karmiloff-Smith, D. Parisi, and K. Plunkett (1996), *Rethinking innateness: A connectionist perspective on development.* Cambridge, MA: MIT Press.

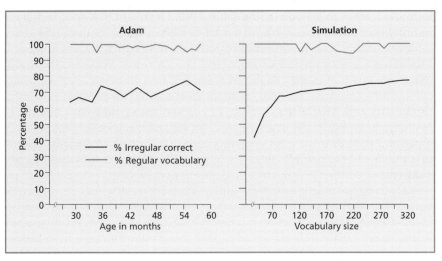

FIG. 8.4 Percentage of correctly pronounced irregular past tenses from the Plunkett and Marchman (1993) simulation compared to those of Adam (Marcus et al., 1992). The level of overregularisation (the micro-U-shaped profile) is similar in both cases. The thick lines indicate the percentage of regular verbs in the child's network's vocabulary at various points in learning. Reproduced with permission from J.L. Elman, E.A. Bates, M.K. Johnson, A. Karmiloff-Smith, D. Parisi, and K. Plunkett (1996), *Rethinking innateness: A connectionist perspective on development.* Cambridge, MA: MIT Press.

reflected the performance of young children. Most importantly, from the perspective of explaining development, Plunkett and Marchman were able to show that the same kind of learning process throughout could give rise to a pattern of learning in which there appeared to be a major change.

In spite of the apparent similarities between c-net learning and that of young children, there would appear to be two important differences between them. C-nets are typically trained with a large number of items and these are all presented in a single training epoch (even if the very first part of training may include only a subset of items). The experience of each presentation contributes equally to learning and all experiences are reflected in the current setting of weights within the network. However, it seems unlikely that such a process of simultaneous learning of many associations occurs in the case of the child. In the case of vocabulary, for example, the evidence suggests that learning is focused with the child concentrating on a small number of words that are of particular salience in terms of the child's own activity. The second difference between children and c-nets is that the latter are given very systematic feedback after each trial. Again this does not appear to reflect the way that children learn. Recent research (see the next section, The Role of Language Input) shows that children are given more feedback about the grammaticality of their utterances than was thought but even the strongest advocate of the significance of feedback for language development would not claim that it ever comes anywhere near the level found in c-net training.

Bray, Reilly, Villa, and Grupe (1997) highlight some of the special challenges that arise in connectionist modelling of developmental phenomena. These include the problems of real versus simulated time and the representation of different levels of learning—the idea that all aspects of learning change with age. Bray et al. discuss ways in which the amount of learning across time can be modified so that, at one extreme, information learned may not be modified and, at the other, modified within trials. With such developments connectionist models should be able to simulate language learning much more accurately.

The role of language input

One important feature that distinguishes inside-out from outside-in theories is the emphasis that they place on children's language environment as a significant contributory factor in their language development. Many studies have attempted to establish the extent to which linguistic input—the language children hear—directly influences language development.

One early hypothesis was that the syntactic complexity of mothers' speech would have a directly effect on the precocity of their children's language development. However two very different observational studies—carried out in Bristol by Ellis and Wells (1980) and in the United States by Gleitman, Newport, and Gleitman (1984)—demonstrated that there is, in fact, very little relationship between purely syntactic measures of maternal speech (i.e. length and complexity of maternal utterances) and children's language development. However, the Bristol project also showed that there were other important aspects of mothers' speech that were related to (and did predict) children's language development. These concerned the relationship between what mothers said to their children and what the children were doing at the time. Most notably, the group of children in the Bristol study who showed the most precocious development—early fast developers—were asked more questions and given more instructions by their mothers than children with less precocious development. The mothers of this group were also more responsive to their children's own utterances, which they tended to acknowledge and imitate more often than the mothers of children whose language development was less precocious. Finally, the early fast developers had more opportunity to hear speech that referred to activities in which they were currently involved. What binds these apparently disparate features of maternal speech together is that they are all concerned with the relationship of individual utterances to the prevailing non-verbal context. In other words, the mothers of children with more precocious language development were more likely to ask questions, give instructions, and generally comment on the activity in which their child was currently engaged.

The Bristol study thus demonstrated that, in the very early stages of learning to talk, mothers who relate their language very specifically to their children's ongoing activity have children with more precocious development. Precisely why this might occur was explained in a study by Harris et al. (1988) which studied the first 10 words children produced and compared the pattern of use of each word with uses of the same word by the mother in the month preceding the child's first use. Children used their first words in ways that very closely mirrored their experience of hearing these words being used by their mothers. In the 40 words studied, there were only three where there was no apparent relationship between a child's use and the mother's use of that word in the preceding month; and in 33 of the cases studied, the child's use was identical to the mother's most frequent use. For example, the first word used by James was "mummy" but, rather puzzlingly, he restricted its use to situations where he was holding out a toy for his mother to take. This unusual use was explained when an inspection of his mother's speech revealed that she most commonly used this word when holding out her hand to take a toy, saying "Is that for mummy?"

It is important to note that this close relationship between children's words and their mothers' speech is of strictly limited duration because, where a child subsequently acquires a new use of the same word, this is much less likely to be related to a preceding maternal use (Barrett, Harris, & Chasin, 1991). This finding was confirmed by Hart (1991) who directly compared early vocabulary with later vocabulary. She found that children's first words tended to be the ones that their parents frequently used when speaking to them—on average these words occurred 30 times in a monthly observation session. However, when the children were six months older, the words that they were acquiring had typically occurred only twice in parental speech during the observation session.

Some effects of input do, however, appear to be of longer duration. Gopnik and Choi (1995) have found that verbs appear earlier, and form a greater proportion of early vocabulary, in the speech of children acquiring Korean than of children acquiring English. Similarly, Tardif (1996) has found that 21-month-old children who are learning Mandarin Chinese have as many different verbs as nouns in their vocabulary compared to the typical noun predominance in the vocabulary of English-speaking children. These patterns reflect a greater preponderance of verbs in the maternal speech of Korean- and Mandarin-speaking mothers compared to English-speaking mothers. Interestingly, such differences in maternal language style appear to stem not only from the structure of the language but also from differences in the amount of labelling. In a study of Japanese mothers, Todo, Fogel, and Kawai (1990) found that cultural norms have an important influence on the way that mothers talk to their children. The mothers in Japan were more concerned with their babies' feelings and emotions and were less concerned with questioning and directing their babies in the manner that is so characteristic of Western mothers. Similar findings are reported by Fernald and Morikawa (1993).

Another effect of input to emerge in recent studies concerns adult correction of children's grammatical errors. The traditional view had been that parents rarely correct grammatical errors and respond mainly to the content of what children say (Brown & Hanlon, 1970). Attempts to correct grammatical errors were considered to be rare and doomed to failure: Many textbooks quote a well-known example from McNeill (1966) of a mother's repeated, but unsuccessful, attempt to correct a child:

Child:	*Nobody don't like me.*
Mother:	*No, Say "Nobody likes me".*
Child:	*Nobody don't like me.*
	(8 repetitions of this sequence)
Mother:	*Now listen carefully. Say "Nobody likes me".*
Child:	*Oh! Nobody don't likes me.*

(McNeill, 1966, p. 69)

Saxton (2000) has shown that children do, in fact, receive more direct evidence about their errors than was previously thought. This is either in the form of, what Saxton has called, "negative evidence" or "negative feedback". Negative

Verb form	Action
Pro/prew (cf. throw/threw) Twisting motion applied with a cross-ended stick.	
Neak/noke (cf. speak/spoke) Repeated clapping motion in which target is trapped between the palms.	
Jing/jang (cf. sing/sang) Striking a target with a beanbag flipped from a spoon.	
Streep/strept (cf. creep/crept) Ejection of a ping-pong ball from a cone-shaped launcher towards target.	
Sty/stought (cf. buy/bought) Prodding action performed with a plastic stick which concertinas on contact to produce a honking noise.	
Pell/pold (cf. sell/sold) Striking action achieved by swinging a beanbag on the end of a string towards target.	

Meanings and past tense alternations of Saxton's novel verb forms. Drawings by Colin Saxton. Reproduced with permission from Matthew Saxton.

evidence is provided when a child produces an incorrect utterance that is immediately followed by an adult utterance modelling the correct form:

Child: I losed *my hands (pulling up hands inside pyjama sleeves).*
Adult: *You* lost *your hands.*
Child: I lost *my hands.*

Negative feedback is when an adult queries a child's utterance:

Child: *The pirate* hitted *him on the head.*
Adult: *What?*
Child: *The pirate* hit *him on the head.*

Saxton has shown that children often reformulate their own utterance following both types of negative input. He argues that the adult model of the correct form is providing children with a contrast between the correct and incorrect forms. One might suggest that such an effect will only be of short duration, with the child reverting to the incorrect form when is no adult model to follow. However, Saxton, Kulcsar, Marshall, and Rupra (1988) have shown, in an experimental setting, that preschoolers will learn the irregular past tense of nonsense verbs (*pell/pold* and *streep/strept*) better when they are presented with negative evidence over a five-week period rather than only the correct form. The methodology of this study was similar to that of Pinker et al. (1987) in using puppets to depict the novel action.

Experimental studies of early grammatical understanding

One important development in the study of grammatical understanding has been the use of the preferential looking paradigm. Hirsh-Pasek and Golinkoff (1996) have used it to examine a number of hypotheses about syntactic development in young children.

In the preferential looking paradigm a spoken sentence is presented at the child's mid-line while two events are presented on screens at either side (see Figure 8.5). Both screens show objects or events that can be plausibly associated with the spoken words. In one study, toddlers heard "See? Big Bird's hugging Cookie Monster" while seeing *Big Bird hugging Cookie Monster* on one screen and *Cookie Monster hugging Big Bird* on the other. If the children look significantly longer at the screen showing the event described in the sentence this is taken as evidence that they associated the sentence with that event and thus are sensitive to the contrast (in this case, word order) being tested. Many essential controls have to be introduced in the series of studies to ensure the children are discriminating only the salient syntactic features of the contrast.

The studies of Hirsch-Pasek and Golinkoff (1996) showed, among other things, that 18-month-old children could distinguish word order (as in the Big Bird–Cookie Monster example). However, the more complex contrast between transitive and intransitive uses of a verb (as in *Look at Cookie Monster turning Big Bird* versus *Look at Cookie Monster and Big Bird turning*) was not distinguished until several months later. Interestingly children first showed a preference for

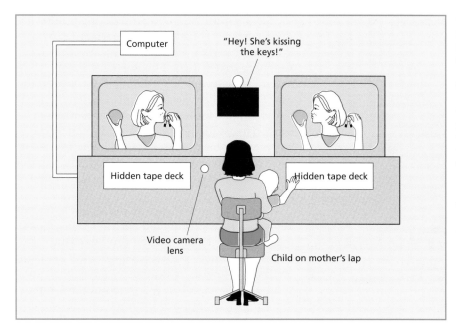

FIG. 8.5 The intermodal preferential looking paradigm showing a sample stimulus set from Experiment 1. On the left screen a woman is kissing keys while holding a ball in the foreground. On the right screen she is kissing a ball while holding keys in the foreground. Reproduced with permission from K. Hirsh-Palek and R.M. Golinkoff (1996), *The origins of grammar: Evidence from early language comprehension.* Cambridge, MA: MIT Press.

the "correct" event only with familiar verbs. This occurred at 23 months but, by 27 months, this preference was extended to unfamiliar verbs.

Overall the results of Hirsh-Pasek and Golinkoff show that, by the age of 24 months, children are beginning to use syntax as a guide to meaning but they are not doing so six months earlier, at 18 months. These findings using the preferential looking procedure thus support evidence from many other studies which show that that there is a significant period of syntactic development at the end of the second year.

The language abilities of chimpanzees

Another source of evidence about the special language abilities of young children comes from a recent study of the language abilities of chimpanzees. Over the last 20 years or so several studies have attempted to teach language to chimpanzees. Since chimpanzees have a very limited ability to produce speech-like sounds because of the anatomy of their vocal tract (see Figure 7.1 on page 148), these studies have made use either of sign language, as in the case of Washoe (Gardner & Gardner, 1971, 1974) and Nim (Terrace, 1979, 1985) who were trained to produce signs from American Sign Language (ASL), or they have used an artificial language communicated via a keyboard (see Premack, 1986 for a review).

The most successful study has been carried out by Savage-Rumbaugh with a young male bonobo (previously called a "pygmy chimpanzee") named Kanzi (Savage-Rumbaugh, McDonald, Sevcik, Hopkins, & Rupert, 1986). The chimpanzees used by the Gardners, Terrace, and Premack were all common chimpanzees (*Pan troglodytes*). There is some evidence that bonobos (*Pan paniscus*) are more intelligent than common chimps and that they also have a more complex social-communicative repertoire. They are thus ideal participants for a study of language learning.

Sue Savage-Rumbaugh holds a board with lexigrams that Kanzi uses to communicate with her. From E.S. Savage-Rumbaugh and R. Lewin (1994), *Kanzi: The ape at the brink of the human mind.* New York: Wiley. Copyright © 1994 John Wiley & Sons, Inc. This material is used by permission of John Wiley & Sons, Inc.

Savage-Rumbaugh had previously trained the chimpanzees, Austin and Sherman (Savage-Rumbaugh, 1986), who communicated through a keyboard that activated geometric symbols. They had to be given explicit training to go beyond the use of a particular visual symbol in a single context. Kanzi differed from Austin and Sherman in that he learned to use the symbol keyboard spontaneously by watching his mother, Matata, being trained to use it. Kanzi was not given formal training in the use of the keyboard, but learned the skill from his mother.

Once Kanzi had learned the symbols on the keyboard, he was provided with a pointing board that could be taken outside the laboratory. The board contained photographs of the symbols on the keyboard (lexigrams) and a particular symbol was selected by touching the board. Kanzi was credited with knowing a lexigram only if he spontaneously produced it on at least nine occasions and also if he provided unambiguous evidence that he was using it appropriately. For example, many of the lexigrams referred to locations and Kanzi showed that he understood them by pointing to the lexigram and then taking a researcher to the correct location. Kanzi was also tested to see if he understood the items in his production vocabulary.

Kanzi comprehended lexigrams before producing them and he often comprehended both the spoken English word and the lexigram before using the lexigram in production. For example, when Kanzi first understood the word "strawberries", he would hurry over to the strawberry patch when the word was mentioned. Later the lexigram for "strawberry" was added to Kanzi's keyboard and he learned to use it to request a strawberry to eat, to ask to travel to the strawberry patch, and he also used it when shown a picture of strawberries.

Overall Kanzi's performance at learning lexigrams was impressive and over a period of 17 months he learned to understand nearly 60 symbols and produce nearly 50. He also regularly produced two and three lexigram combinations such as "Grape eat", "More drink", and "Apple me eat". He could also understand the difference in meaning between two similar combinations such as "Chase Kanzi" and "Kanzi chase".

Kanzi's success in learning language marked a significant improvement on previous studies not only because he learned the meaning of words spontaneously—through observation of his mother, Matata—but also because he appeared to understand lexigrams before using them himself. Another important difference between Kanzi and chimpanzees who took part in earlier studies was that, at the age of two years, he began to show signs of understanding *spoken* English and his ability in this regard became a major focus of study.

Savage-Rumbaugh adopted exceptionally strict criteria for determining competence in both comprehension and production in order to offset criticism that she and her colleagues were overestimating Kanzi's ability. The testing of comprehension was equally rigorous and used double-blind procedures in which Kanzi had no visual contact with the experimenter who was presenting the stimuli.

Seidenberg and Petitto (1987) have argued that Kanzi's use of lexigrams was not genuinely symbolic and that it was fundamentally different from young children's early vocabulary learning. However, both Savage-Rumbaugh (1987) and Nelson (1987) have convincingly argued that Kanzi's understanding and use of lexigrams is much closer to that of young children than Seidenberg and Petitto claim. Nevertheless, although Kanzi's performance is very impressive, it pales into insignificance when compared with the very rapid vocabulary learning that occurs in young children (see Inside-out Theories, earlier in this chapter).

The study of Kanzi entered a second phase when Savage-Rumbaugh and her colleagues decided to investigate Kanzi's understanding of simple sentences and to compare this with that of a child called Alia who was the daughter of one of the researchers (Savage-Raumbaugh et al., 1993). Alia was exposed to spoken English from birth and to lexigrams from the age of three months. She was brought to the laboratory and played with her mother every afternoon in an environment that was very similar to Kanzi's.

Alia and her mother (who looked after Kanzi in the mornings) took part in similar games and activities to those provided for Kanzi. Alia watched many of the same videotapes that Kanzi saw, carried out many of the same computer-based tasks and she also visited many of the outside locations that Kanzi was taken to. All these activities were designed to foster understanding of both spoken English and the lexigram vocabulary.

Between the ages of 18 months and two years Alia was tested on exactly the same set of sentences as Kanzi using an identical procedure in which the test item was presented via headphones (see Figure 8.6) so that Kanzi and Alia did not receive any unwitting non-verbal cues from the experimenter. The sentences were of a number of different types but they all required Kanzi and Alia to carry out instructions involving familiar objects, locations, and people (see

FIG. 8.6 Sometimes Kanzi received spoken instructions through headphones. Photograph by Mike Nichols.

Figure 8.7). The results of this part of the study were very interesting and they provoked a great deal of discussion because they suggested that Kanzi's level of understanding was as good as Alia's and, for sentences like *Go outdoors and find the carrot* and *Go get the rock in the play yard*, it was actually better. The table below summarises Kanzi's and Alia's performance across the different types of sentence.

Word order was systematically contrasted so that, for example, both the sentences *pour the lemonade in the coke* and *pour the coke in the lemonade* were presented, as were *make the doggy bite the snake* and *make the snake bite the doggy*. Both Kanzi and Alia were able to use word order to distinguish the meaning of sentences involving the same lexical items and Kanzi was significantly better at sentences involving the retrieval of items from a specified location—perhaps because this was a major activity in his daily life. (Savage-Rumbaugh concludes that the diversity of sentence types in the "All other category" made it difficult to draw firm a conclusion about Kanzi's apparently superior performance.) Being able to use word order as a guide to meaning is an impressive achievement and Kanzi (and other bonobos whom Savage-Rumbaugh continues to study) have shown greater facility with this aspect of language than any other primate. However it is important to remember that word order

COMPARATIVE PERFORMANCE OF KANZI AND ALIA ON COMPREHENSION OF SENTENCE		
Sentence type/example	**Kanzi % correct**	**Alia % correct**
Put object X in/on transportable object Y *Put the pine needles in the backpack*	63	73
Put object X in/on non-transportable object Y *Put the clay on the vacuum*	77	71
Give (or show) object X to animate A *Give the pillow to Sue*	78	84
Give (or show) object X and object Y to animate A *Show me the ball and the cereal*	37	57
Do action A on animate A *Hide the toy gorilla*	91	91
Do action A on animate A with object X *Tickle me with a stick*	76	61
Do action A to object X (with object Y) *Stab your ball with the sparklers*	82	63
Announce information *Nathaniel is going to chase Alia*	67	83
Take object X to location Y *Take the can opener to the bedroom*	78	71
Go to Location Y and get object X *Go outdoors and find the carrot*	82	45
Go get object X that's in location Y *Go get the rock in the play yard*	77	52
Make pretend animate A do action A on recipient Y *Make the doggy bite the snake*	67	56
All other sentence types *Open the jello and pour it in the juice*	78	33
Adapted from Savage-Rumbaugh et al. (1993).		

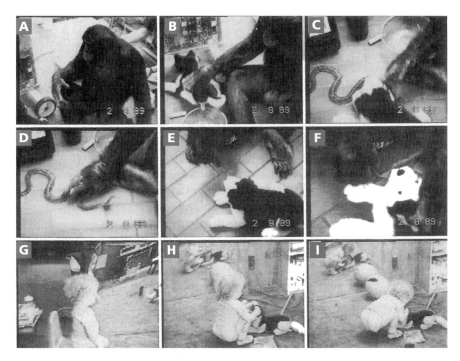

FIG. 8.7 Kanzi and Alia respond to the sentence "Can you make the doggie bite the snake?" (a) Kanzi listens to the sentence; (b) Kanzi picks up the dog; (c) Kanzi places the dog near the snake; (d) Kanzi picks up the snake; (e) Kanzi moves the snake towards the dog; (f) Kanzi puts the snake's head in the dog's mouth, and using his thumb, closes the dog's mouth on the snake's head; (g) Alia listens to the sentence; (h) Alia approaches and looks at the dog; (i) Alia bites the dog herself. Reproduced with permission from E.S. Savage-Rumbaugh and D.M. Rumbaugh (1993), The emergence of language. In K.R. Gibson and T. Ingold (Eds.), *Tools, language, and cognition in human evolution* (pp. 86–108). Copyright © Wenner-Gren Foundation, published by Cambridge University Press.

alone does not provide syntax in English and so it may not be correct to conclude that Kanzi's language comprehension is identical to that of a two-year-old child. Savage-Rumbaugh et al. did not investigate morphological knowledge which is, as we have seen, essential for an understanding of the syntactic relations among words.

Bates (1993, p. 223) describes the two-year-old child as "on the threshold of full-blown syntactic processing". This is because, for the child, the mastery of morphology is beginning and it is this that paves the way for syntactic development. However, there seems to be little evidence that bonobos are capable of passing over the threshold to a similar level of morphological competence. One strong piece of evidence to support this view is that over the entire period that Kanzi was tested his mean length of utterance (MLU) did not go above 1.15 morphemes, showing that he seldom combined lexigrams in his own language output. Alia, however, progressed from an MLU of just under two morphemes at 18 months to over three morphemes at two years. Interestingly, Alia also started to pick out lexigrams before she could talk, underlining the fact that young children's ability to produce spoken language is initially held back by the difficulty of producing speech sounds (see The Development of Babbling, in Chapter 7).

Vocabulary development in the school years

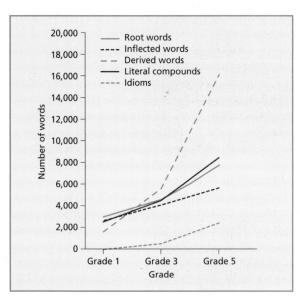

FIG. 8.8 Mean estimated number of words known for each morphologically defined word type as a function of grade. From J.M. Anglin (1993), Vocabulary development: A morphological analysis. *Monographs of the Society for Research in Child Development*, 58(10), 65.

Children continue to learn new words throughout the preschool period and into the school years. Anglin (1993) has estimated that, on average, children's vocabularies grow from 11,000 words at age 6 to 20,000 words at age 8 and to 40,000 words at the age of 10 years. Anglin derived his estimates by asking children to define a carefully selected set of words that represented the different classes of word and so he was not only able to provide an estimate of total vocabulary but also of vocabulary composition. Figure 8.8 summarises Anglin's findings and shows that, from grade 3 (age 8 years) to grade 5 (age 10 years), the greatest increase was in the number of derived words that the children knew. Having learned the root word, the children were then able to work out the meaning of others words derived from the root. Although first graders (of 6 years) could do this to some extent (particularly with prompting), the fifth graders were very proficient. Here are two examples from Anglin's study in which a first- and a fifth-grade child explain the meaning of *sourer*:

First-grade child (p. 89)

Adult:	Can you tell me what the word sourer means?
Child:	Um, a lemon's sour.
Adult:	Mmm.
Child:	And more than um an orange.
Adult:	And when you say that a lemon is sour, what do you mean by the word sour?
Child:	Well I mean that I taste it um, you don't hardly like it ...
Adult:	Can you use the word sourer in a sentence to show me you know what it means?
Child:	A lemon is s-, sourer than an orange.

Fifth-grade child (p. 91)

Adult:	What does the word sourer mean?
Child:	Like you eat something and it tastes really like, not sweet ... like you can hardly keep it in your mouth. It's like a lemon. A lemon tastes like that. And gum ... and then there's other gums and they really taste sour ... sourer.
Adult:	Can you tell me anything more about the word sourer?
Child:	Say you have something ... say you have a lemon and it's sour and you have something ... a plum—and it's sourer than the lemon. So it's really worse than the lemon. It's really bad to eat.

What Anglin's study shows is that an understanding of morphological relationships is important for continuing vocabulary growth just as it is for the growth of grammatical competence. Research into reading ability has also highlighted an understanding of morphology as a key component in the development of good spelling skills (see Chapter 12, Learning to Read and Spell).

Conclusion and summary

Towards the end of the second year of life children begin to acquire morphology. The acquisition of morphological knowledge marks an important milestone in language development because it is an essential component of mastering grammatical rules and also in the development of vocabulary. Evidence from chimpanzee studies suggests that the ability to master morphology remains a uniquely human ability.

Both inside-out and outside-in theorists have attempted to explain how morphological and syntactic knowledge is acquired. Inside-out theorists argue for innate, language-specific knowledge, while outside-in theorists claim the children learn language on the basis of more general processes that are cognitive or social in origin. There is considerable evidence that children are able to extract and generalise—and overregularise—morphological regularities and to categorise types of word according to their grammatical function, but the root of this ability remains a continuing source of controversy.

Recent studies of the influence of linguistic input on morphological development have found that children can make use of negative evidence, which signals that they have produced an incorrect from. This suggests that children can correct their own speech following to produce, for example, *hit* rather than *hitted*. However, it is important to remember that effects such as these are found for grammatical forms that children are already in the process of mastering, and attempts to encourage children to produce adult forms that are well outside their competence will invariably fail.

Further reading

- Barrett, M. (1999). *The development of language*. Hove, UK: Psychology Press. This edited book provides chapters on different aspects of language development. The chapters are written for undergraduates.
- Bishop, D. (1997). *Uncommon understanding: Development and disorders of language comprehension in children*. Hove, UK: Psychology Press. Although this book focuses on the development of specific language disorders, it provides a good insight into normal language development and assessment.
- Fletcher, P., & MacWhinney, B. (1995). *The handbook of child language*. Oxford, UK: Blackwell. This book is written for advanced undergraduates but it is an excellent starting point for finding out about the development of languages other than English.
- Hoff-Ginsberg, E. (1997). *Language development*. Pacific Grove, CA: Brooks-Cole. Provides an introduction to language development for undergraduates.
- Pinker, S. (1994). *The language instinct: The new science of language and mind*. London: Penguin Books. This influential book, which was written for a lay audience, provides a strongly nativist account of language development.

CHAPTER 9

CONTENTS

Cognitive development in the preschool years

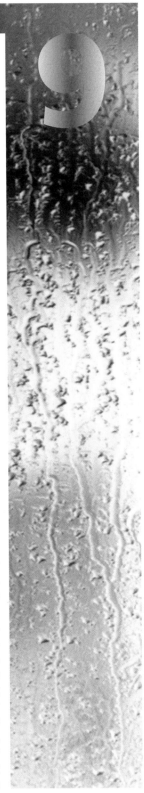

In this chapter we will consider some of the major changes that occur in the cognitive abilities of preschool children. We are taking this period as spanning the ages from two to six years. In most countries children do not begin formal schooling until they reach the age of six or even older and, as we will see, this age marks a major transition in ability. Rather unusually formal schooling begins from the age of five years in the United Kingdom and it remains an open question as to whether this is an appropriate age.

The major changes that occur in cognitive ability at age six were first highlighted by Piaget. We begin this chapter by describing Piaget's account of preoperational reasoning and then discuss some of the criticisms of his argument. We then go on to consider some more recent work on children's reasoning abilities during this period and their ability to distinguish appearance from reality. Finally we consider the development of children's drawing ability in the preschool period.

Piaget's theory of preoperational reasoning

In Piaget's theory, the period from two and a half to six years is known as the *preoperational stage*. According to Piaget, the preoperational period is a time during which children gradually acquire systematic, logical thinking, although many important developments do not occur until after six when children move into the next stage of *concrete operations*.

According to Piaget, the main changes that occur during the preoperational period are in the organisation of thinking into a system of mental operations. By the end of the sensorimotor stage (see Chapter 5, Cognitive Development in Infancy) the infant has developed complex co-ordinated actions but these have not yet been internalised as mental operations. Mental operations, according to Piaget, are the internalised forms of actions that the infant has already mastered, for example in ordering, combining, and separating things in the physical world. Although the young child can reason about simple problems, the system of mental operations lacks critical linkages, such that it is not totally internally consistent. For instance, the child may not be able to reverse the logic of a train of thought. So, for example, the three-year-old knows that she has an older brother, but she may not realise that the relationship simultaneously entails her brother having a younger sister! In this example, thinking proceeds in only one direction and is irreversible.

The key feature of preschool-age thinking, according to Piaget, is that the child is able to focus only on one salient feature of a problem at a time. Piaget argues that the child is dominated by the immediate appearance of things and, as a consequence, thought is prelogical. The limitations of thinking in the preoperational stage are best illustrated by children's performance in **conservation tasks**. These were invented by Piaget as a way of showing the limitations of preschool children's thinking. The conservation tasks are so effective at demonstrating the difference between a preoperational child and one who has acquired concrete operations that they have become one of the most well-known aspects of Piaget's very extensive research.

Conservation tasks, as their name implies, test children's ability to apply the principle of conservation. To have the concept of conservation means that the child understands that the basic properties of matter—volume, number, and weight—are not altered by superficial changes in their appearance. The best-known example is probably conservation of volume, which involves judgements about the amount of water in three transparent containers, A, B, and C.

In Piaget's original conservation task the experimenter begins by showing two equal quantities of water in identical beakers A and B. Children will tell you that the amount of water is the same. Then B is poured into a third beaker C, of different shape, so that the water level is higher (or lower) than before. Preschool children will then say there is more water in the jar with the higher level. This is because they have failed to compensate a change in the height of the liquid by the change in the width that results from the water being poured into a differently shaped jar. Nor can children of this age understand the important principle of **reversibility**, that is, if the water is poured back into the original jar then the level will once again be the same. Preoperational children are said not to be able to imagine the sequence of changes in the appearance of the water in the successive jars that would accompany a reversal of the height of the liquid to its original level.

The same lack of conservation arises with experiments on number (discontinuous quantity), where rows of counters are said to change in numerosity depending on their arrangement in space and even the length of a piece of string (continuous quantity) is said to depend on whether it is stretched out straight or coiled! Figure 9.1 shows some examples of Piagetian conservation problems.

As you might expect, the limitations of thinking in preschool children are very widespread and can be illustrated in many tasks other than those involving conservation. Another well-documented task is the class inclusion problem, which is a test designed to assess whether the child can simultaneously think about parts and wholes. For example, the child is shown a necklace of ten wooden beads, seven of which are painted brown and three white. Piaget asks the child "Are there more brown beads or beads?" The child typically answers that there are more brown beads than beads. Piaget says that when the child thinks about the whole class (beads) she cannot simultaneously think about the parts (i.e. the subsets brown beads, white beads). The child can compare parts with parts but not parts with wholes because thinking remains a succession of

KEY TERMS

Conservation tasks: Tests designed to see whether the child understands that some properties of an object or substance remain fundamentally the same even when there are external changes in shape or arrangement.

Reversibility: The child has an understanding that actions can be reversed.

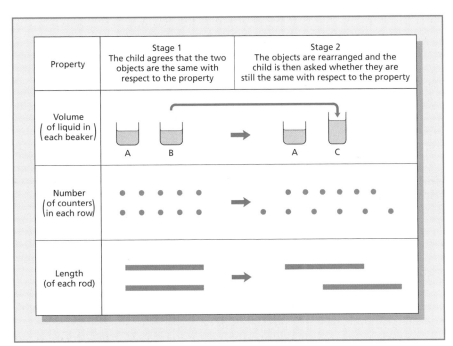

FIG. 9.1 Examples of Piagetian conservation problems.

separate views of things (these are called "centrations" in Piaget's terminology). This separation precludes reasoning about the relations between parts and whole.

Further evidence of preoperational children's inability to compare different views comes from his studies of **egocentrism**. At its simplest, egocentrism can be defined as looking on the world only from one's own position. It implies an inability to differentiate between one's own point of view and other possible points of view. As Piaget described it, this involves an inability to decentre from a particular point of view. In general, egocentrism means that the child is unable to differentiate what is **subjective** (this means what is strictly private or personal) from what is **objective** (i.e. a matter of public knowledge, something we know for certain to be true). It is just as well to be clear that egocentrism does not refer to selfishness as a personality trait. It is simply the unconscious adoption of one's own perspective through failure to realise that other perspectives exist.

Piaget's most famous demonstration of egocentrism comes in preschool children's performance in the three mountains task devised by Piaget and Inhelder (1956). The task involves children assessing both their own viewpoint of a mountain and that of an observer who is at a different position from themselves. Children's performance in the three mountains task is described in the box overleaf.

A final example of Piaget's investigation of thinking in preschool children comes from his interviews in which children were asked probing questions about their understanding of **animism**. Animism can be defined as attributing life to inanimate objects. Piaget (1929/1973) argued that children's answers do not simply reflect lack of knowledge. In his view children egocentrically assimilate what they do not understand to something that they do.

KEY TERMS
Egocentrism: To consider the world entirely from one's own point of view.
Subjective: Private or personal knowledge.
Objective: Public knowledge; true.
Animism: The attribution of feelings to non-living things.

Piaget's three mountains task

Piaget and Inhelder developed the three mountains task in their laboratory on the shores of Lake Geneva. A large mountain, called La Saleve, is visible across the lake from the city of Geneva and it is known to everyone locally, including the children tested by Piaget and Inhelder. The three mountains task uses a 3-D model of the mountain and surrounding peaks. In the diagram in Figure 9.2 a child is seated at position A and asked to represent both her own view and the view of a doll placed at positions B, C, and D. Children can be questioned about their own perspective and that of the doll either by arranging three pieces of cardboard shaped like the mountains, selecting the doll's view from one of ten pictures depicting different points of view or by choosing one picture and deciding where the doll must sit with respect to the model to have that view.

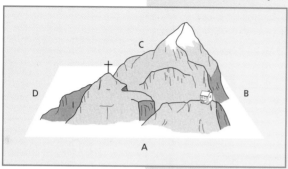

FIG. 9.2 Piaget's three mountains task; one mountain has a cross on top, another a house, and another a peak covered in snow. Children of various ages had to choose an appropriate photograph of the view for a person standing at locations A, B, C, and D.

Piaget and Inhelder described a sequence of stages in the development of perspective-taking ability. Children of under four years old simply do not understand the meaning of the questions. Between four and six years children fail to distinguish between their own view and a doll's view. Consequently they always choose their own view whatever the perspective of the observer. The first signs of discrimination between viewpoints occur at about six years when children show that they are aware of the distinction but cannot specify what it is. Between seven and nine years, when children are in the stage of concrete operations, they are able to understand some relationships between their own viewpoint and that of the doll. Initially it is the relationship between being in front of or behind the mountain that they can recognise but transformations in the left–right perspective remain problematic. It is not until eight years that children become capable of dealing with all changes in perspective. All the transformations involved in a change of viewpoint are considered simultaneously and the child gives the right answer.

In this classic demonstration, then, children below eight years are considered egocentric because they are "rooted in their own position" and cannot imagine any position other than their own.

In Aristotle's original definition, animism refers to the view that the "soul (anima) is the cause or principle of life" (Baldwin, 1905). Animism is said to be characteristic of children's thinking until about the age of 10 years. According to Piaget, anything that has no obvious physical cause is believed by the preschool child to be in some way animated. Piaget suggests that children indiscriminately take activity as a criterion for life and they consequently attribute intentions to anything that can move, even inanimate objects like the wind, or a candle flame. He gave many charming examples of animistic thinking from his interviews with young children. Here is one:

Piaget: *Can the wind feel anything?*
Child: *Yes.*
Piaget: *Why?*

Child: *Because it blows.*
Piaget: *Can the water feel anything?*
Child: *Yes.*
Piaget: *Why?*
Child: *Because it flows.*

Questioned closely by Piaget, the child seems to attribute life to inanimate objects because they show spontaneous movement. To be sure, this is not a bad criterion for being alive, but it is incomplete. Piaget says children assimilate the world to their own ego and in that sense thinking is intuitive rather than fully rational. Here is another example:

Piaget: *What does the sun do when there are clouds*
          and it rains?
Child: *It goes away because it is bad weather.*
Piaget: *Why?*
Child: *Because it doesn't want to be rained on.*

This example also shows egocentrism because the child attributes both will and consciousness to an inanimate object.

Criticisms of Piaget's tests of preoperational thinking

At first sight, then, preschool children are quite illogical in their failure to reason about simple conservation or class inclusion problems or to differentiate their own point of view from that of others. But to what extent are children being led into these answers by the manner of questioning or by the rather abstract tests of reasoning that Piaget devised? It may not be the case that children actually believe that the volume of a liquid changes when it is poured from one container to another or that inanimate objects are alive. Piaget's results might have other explanations.

One possibility is that young children, who have limited knowledge of the physical world, may not yet understand relatively complex terms such as "alive" or "same" and simply make an intelligent guess when confronted with a question that they do not fully understand. It could even be that the very questions that are asked by the adult steer them towards one answer rather than another. If such problems significantly affect preschool children's performance in Piagetian tasks then simplified versions of the same tasks—involving more familiar scenarios and less complex language—might reveal unsuspected abilities.

Critics of Piaget, especially Margaret Donaldson (1978) and, more recently, Siegal (1997) take the view that much of children's difficulty in reasoning stems not from an inability to think logically, precisely for the reasons that we have hinted. Donaldson has argued that the traditional Piagetian tasks make little sense to the preschool child while Siegal has shown that performance may be strongly affected by relatively subtle changes to the wording of questions that children are asked. Their arguments are quite subtle. It is not just that the child lacks knowledge of language which leads them into error: Children's errors arise in an active attempt to discover what the adult actually means by the questions being asked in the social context established for the task.

In her book, *Children's Minds* (1978), Margaret Donaldson argues that preschool children are very much more competent than Piaget gives them credit for. She suggests that Piaget's testing situations are too abstract and do not connect with young children's everyday, social experience. Consequently, performance in the standard Piagetian tasks underestimates children's ability to reason. Donaldson suggests, instead, that children should be tested in situations that make "human sense" to them. By human sense she means that the child should be tested on problems that are couched in the social terms familiar to the child in everyday life, rather than in the abstract rather unfamiliar ways that have been adopted.

Donaldson argues that young children do understand other people's feelings and so socially based tasks that tap this ability will give a rather different estimate of preschoolers' thought processes than Piaget's rather "cold-blooded" tests of intellectual development. One example, that she discusses extensively in her book, is an experiment on childhood egocentrism by Hughes in which a child has the task of "hiding" a boy doll from a policeman doll. The task is shown in Figure 9.3. It comprises a model made of two walls, intersecting as a cross. Children aged from three and a half to five years played a game which involved hiding a boy doll in one of the quadrants formed by the walls, so that the boy doll could not be seen from the position of a policeman doll, also placed in the model. In the example shown in Figure 9.3a two quadrants were visible and two hidden from the policeman's position. In Figure 9.3b, with two policemen, only one hiding place (location C) is concealed from the gaze of the policemen.

Even the youngest children (aged three) were 90% correct in identifying whether the policeman doll(s) could see the boy. In more complex arrangements, with up to six sections of walls and three policemen stationed at various positions, four-year-olds still showed 90% correct performance. These results seem impossible to reconcile with Piaget's theory that the egocentric child cannot understand the possibility of other points of view.

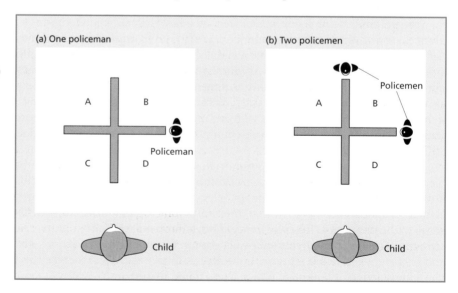

FIG. 9.3 Hughes' perspective-taking task, showing the experimental set up for (a) the one-policeman condition and (b) the two-policemen condition. Adapted from Donaldson (1978).

However, to evaluate Donaldson's claims about the implications of this task more carefully it is necessary to distinguish between two aspects of the test. We need to ask (1) whether children are aware that independent viewpoints exist and (2) whether the child can imagine what someone else would see from a different position.

Donaldson's results provide convincing evidence that even the youngest children could appreciate the possibility of different viewpoints. This must mean that preschool children cannot be considered completely egocentric. However, as was discussed earlier (see Chapter 7, The Beginnings of Language Development), babies can work out where someone else is looking or pointing. So, the ability discovered in Hughes' task may, in part, be explained by a relatively elementary understanding based on knowledge of lines of sight and in part by knowledge of hidden objects. Young children may be able to say whether the boy would be visible or invisible from the various positions of the policemen simply by working out whether the policeman's line of sight is blocked by a wall. Thus, the non-egocentric skills in determining whether another person's viewpoint is occluded or not, which four-year-olds demonstrate in the policeman task, may actually require only a slightly more advanced level of understanding of spatial relationships than the skills already demonstrated when babies search for a hidden object. The ability demonstrated may not require the child to imagine the particular view that would be perceived from any particular position.

In other words, Donaldson may not be correct to argue that her simplified task, in making human sense, is equivalent in difficulty to Piaget's three mountains task. In the latter case, the question is not whether something can be perceived but what can be perceived from positions other than the child's own.

In a review of this area, Cox (1991) discusses what young children can represent. She agrees both with Piaget and with Donaldson that the three mountains task requires the simultaneous co-ordination and transformation of a number of spatial relations in the display. She argues that young children do have the capacity to understand that points of view can be different for different people looking at the same scene (see the previous box, on page 188). However, young children do have difficulty in determining precisely what can be experienced from a different perspective. Here the problem she identifies is that different perspective-taking tasks may be of differential difficulty. For example, with objects such as a doll that have an easily identifiable front, back, and sides, children may find it relatively easy to specify what would be seen from any position. In the three mountains task, however, not only are the mountains symmetrical (i.e. they do not have a "front" and "back") but also children must imagine the relationship between them. Furthermore, the mountains occlude each other differently, from different viewpoints. The requirements of the three mountains task are thus much more complex than the policeman test.

Cox concludes that knowing how more complex scenes of this kind appear to another observer is rather a late appearing ability. However, she does suggest that children between four and six years tend to select their own view in the three mountains task simply because this happens to be the view that differentiates the three mountains most clearly. Children are not "stuck" with their own view, as some interpreters of Piaget imply. Rather, children choose the best view of the scene. All of this leaves Piaget's concept of spatial egocentrism partly intact and partly modified. The modified aspect is that even four-year-old children understand that different viewpoints on the world exist. However, Piaget is on stronger ground in arguing that there are stages in the child being able to specify what can be seen from any particular viewpoint other than the child's own.

The fact that Donaldson, Siegal, and many other critics may be on much stronger ground than Piaget concerns the contextual effects of social interaction and language on children's performance on typical Piagetian tasks. Here, the basic argument is that young children don't necessarily know what words mean in the test interview, independently of the context in which they are uttered. In fact, the context is essential to the child in interpreting what the adult intends.

Interestingly, Siegal (1997) notes that Piaget was very aware of the difficulties inherent in asking children questions and his aim was always to ask questions that were similar to those that children of the age being tested would spontaneously ask. Piaget also sought to avoid repeated questioning and lengthy interviewing. The problem remains, however, that it is not always possible to be sure that children have interpreted a question exactly as the experimenter intended without very careful testing of question wording. For example, Karmiloff-Smith (1979) showed that relative terms like "same" and "different" and "all" are not fully understood until children are around the age of six years. For example, three-year-olds interpret *same* as meaning the "same kind" so, when asked to act out (using small toys) a sentence in which a boy pushed a cow and then "a girl pushed the *same* cow", they will first touch one cow and then a different but identical one. Understanding of "same"—and of *other*—slowly develops over the next three years so that, by the age of six years, children could reliably interpret both terms correctly.

Siegal (1997) discusses how children's responses can be influenced not only by the way that questions are worded but also by the conversational context. He points out that the repeated questioning that characterises standard conservation tests violates the normal rules that govern conversation. For example, the very act of asking whether something is "the same" implies that it is not since the question is otherwise redundant.

Siegal cites a study by Siegler (1995) in which children aged between four and a half and six years were given a series of conservation problems. All the children were unsuccessful on the conservation tasks—as you might expect—but then they were given one of three kinds of training. One group was given feedback on the accuracy of their responses, a second was also given feedback but in addition they were asked to explain their reasoning, and the third group was asked to explain the reasoning behind the experimenter's judgement of their own answer. The children in the third group performed best and Siegler's analysis of the overall responses in his study suggested that being encouraged to take on the perspective of the experimenter contributed most to children's developing insights into the nature of conservation. Siegal argues that the reason for the efficacy of this third condition is that it sets a context for the repeated question asking, since they can see why the experimenter behaves as he does in the task. Siegal argues for an experimental context in which the child and experimenter can collaborate in their search for the correct answer rather than the traditional relationship in which children may be induced to provide an answer that they know to be incorrect.

The now famous McGarrigle and Donaldson (1974) "naughty teddy" study can be seen as providing a more naturalistic context for the number conservation task. As in the original task, the experimenter sets out two rows of counters and these are adjusted until children agree that both contain the same number. Then, under the control of the experimenter, a glove puppet known as "naughty teddy" rushes in and moves the counters in one row so that it is now longer than the other row. Children are then asked whether the two rows contains the same or a different number of counters. In the standard conservation task most children between four and six years think that the number of counters has changed, but they give the correct answer, that the number of counters remains the same in the two rows, when "naughty teddy" has moved the counters

When the adult deliberately rearranges the display, and asks repeated questions about number, the child is likely to assume that this action is related to the question about whether the number is the same or different. However, when the rearrangement is made to appear accidental, children are less likely to assume that Teddy's action is directly related to the question that is being asked and so will say what they think the answer is.

It would appear, however, that the "naughty teddy" task also has its own methodological problems that make it difficult to interpret the apparent improvement in children's performance. Moore and Frye (1986) used this paradigm to explore five-year-olds' performance in both the standard task (where "naughty teddy" rearranges the counters) with an alternative version where additional counters were added. The children behaved as they had done in the original McGarrigle and Donaldson study when the counters were rearranged, and so were able to appropriately conserve number. However, the children gave an incorrect response in the condition where more counters were added and said that the number remained the same. Moore and Frye also showed that giving the children a reason to ignore the intention of the experimenter in asking the question did not improve their performance as would have been predicted by McGarrigle and Donaldson's explanation. Thus it would appear that, at five, children are still have significant problems in distinguishing length from number in this counter conservation task.

Another aspect of Piaget's account of thinking in preoperational children that has been criticised is his claim about animistic thinking. Carey (1985) showed that four-year-olds are often inconsistent in their attributions of animism. For example, children sometimes say that a table is alive because it has legs and, at other times, that it is not alive because a table does not have a face and therefore cannot breathe. Such anthropomorphic justifications are as common as those couched in terms of movement or activity and seem to reflect judgements based on the familiar properties of living people.

Carey suggests that young children may judge the meaning of the word "alive" by comparison with things being "dead" or out of existence. For example, she describes an interview with a four-year-old who said "A ball is living when it goes up in the air but when the ball goes down it dies dead" or "The moon is dead today but tonight it lives". Being in motion or being observable seem to be the criteria the child adopts in these cases. Functional properties are also associated with the child's concept of life: "A table is alive because you can eat on it". Such justifications, in terms of observable or functional properties are biologically relevant in the sense that they highlight existential criteria and they also underscore the salience of other people as exemplars of living things. Thus, Carey's four-year-olds do have an idea of animate versus inanimate objects, based on autonomous movement and functional integrity, but they do not have a well-formed concept of living things as distinct from inanimate objects. Consequently, they will sometimes deny that plants are alive because plants don't move or they will say that a button is alive because it can fasten things. The implication is that children have an intuitive biology but they simply don't know enough biology to classify plants and animals into the single superordinate category of living things.

Finally, it has been suggested by Carey that animism in childhood might be an attempt to characterise the world by an intuitive biology, rather than as the result of incomplete logical development. Both for adults and children there are unclear cases of what is alive when it may be necessary to consult an expert biologist for a decision. Strict rules apply, based on morphology, the means of reproduction, digestion, and so on. In marginal cases, to determine whether some aspects of nature are animate or inanimate is a difficult task. Young children are, in a sense, grappling with a similar problem at the outset of acquiring their biological knowledge.

Problem solving

Children's ability to solve problems undergoes significant changes between the ages of two and six years. The first systematic attempts begin with means–ends analysis during infancy (see Piaget's Theory of Infant Cognition, in Chapter 5) when nine-month-old babies will pull on a cloth in order to retrieve a toy that they cannot reach directly (Willatts, 1990). Means–ends problem solving imposes a high cognitive load because of the necessity to generate, order, and remember subgoals. This was clearly demonstrated by Bullock and Luetkenhaus (1988) who studied young children's ability to stack disks in order to copy a tower built by an adult. The youngest group (aged 17 months) were able to stack disks but did not attempt to copy the adult model. Copying was not evident in most children until 26 months. A similar pattern of development was evident in the children's monitoring of their own performance and their correction of mistakes. At 17 months, just under half the children corrected the position of a single disk on at least one trial but only 9% showed evidence of monitoring the overall outcome. By 26 months almost all children corrected the position of at least one disk and 85% carefully stacked all the disks on at least one trial. The most interesting aspect of this study was the children's reaction to their own performance. Only 36% of 17-month-olds smiled or frowned after building their tower but among the oldest children, aged 32 months, such reactions were evident in 90% of cases. This suggests that, as children approach the age of three, they are beginning to understand that there is a correct solution to a problem.

Means–end problem solving clearly develops significantly in the early toddler years but many important changes in children's ability do not occur until the preschool period. For older children the Tower of Hanoi puzzle is often used to study means–ends problem solving. The puzzle (shown in Figure 9.4a) can be made more or less difficult and in its most challenging form can continue to pose a problem for adults. On the first peg there is a series of disks of increasing size, placed with the largest disk at the bottom. The children's

playdoh:cut playdoh) can even be completed by three-year-olds. Much of the difficulty of an analogy lies in recognising the correspondence between the new problem and that encountered earlier. This was well illustrated by Brown, Kane, and Long (1989) who gave four- and five-year-old children the "Genie" problem invented by Holyoak, Junn, and Billman (1984). In this task a genie needs to move some precious jewels to a new location. In order to avoid damaging the jewels he must move them by rolling his magic carpet into a tube and then rolling the jewels through it. In the study by Brown et al. the children were shown the Genie problem with the aid of toy props. The magic carpet was represented by a sheet of paper. The children and experimenter acted out the solution. One group of children also answered questions that were intended to allow them to extract the goal structure of the problem: "Who has a problem?", "What did the genie need to do?", and "How does he solve this problem?" A control group did not receive the questions.

Having gone through the solution to the Genie problem the children were than given another problem involving an "Easter bunny" who needed to deliver a lot of Easter eggs to children. He needed the help of a friend, as he had left the delivery rather late, but the friend was on the other side of the river from the bunny. This meant that the eggs had to be transported across the river but they had to be kept dry. The bunny had a blanket (represented by a piece of paper) and the solution, by analogy with the Genie problem, was to roll up the paper into a tube so that eggs could be rolled across to the other side of the river.

Brown et al. found that 70% of the children who had answered the questions while seeing the solution to the Genie problem spontaneously saw the analogy between the earlier problem and the new one, whereas only 20% of the children in the control group, who had not answered the questions, did so. This highlights the difference between merely having appropriate experience and realising that this experience is relevant to a new problem. Brown et al. argue that what is important is for children to have represented the relational structure of the previously encountered problems in memory. Questioning by the experimenter allowed children to uncover the relational structure.

Goswami (1998) notes that these findings have important implications for education because they suggest the children learn best when they are given a series of examples of a particular concept within an explicit framework that emphasises the relational similarity among the examples. Teaching in this way actively encourages children to look for analogies. Studies of the teaching of maths in different countries provides evidence of the importance of such an approach since children seem to learn better when they are required to think about solutions and their general applicability (see Chapter 13, Learning to Do Mathematics).

Recent research shows that, with suitable examples, preschool children are also capable of **syllogistic reasoning**. Syllogistic reasoning requires deduction from premises to a conclusion, as in the following example from Dias and Harris (1990, p. 308):

All cats bark.
Rex is a cat.
Does Rex bark?

KEY TERM
Syllogistic reasoning: The inference of a logical conclusion from two premises.

The answer is, of course, "Yes Rex does bark", since this is the only conclusion that can be drawn from the two premises. Note that, in this example, the conclusion is actually inconsistent with real world knowledge. If children's ability to deduce a conclusion from premises is to be assessed it is essential that they are given examples where they cannot guess the correct answer on the basis of their general knowledge. However, it is equally important that the deduction of the premise seems sensible to children so, when Dias and Harris presented this and other syllogisms, they explained to the children that they should pretend they were on another planet where everything was different. The premises were said by the experimenter using a special intonation that emphasised the make-believe setting. Under these conditions four- and five-year-old children were able to solve the syllogisms and in a follow-up study (Dias & Harris, 1990), even four-year-olds could deduce the correct conclusion. However, when the same premises were presented without any appropriate context, five- and six-year-olds were not able to solve the syllogisms correctly unless they involved real world knowledge such as:

> All cats miaow.
> Rex is a cat.
> Does Rex miaow?

Evidence from deductive reasoning studies like this one provides another example of children's superior performance with a task that makes sense rather than a task that is purely logical.

Appearance and reality

In Chapter 5, Cognitive Development in Infancy, we considered the idea that perception puts children in direct contact with the real world. The argument is that, since perception specifies the real world, developing children are necessarily dependent on what they perceive in order to build up a fund of knowledge. However, appearances can be deceptive. Piaget asked whether children can conceive of the possibility that perception may be misleading or whether they inevitably take whatever they perceive to be real.

The difference between appearance and reality runs through many aspects of cognition. One key study in this area was carried out by Flavell and his colleagues (Flavell, Miller, & Miller, 1993). They showed children a piece of sponge that had been carefully painted to look like a rock. The child was allowed to squeeze the "rock" and discover that it was actually spongy. The child was then asked two questions. The first was a **reality question** ("What is this, really? Is it really a rock or really a piece of sponge?") and the second an **appearance question** ("When you look at this with your eyes right now, does it look like a rock or does it look like a piece of sponge?").

The majority of three-year-olds gave a similar answer to both questions: They thought that the object was really a sponge and that it looked like a sponge. By contrast, the majority of four-year-olds were able to state that it really was a sponge but it looked like a rock. Perner (1991) has reviewed many studies of this type and suggests that the realism of the three-year-olds leads them to understand the question in the following fashion: "When you look at this right now, are you looking at a rock or looking at a piece of sponge?" and, naturally, they answer "A piece of sponge". By four years, however, children are beginning to acquire a notion of misrepresentation and they can understand how the sponge can look "as if" it is a rock.

A particularly striking study of the appearance and reality distinction, that supported Piaget's original observations, was carried out by De Vries (1969). De Vries had a very well-behaved black cat called Maynard. Three-year-olds were encouraged to play with Maynard and get to know him. Then, Maynard's face was placed behind a screen, although his tail was still visible, and a realistic mask of a dog was strapped onto the cat's head. De Vries told each child: "Now this animal is going to look quite different. Look, it has a face like a dog." When the screen was removed she asked the child "What kind of animal is it now?" "Is it really a dog, can it bark?" Three-year-olds focused almost entirely on the cat's appearance and some said he had actually become a dog. The four- and five-year-olds were confused, whereas six-year-olds did not believe that a cat could become a dog.

These apparently compelling examples of the limits of preoperational reasoning are subject, however, to the same criticisms as the other studies we have already discussed. The experimenter is deliberately misleading children in an attempt to assess their knowledge, and consequently the task may underestimate children's capabilities.

Children's drawing

Another important line of evidence about children's unfolding cognitive abilities comes from studies of their drawings. The significance of children's drawing as a marker of emerging cognitive processes was vividly described by Freeman (1980) in his book, *Strategies of Representation in Young Children.* Freeman showed that the planning strategies used in children's drawings could be experimentally analysed to reveal a developmental progression in the acquisition of the various subskills that are required for successful drawing. These include sequencing, organisation, and orientation. Freeman showed that understanding how these subskills develop allows an understanding of the most striking feature of young children's drawings—that they "look so queer".

This view of the cognitive significance of children's drawing emerged relatively recently in developmental psychology compared with some of the other traditional markers of cognitive development that we have already discussed. The main reason for this relatively recent interest in drawing is that there had previously been a strong tendency to treat children's drawings "as if they were direct translations of mental states and images onto paper" (Thomas, 1995, p. 107). On this (mistaken) view a picture is considered merely as a copy of the scene that is represents. This view, though, is clearly not adequate to explain children's drawings that look very different from what they are representing and which vary with the age of the child. Freeman's (1980) view—and that of later researchers such as Thomas (1995)—is that a more accurate way to think of children's drawing is as a pictorial construction of what they observe. Thomas (1995) argues that pictorial constructions are often copied from memory or from other pictures so that, at a given point in development, children will tend to draw in a rather similar way.

Kellogg (1970) recorded many examples of the drawings children produce between 18 months and three years. During this period children begin to make marks on paper and to progress to a variety of more complex patterns. Such marks cannot be easily identified and Kellogg did not consider them to be representational. However, other authors (e.g. Campbell & Harrison, 1990; Matthews, 1990) have argued that even children of this young age may intend to represent something even though their picture is not recognisable to adult observers. However, this is not always the case and both Luquet (1927) and Freeman (1987) report that young children often change their interpretation of the same drawing from one occasion to the next. Indeed, three-year-old children sometimes complete a drawing before deciding what it is—a phenomenon that Luquet described as "**fortuitous realism**".

Luquet (1927) was one of the first people to study children's drawing. He argued that drawing passes through several stages. Following the "*fortuitous realism*" of the scribbling stage, comes the stage of "**intellectual realism**". Although the drawing of preschool children bears some resemblance to what is being depicted, its primary purpose is to represent an object by symbolic means. Luquet argued that young children, by combining simple geometric elements, are drawing "what they know" rather than what they see.

Intellectual realism gradually gives way to "**visual realism**", as children attempt to master the intricacies of representing life-like three-dimensional objects within the spatial constraints of the two-dimensional picture plane. Freeman and Janikoun (1972) provided some evidence for a transition from intellectual to visual realism. They asked children to draw a cup which was presented in such a way that the handle could not be seen but a prominent feature, a flower decoration on the cup, was in full view. Children below eight years included the non-visible handle and omitted the visible flower decoration from their drawings. They know that a cup has a handle and their drawing symbolically depicts what they know about cups. Children aged over eight years omitted the handle and included the flower, since, it is argued, they draw realistically what they can see from a particular viewpoint. Note however that another interpretation of this study is that the younger child simply prefers to draw the symbol for a cup rather than the cup as seen from a particular viewpoint.

Ingram and Butterworth (1989) showed that children as young as three years would attempt to draw a pair of plain wooden blocks of different sizes from a particular viewpoint. The blocks were presented in different positions (either vertically one on top of the other, horizontally one next to the other, or in-depth, one behind the other). The finished drawings of the vertical pile and of the in-depth file were both drawn in the vertical plane and the finished products were virtually indistinguishable. However, the process of drawing revealed that the children had different pictorial strategies for depicting height and depth. Piles were drawn with the bottom block first, then the second block drawn above and touching the first block. Files were also drawn vertically but the near block was always drawn first and the far one second and not touching the first. Thus even the three-year-olds were preserving something of the specific spatial viewpoint in their drawings. Furthermore, the different temporal order of production of the blocks shows that different spatio-temporal 3D processes may still result in very similar 2D products. Not until about five years of age did the children begin to represent depth by perspectival interposition of the cubes. These data, illustrated in Figure 9.6, show that even young children are attempting a visually realistic depiction which includes the point of view of the observer.

Ingram and Butterworth (1989) showed that this early visual realism can easily be suppressed in favour of intellectual realism. Facial features were added to the blocks so that the pair of blocks resembled a doll. In whatever orientation the blocks with doll features were presented, children between three and seven years always drew the doll vertically. In fact, some of the youngest children drew the featured blocks as a vertical tadpole figure, just a head and legs, even though the model had a body and lacked arms and legs! Such tadpole drawings never occurred with the blocks without features.

It seems that the blocks alone lack any symbolic significance and, hence, even young children can depict them realistically in a drawing. However, as soon as human features are added, the child invariably draws the person schema, in the typical frontal vertical orientation. These data suggest that drawing some types of objects does involve conceptual knowledge, consistent with Luquet's theory of intellectual realism. However, even very young children, at Luquet's stage of fortuitous realism, will draw what they see from a particular viewpoint if the overwhelming effects of the symbolic representation can be circumvented.

Kellogg (1970) collected over 8000 drawings and found that it was possible to classify early drawings into 20 basic types which are very similar worldwide (see Figure 9.7). These simple forms include geometric shapes such as circles, squares, triangles, crosses, and simple combinations such as the mandala (a cross enclosed by a circle) and sun drawings (a circle with straight lines radiating in all directions). These geometric shapes are the basic elements which, in combination, form the first graphic symbols. On this theory, graphic symbols arise from non-symbolic precursors

Other theorists suggest that even the earliest geometric shapes may have symbolic significance for the child. Golomb (1992) argues that simple shapes are non-conventional signifiers in their earliest origins. A circle, for instance, can signify the general solidity of three-dimensional objects. On this view, the perceptual abilities and the motor skills of infancy form the foundations for graphic representation. Golomb (1992) suggests that children move on from scribbling to the use of geometric shapes, like circles in drawing, because the shapes can effectively serve as memory aids for what the representation is intended to depict. Thomas

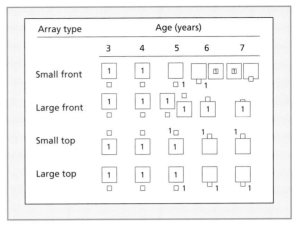

FIG. 9.6 Children's representation of depth in drawing. Reproduced with permission from N. Ingram and G.E. Butterworth (1989), The young child's representation of depth in drawing: Process and product. *Journal of Experimental Child Psychology*, *47*, 356–379.

FIG. 9.7 Children's early drawings. Reproduced with permission from R. Kellogg (1970), *Analyzing children's art*. Mountain View, CA: Mayfield Publishing Company.

FIG. 9.8 A tadpole person.

and Silk (1990) point out that another reason why circles are so universally common in young children's drawings is that they are easy to make.

The circle usually plays an important part in children's early drawings of the human figure. The simplest drawing of a person is a "tadpole figure" comprising a circle for the head and two vertical lines for legs (see Figure 9.8). A little later a differentiated head and trunk will be drawn, sometimes with arms added. Gradually, as children get older, more features are added and the figure becomes more accurately proportioned. It is remarkable that congenitally blind children, when asked to draw the human figure, also do so using combinations of circles and straight lines, just like the sighted child (Millar, 1975).

As Thomas (1995) points out, it seem unlikely that children's knowledge of the human body develops in line with their drawings. Freeman (1987) has shown that four-year-old children do not believe that people really have arms growing out from their heads even though they often depict people in this way. Indeed when discrepancies between a child's drawing and a real person are pointed out the child will often admit that the picture is not an accurate reflection of reality. Another important feature of early drawing of people— and of familiar objects such as a house or a tree—is that they are "schematic" in the sense that children tend to follow the same general plan every time they make a drawing. Thus a four-year-old might distinguish a person from a cat by the addition of hair to the former and a tail to the latter while using identical body outlines, as in the example in Figure 9.9.

The obvious question that immediately follows from the observation that children up to the age of eight make schematic drawings is *why*? One answer is that much of children's drawing is based on copying other pictures. It is certainly the case that children very seldom draw from life and, as we have already noted, there is a great deal of similarity in the pictures drawn by the same child at a particular stage in development. So it seems likely that children tend to copy their own previous efforts. A study by Wilson and Wilson (1984) suggests that the original model for such copies comes from the pictures that are available in a particular culture. They found that children in an Egyptian village drew people using a few distinctive shapes for head and trunk and a standard way of drawing arms and legs. Wilson and Ligtvoet (1992) studied tree drawing in seven- to nine-year-old children in a number of different cultures. There were interesting differences between cultures but high consistency in style within a culture. The authors argue that the strongest influence on style was the pictures that were available for children to copy.

If we accept that culturally available models have a strong influence on children's drawings this still does not explain why depictions in drawing change with age. Thomas (1995) argued that young children have only a small number of schema available and, equally importantly, a limited capacity to adapt them. Silk and Thomas (1986) asked children

FIG. 9.9 A four-year-old's drawing of her cat and herself. The cat and the child have been drawn with identical bodies, arms, and legs, but the cat has been given pointed ears and a tail, while the little girl has a hair band and hair.

of different ages to draw a man and a dog. The youngest children drew the man and the dog according to the same basic formula (see Figure 9.10) but there was increasing differentiation with age. Interestingly, the dog often displayed human features (such as eyebrows) but the man was never depicted with doglike features. Silk and Thomas also found that, even in the youngest children, the dog and man were differentiated by size, with the dog being drawn as smaller than the man, suggesting that the children were fully aware of a need to distinguish the two. Size appears to be one of the first ways in which children first begin to make an accurate distinction in their drawing. Arguably this is because a drawing can be changed in size without modifying the schema.

FIG. 9.10 Drawings of a man and a dog at different ages. Reproduced with permission from A.M.J. Silk and G.V. Thomas (1986), Development and differentiation in children's figure drawings. *British Journal of Psychology, 77,* 399–410.

It is interesting to note, however, that in the drawing shown in Figure 9.9 of Francesca (the author's daughter) and her cat, both are shown of equal size. This may be because the cat in question was the family pet and a very important companion to Francesca. His personal significance was evidenced by the fact that a simplified form of his name—Ta-Ta (Tarquin)—was Francesca's first word to be produced when the cat came into the room. It would be interesting to compare children's drawings of cats and dogs in general with ones that they made of valued family pets to see whether the latter are shown as larger than the former.

How to improve children's drawing of the human figure

The actual sequence in which the parts of a drawing are executed can affect the accuracy of children's drawing. When they are drawing a person most children start at the top and then work down to the bottom of the page since this allows them to see what they have already drawn. Thomas and Tsalimi (1988) were interested in the possibility that this pattern of working might contribute to children's tendency to exaggerate the size of the head. They observed that children would invariably begin with the head and work down if asked to draw a person. Many of the children did not leave sufficient space to complete the rest of their picture to scale. Thomas and Tsalimi managed to persuade some of the children to start by drawing the truck instead and, in every case, the second drawing was more accurate. Some examples are shown in Figure 9.11.

FIG. 9.11 Effects of order of drawing head and trunk on their relative proportions. Reproduced with permission from G.V. Thomas and A. Tsalimi (1988), Effects of order of drawing head and trunk on their relative sizes in children's human figure drawings. *British Journal of Developmental Psychology*, 6, 191–203.

Headfirst Girl (5:5)

Trunkfirst Girl (5:4)

Headfirst Girl (7:9)

Trunkfirst Girl (7:10)

An exceptional talent for drawing

Selfe (1983) studied an autistic child called Nadia who was exceptionally gifted in drawing. By the age of five years Nadia was drawing pictures of horses, cockerels, and cavalrymen from memory in realistic perspective. Nadia lacked language and her gross motor development was very retarded, yet she could produce exquisite drawings. Selfe argues that Nadia's drawings differed so much from those of normal children precisely because Nadia was unable to consider the objects symbolically. She drew the objects in a visually realistic manner, altogether lacking intellectual realism. Figure 9.12a shows Nadia's drawings at the age of three and a half years.

Selfe (1983) subsequently identified a small number of other graphically gifted children, for example, Stephen could draw buildings as complex as the Kremlin Palace in realistic detail, both from memory and directly. She argues that these gifted autistic artists attend particularly to the spatial aspects of the picture in their graphic representations. These autistic children are concerned to represent single fixed viewpoints in elaborate detail and they are able to do so because

FIG. 9.12   Nadia's drawings at (a) age 3½, and (b) age 25. Reproduced with permission from L. Selfe (1995), Nadia reconsidered. In C. Golomb (Ed.), *The development of artistically gifted children: Selected case studies*. Hillsdale, NJ: Lawrence Erlbaum Associates Inc.

there is no interference from symbolic processes that lead normal children to produce drawings that are pictographic.

Since her original study, Selfe (1995) revisited Nadia when she was in her 20s. Selfe found that drawing no longer held the excitement or pleasure for the adult Nadia that it had when she was six years old. When she was coaxed into drawing she drew rather stereotyped and unremarkable pictures (see Figure 9.12b).

Conclusion and summary

Piaget's account of children's thinking in the preschool period, which seeks to describe universal stages of development, emphasises the child's lack of logical consistency, difficulty in adopting others' perspectives, reasoning about appearance and reality, or about cause and effect. An inability to deal with more than one perspective at a time seems to lie at the heart of all these difficulties.

Although Piaget's own observations have been replicated many times, more recent research suggests that, when preschool children are given tasks that are more familiar and less abstract, their performance improves. Donaldson was in the vanguard of contemporary critics of Piaget in her demonstrations that preschool children are more competent in their reasoning than Piaget gave them credit for with tasks that draw on the children's everyday experience. Siegal's work shows that careful choice of language is also important, as is the need to make the experimenter appear less like an inquisitor who knows the right answer.

Research on problem solving also shows that preschoolers' performance improves if the rules that underlie a task, such as the Tower of Hanoi problem, are made more concrete. Children were able to solve the Klahr and Robinson version, which used tin cans, better than the traditional version using disks. Preschool children are also better at adopting a "hill-climbing" strategy than a "means–ends" analysis when they are asked to solve a problem.

Recent research has emphasised individual differences in the use of strategies. These differences exist not only among different children of the same age but also across different domains of knowledge within the same child. Children who have a particular area of expertise typically show much better organisation of information about that topic which they can use to deal with new situations. Preschoolers are good at making analogies between a previous situation and a new one. The problem they often have is in recognising the relationship. Training children to reflect on the goal structure of a problem can improve their ability to make analogies.

Appropriate training can also improve children's drawing abilities. Certainly there is good evidence that preschool children recognise a difference between what they have drawn and how things really are. In other situations, however, they may be unsure of the distinction between reality and appearance, as demonstrated in appearance–reality tasks.

Further reading

- DeLoache, J.S., Miller, K.F., & Pierroutsakos, S.L. (1998). Reasoning and problem solving. In D. Kuhn & R.S. Siegler (Eds.), *Handbook of child psychology: Vol. 2. Cognition, perception, and language* (W. Damon, Gen. Ed.; pp. 801–850). New York: Wiley. This chapter, intended for advanced undergraduates, provides an authoritative account of recent research on the development of problem-solving skills.
- Flavell, J.H., & Miller, P.H. (1998). Social cognition. In D. Kuhn & R.S. Siegler (Eds.), *Handbook of child psychology: Vol. 2. Cognition, perception, and language* (W. Damon, Gen. Ed.). New York: Wiley. This chapter reviews the development of social cognition from infancy through the school years. The chapter is intended for advanced undergraduates.
- Goswami, U. (1998). *Cognition in childhood*. Hove, UK: Psychology Press. This undergraduate textbook is a good introduction to the development of cognition.
- Lange-Kuttner, C., & Thomas, G.V. (1995). *Drawing and looking*. Hemel Hempstead, UK: Harvester. This edited book discusses the development of children's drawing abilities. The chapter by Thomas is particularly useful.
- Selfe, L. (1995). Nadia reconsidered. In C. Golomb (Ed.), *The development of artistically gifted children: Selected case studies* (pp. 197–236). Hillsdale, NJ: Lawrence Erlbaum Associates Inc. Selfe's study of Nadia's outstanding skill at drawing is now well known. In this chapter, Selfe describes a return visit several years later when she discovers that the adult Nadia has lost most of the exceptional skill that she showed as a child. In this chapter, Selfe reflects on the initial reaction to her study of Nadia—diagnosed as autistic—and considers possible explanations for her unusual talents.

CONTENTS

Social development in the preschool years

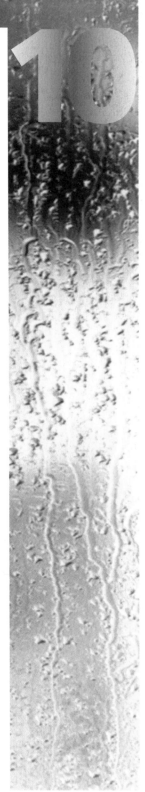

The continuing development of self-recognition

We saw in Chapter 6, Early Social Development, that, by the time they reach the age of two years, children will remove a dab of rouge from their face when they see their own reflection. This has been taken as evidence that children are able to recognise their own reflection by this age. However, recent research by Povinelli, Reaux, Bierschwale, Allain, and Simon (1997) has shown that the process of self-recognition continues to develop over the preschool period. They used a novel variation of the rouge removal task with children aged three, four, and five years to see how children interpret images of themselves on videos.

Povinelli et al. tested children on two successive occasions, one week apart. On the first visit, one experimenter surreptitiously placed a sticker on the child's head and then a video-recording was made of the child playing an unusual game. The sticker was then removed without the child knowing. One week later the same children were filmed playing a different game in a distinctively different location from their earlier visit. Again a sticker was surreptitiously placed on the child's head. Then, after a three-minute delay, half the children were shown the recording made at the previous visit and half were shown the recording made only three minutes before. The point of the two contrasting locations and the choice of different games for each visit was designed to emphasise that two different visits were involved.

After the brief delay the majority of four- and five-year-olds (but not three-year-olds) reached to remove the sticker from their head when they were shown the recording made a few minutes earlier. This showed that they recognised the continuity of self over the three-minute gap. However, when shown the recording made on the previous visit, they were unlikely to try to remove the sticker.

Four- and five-year-olds would also refer to the video image using the first pronoun "me" or their own name. In contrast, the three-year-old often said that the sticker was "on his (or her) head", implying that they did not recognise the continuity of self. This is in marked contrast to their ability to recognise themselves in a mirror—which is well established by two years—when they can rely on the spatio-temporal contiguity between their own action and that in the mirror.

Three-year-olds were as likely to try to remove the sticker when the film was of the session a week earlier as they were when it was of the immediately preceding play session. In other words, they recognised themselves on the video-recording but they did not take into account the contextual information—location and game—that distinguished between a very recent recording and one made a week ago. They treated both older and more recent images as equivalent. Four- and five-year-olds, however, did not treat the images of themselves as equivalent. Almost all older children attempted to remove the sticker in the recent condition while very few attempted to do so when they saw the recording made the week before.

A series of developmental changes may underlie these differences in performance between two and five years (Povinelli, 1995; Povinelli et al., 1997). As we have noted, children can recognise themselves in mirrors (and photographs) by the age of two. But, even at three, young children have difficulty in relating the present self to the past self in delayed visual feedback. This latter situation requires the child to consider two simultaneous perspectives on self—self as it is now and self at a previous time. The capacity to link the present and past self is still incompletely developed at three years. Povinelli (1995) suggests that three-year-old children lack the "duplicated self" that enables older children to connect "me experiencing now" with "me experiencing then". Such an autobiographical self emerges at four. At this age children simultaneously consider the present and immediately past states of self; and previous states of the self can be linked to present states. Thus, by the end of the preschool period, children have developed a sustained view of themselves.

The development of pretend play

We saw in Chapter 6, Early Social Development, that pretend play emerges in the second year of life. During infancy, pretending mainly tends to revolve around object play but, during the preschool years, children begin to expand their abilities as pretend play becomes an increasingly important and elaborate activity. It is common to class pretend play as a cognitive activity—as indeed it is—but what is often overlooked is that the great majority of pretend play is also social. Young children engage in *shared* pretence in which they and a partner move from the real into an imaginary world. From this perspective, pretend play can be viewed as an important social activity.

One reason why there has traditionally been an emphasis on the cognitive significance of pretend play is that Piaget's seminal account is very much concerned with this aspect. Piaget (1936/1952) made extensive observations of his own three children at play in early childhood. We mention some examples later. Piaget used the examples to highlight stages in what he describes as **"symbolic play"**. However, if you read Piaget's examples carefully you can see that his children's imaginary play was often part of a complex social interaction. This is an aspect that Paul Harris (2000) highlights in his recent book, and we will return this important dimension of pretend play at the end of this section.

According to Piaget, the essential difference between the physical play of infancy and the symbolic play of early childhood is that symbolic play serves to practise the imagination. Piaget divided symbolic play into two main stages, up to four years (stage 1) and from four to seven years (stage 2). Stage 1 has three sub-stages.

In sub-stage 1 children project symbolic schemas onto new objects. A symbolic schema is a mental representation that preserves the most distinctive aspects of an object. In the earliest examples of symbolic play, the child applies familiar actions to new objects. For example, Jacqueline at 1;7 said "cry , cry" to her toy dog and imitated the sound of crying. She then went on to make her toy bear and toy duck cry. A few days later she made her hat cry. Such examples illustrate how, in the early stage of symbolic play, young children reproduce their own actions in a make-believe situation.

A second type of symbolic play, observed at the same age, involves projection of imitative schemas onto new objects. These schemas are not derived from the child's own activity, as in the case of Jacqueline making her toys "cry", but they are borrowed from activities that have been observed in other people. For example, when Jacqueline was nearly 22 months old she rubbed the floor with a seashell, then with a cardboard lid, in the manner that she had previously observed the cleaner cleaning the floor.

In these first two types of play that appear in sub-stage 1, the child's action is closely related to the prop. In sub-stage 2 the action becomes increasingly independent of the prop as the child's action (signifier) begins to separate from what is signified. Piaget noted two different types of play in sub-stage 2. The first involves objects but, unlike the examples from sub-stage 1, the identification of the pretend object precedes its use in action and hence the child achieves greater distance from the "here and now" through imagination. Examples of this type of play with objects are again from Jacqueline who, at the age of just over two years, moved her finger along the table and said, "finger walking, horse trotting". At 2;3, she held a brush over her head and said "It's an umbrella".

The second type of play in sub-stage 2 involves games of imitation. At 1;10 Jacqueline pretended to play hide and seek with a cousin, Clive, who was not present and whom she hadn't seen for two months. She pretended to be her cousin and imitated him strutting up and down. At 2;4 she pretended to be her mother and said to Piaget, "Come kiss mummy", and then kissed him. Such imitative games can become very complex. At the age of four Lucienne stood stock still as she imitated the sound of bells. Piaget put his hand over her mouth in an attempt to make her stop. She pushed him away angrily and said "Don't. I'm a church".

In sub-stage 3 play involves the combinations of symbols of increasing complexity. Such play begins when, at the simplest level, the child transposes real scenes with imaginary ones. For example, when she was two and a half years old Jacqueline prepared an imaginary bath, using an empty box as the bath and a blade of grass as a thermometer. She plunged the grass into the big box and declared the water too hot. She waited and then tried again declaring "That's alright, thank goodness". At three and a half she constructed an imaginary ants' nest from pine needles, complete with imaginary furniture, a family of ants, and imaginary macaroni in the cellar.

Towards the end of the preschool period the whole character may be imaginary. At 3;11(20) Jacqueline invented a composite animal that she called "aseau". This animal was part bird, part dog with long hair, and it had moral

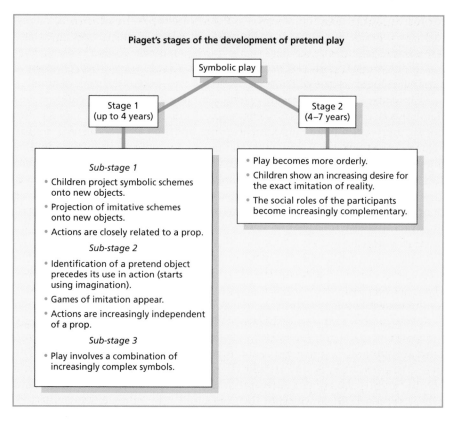

Piaget's stages of the development of pretend play

Symbolic play

Stage 1
(up to 4 years)

Stage 2
(4–7 years)

Sub-stage 1
- Children project symbolic schemes onto new objects.
- Projection of imitative schemes onto new objects.
- Actions are closely related to a prop.

Sub-stage 2
- Identification of a pretend object precedes its use in action (starts using imagination).
- Games of imitation appear.
- Actions are increasingly independent of a prop.

Sub-stage 3
- Play involves a combination of increasingly complex symbols.

- Play becomes more orderly.
- Children show an increasing desire for the exact imitation of reality.
- The social roles of the participants become increasingly complementary.

authority ("You mustn't do that, aseau will scold you"). Piaget says this is an example of "infantile totemism", also described by Freud, as the invention of animals that dispense justice. Piaget also describes many other examples of play in which the child, through make-believe, comes to understand unpleasant situations, or emerges victorious against the threat of failure. In all these cases reality is assimilated to the needs of the ego.

As children move into stage 2, at the age of four years or so, there is an interesting change in this kind of fantasy play. Piaget argues that symbolic play becomes more orderly and children show an increasing desire for exact imitation of reality and the social roles of the participants in symbolic play become increasingly complementary. In one of Piaget's observations, Jacqueline (aged four and a half) decided that she and her sister, Lucienne, would pretend to be Joseph and Therese, two of their local friends. In the course of the play Jacqueline reversed the roles so that she was Therese and Lucienne was Joseph. The play continued with meal-time scenes and other imaginary activities. At this age children spend a great deal of time acting out their everyday activities such as being taught at nursery school, going shopping, or being examined by a doctor.

Given that pretend play has such an important role in the preschool period, it is legitimate to ask what function it serves. Why do young children enjoy pretending and why do they engage in increasingly elaborate games with age? Harris (2000) points out that Piaget saw pretend play as an immature form of thinking that eventually gives way to logical thought. He argues for a very different account, beginning with an important reminder that pretend play does not emerge until the end of infancy—as Piaget observed—by which time young children already have a surprisingly sophisticated understanding of the relationship between make-believe and reality. In other words, "pretend play is not an early distortion of the real world but an initial exploration of possible worlds" (Harris, 2000, pp. 27–28).

Harris describes a number of studies that show the extent to which young children can engage in pretence. For example, two-year-olds can interpret the same prop—a toy brick—as standing for one thing in one game of make-believe—food—and as something else—soap—in a new game. They can also interpret pretend actions as though they have actually happened and so are able to wipe up pretend spillages; and to determine what an animal would look like after being covered with imaginary talcum powder. An even more impressive finding was that, when two-year-olds watched an adult acting out imaginary episodes such as making a naughty teddy pour tea over a toy monkey's head, they described the imaginary action rather than what had actually happened. So they said that naughty teddy had "poured tea over the monkey" rather than saying that teddy had lifted up an empty teapot, lifted it above the monkey, tilted it, and put it down. They also said, when questioned, that the monkey's head was "wet".

Harris argues that young children apply their knowledge of cause and effect in the real world to the play situation. Yet, at the same time, they are aware that the way that cause and effect work during pretence is different from reality. For example, in pretend pouring no liquid is involved. However, children are easily able to join in games of pretence with a play partner where they are engaging in shared pretence in which reality is temporarily suspended. What makes such play rewarding for young children is not only that they are pushing the boundaries of reality, and entering the realm of the imagination, but that they are doing so with a play partner with whom there is a mutual suspension of belief.

Fantasy and imagination

Young children often invent complex fantasies. An important question is whether they draw a firm line between fantasy and reality in the preschool period. As we have noted, Harris (2000) argues that they do. However, there has been some inconsistency in research findings.

One line of evidence suggests that preschoolers reliably distinguish between things that are imagined and those that are real. Woolley and Wellman (1993) found that three- to five-year-olds draw a clear distinction between real physical objects and objects that they have imagined: They understand that you can see, touch, and act upon a real object but you cannot do any of these things with an object that is imaginary. Woolley and Wellman also found that, when three- to four-year-olds were asked to judge whether an object that that they had imagined really existed, most correctly said that is did not.

The other line of evidence comes from Paul Harris and his colleagues who have investigated children's beliefs in monsters and witches. Harris, Brown, Marriott, Whittall, and Harmer (1991) carried out a study in which children aged between four and six years were asked to imagine that there was either a bunny or a monster inside a real box. The experimenter then left the children alone in the room with the box and observed their behaviour with a hidden video camera. Although the children had earlier denied that the monster or bunny were real, a number of them went to look inside the box after the experimenter had gone out. When the children were later questioned about their behaviour they admitted to wondering about the contents of the box. A similar pattern was found by Johnson and Harris (1994) when children were asked to imagine a fairy or ice-cream in a box.

Woolley and Phelps (1994) point out that there a number of methodological differences between these two sets of studies which may explain why they point to different conclusions. The Harris studies involve behavioural as well as verbal measures of children's belief; and they explore attitudes to fantasy figures as well as the imaginary real objects studied by Woolley and Wellman. Woolley and Phelps used a different task from that of previous studies, involving four boxes. The first box that children looked into (real box) contained a real object such as a sock. The second (empty box) was empty. The third box (imagination box) was also empty but children were asked to imagine that there was an object in it that was the same as in the real box (e.g. a sock). The fourth box (unopened box) was never opened. Three items were used across trials. One was positive—an object that the children liked (a toy car), one was negative (a bug), and the third (the sock) was neutral.

Children aged between three and five were asked to look in each box in turn and to imagine that the relevant object was inside the imagination box. The children were then asked if the object was *really* in the box. Then another experimenter came into the room and asked for the object (e.g. a sock) that the children had just imagined. When the children gave the experimenter one of the boxes (which was almost always the real box), she asked the children whether there were any more socks (or toy cars or bugs) in any of the other boxes. This continued until the children said that there were no more objects left.

Woolley and Phelps found an interesting discrepancy between children's response to the question about whether an imaginary object was *really* in the box and their selection of the imagination box to give to the experimenter. Nearly 40% of children aged 3;0 to 3;6 said that the imaginary object really was in the box but only 4% gave this box to the experimenter. Children of over 3;6 said that the imaginary object was really in the box 24% of the time but they chose the imaginary box only 2% of the time.

In a second study Woolley and Phelps asked children to imagine the same objects as before but this time the real box contained a different object. This manipulation significantly increased the number of children who elected to give the experimenter the imaginary box. The younger children (3;11 and under) gave the box to the experimenter 33% of the time while four- and five-year-olds selected it on 14% of trials.

Woolley and Phelps conclude that, although young children have an understanding of the difference between real and imaginary entities, this understanding is fragile and different situations will lead children to respond in different ways. Where magical thinking is encouraged and there is less of a firm grounding in reality, children are more likely to act as though imaginary entities are real. This view is supported by Subbotsky (1994) who questioned four- to six-year-old children about an impossible event—being able to stretch a hand through the glass wall of a box to get at its contents. When the children were initially asked about this event most said that it was impossible but, after they had heard a fairy tale about a glass magic box whose walls could be made "just like air" by saying "magic words", 82% of the four-year-olds, 58% of five-year-olds, and 20% of the six-year-olds said the magic words and tried to reach through the walls of the box when the experimenter went out of the room. Many of these children also expressed disappointment when the magic words had no effect. In a control group, who did not hear the fairy tale, only one child attempted to gain access to the box by magic when left alone.

Imaginary worlds

The verbal imagination can create extensive imaginary worlds. Cohen and MacKeith (1991) collected adults' memories of imaginary worlds of childhood. They found that some people had invented extensive "paracosms" (imaginary worlds) as early as three years of age. These imaginary worlds might be a farm, an island, whole countries, extensive railroad systems, or even Baltic States! They may be secret, or shared with brothers and sisters.

One of the best documented accounts of the creation of childhood paracosms comes from the Brontë children who recorded the events that took place in a number of imaginary worlds, the most famous of which was Gondal. The three Brontë sisters, Charlotte, Emily, and Anne, who later became renowned novelists, and their brother, Branwell, wrote many stories about their imaginary worlds in tiny notebooks. At the time they were writing, in the first half of the 19th century, the detailed documentation of complex adventures taking place in a fantasy kingdom was not unusual. Barker (1994), in her biography of the Brontës, notes that John Ruskin—an exact contemporary of the Brontës—wrote a similar miniature book and the Winkworth children, who grew up in Manchester at the same time as the Brontës, also documented a fantasy land. In all three cases the stories that the children wrote were strongly influenced by their own reading but the Brontës were unusual in their total absorption in their fantasy world. They were also unusual in that the fantasy play that revolved round Gondal persisted into adulthood. Barker records that, as late as their mid 20s, Emily and Anne Brontë spent a long train journey playing out a Gondal fantasy in which they pretended to be escaping prisoners. The obsession with Gondal ultimately bore fruit in Emily's famous novel *Wuthering Heights*, which, according to Barker, is "pure Gondal".

Transitional objects

Play has an important role in emotional development. Many children have a favourite soft toy, or perhaps a piece of cloth, to which they are particularly attached. The cartoon character Linus, in the Peanuts comic strip, carries his security blanket at all times. Psychoanalysts call such favourite things "transitional objects" because they are thought to help the child to bridge the transition between close physical contact with mother in infancy and the movement away from the caretaker as the toddler becomes autonomous. Winnicot (1971) suggests that these special possessions serve as a kind of substitute for the mother. They act as imaginary companions which the child can invest with her own ideas, emotions, hopes, and fears. Psychoanalysts often use symbolic play as a means to reveal the causes of maladjusted children's difficulties.

Gender differences in play

As we have noted, play in the second and third year becomes increasingly social with the beginnings of reciprocal and complementary role taking. Furth and Kane (1992) suggest that symbolic play has the important function of informing children of the societal framework within which they live. By the age of four to five years, child use social play to explore shared societal values, traditions, and customs.

Preschool children use play to explore familiar roles such as teacher, cook, mechanic, bus driver, car passenger, doctor, or nurse. Such functional roles may be combined with family roles of mother or father. Preschool children tend to adopt these roles along gender appropriate lines (Garvey, 1977). Girls typically choose roles normally occupied by females, whereas boys are more likely to take the male part in play. Symbolic play may therefore contribute to the acquisition of gender identity.

Gender is a biological attribute that shapes the social roles that the child can explore in symbolic play. Conventional social roles in turn provide a symbolic framework within which the developing child can explore gender identity. The biological basis of gender is becoming known through modern genetics. The sex chromosomes of female mammals, including humans, are identical XX chromosomes, whereas males have different XY chromosomes. The complex embryological processes and hormonal factors that organise masculine and feminine morphology are well described in Cairns (1979).

Social differentiation of boys and girls occurs in the ways they are dressed, in how they are named, and in the many ways in which parents socialise them. The social learning theorists, Bandura and Walters (1963), argue that parents in many cultures provide play materials that are, wittingly or unwittingly, sex typed. In Western society little girls are given toy kitchens and baby dolls, whereas little boys are given toys cars and Action Man figures. Rheingold and Cook (1975) found that, from age two to age six, boys' bedrooms contained more vehicles, machines, weapons, and sports equipment, whereas girls' bedrooms contained more dolls, dolls' houses, and play household items. The girls' bedrooms also contained more floral furnishings and ruffled fabrics than the boys. Interestingly there was no sex difference in the number of soft stuffed toy animals, which were equally popular with boys and girls.

Children show clear preferences for particular types of toy very early on. Lloyd and Duveen (1990) carried out a study of 120 children aged between one and a half and three and a half years. The children were videotaped while playing with a familiar peer and their choice of toys was noted. The toys included ones that the parents judged to be typically boy toys and others that parents judged as typically girl toys. There was an interesting difference between boys and girls in their toy selection. Boys spent significantly longer playing with boys' toys but girls spent a roughly equal amount of time playing with both types of toy. When the play patterns with same-gender and opposite-gender peers was compared there was another striking difference between boys and girls. Lloyd and Duveen compared the number of toy choices that were congruent with children's own gender (paradigmatic choices) with toy choices that were incongruent with their own gender (syntagmatic choices). Figure 10.1 shows the results of this study. When two boys played together, almost all toy choices were paradigmatic, that is, the boys chose boys' toys. When two girls played together there were slightly more paradigmatic than syntagmatic choices but the difference between the two was considerably less than for the boy–boy pairs. When a boy played with a girl there was similar pattern, that is, the boy chose gender-appropriate toys a little more often than gender-inappropriate. When a girl played with a boy, however, she was likely to choose boy toys more often than girl toys.

Lloyd and Duveen also found evidence of such an asymmetry in a card-sorting task in which children aged between two and six years were asked to decide whether a picture was of a boy toy or a girl toy. The toys had consistently been judged as either masculine (fire engine, construction trucks, fireman's helmet, briefcase, peg bench and hammer, guns, and a garage) or feminine (iron, comb, brush and mirror, large white hat, shopping bag, saucepans and cooker, dolls with cradle, and a teaset) by adults. Four-year-old boys were better at sorting pictures of masculine toys than feminine

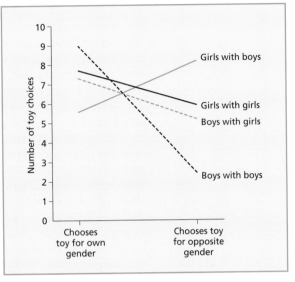

FIG. 10.1 Comparison of toy choices between those congruent with children's own gender and those incongruent with own gender. Adapted from Lloyd and Duveen (1990).

toys whereas girls showed no such difference. As might be expected both boys and girls showed increasing ability with age. Lloyd and Duveen report that children found it easier to sort pictures of people according to gender than to sort toys. Children as young as 18 months could appropriately match the gender-marked nouns mummy, daddy, lady, man, girl, and boy to a picture of a male or a female.

There has been much debate about why girls and boys show differences in play. Part of the reason—as we noted in Chapter 6, Early Social Development—is that parents tend to treat boys and girls differently. Not only do they often provide different toys but they also dress boys and girls differently and give them different hairstyles. Interestingly, although there have been major changes in both of these two aspects of children's appearance over the last century, the appearance of girls and boys still remains distinct, even though girls now often wear trousers and boys wear brighter colours.

The development of gender identity

How is the basic biological predisposition to be male or female channelled in the formation of gender identity? Gender identity is about how children understand and interpret their sex role. Perhaps the best-known theory of the development of **gender identity** is that of Sigmund Freud (1938) who argued that identification with the parent of the same sex is the main process by which the child acquires gender identity. Freud conceived of gender identity as a natural outgrowth of the process of attachment of the child for the mother.

Freud took as a metaphor for gender identification the Sophocles tragedy in which Oedipus unknowingly murders his father and marries his mother. He argued that, between the fourth and sixth year, the male child must resolve the Oedipal conflict. The boy desires to take the place of his father in order to possess his mother sexually. The Electra conflict is the equivalent process for girls. In

Why is it that girls are more likely than boys to play in a toy house? Copyright © Popperfoto.

order to resolve the feelings of guilt and fear that arise from the child's fantasies about replacing the envied parent, the child represses the forbidden desire and identifies with the parent of the same sex. The concept of identification is similar in some ways to imitation, in that boys emulate the father figure, whereas girls emulate the mother, incorporating the admired characteristics of the sex role model into their own identity.

There is a problem however with supposing that masculinity or femininity is a single bipolar dimension. The qualities associated with men and women overlap significantly and any one individual may embody some properties of each. Furthermore, some occupational roles may be arbitrarily related to gender. Some roles are filled by different sexes in different cultures, as in the case of female engineers who are much more common in Russia than in the West. The Freudian account may be limited because it tends to take as a package aspects of personal identity that can be separated. Labelling the self as male or female, the choice of behaviours considered appropriate to a particular sex, identification (wishing to be similar to the same sex parent), and the child's sexual orientation are treated as inseparable aspects of the same process.

Piaget (1936/1952, p. 189) addressed Freud's theory in his observations of the preschool child's play and dreams. Although he readily admits that play may reveal unconscious symbolism in children and that their dreams and nightmares may reveal their fears, he was rather sceptical of Freud's particular interpretation of childhood symbolism. Piaget suggests that the child's conscious intellectual processes may be more important than the unconscious repression of unacceptable thoughts about the parent in arriving at an understanding of gender identity.

Kohlberg (1966), a follower of Piaget's, has argued that the whole process of developing gender identity stems from children's interest in classifying other objects and persons as similarly "girlish or boyish". In his account, gender role development comes about as a consequence of children's attempts to classify the sex role behaviour that they observe.

Kohlberg outlined three stages in this process, beginning with gender labelling, which occurs during the period between two and three and a half years of age. During this first stage children slowly become aware that they are a member of a particular sex. Initially they learn about the labels that are attached to them and then they begin to discover that the same labels apply to other people. This developing understanding goes hand in hand with an increased understanding of gender labels such as *man, woman, boy, girl.*

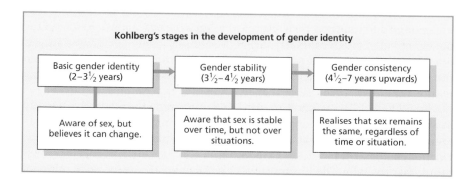

Kohlberg's stages in the development of gender identity

Basic gender identity (2–3½ years)	Gender stability (3½–4½ years)	Gender consistency (4½–7 years upwards)
Aware of sex, but believes it can change.	Aware that sex is stable over time, but not over situations.	Realises that sex remains the same, regardless of time or situation.

Kohlberg's next stage is gender stability, which spans the period from three and a half to four and a half years. In this stage children develop an understanding of the durability of their own gender and that of others. However, they tend to focus on physical appearance and may think that a person who changes into opposite-gender clothes has also changed sex (Emmerich, Goldman, Kirsh, & Sharabany, 1977). As we will see, this tendency to be swayed by appearance in the preschool period is not restricted to children's view about a person's gender. Similar confusions arise when children of this age make judgements about whether a cat is still a cat when it is wearing a dog mask (De Vries, 1969; see Appearance and Reality, in Chapter 9). Gender consistency, the third of Kohlberg's stages, does not appear until around four and a half when children begin to understand that people remain male or female in spite of changes in their appearance.

In a similar vein, Fischer and Lazerson (1984) argue that young children do not understand age or sex roles until about four years. Children can then think about age or sex roles considered separately but dealing with both at the same time may confuse them. For instance, the little boy who says that when he grows up he wishes to become a "mummy" may simply be having difficulty in co-ordinating two aspects of the representation of age and gender. Such cognitive accounts of gender identification very much reduce the significance of the symbolic sexual aspects of Freud's Oedipal theory.

Another alternative to Freud comes from **social learning theory**, which was derived initially from the ideas of the behaviourist school including those of Watson and Skinner (see Learning or Maturation: The Rise of Opposing Schools, in Chapter 2). The ideas behind social learning theory were set out by Bandura and Walters (1963) and subsequently expanded and revised by Bandura (1973, 1977, 1986). Social learning theory emphasises the role of social influences on development, particularly observational learning. Bandura and his colleagues pointed out that children have many potential models for their own behaviour in that of their parents, older siblings, teachers, and familiar figures on television. They argue that, by observing the behaviour of these

KEY TERM

Social learning theory: The view that behaviour can be explained in terms of both direct and indirect reinforcement.

models and its consequences, children can learn about social norms and expectations such as gender-appropriate behaviour. However, since children are able to observe both same-gender and opposite-gender behaviour, social learning theory has to explain how it is that children focus on the models and behaviour that are appropriate for their own gender. We have seen that parents tend to treat girls and boys differently from an early age so part of the explanation is that gender-appropriate models are presented more often than gender-inappropriate ones. Bandura (1977, 1986) also claims that children attend selectively to models and take account of the gender and gender-typicality of a model's actions.

There is some evidence to support this latter claim. In a study by Perry and Bussey (1979), men and women engaged in a series of neutral activities (such as selecting an apple or a pear) that were watched by a group of children aged between eight and nine. The children were then given the same choices as the adults and they were more likely to select an item that had been preferred by an adult of the same gender. However, modelling studies of this kind have been criticised (see Durkin, 1995) because of their artificial nature. Adults do not often provide such clear opportunities for children to model their behaviour. More seriously, social learning theory does explain how children make a link between their own gender and that of others. This is better explained by a more cognitive developmental account such as that of Kohlberg or, more recently, the work of Maccoby (1990b).

Social cognition and theory of mind

Social cognition is the term given to knowledge about people and their affairs. As the term suggests one can view social cognition as being on the boundary of social and cognitive development. We have already noted one important aspect of social cognition in our discussion of the development of gender identity. Another key aspect of social cognition concerns understanding of other people's mental states—understanding what other people think and believe. The preschool period marks an important milestone in children's social cognition because between the ages of three and four children acquire what has become known as a "theory of mind".

The notion of "**theory of mind**" came to prominence in psychology following a seminal experiment by Premack and Woodruff (1978) that attempted to test whether chimpanzees have a theory of mind. According to their definition someone has a theory of mind if they "impute mental states" to themselves and others. Discussion of the Premack and Woodruff paper led to the suggestion by a number of philosophers (including Bennett, Dennett, and Harman) that chimpanzees and children could be tested to see if they had a "theory of mind" by giving them a **false belief task**. The essence of the false belief task is that the observer is privy to some crucial information that a second person (or chimpanzee) does not have. If the observer has a theory of mind then he or she will realise that the behaviour of the second individual will be consistent with their lack of information rather than with the information held by the observer.

There are now a number of false belief tasks that have been developed for use with preschool children. Wimmer and Perner (1983) used a task in which children are shown a Smarties tube that (disappointingly) contains pencils rather than Smarties. Children are asked what another child, who has not seen inside the Smarties tube, will think is inside. The correct answer is, of course, "Smarties" since this is what the appearance of the tube suggests. However young children typically say that another child will think that the tube contains pencils even though there is no way of telling this without looking inside. Another task that has been used in many studies is the Sally–Anne test (Baron-Cohen, Leslie, & Frith, 1985) in which a girl doll (Sally) hides a marble and then goes for a walk. A second doll (Anne) then moves the marble while Sally is still away and so cannot see what has happened (see Figure 10.2). The children are asked where Sally will look for the marble. In this task, as in other tests of theory of mind designed for children, it is important to ask a series of control questions to ensure that they remember the real location of the marble as well as being able to predict where the doll will look.

Three-year-old children almost always fail theory of mind tasks. In the Sally–Anne test they say that the girl doll will look in the new location for the marble rather than the original location in which she placed it and where she would expect it to be. In the Smarties task three-year-olds say that another child will expect there to be pencils in the tube. Four- and five-year-olds, however, normally pass both the Sally–Anne and Smarties tests indicating that they are able to distinguish between their own knowledge and that of another person. Performance in other tasks provides a similar picture. For example, three-year-old children are not able to learn a game involving two boxes, one empty and the other containing sweets. In order to succeed at the game the children must deceptively point to the box that does not contain sweets rather than to the one that does, otherwise another child will be given the sweets. Russell, Mauthner, Sharpe, and Tidswell (1991) attempted to train three-years-olds to deceptively point to the "wrong" box but, time after time, they pointed to the box with the

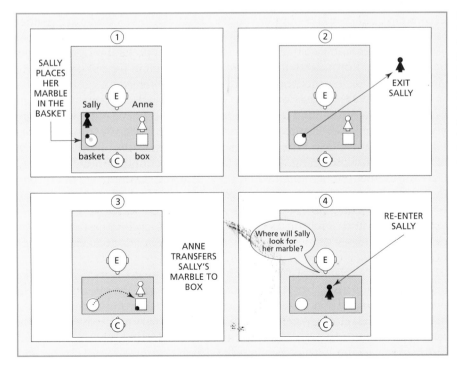

FIG. 10.2 The Sally–Anne test. C denotes the child observer, and E is the experimenter. Reproduced with permission from H. Wimmer and J. Perner (1983), Beliefs about beliefs: Representation and the constraining function of wrong beliefs in young children's understanding of deception. *Cognition, 13*, 103–128. Copyright © 1992 Macmillan Magazines Limited.

sweets only to see them being given to their opponent. By contrast, four-year-olds soon picked up the rules of this deception game.

Interestingly, performance on theory of mind tasks is closely related to understanding of the appearance–reality distinction that we discussed earlier. Young children who can distinguish between the rock-like appearance of the sponge and its real substance can also pass theory of mind tasks whereas those who think the sponge really is a rock also fail theory of mind tasks. What links these two kinds of task together is that they both involve the pitting of an erroneous mental impression against a known reality (Flavell et al., 1993). This suggests that three-year-olds have a general difficulty in entertaining two competing representations.

One special group of children appear to have a more specific difficulty with theory of mind tasks. These are children who are autistic. **Autism** is more frequent among boys and it is accompanied by mental retardation in approximately 75% of cases, although a minority of high functioning autistic children have intelligence in the average, normal range (Frith, 1989). This latter group can be tested on theory of mind tasks. Many studies have now shown that the great majority of high functioning autistic children fail theory of mind tasks (Baron-Cohen et al., 1985). This has led to the proposal that autistic children have a specific deficit in theory of mind. (The box on pages 225–226 describes a study that compares autistic children with deaf children and normally developing children on theory of mind tasks.)

Other authors have argued for a more general deficit in autism. Another important symptom is an abnormal lack of imaginative "pretend" play (Frith, 1989; Hobson, 1993). Leslie (1991) has argued that autistic children lack the ability to suspend belief in order simultaneously to consider the real and symbolic properties of objects. Normal children know that a banana remains a banana, even when they are pretending that the banana is a telephone (see Chapter 9, Cognitive Development in the Preschool Years). Leslie argues that autistic children cannot "decouple" the properties of the real object from its mental representation, so that the object can take on pretend properties. This basic deficit makes autistic children excessively literal in their understanding since they cannot consider reality "as if" it were different.

Hobson (1993) argues for a more general difficulty in autism that can explain why theory of mind tasks are problematic. He points out that there are important ways in which autistic children do not relate normally to their parents even though they appear to react in the same way as mentally retarded children of the same age in the strange situation test where the child is briefly separated from the mother (Sigman & Ungerer, 1984). Autistic children may not turn to their parents for comfort, nor do they seem interested in sharing experiences, nor in caring for their parents. They also have difficulty identifying emotional expressions in films (Hobson, 1993). Problems of this kind suggest that autistic children have a more general problem in interpreting the intentions and feelings of other people.

This wider explanation of autistic children's failure in theory of mind tasks is consistent with a number of studies that have explored the role of families in promoting theory of mind. Ruffman, Perner, Naito, Parkin, and Clements (1998) have shown that children with older brothers or sisters succeed in theory of mind tasks at an earlier age than only children or those with a younger sibling. Ruffman et al. argue that older siblings provide opportunities through play and discussion for younger children to learn about the mental states of others. The general view that older members of the family are important for developing theory of mind is in line with an earlier study by Cutting and Dunn (1999) that examined performance in theory of mind tasks as well as emotional understanding and language ability. They found that language ability and family background—parental occupational class and level of mother's education—contributed significantly to both theory of mind and emotional understanding. However, Cutting and Dunn did not find that the number of siblings made a difference—a finding that may well be explained by the fact that it is older, more experienced, siblings who appear to be important. The role of the family in the development of theory of mind is also an important feature of Peterson and Siegal's (1998) view (see the box below) about the role of conversation.

The idea that children learn about other people's mental states by observation and interaction also fits in with the view of other authors (including P.L. Harris, 1992; Johnson, 1998) who have argued against the use of the term "theory" in "theory of mind". They claim that children do not have a theory about other people's mental states. Their explanation is that children are aware of their own mental states and can infer the mental states of other people through a kind of role-taking or simulation process. P.L. Harris (1992) stresses the importance of mental simulation in the development of social cognition.

Do deaf children have a theory of mind?

As we have noted, autistic children fail theory of mind tasks. Several studies have shown that deaf children of normal intelligence also tend to fail standard false belief tasks. Peterson and Siegal (1998) argue that this is because most deaf children come from hearing families and so very often they do not have as much language exposure as either a hearing child or a deaf child growing up in a deaf family where signing is used. The majority of deaf children from hearing families do not, therefore, have the same conversational experience as hearing children and so have less opportunity to acquire an understanding of the content of other people's thoughts and feelings. The idea is that children and their parents, peers, and teachers talk about what they are feeling and thinking so that the children can come to appreciate the potential discrepancy between their own perceptions and knowledge—mental states—and those of others. Peterson and Siegal also suggest that children's conversational inexperience both at home and at school may well restrict deaf children's ability to perform standard false belief tests. If this is the case, deaf children will find tasks that have high linguistic demands (such as a standard false belief task like the Sally–Anne test) particularly difficult and so they should do better in tasks that do not require the understanding of complex language.

Peterson and Siegal (1998) compared the performance of high functioning autistic children, normal three-year-olds, normal four-year-olds, and pre-linguistically severely/profoundly deaf children from hearing families on a number of false belief tasks. Most of the deaf children had relatively poor language skills. In Experiment 1, Peterson and Siegal used a modification of the standard Sally–Anne false belief task and a false photograph task (Zaitchik, 1990). In the false belief task a girl doll hid a marble and then went away. A boy doll then moved the marble. The children were asked where the girl doll would look for the marble. In the false photo task, the child photographed a Duplo doll in the bath. The doll was than moved to a bed and children were asked to predict where the baby would be in the photo that they had taken.

Normal four-year-olds performed significantly above chance on the Sally–Anne test, as you would expect, but the performance of the children in the other three groups—younger normal, autistic, and deaf children—was not significantly above chance. However, in the false photo task, all four groups performed significantly above chance and there were no significant differences among them.

In Experiment 2, Peterson and Siegal used three tasks that made minimal linguistic demands on the children. All three tasks were acted out with Duplo dolls and they used a similar scenario and similar language in the control and test questions and during the enactment of the scenario. In the false belief task, a Mother doll goes to get a hair ribbon to match the colour of the daughter doll's pink dress. Unbeknown to her, the daughter doll changes into a green dress. The child is asked to choose, from a pink and a green ribbon, which colour ribbon the mother selected. In the false photo task, a boy doll photographs the girl doll in a green dress. As before, the girl doll then changes (this time into a yellow dress). The child is then shown two pictures, one of the doll in a green dress and one of the doll in a yellow dress, and asked which is the photo that the boy took. In the false drawing task, a Dad doll paints the girl doll in a yellow dress. She then changes into a blue dress. The child is asked to choose between pictures of a doll in yellow dress and in a blue dress as being the one that Dad painted. The false belief and false drawing tasks both produced similar results to the false belief task in Experiment 1, with only normal four-year-olds performing above chance. However, all groups except the normal three-year-olds passed the false photo task.

These results show that, even in a simplified version, false belief tasks are problematic for deaf children as well as those who are autistic. Why, however, did children in both of these groups succeed with the false photo task? At first sight there do not appear to be many differences between this task and the false picture task. However, a real camera was flashed and clicked when the photo was taken, whereas the Dad doll did not actually paint a picture. Peterson and Siegal suggest that the flashing camera may have drawn children's attention to the fact that a particular state of affairs was being permanently recorded. They also argue that the Polaroid snapshot provided the child with a physical record of the scene that may have served as a strong cue during the false belief question. However, as there was also a physical record of the scene in the false picture condition, children must have treated the picture as a more powerful record than the photo if this explanation is correct. This does seem possible but further research would be needed to determine whether children view photos and pictures differently. It is certainly possible that even three-year-olds consider photos as an accurate record in a way that a picture is not.

One final point to note about the Peterson and Siegal (1998) study is that it focused on deaf children with poor language skills. A subsequent study (reported in Peterson & Siegal, 2000) showed that deaf children who had learned to sign in infancy were much better at theory of mind tasks than deaf children with poor language skills.

Prosocial behaviour

Prosocial behaviour is voluntary behaviour that is intended to help someone else. Once children go to school, considerate behaviour towards other children is actively encouraged and is normally part of the school ethos. However, well before explicit admonitions to engage in prosocial behaviour at school, there is evidence that children will act in a kindly way towards others, for example, by sharing toys or food or comforting a child who is crying. In the preschool years, it is natural to look for links between the prosocial behaviour of young children and that of their parents. There are also interesting differences in prosocial behaviour depending on the position that a child occupies in a family.

Reliable evidence for the relationship between the prosocial behaviour of young children and their parents has proved difficult to obtain. On the one hand there are studies that rely on parental report—these have the usual problems of potential unreliability. On the other hand, there are laboratory-based studies. Here the problem is in deciding whether such studies have ecological validity, that is, whether they reflect young children's real prosocial behaviour. Taken together, however, these two lines of research do suggest a link between the behaviour of parents and their children.

Eisenberg, Wolchick, Goldberg, and Engel (1992) found that there was a positive correlation between fathers' reports of their own prosocial values and their children's observed prosocial behaviour in preschool. However, perhaps surprisingly, there was no such link with mothers' reported values. Other studies have questioned adults, who have performed acts of exceptional altruism, about the prosocial values of their parents. Oliner and Oliner (1988, cited in Eisenberg & Fabes, 1998) questioned people who rescued Jews in Nazi Europe and found that many reported their parents as having strong views about the importance of extending ethical values to all people, irrespective of their race or religion. Interestingly, compared with a control group, rescuers did not report differences in parental attitudes to issues that did not affect prosocial behaviour, such as honesty. This suggests that it is a specific parental emphasis on how to treat other people that affects the development of prosocial behaviour.

Laboratory-based studies of prosocial behaviour have investigated social modelling. Children see a model perform a prosocial act—such as donating the winnings from a game to other children—and their own behaviour is then compared to that of a control group who did not observe the modelling. An overview of these studies (Eisenberg & Fabes, 1998) suggests children who observe a generous or helpful model are more generous and helpful themselves. Not all adults are equally good models, though, and preschool children are more likely to model the prosocial behaviour of the adults who care for them over extended periods. For any preschoolers, then, parents will provide important models for interaction with others.

Children who have a younger sibling have an ideal opportunity to learn about caring for others. Birth order is important because older siblings are often encouraged to care for their younger siblings who, in turn, learn to co-operate in these ministrations. Preschoolers who have a younger sibling will often comfort them if they show signs of distress (Howe & Ross, 1990) and even one- and two-year-olds have been found to exhibit prosocial behaviour towards their siblings (Dunn & Kendrick, 1982). Several studies have found that older sisters

> **KEY TERM**
> **Prosocial behaviour:**
> Altruistic behaviours such as sharing, helping, caregiving, and showing compassion.

are particularly likely to engage in prosocial behaviour (see Eisenberg & Fabes, 1998 for a review). Interestingly, the caring attitude of an older sibling towards a newly arrived younger sibling is strongly affected by the mother's preparation for the arrival of the baby. Dunn and Kendrick (1982) found that when mothers discussed the feeling and needs of the newborn with the older child, that child was more nurturant towards the new baby. The positive, nurturant attitude engendered at birth tended to persist, with behaviour following the birth predicting prosocial behaviour three years later. This finding underlines the view that, for young children, parental influence on this kind of behaviour is very important.

The formation of friendships

During the preschool period, when many children come into contact with their peers in play groups and at nursery, children express preferences for some children over others to be their play partners. Studies of choice of playmates show that young children tend to be attracted to children who are similar to them in age, sex, and behaviour (Rubin, Lynch, Coplan, Rose-Krasnor, & Booth, 1994, cited in Rubin, Bukowski, & Parker, 1998).

Once early friendships are formed, children behave differently with their friends than with other children in the group. Preschoolers seek out their friends and interact more with them, often initiating interactions. Perhaps less predictably, friends often play in more complex ways than non-friends (Hinde, Titmus, Easton, & Tamplin, 1985), and they tend to be more co-operative in their play.

Friendships are often volatile in the preschool period and studies by Hartup and his colleagues have shown that there are more conflicts between friends than other peers (Hartup & Laursen, 1992). Presumably this is because friends spend much more time together than non-friends. However, Hartup's work also shows that friends make more use of negotiation and disengagement in their resolution of conflicts than do non-friends; and conflicts are more likely to be resolved to mutual satisfaction. This is reflected in the finding that, after conflicts are resolved, friends will tend to stay close to each other and to carry on interacting, whereas disputes between non-friends usually end in separation. We discuss the development of friendships in more detail in Chapter 14, Social Development in the School Years.

Conclusion and summary

During the preschool years there are significant changes in many aspects of children's social understanding and behaviour. Toddlers can recognise themselves in a mirror but, over the next two or three years, they develop an increasingly sophisticated understanding of self as they learn to connect their experiences over time. The emergence of an "autobiographical self" at around four years marks an important point in development.

Pretend play becomes increasingly complex as the relatively simple object-based play of the toddler gives way to sustained fantasy play involving long sequences of events and, often, several characters. At the end of the preschool period, these games of pretence are often rooted in detailed observation of social situations such as attending playgroup or visiting the doctor. At the same time children become increasingly interested in magical characters such as witches, fairies, and ghosts, although sometimes the boundaries between the real and the imagined can become a little blurred,

Gender differences in play are present throughout the preschool period—and often become more marked—with boys and girls typically showing preferences for what are considered to be gender-appropriate toys and activities. An understanding of what it is to be a boy or a girl develops over this period so that, by the age of four and a half, children understand that gender is fixed. Understanding of other people also develops and, at around the age of three and a half, children show an important development in their ability to distinguish between their own belief and that of another person. Success in theory of mind tasks is closely related to success in distinguishing between appearance and reality (described in Chapter 9), suggesting that there is a general change in ability to maintain and compare two competing perspectives during the preschool period.

During the preschool period children begin to show increasing amounts of prosocial behaviour towards other children. They also establish friendships and spend more time with particular children who are usually similar to them in age and behaviour. Friendships are frequently with a child of the same sex, and observation of free play in groups of preschoolers often reveals a clear separation of boys and girls according to toy choice and preferred activity.

Further reading

- Campbell, A., & Muncer, S. (1998). *The social child*. Hove, UK: Psychology Press. This edited book, written for undergraduates, contains useful chapters on many different aspects of social development through childhood.
- Durkin, K. (1995). *Developmental social psychology*. Oxford, UK: Blackwell. This book, which is suitable for first- and second-year undergraduates, provides a comprehensive account of social development.
- Eisenberg, N., & Fabes, R.A. (1998). Prosocial development. In N. Eisenberg (Ed.), *Handbook of child psychology: Vol. 3. Social, emotional, and personality development* (W. Damon, Gen. Ed.; pp. 701–778). New York: Wiley. This is an authoritative and detailed chapter that reviews recent research on prosocial development from infancy onwards. It is intended for advanced undergraduates.
- Harris, P.L. (2000). *The work of the imagination*. Oxford, UK: Blackwell. This thought-provoking book, which summarises the author's own work in this area, reassesses children's capability for imagination from a very young age and discusses the important role of imagination in development. The book is suitable for advanced undergraduates.
- Ruble, D.N., & Martin, C.L. (1998). Gender development. In N. Eisenberg (Ed.), *Handbook of child psychology: Vol. 3. Social, emotional, and personality development* (W. Damon, Gen. Ed.; pp. 933–1016). New York: Wiley. This detailed chapter examines gender development from infancy onwards. It is intended for advanced undergraduates.

Part 4

The school years

CHAPTER 11

Cognitive development in middle childhood

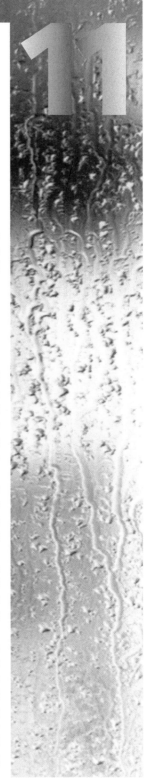

In this chapter we consider cognitive development during the school years, the period from approximately six years to adolescence. As in the previous stages we have discussed there are both biological and social markers for this period that we will refer to as middle childhood.

Social and biological markers of middle childhood

Middle childhood coincides in many societies with the beginning of formal schooling and being allowed a relatively unsupervised life, on a bicycle, in a playground or in the classroom or perhaps helping with younger brothers and sisters. During middle childhood there is an increasing emphasis on peer relations to complement the parent–child and other family relations in the life of the child. Cole and Cole (2001) estimate that 40% of the waking time of six- to 12-year-olds is spent with peers.

There is continued physical growth, with a gain in height of two to three inches per year for both boys and girls. At six years children are about three and a half feet tall and weigh about fifty pounds; by thirteen they are about five feet tall and weigh a hundred pounds. Boys double in strength during this period.

A little noticed biological marker for entry into middle childhood is the eruption of the first adult teeth as the milk teeth are replaced. It is not clear that there is any necessary psychological significance to this event but as it is universal it provides a convenient and easily observable biological benchmark for a new stage in development.

There are other biological reasons for supposing a stage transition to have occurred. There is a growth spurt of the brain between the ages of five and seven years, especially in the region of the frontal lobes. This part of the brain has an important role in planning and in the sequential organisation of actions and thoughts. The Russian psychologist, Luria (1959), a student and life-long follower of Vygotsky, developed a test in which the child has to follow instructions to activate or inhibit behaviour. The simple task requires the child to squeeze a rubber ball when a light comes on, according to the following instructions:

Squeeze the ball when you see a green light.
Don't squeeze the ball when you see a red light.

Preschoolers get confused by these instructions and tend to squeeze the ball whenever they see a light come on, regardless of its colour. Verbal instructions serve to activate their behaviour but do not serve to inhibit it. Eight-year-olds, however, have no difficulty with the task and can follow the instructions perfectly. Luria argues that children have become able to use language to regulate their own behaviour. Language now serves both to activate and inhibit activity. In Vygotsky's theory, once language takes on this self-regulatory function it is internalised as verbal thought. From a Vygotskian perspective, verbal regulation of behaviour is a major feature of the stage transition from early to middle childhood (see Chapter 2, Developmental Psychology in the 20th Century).

Another factor that may contribute to the stage transition occurring in middle childhood is a change in memory capacity, or perhaps simply in the efficiency with which children use their memory. Children may become more aware of the strengths and limitations of their own memory and this may lead to conscious rehearsal of material to be remembered. Such knowledge about the operation of one's own abilities is known as **metacognition**. In the case of metamemory (knowledge about the operation of memory), children have learned that rehearsal helps in remembering information, which results in improvement on tasks requiring memory for large amounts of material (Kail, 1990). For a detailed discussion of the important changes in memory that occur see Goswami (1998).

Another consideration is the increased amount of knowledge that the child can bring to bear on problem solving in middle childhood. Chi (1978) showed that 10-year-old chess experts had a better memory for the positions of the chess pieces than college students who were only novice chess players. The children, having greater knowledge of chess, could remember more about it than the adults. This example also raises the possibility that changes in development may not always have the across-the-board quality of a stage transition but may sometimes reflect knowledge of specific domains.

The main evidence that the middle childhood period does indeed comprise a new stage of development comes from Piaget. Middle childhood encompasses Piaget's stage of *concrete operations* in which children begin to use logical rules to solve problems.

Piaget's theory of concrete operational reasoning

Although there is clear evidence preschoolers are more competent in many reasoning tasks than Piaget suggested (see Chapter 9, Cognitive Development in the Preschool Years), there remain many problems that preschool children find difficult but that children of school age readily solve. Perhaps the single best indicator that children have entered Piaget's concrete operational stage is that they can now solve conservation problems. Conservation refers to the child's understanding that quantitative relationships between two objects are conserved, or remain invariant, despite irrelevant changes in the appearance of the objects. An irrelevant transformation is any change other than addition or subtraction from the original quantities. There are a number of different conservation tasks, relating to the understanding of physical quantities such as mass, weight, and volume.

School-age children comprehend conservation as self-evident and will say, in the conservation of liquid quantity task for example, that the amount of water in the two differently shaped jars remains the same because nothing was added or taken away when the water was poured into the differently shaped container. Furthermore, if the water in the short flat jar were to be poured back into the tall thin one, children know that the levels in the two tall thin jars would once more be the same. Children also know that the change in the height of the liquid was accompanied by a correlated change in its width and this accounts for the change in appearance.

According to Piaget, the stage transition from preoperational to concrete operational reasoning is a shift from reliance on perception to reliance on logic. The conservation problems, which caused such difficulty before, are now solved because children can reason that, if nothing was added or taken away, the amount must be the same. Similarly, mentally reversing the sequence of steps (i.e. imagining the water being poured back into the original container) enables children to conclude that nothing can have changed simply as a result of pouring the water into a new container.

The fact that children are no longer perceptually dominated by one aspect of the display (the height of the liquid) means they can take into account the possibility that the perceived changes in height and width co-vary. This new-found ability to comprehend the logical necessity of conservation enables children to justify their conclusions. This qualitatively new behaviour is Piaget's main reason for arguing that a stage change has occurred in cognitive development.

Piaget defines a logical operation as an internalised, mental action that is part of a logical system. According to Piaget, thought during the concrete operational stage is more flexible than in the preoperational stage because children can mentally retrace their steps—thought is reversible—within an internally consistent set of mental operations. However, cognitive development is not yet over. The thinking of children who are in the concrete operational stage remains limited because of the need for concrete objects to support thinking. According to Piaget it is not until adolescence that thinking becomes capable of tackling purely hypothetical problems (see Chapter 15, Adolescence).

The system of logical concrete operations involves two different sets of rules that allow the child to reverse imagined sequences of actions and their observed consequences. These are identity (I) and negation (N) (I/N rules) or reciprocal (R) and correlative (C) (R/C rules). Children at the stage of concrete operations can solve concrete problems that separately involve either I/N or R/C reversible reasoning. These reversible mental operations can be illustrated by the conservation of liquid volume task.

In the conservation of volume task, two identical quantities of water, initially in identical containers, are shown to children who affirm that the amounts are the same. Then one jar is emptied into a container of a different shape and children are asked whether the amounts of water are the same or different in the two jars. Preoperational children, who Piaget maintains are dominated by perception, mistakenly focus on the height of the liquid and conclude that the volume has changed after it was poured. However, children who have attained concrete operations, are not misled by this change in the appearance of the liquid. They know the volume is the same and often justify their judgements by saying "If the water were to be poured back, the levels would be just the same as before" (justification by the negation rule) or "The water in this jar is taller but this one is wider" (justification by the correlative rule).

Children's ability to justify their conclusion shows that they understand the reversibility of the actions and the associated transformations that were observed. In other words, they know that the volume of water must remain invariant under these perceptual-motor transformations. A limitation however is that children can only justify their conclusions with respect to one or the other of the reversibility rules. Not until formal operations are the I/N and R/C operations co-ordinated hierarchically.

The I/N and R/C operations can be illustrated in the conservation of liquid quantity task as follows:

I = *Identity*. It is the same water poured into a new jar.
N = *Negation*. The water is poured back into the original jar.
R = *Reciprocal*. Two sets of operations, such as pouring the water and then pouring it back are the reciprocal of each other.
C = *Correlative*. Changes in one aspect (e.g. the height of the liquid) are compensated by change in another aspect (e.g. the width of the liquid).

Another approach to the logical necessity of conservation, which may actually be broadly consistent with Piaget's position, has been proposed by Bruner et al. (1966). He suggests that children reason that the amount must be the same because it is "the same water". On this view, the qualitative judgement of identity may enable children to arrive at a logical conclusion about quantitative identity across the observed transformation.

The basis of this logical justification can be expressed in the following way:

1. There are two identical jars containing water to the same height and width (see Figure 9.1 on page 187). Thus jar A = jar B. They are in 1:1 correspondence. Therefore the amount of water is the same in the two jars.
2. The water is poured from jar B to jar C. It is the same water (qualitative identity) and nothing was added or taken away.
3. If A=B and B=C then A=C.

It is logically necessary that the amount of water is the same in jars A and C. The deduction enables children to justify the conclusion that the volume of liquid is conserved across a transformation in its appearance. On this account the deductive inference A=C provides the sense of logical necessity that the amount *must* be the same. This in turn allows the child to offer a logical justification according to one of the I/N or R/C reversibility rules (see Brainerd, 1978 for an extensive discussion). Although Piaget's and Bruner's accounts differ slightly in their emphasis, they are actually similar in that each requires the child to be in possession of an internally coherent set of logical operations for solution of the conservation task.

Other important logical operations that children acquire during the period of middle childhood are seriation, **classification,** and numeration. *Classification* refers to the hierarchical ordering of objects into superordinate classes and subclasses. Piaget's famous (or infamous) example is the class inclusion problem (described in Piaget's Theory of Preoperational Reasoning, in Chapter 9) where the child is questioned about a necklace made up of seven brown and three white beads. When six-year-old children are asked whether there are more beads (superordinate class) or more brown beads (subordinate class) they typically reply that there are more brown beads than beads. However, by eight years, children understand that the questions refer to different aspects of the problem, the set and the subset.

Seriation refers to the understanding of relationships of position both in space and in time. Acquiring the logic of seriation allows children to order objects according to spatial dimensions such as height, length, width, or according to when events occurred in time. Seriation, in turn, enables the logical operation of **transitive inference** where, for example, children can work out the relative length of two sticks by employing a third stick of intermediate length. This type of measurement problem can be described in the following way:

If stick A is longer than stick B, and stick B is longer than stick C which is the longest?

The solution is that if A>B; and B>C; then A>C. We deduce that A must be the longest stick from the dual relationship of B with A and C. To solve transitive inference problems children must be able to store all the relevant information in memory and comprehend the double relationship of the comparison term, B, with its neighbours A and C. Piaget argued that children cannot solve transitive inference problems until the beginning of concrete operations and as such they do not understand the logical necessity of the relations between the A and C terms (see the box on pages 241–243 for a link with the conservation task).

Numeration emerges from the combination of classification and seriation. Preschool children do understand something about number and may be able to count small sets of objects. According to Piaget the main gain during the concrete operational stage is that serial ordering and classification enable children to comprehend numbers as a sequence and to classify them as a set of classes and subclasses. For example, a group of eight counters can also be understood to comprise two groups of four, or four groups of two counters; and this provides the logical foundation for learning about multiplication and division (see Chapter 13, Learning to Do Mathematics).

Again, there has been much controversy over whether or not children have these abilities before the concrete operational stage. As these problems have particular significance for educational practice they have received a great deal of empirical investigation both in Western cultures and cross-culturally.

Piaget's claim generated a great deal of controversy because it has important implications for teaching about numbers and measurement. Numbers occur in a serial order. In measurement, a ruler necessarily serves as the B term in serial comparisons between objects to be measured. So Piaget's conclusions suggest that children will not be able to measure things until they have attained concrete operations.

KEY TERMS
Classification: Understanding the hierarchical sequence of objects by grouping them in classes and subclasses.
Seriation: Understanding spatial and temporal sequences.
Transitive inference: Understanding the relation between objects.
Numeration: Understanding the sequence of numbering.

Criticisms of Piaget's account of concrete operational reasoning

The first major criticism of Piaget's account of transitivity was made by Bryant and Trabasso (1971). They showed that children could solve transitivity tasks at a rather younger age than Piaget proposed. Bryant and Trabasso used a version of the transitive inference task in which five rods of different lengths and colours, A>B>C>D>E, were serially compared. The rods were kept in a block of wood with holes drilled into it, so that the longest rod (which was red, let us say) was at the left, with successive rods of reducing length to the right. Each rod protruded by exactly the same amount above the surface so children could only see how long the rods actually were when the experimenter took them from the block, in pairs, and showed them to the child.

Four-year-old children were given extensive training in which pairs of rods were serially removed from the block and they were shown that the red rod was longer than the white one next to it, the white rod longer than the green one next to it, and so on. The children were tested on their knowledge of the relative lengths of adjacent pairs while the rods were concealed in the block.

After training the children had learned all the relationships between adjacent pairs, i.e. that the red rod A was longer than the white one B; the white one B was longer than the adjacent green one C; the green one C was longer than the blue one D; and the blue rod D was longer than the pink one E. In other words the children knew that A>B, B>C, C>D, and D>E. Then came the critical tests in which the children were asked about non-adjacent pairs. The questions were: Which is longer, A or C and C or E? Children gave the correct answer to both these questions, showing that they had deduced that A>C and C>E. However, the critical question was: Which is longer, B or D? The answer to this question is crucial. In the training phase, both B and D rods had equally often been named by the child as longer or shorter than the adjacent rods A, C, and E. If children can get this B?D question right, it cannot be because they are simply repeating a verbal label that they have heard before. In fact, children did give the right answer, B>D, and so Bryant and Trabasso argued that young children's problem is not with transitive inferences but with memory limitations that conceal their underlying capacity for logical reasoning. This criticism of Piaget is similar to that of Donaldson (see Chapter 9, Cognitive Development in the Preschool Years) in that it proposes a distinction between an underlying competence and the child's actual performance on reasoning tasks.

Russell (1978) has reviewed criticisms of the Bryant and Trabasso conclusion that children can make transitive inferences when they are only four years old. One possibility is that the children may simply have imagined all the rods, rather like imagining all the members of a family of five people of different height, then they directly read off the relative heights of any pair from the mental image. Russell says such a solution would not require any understanding of the logical necessity of transitive inference. This solution is arguably consistent with Piaget's theory that preoperational children rely on the appearance of things when reasoning. However, in this case, the appearance of the rods in visual imagery actually allows the child to arrive at the correct answer. This weakens Piaget's case since it is quite possible that inferences do require visual imagery, even in adults.

In another approach to the question of whether young children can make transitive inferences, Bryant and Koptynskya (1976) studied spontaneous measurement in preschool children. They presented children with a wooden block with a four-inch and a six-inch hole bored into it. Children had to work out which hole was deeper using a ten-inch measuring stick with a red portion four inches long at either end and a two-inch yellow band in the middle. When the stick was dropped into the deeper hole, the yellow band disappeared, whereas when it was dropped into the shallow hole, the yellow band protruded above the surface. The relative position of the yellow band could thus be used as a comparative measure of the depth of the two holes.

Four-year-olds had no difficulty stating that the six-inch hole was the deeper of the two holes. Bryant and Koptynskya argued that this shows not only that children are capable of simple measurement but that they can also use the measuring stick transitively to make the inference that the six-inch hole is the deeper. The child's reasoning would be as follows: One hole "swallowed up" the yellow band, whereas the other hole did not. Since more of the stick was accommodated that hole must be the deeper.

It is difficult to decide exactly how young children are able to perform correctly in these two studies of transitive inference. However, even if children are actually solving transitive inference problems through visual imagery, this may not be entirely consistent with Piaget's theory of logical development. Piaget argued that perception, in the absence of logical operations, is inadequate for understanding reality. It is only on the argument that perception is not adequate that it follows that preoperational children are dominated by the incidental aspects of what they experience. More pertinent, perhaps, is the criticism that the tasks used to demonstrate transitive inferences in preoperational children actually structure the problem space for the child, whereas, in Piaget's tests, the child is expected spontaneously to come up with the right solution (Russell, 1978).

Bryant (1974) actually made a much more extensive argument for the adequacy of perception in understanding the world. His theory, based on a great deal of experimental evidence, is that perception in young children is adequate for understanding the relationships between objects but it is poor in providing absolute information. For example, a four-year-old can easily tell which of two rows contains relatively more counters when both rows are arranged so that each counter is opposite a corresponding counter in the adjacent row. However, the same child would have difficulty knowing the absolute value that one row contains ten counters and the other contains eight. In fact, Bryant follows the French psychologist, Alfred Binet, in arguing that perception operates logically by a process of unconscious inference. All in all, the weight of the evidence suggests that perception in infancy and early childhood is adequate to perceiving objects and relationships between them.

At least three theories of the transition from preoperational to concrete operational thinking are possible on the evidence to date. The matter is not yet resolved but it may be useful to list the main alternatives before going on to consider other evidence.

1. The boundary between preoperational and concrete operational thinking may not be as strict as Piaget thought. For some problems, such as conservation, or transitive inference, younger children may be able to reason adequately but they also have to overcome the unfamiliarity of the social situation (Donaldson) and/or limitations in memory (Bryant) to reveal this ability. This type of explanation implies that there isn't really a stage transition at age seven. In solving Piaget's tasks, children need only apply pre-existing logic to non-social situations and/or develop the requisite memory capacity.

2. A second possibility is that Piaget was wrong about perception and its relationship to the development of thinking but he was right that concrete operations is nevertheless a separate stage. Given appropriate training and contextual support of the kind described in Chapter 10, Social Development in the Preschool Years, younger children can solve problems that are similar to Piaget's concrete operational tasks. However, they do so only under the special circumstances that apply in these studies. This competence may be restricted to the perception of the relationships among the elements of a task and children are not able logically to justify their conclusions.

    This view combines some of the newer evidence for the adequacy of perception in young children with Piaget's arguments about the importance of logical justification. On this view, a stage transition does occur. The new-found ability for logical justification in children aged from seven to twelve years need not mean that preschool children lack the ability for logical reasoning, but they may have difficulty with logical justification. However, this leaves unexplained the new ability for logical justification.

3. A third possibility combines the second explanation with a Vygotskian alternative. There may be a stage transition from perceptually based to verbally based reasoning. This argument comes from the observation that many of the abilities revealed in preschool children's reasoning (see Chapter 9, Cognitive Development in the Preschool Years) occur only under conditions where any ambiguity between the verbal and non-verbal communication between adult and child is eliminated. A similar possibility exists in the Bryant and Trabasso training study where the requirements of the task were made absolutely unambiguous. Hence it is possible that children move through the zone of proximal development (see Chapter 2, Developmental Psychology in the 20th Century) from non-verbal to verbal thought when they become able to map their perceptual experience into language. This in turn might enable verbal justification of conclusions once the logical requirements of the task can be consciously formulated in verbal terms. Such an account would combine aspects of the observations of Donaldson, Bryant, and Piaget with Vygotsky's theory.

Piagetians might still argue that the onset of concrete operations enables the child to take perspectives in a more flexible way and to keep more than one aspect of the task in mind. They might suggest that a decline in egocentrism would contribute to more effective communication because children would be better able to select the salient attributes of the situation in justifying their conclusions. However, Piagetians would have difficulty in explaining away all the contradictory evidence we have reviewed so far.

Piaget's concrete operational stage is intended to be a description of a universal feature of development. What is crucial is not the exact time at which the child enters a stage, but that the sequence of sensorimotor, preoperational, concrete operational, and formal operational stages should always occur in the same order and universally, since they are supposedly universal modes of human intellectual development.

Dasen (1972) reviewed a large number of studies of concrete operational reasoning in non-Western children and adults. In general, children in non-industrialised societies show a one-year lag in their entry into concrete operations, by comparison with children from industrialised societies. This suggests that there may be a cultural contribution to the rate of development but the lag does not undermine Piaget's basic argument for universality. However, detailed analysis shows there are many exceptions and variations from culture to culture. Performance on some Piagetian tasks may depend on whether children have attended school and it could even be that Piaget's reasoning tasks reflect the cognitive style demanded by Western industrialised society (see the following box).

Cross-cultural comparisons of concrete operational reasoning

Looking more closely at particular concrete operational tasks reveals a surprising variation both within and between different societies in children's ability to solve concrete operational problems. Dasen (1972) reports, among other tasks, on conservation of quantity, weight, volume, and length and the ability to carry out seriation. These tasks have been administered at one time or another to Australian rural and urban Aboriginal children, to New Guinea Highlanders, to Chinese children in Hong Kong, to Canadian Eskimos, to adults from Amazonian tribes, to schooled and unschooled members of the Wolof people in Senegal, to illiterate adults in Sardinia, and to Zambian children.

While all these groups succeeded in passing Piagetian concrete reasoning tasks—suggesting that acquiring at least some concrete operations is universal—there was a very great variation among the different groups. Rural, unschooled Aborigines, with a little training, can solve conservation tasks but they lag about three years behind schooled, urban children. In some tasks, even adults failed and in other tasks, children performed better than the adults, as if the adults eventually developed quite different reasoning strategies in different cultures.

In evaluating such evidence it is important to take into account the possibility that the experimenter may not be presenting tasks clearly. Performance on Piagetian tasks by people in traditional cultures improves when native speakers are used to carry out the tests. It is also important that, if necessary, tasks are adapted so that they use materials that are familiar to the children being tested. It is easy to forget that, when Piaget and his collaborators first developed tasks for testing children's understanding of concrete operations, they chose items that were very familiar to the children attending school in the area round Lake Geneva. Such materials may seem very strange when presented to children from a different culture. For example, the original three mountains task that we described in Chapter 9 (see Figure 9.2 on p. 188), made use of a familiar scene depicting a well-known local mountain. However, for children who have not grown up with mountains in their daily view, the task immediately becomes less familiar.

Dasen suggests that there are two major factors that can explain cultural variations in performance on tasks that tap concrete operations. These are whether or not children attend school and the extent to which they have had contact with Western cultures. Thus, children in New Guinea and Senegal, who attended Western type schools, were comparable to Western children in the attainment of concrete operations, whereas unschooled children from the same cultures were much slower in attaining a similar level of performance. This suggests that schooling may have a special effect in the attainment of concrete operations. On the other hand, schooling may simply serve to bring the individual into contact with Western intellectual values. Where the society already holds such values, schooling may not significantly influence the onset of concrete operations. Thus, unschooled Chinese children in Hong Kong, which has for long been in European contact, performed comparably to schooled Western children on Piagetian tests of concrete operational reasoning.

Cole and Cole (2001) argue that problem-solving tasks have specific settings, or contexts, which interact with basic cognitive processes. Even if logical operations are universal, their expression depends on the particular setting. Schooling provides a particular setting for the development of memory and reasoning in Western children. Cole and Cole argue that the method of teaching in schools creates a metacognitive awareness of the basic principles for ordering information. This contributes to children's intellectual skills in domains where much information of an impersonal kind needs to be remembered. However, where complex information of a personal kind is to be remembered, unschooled children and adults may display very good memory because they are experts in their own specialised contexts. Thus, unschooled Mayan children from Guatemala can remember better up to 20 objects placed in a diorama of a Mayan village than can schooled Western children (Rogoff & Waddell, 1982).

We will see in Chapter 13 (Learning to Do Mathematics) that cultural emphasis on schooling has a very important influence on the development of cognitive skills in middle childhood. Stevenson, Lee, Chen, Stigler, Hsu, and Kitamura (1990) found that children in Chinese primary schools spent four times as many hours on their homework as children of the same age in the United States and twice as many hours as their peers in Japanese schools. According to their parents, American children were frequently given chores to do at home whereas this was not common among the Chinese and Japanese children. In a commentary on the findings of Stevenson et al., Hatano (1990) notes that different countries place different emphasis on the cognitive achievements that they value in children. Thus, there are important cross-cultural variations both in the value placed on the ability to solve particular kinds of problem and in beliefs about the kinds of problems that should be presented to children of a given age. This will lead to experiences of problem solving that vary from culture to culture and so to differences in performance on the traditional Piagetian tasks that assess mastery of concrete operations.

All this evidence raises the basic question of whether it is specific school training, or the more general demands of life in Western societies, which creates the concrete operational mode of thought with logical justification at its core. Could Piaget have mistaken a culturally specific Western form of intellectual adaptation for a biological universal?

Developmental changes in problem solving

During the school years children show considerable development in their ability to plan and monitor their solutions to problems. By five years of age children are planning recurrent daily activities such as laying out their clothes for the morning (Kreitler & Kreitler, 1987). However, the ability to plan ahead in solving a problem seems to be a relatively late-acquired skill especially when the problem is unfamiliar. Gauvain and Rogoff (1989) looked at the organisation and planning shown during a task in which children had to retrieve a series of items from the shelves of a toy grocery store. Most five-year-olds searched item-by-item which meant that the entire search took a long time. Nine-year-olds, however, carried out a much more systematic search in which they first scanned through the entire store to see where different types of item were located and then carried out an efficient search using this knowledge.

One task that involves careful planning is route finding. Fabricus (1988) used a route-planning task in which children were asked to devise a route that would allow then to retrieve a specified set of objects without any backtracking. It was not until the age of at least five that children were able to devise a suitable route. However, route-planning ability seems to vary from culture to culture. Western children do not usually have to find a route as they are invariably taken from place to place by their parents. However, eight-year-old Navajo Indian children proved to be much better at solving route-finding problems than their non-Navajo peers (Ellis & Schneider, 1989).

Siegler (1981) has attempted to explain how problem-solving ability changes during the school years by investigating children's ability to solve problems using a balance beam. We have already discussed some of Siegler's findings in Chapter 3, Observing and Modelling Developmental Change, when we introduced the idea of connectionist modelling. There is a drawing of a balance beam in Figure 11.1. The balance beam, which is pivoted in the middle, has a number of pegs spaced at equal intervals on either of the fulcrum. Weights are placed at different peg positions and children are asked to predict which side of the balance will go down. The answer to this question is determined by two factors—the total amount of weight on each side of the balance and the distance of those weights from the fulcrum. Solving the balance beam task, and making the correct prediction about which side will go down, therefore depends on combining information about two different dimensions. Given that preoperational children have difficulty in combining information in this way, Siegler predicted that five-year-olds would make incorrect predictions because they would attend to only one dimension. Siegler assumed that this dimension would be weight rather than distance from the fulcrum since this is a more visibly evident variable in the balance beam task.

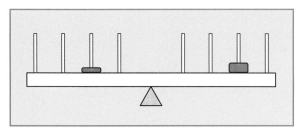

FIG. 11.1 A balance beam.

Siegler (1976) predicted that children would use one of four rules to predict which side of the balance beam would tip down. These are shown in the table below. These different rules are increasingly successful in solving a range of balance beam problems but, interestingly, improvement in success rates is not uniform across specific balance beam tasks. For example, the least sophisticated rule (rule 1) will produce the correct answer only when both weight and distance from the fulcrum are equal or when distance is the same but one side has a heavier weight than the other; and only the most sophisticated rule (rule 4) will make the correct prediction with all possible combinations of weight and distance (see Figure 11.1). However, children who are following rule 3 will actually perform *less* accurately than those following rule 1 in situations where there is a conflict between weight and distance but the side with more weight is the one that will go down. Presentation of a range of different weight x distance combinations can therefore reveal which rule children are following.

In Siegler's original study more than 80% of five- to seventeen-year-olds consistently used one of the four rules. Five-year-old children mostly used rule 1. Nine-year-olds most often used either rule 2 or rule 3, and those over thirteen usually used rule 3. Very few children used rule 4. Since Siegler's original study a number of other studies have shown similar sequences of rule following in this task (e.g. Damon & Phelps, 1988; Marini, 1992; Surber & Gzesh, 1984).

Overall, performance in the balance beam task can be seen as providing evidence for the claim that there is a major change in children's ability to deal with two conflicting task dimensions between the ages of five and nine as Piaget originally claimed. However, as we saw for preschool children (see Chapter 9, Cognitive Development in the Preschool Years), appropriate training can improve performance. Siegler (1976) gave children, aged between five and eight, feedback on balance beam problems. The children were asked to predict which side of the beam would go down and were then shown what would actually happen. (This can be done by releasing a lever that locks the beam in a

---

RULES FOR SOLVING BALANCE BEAM PROBLEMS

Rule 1   If the weight is the same on both sides, predict that the scales will balance. If the weight differs, predict that the side with more weight will go down.

Rule 2   If one side has more weight, predict that it will go down. If the weights of the two sides are equal, choose the side with the greater distance (i.e. the side with the weight furthest from the fulcrum).

Rule 3   If both weight and distance are equal, predict that the scale will balance. If one side has more weight or distance, and the two sides are equal on the other dimension, predict that the side with the greater value on the unequal dimension will go down. If one side has more weight and the other side more distance, muddle through or guess.

Rule 4   Proceed as rule 3, unless one side has more weight and the other side more distance. If so, calculate torques by multiplying weight x distance on each side. Then predict that the side with the greater torque will go down.

Table from "Three Aspects of Cognitive Development" by R.S. Siegler, in *Cognitive Psychology*, Volume 8, 481–520, copyright © 1976 by Academic Press, reproduced by permission of the publisher.

level position.) Feedback was given on three types of problem. Some children received only problems where rule 1 would always make the correct prediction. Other children were given problems where the weights were the same but distance varied (distance problems). These can only be solved using rule 2. A third group received problems where there was a conflict between weight and distance (conflict problems). These can only be solved using rule 3.

As predicted, children who were given only problems that could be solved with rule 1 continued to use this rule after the feedback session but children who had received distance problems were able to use rule 2 in new problems. The most interesting group was the third group to whom the most difficult problems—involving conflict between weight and distance—had been presented during the feedback session. They younger children—aged five – did not make any progress in their solutions to balance beam problems but many of the eight-year-olds were able to advance to rule 3. This is a very significant advance.

Siegler was interested in trying to pinpoint what is was that enabled the older but not the younger children to make this impressive developmental progression. Inspection of videotapes of the children solving problems where weight and distance were in conflict showed an important difference between the five- and eight-year-olds. The younger children—still in the preoperational stage—seemed to treat the sides of the fulcrum as two separate piles of weights, whereas the older children—who were capable of concrete operational thinking—seemed to encode information both about weight on either side of the fulcrum and the distance between each pile of weights and the fulcrum. An experimental test confirmed that the younger and older children were indeed encoding the balance beam array differently. Siegler (1976) showed the children an arrangement of weights on pegs which was then hidden behind a board. The children were asked to "make the same problem" with their own balance scale and set of weights. The eight-year-olds could usually put the correct weights onto the correct pegs—showing that they had encoded both weight and distance—whereas the five-year-olds usually selected the correct weights but put them on the wrong pegs.

Siegler then taught a group of five-year-old rule 1 users to encode distance as well as weight before giving them feedback training on balance beam problems where weight and distance were in conflict. This time, 70% of the five-year-olds were able to benefit from their experience with conflict problems and were able to use rule 3 after the feedback session. This impressive finding highlights the importance of encoding appropriate information in problem-solving and it illustrates once again that getting relevant experience can aid the development of specific problem-solving skills.

Conclusion and summary

Middle childhood is the period from six years to the onset of adolescence. Piaget saw this period as a discrete stage of intellectual development and he argued for a discontinuity between the preoperational reasoning of preschool children and the concrete thinking that is typical of school-age children. The major logical operations that children acquire as they develop an understanding of concrete operations are conservation, seriation, classification, and numeration. These operations require children to apply logical rules to classify and order things in the world. A key aspect of concrete operational thought is that children can simultaneously take account of two different dimensions—an ability that is usually beyond the grasp of preschoolers.

The main reason for supposing that some new capacities have been acquired as children enter middle childhood is that they are now able to provide a logical justification for the conclusions that they draw. The nature of the transition to concrete operations and the extent to which it involves specifically verbal reasoning processes remains a matter of debate and it might be wise to recognise that being able to explain something in words is a relatively late achievement. Children may well be able to solve a problem before they can provide a logical justification for their correct solution.

Since Piaget carried out his original studies it has become increasingly clear that educational and cultural factors have a very important role to play in the cognitive abilities of children of primary school age. There is a large variation in children's ability to carry out concrete operational tasks in different cultures, which suggests that education and experience play an important part in determining the age at which concrete operational thought is attained.

For many cognitive tasks, specific training can improve performance, as Siegler (1976) showed for the balance beam problem. What is often important is cueing children as to the appropriate variables to consider in a particular problem and giving them a suitable strategy to use. At this level, the view that emerges of children's cognitive development in middle childhood is very similar to the one that we presented of preschoolers (see Chapter 9, Cognitive Development in the Preschool Years). Right across both periods of development it is clear that, with the right kind of support, children can often be guided towards better performance in a task than they could manage on their own. One difference that we might point to, however, is that middle childhood brings with it an increasing ability to select appropriate strategies for solving a particular problem.

One important aspect of successful problem solving that children acquire is the ability to combine and interleave the knowledge about different domains. The knowledge of preschool children appears to consist of rather separate schemas whereas, in older children, separate strands of knowledge become increasingly inter-related. There have been a number of attempts to capture the nature of this inter-relatedness. Karmiloff-Smith (1992) argues for a notion of representational redescription (RR) in which information that a child has learned about a particular process is made available to other parts of the cognitive system. The RR model was developed to explain how the way that children represent knowledge becomes increasingly flexible and more capable of being manipulated. Case (1998) also presents a model in which patterns that are common across problems can be extracted and fed into the solution of new problems. What these two rather different approaches have in common is that, like Siegler (1976), they advocate a non stage-like account of development. As we saw in the first part of Chapter 3—where we discussed the dynamic systems approach, the connectionist approach, and information processing approaches—such accounts are becoming increasingly influential in developmental psychology. They perhaps have the most to offer in explaining the differences that are evident in the thinking of preschoolers and older children.

We have seen in this chapter that schooling exerts a powerful influence on development in middle childhood. During this period, children receive very intensive training in specific areas of cognition and, unlike infancy and the majority of the preschool period, much of the development in middle childhood occurs against the backdrop of explicit education. In the next two chapters we turn to two areas of cognitive knowledge that occupy a large part of the school curriculum. These are literacy and numeracy.

Further reading

- DeLoache, J.S., Miller, K.F., & Pierroutsakos, S.L. (1998). Reasoning and problem solving. In D. Kuhn & R.S. Siegler (Eds.), *Handbook of child psychology: Vol. 2. Cognition, perception, and language* (W. Damon, Gen. Ed.; pp. 801–850). New York: Wiley. This chapter, intended for advanced undergraduates, provides an authoritative account of recent research on the development of problem-solving skills during the school years.
- Dunn, J. (1984). *Sisters and brothers*. London: Fontana. This book describes Dunn's classic study of the development of sibling relationships.
- Goswami, U. (1998). *Cognition in childhood*. Hove, UK: Psychology Press. This undergraduate textbook provides a good introduction to the development of cognition.
- Harris, P. (1989). *Children and emotion*. Oxford, UK: Blackwell. This book, which summarises the author's own work, provides a persuasive and engaging account of children's emotional development.
- Turiel, E. (1998). The development of morality. In D. Kuhn & R.S. Siegler (Eds.), *Handbook of child psychology: Vol. 3. Cognition, perception, and language* (W. Damon, Gen. Ed.; pp. 863–932). New York: Wiley. This detailed chapter examines moral development from infancy onwards and describes the range of approaches that have been used to characterise and assess moral development. The chapter is intended for advanced undergraduates.

CHAPTER 12

Learning to read and spell

In the early school years, children spend a great deal of time learning to read and spell. As we shall see in this chapter, how easy it is for children to become good at reading and spelling depends not only on how clever they are, or how they are taught, but also on the relation between letters and sounds in the written language that they are learning.

Orthographic regularity

The majority of modern languages are written using an alphabet. Readers of this book will be familiar with the Roman alphabet, which is used for writing English and many other European languages. However, even within Europe, other alphabets are used such as those in Greek and Russian. Languages with alphabetic scripts all represent the sounds of the spoken language through letters but the relation between sound (**phonology**) and spelling (**orthography**) is very variable. In some languages, such as Italian or Spanish, there is a very consistent relation between phonology and orthography. This means that a particular sound always has the same spelling so that once children have learned all the relations between spelling and sound it is possible for them to spell any word that they hear and to read any word that they see written down. Languages like Italian or Spanish are described as having high **orthographic regularity** for both reading and spelling.

Reading and spelling are not always mirror images of each other. Modern Greek has high orthographic regularity for reading—comparable to that of Italian or Spanish—since each **grapheme** (letter) is always pronounced in the same way. However, unlike Italian or Spanish, Greek has much greater orthographic irregularity for spelling because vowels can be spelled in more than one way. One important reason for this discrepancy between reading and spelling is that the written form of Greek has remained unchanged from antiquity, whereas the spoken form has changed very considerably. Modern Greek spelling thus sometimes reflects the way that ancient Greek sounded rather than the sound of modern pronunciation. Somewhat similar changes can be found in English spelling (see the box on pages 260–261).

English differs from all three languages that we have considered so far— Italian, Spanish, and Greek—in that it is highly irregular for both reading and spelling. This is because English has an inconsistent relation between spelling

KEY TERMS
Phonology: The sound system of language.
Orthography: The system of writing.
Orthographic regularity: A consistent relationship between the sounds of a language and the method of writing them down.
Grapheme: Symbols such as letters that serve to distinguish words; usually represent phonemes.

and sound. This inconsistency is very evident in the case of a letter sequence such as OUGH. This is pronounced differently in *cough, bough, through,* and *enough.* However, even in less extreme cases there are often two different ways to pronounce a letter string. Consider, for example, AVE (as in *have* and *wave*) and IND (*wind* can be pronounced in two different ways). For many letter sequences in English, one pronunciation is more common than any other. Words that contain only letter sequences (graphemes) with the common pronunciation are called **regular words**, and words that contain at least one less common pronunciation are known as **irregular words**.

Theories of learning to read

The first theories of learning to read were concerned only with English. As we shall see later in this chapter, these theories have to be modified to account for learning to read alphabetic scripts with greater orthographic regularity than English.

One of the first and most influential theories about how children learn to read was developed by Frith (1985), who revised an earlier theory devised by Marsh (Marsh, Friedman, Welch, & Desberg, 1980). Frith proposed a three-phase theory of development in which children use a different reading strategy in each phase. In the first phase, children build up a sight vocabulary of words, which they recognise on the basis of their overall appearance. Frith called this kind of early reading *logographic*. Children who read using a **logographic strategy** recognise whole words and do not pay attention to individual letters. This means that children can only read words that they already know and are unable to make any attempt at reading unfamiliar words. When children are taught to read words on "flash cards"—cards with single words printed on them in large letters—they are being encouraged to use a logographic strategy.

In Frith's second phase of learning to read children begin to pay attention to individual letters and they learn how to convert graphemes (letters and letter strings) into phonemes using an **alphabetic strategy**. This new strategy of using letter-to-sound rules means that children can begin to guess how to pronounce unfamiliar words by looking at the sequence of letters they contain. However, even when they are good at using an alphabetic strategy, children will only be successful at pronouncing regular words. They will continue to mispronounce irregular words that they have not already learned.

Frith's final reading phase is called the *orthographic* phase. Children develop an **orthographic strategy** where words are broken down into orthographic units, strings of letters that commonly go together such as IGHT. These orthographic units are larger than those used in the alphabetic phase and they are not converted to individual phonemes. By using an orthographic strategy children are able to pronounce regular words that are similar in structure to words that they already know. For example, if a child can already read LIGHT, then it is possible to make a good guess about the pronunciation of words such as MIGHT and SIGHT. The orthographic strategy does not, however, replace the alphabetic strategy which children will continue to use for pronouncing new regular words.

Other authors (e.g. Seymour & Elder, 1986) have argued that children first begin to read by building up a sight vocabulary of environmental words that are recognised on the basis of overall word shape (see Beech, 1989) for a review).

This stage appears to be particularly important when children are learning to read an irregular language like English in which there is an inconsistent relation between letters and sounds. However, it is now clear that teaching methods have an important influence on the early reading strategies that children adopt. If early teaching emphasises a whole word approach to reading then children are more likely to use a logographic strategy when they first began to read, as Seymour and Elder (1986) found in a study carried out in Scotland. However, if children are taught to sound out letters when they first begin to read, then they will pay much more attention to individual letters in words and they will not use a purely logographic strategy (Connelly, Johnston, & Thompson, 2001).

Several studies show that children use an alphabetic strategy for reading. In one well-known study, Doctor and Coltheart (1980) asked children aged between six and ten years to read sentences and to decide whether or not they made sense. Some of the sentences sounded correct but were not, for example, "The sky is BLEW" and "She BLUE up the balloon". Doctor and Coltheart argued that, if children were using an alphabetic strategy for reading and converting letters to sounds, then both of these sentences would appear to make sense. However, if children had moved on to using an orthographic strategy, in which words were no longer sounded out, these sentences should correctly be identified as not making sense.

Doctor and Coltheart found that six- and seven-year-old children mistakenly judged the sentences that sounded correct as making sense but the older children were not confused by how a sentence sounded. They correctly rejected sentences that merely sounded correct. Doctor and Coltheart thus argued that the younger children were using an alphabetic strategy for reading.

There is considerable controversy about whether children do use an alphabetic strategy for reading so it not surprising to find that Doctor and Coltheart's experiment has attracted a great deal of criticism. One problem is that the study only provided indirect evidence that children were actually sounding out words when they were reading. Another problem has been highlighted by Goswami and Bryant (1990), who have argued that the results actually suggest that the children were paying some attention to the spelling of words rather than just relying on their sound. They point to one of the control conditions in the experiment which used nonsense words that sounded correct, for example, "She BLOO up the balloon". If children were merely sounding out words in order to read them, then a nonsense word that sounded right should be treated in the same way as an incorrect real word (BLUE) that sounded right. However, as Goswami and Bryant point out, even the six-year-olds did not treat these two types of incorrect sentence in the same way. They were much more

---

Frith's theory of learning to read

Logographic stage

- Child builds up a sight vocabulary of words that are recognised by their overall appearance.
- Child does not pay attention to individual letters.
- Child can only read words that he or she knows.

Alphabetic stage

- Child starts paying attention to individual letters.
- Child learns how to convert graphemes into phonemes by the use of the alphabet and letter-to-sound rules.
- Can attempt to pronounce unfamiliar words.
- Will be successful at pronouncing regular words, but unsuccessful with irregular words.

Orthographic stage

- Child develops an orthographic strategy and breaks words down into orthographic units.
- These units are larger than those in the alphabetic stage and are not converted to individual phonemes.
- Child can pronounce irregular words that are similar in structure to a known word.
- The alphabetic strategy is still used to pronounce new words.

likely to reject sentences with correct sounding nonsense words than they were to reject sentences with incorrect real words.

There may, however, be a problem in comparing children's responses to real and nonsense words. For example, children may be able to distinguish between words that they have seen before and other letter strings (nonwords) that they have not seen before and so can correctly reject nonwords. However, even this ability requires that children know something about what words look like so it is legitimate to see whether there is more direct evidence that children pay attention to visual cues in the early stages of learning to read. This was the aim of a study by Kimura and Bryant (1983).

Kimura and Bryant asked whether seven-year-old children use visual strategies for reading. They presented picture–word pairs in which the word either corresponded or did not correspond to the picture. The children were asked to sort the cards into two piles according to whether picture and word matched. There were two important manipulations. First, the children either carried out the task silently or while repeating an English word over and over (concurrent vocalisation). Second, in half the non-matching cases, the word looked very similar to the correct word. Kimura and Bryant argued that if children were reading by recoding letters into sounds then they would perform more slowly and less accurately with concurrent vocalisation and, if they were taking account of the visual appearance of words, then they should take longer to sort non-matching pairs where the word looked very similar to the correct word. Visual similarity did impair performance but concurrent vocalisation did not have an effect. Kimura and Bryant thus concluded that the children were not recoding letters into sounds in the sorting task but they were taking account of the visual properties of the words. This is, of course, the opposite conclusion to the one reached by Doctor and Coltheart (1980).

It is interesting to compare the methodology of these two studies since this can shed some light on why they present different views of the way that seven-year-old children read English. One important difference is that Doctor and Coltheart tested for alphabetic reading by using inappropriate words and nonwords that sounded correct, whereas Kimura and Bryant used concurrent vocalisation. It may well be that these two procedures are not testing exactly the same phenomenon. For example, although many other studies have shown that concurrent vocalisation interferes with children's ability to retain items in verbal short-term memory, it is not necessarily the case that this kind of interference will affect letter-to-sound conversion in reading. Furthermore, there is evidence from other studies using lexical decision tasks—where words and nonwords are presented on a computer screen and the task is to decide as quickly as possible which items are real words—that children with a reading age of seven years are affected not only by nonwords that sound like real words but also by orthographic regularity. In this latter effect, words that have a regular spelling pattern are easier to recognise than matched words that have an irregular spelling pattern (Harris & Beech, 1994). The regularity effect is also evidence of alphabetic reading, or phonological recoding as it is sometimes known.

If we accept that seven-year-old children do read alphabetically then we must also accept that they are making use of visual cues as well, since both Doctor and Coltheart's data and the result of the Kimura and Bryant study seem to indicate this. Thus it appears that, by seven years, children are using both visual and phonological strategies as they learn to read. Indeed it seems likely that, even at an earlier age, children will rely on both visual cues and letter–sound conversion in order to read, although the extent to which they make use of these strategies early on will almost certainly be influenced by their reading experience in the classroom.

Another theory about the early stages of learning to read comes from Goswami and Bryant (1990), who have proposed a radical alternative to Frith's model. They suggest that, rather than developing an alphabetic strategy after logographic reading, children develop a strategy of reading by analogy. This strategy initially relies on children's knowledge of rime and onset. In monosyllabic words, the onset is the first sound and the rime is the rest of the word so, for example, the onset of HAND is H and the rime is AND. Reading by analogy involves making comparisons among words that have similar spelling patterns and thus similar rimes. For example, a child who knows how to pronounce BEND and TENT may be able to read BENT using the analogy of the onset B in the first word and the rime ENT in the second. This use of larger units helps overcome some of the problems that are raised by the irregular pattern of grapheme–phoneme correspondences found in English.

In a series of studies, Goswami has shown that even five-year-old children can read by analogy. In her first experiment (Goswami, 1986), she initially presented children with a series of words to check that they were unable to read them at start of the experiment. Then Goswami presented one of the unfamiliar words as a cue (e.g. WEAK) and explained how it was pronounced. Next she presented the children with a series of other unfamiliar words that shared something in common with the spelling of the cue word. Some words (e.g. BEAK) shared a common rime with the cue word, others shared a common onset and part of the rime (e.g. BEAN). Goswami predicted that children should be able to read both of these kinds of words if they were able to read by analogy. In addition, the children were also presented with control words that shared letters in common with the cue word but did not have a common rime or onset and part rime (e.g. BASK and LAKE). Goswami found that the five-, six-, and seven-year-old children could all read more analogy words than control words. However, the youngest children could only read the words that shared a common rime with the cue word while the older children were also able to read words that shared an onset and part rime. This suggests that the use of analogy becomes more flexible with age.

Various criticisms of Goswami's experiments have been made. One important concern is whether reading by analogy is a real strategy that children spontaneously adopt in the course of learning to read or whether it is a strategy that is only induced by the experimental paradigm. Another issue, raised by Ehri and Robbins (1992), is whether children might require skills other than rime-onset awareness in order to be able to read by analogy. They suggest that reading by analogy is only possible once children have already developed sufficient decoding skills to be analytic about spelling.

This issue of what basic skills might be necessary for learning to read also applies to the development of the letter-to-sound decoding skills that are required for alphabetic reading. In this case it has been suggested that a more basic ability to segment and manipulate the component sounds of words is a necessary prerequisite for alphabetic reading.

One way to try to understand how the various component skills for reading come together is to consider studies that assess preschool children on a number of tasks before they begin reading instruction and then see which abilities best predict how well the children learn to read. These kind of longitudinal studies have also proved very useful in comparing the predictors of reading success for different alphabetic scripts. Before considering this issue, however, we need to consider how learning to read varies with orthographic regularity.

Learning to read alphabetic scripts

Children who learn to read an orthographically irregular script such as English take several years to become competent readers and spellers. Indeed, even adults will sometimes come across new words when they are reading and not be sure how to pronounce them and they may also hear a new word and wonder how it is spelled. These difficulties stem from the fact that there are so many irregular words in English that it is often not possible to be certain about pronunciation or spelling.

We might expect to find that children will learn to read and spell more rapidly if they are dealing with a script with a high level of orthographic regularity. This is not only because learning the relation between sounds and letters will be easier if that relation is consistent; but it is also because, once children have learned all the links between letters and sounds, they will be able to pronounce most or all of the new words they come across. In other words, for a highly regular orthography children may only have to develop an alphabetic strategy in order to become a fluent reader and speller.

Italian is highly regular for both reading and spelling. Thorstad (1991) found that Italian children learn to read much faster than English children of comparable ability and were reading fluently by the end of their first year at school. A similar pattern has been found by Cossu (1999). Thorstad also found that all the Italian children he studied, even those who were 10 years old, used an alphabetic strategy and converted letters to sounds in order to read an unfamiliar word. Since, for Italian, such a strategy is always successful the children did not need to acquire strategies for reading irregular words.

There was another interesting difference between Italian and English children. Italian children could spell all of the words that they could read and even some that they could not read. For the English children, however, spelling always lagged behind reading: There were many words that they could read but could not spell. The most likely explanation for this difference is that the letter-to-sound rules that Italian children learn can be applied equally easily to both reading and spelling. This means that they can be taught to spell words at the same time that they learn to read them. Thorstad found that Italian children spent most of their first year at school writing and then reading what they had written. The irregularity of English orthography, by contrast, means that children not only have to learn how to read many irregular words but also how to spell them. For this reason the first year at school tends to concentrate on reading rather than spelling.

We saw earlier in this chapter that Greek is highly regular for reading but not for spelling. This suggests that children will make very rapid progress in learning to read Greek—comparable to that in Italian—through the early development of an alphabetic strategy but that progress in spelling will be slow and comparable to that in English or Swedish. Harris and Giannouli (1999) found exactly this pattern. Greek children were fluent readers at the end of their first year of reading instruction and, even after only six weeks at school, they were showing clear evidence of the use of an alphabetic strategy. The children's rapid development of an alphabetic strategy for reading was encouraged in the classroom where teaching concentrated on the relation between sounds and letters. However, the same children were relatively poor at spelling and continued to make a large number of errors until they were 11 years old.

Learning to read non-alphabetic scripts

Some writing systems do not make use of letters but, instead, represent a word by means of a symbol. The most well-known examples of writing systems of this kind—known as *logographic*—are Chinese and Japanese. Learning to read a logographic writing system is a very time-consuming process since these systems contain a very large number of symbols and each symbol (or group of related symbols) has to be learned individually. Indeed, the majority of Chinese and Japanese adults never learn to read all of the symbols and it takes children considerably longer to become fluent readers of Chinese or Japanese than Italian or Spanish. As a result various simplifications have been introduced into the writing systems of both China and Japan including the development of a syllabic system of writing in which each syllable in the language is represented by one symbol (DeFrancis, 1989). In China the syllabic system was introduced in 1958 and was known as *Pinyin*. In Japan the syllabic script is known as *kana* and the original logographic script is known as *kanji* (see the box overleaf).

Japanese children learn to read a text initially only in kana, and gradually learn to read a text involving Chinese kanji characters with the help of kana (Akita & Hatano, 1999). Kana characters each represents a *mora* (which is more or less equivalent to a syllable). It is easy for young children to learn to read in a syllabic system of writing because, as we saw earlier, children become aware of syllables before they learn to read. The use of syllabaries is appropriate for Japanese because there are fewer kinds of syllable than in European languages and so only 71 characters are needed to represent all the possibilities. There is, however, a problem with the use of a small number of syllabary characters in Japanese because this produces many homonyms (words that sound the same but have a different meaning), and so educated Japanese people use the Chinese kanji characters to distinguish them.

It is common for Japanese children to be able to read and write all the characters in the kana script by the time they go to school. Initially reading instruction concentrates only on kana characters but, once children are fluent in these, they are slowly introduced to kanji characters. Sakamoto and Makita (1973) report that Japanese children are expected to learn 46 kanji characters in their first year at school, 105 in their second year, 187 in their third year, 205 in their fourth, 194 in their fifth, and 144 in their sixth year. In junior high school they learn another 969 characters. Children's books sometimes use kana characters next to unfamiliar kanji characters to assist reading (see the box overleaf).

Kimura and Bryant (1983) compared Japanese children reading kanji and kana and showed that they use different strategies for reading the syllabic kana script and the logographic kanji script. Kimura and Bryant were able to demonstrate this by giving seven-year-old Japanese children cards with words and pictures on them. The children had to sort the cards as correct or incorrect where a correct pair was one in which the word and picture corresponded and an incorrect pair was one in which they did not. In half the incorrect pairs the word looked very similar to a word that matched the object. Children who were using a logographic (visual) strategy should be affected by visual similarity and tend to count a similar looking word as correct. Kimura and Bryant also tested to see whether the children were using an alphabetic strategy by getting them to repeat a syllable out loud while they were doing the sorting task. Repeating a syllable over and over again—**concurrent vocalisation**—makes it much more difficult to convert letters to sounds and so should interfere with alphabetic reading.

Kimura and Bryant found that the vocalisation task did not affect the children while they were reading the kanji words but visual similarity did. This suggests that the children were using a logographic strategy for reading kanji. However, the reverse pattern occurred with kana. Here, the children were not affected by visual similarity but were affected by the concurrent vocalisation task and performed more slowly and less accurately. Thus, they appeared to be using an alphabetic strategy for reading kana.

Writing in Japan

The Japanese writing system was borrowed, over several centuries, from different areas of China. The borrowed Chinese characters were used in two ways. Sometimes both the symbol and an approximation of its Chinese pronunciation were used in Japanese. These characters were known as *kanji*—a name derived from the Chinese term for Chinese characters, which was pronounced "kanzi" (DeFrancis, 1989). In other cases Chinese characters were used to represent the sounds of Japanese. These characters were known as *kana* and they stood for the syllables within a word. A multi-syllabic word would thus be represented by two or more kana characters. The first Chinese–Japanese dictionary was compiled in the ninth century by Kukai, a Buddhist priest, who also invented the first syllabary.

From the outset, the Japanese writing system contained both kanji and kana characters. Over time the use of kana to represent Japanese syllables became standardised and, in modern Japanese, two different syllabaries of kana characters are in common use throughout Japan. These are *hiragana* and *katakana*. Hiragana (which was the syllabary originally complied by Kukai) is used in conjunction with kanji characters, whereas katakana characters are mainly used for writing foreign loan words such as terebi (TV) and keiki (cake).

Modern Japanese writing still combines the use of kanji and kana but this makes the system very difficult to learn. Popular publications, aimed at a mass audience, and some children's books make use of a technique in which every kanji character has small hiragana characters placed vertically to the right of it to assist in pronunciation.

In the 1950s the number of kanji characters used in published material was greatly reduced and the abandoned characters replaced by kana. Since then there has been a gradual increase in the use of kana. Bank statements and bills for gas and electricity are all in kana and word processors are designed for the typing

KEY TERM
Concurrent vocalisation:
Repetition of a syllable at the same time as reading.

of kana even though they can output the equivalent kanji characters. As a result some Japanese people are forgetting how to write many of the kanji signs and it is possible that, some time in the future, the traditional Japanese writing system may fall into disuse.

Predictors of reading success

Two of the earliest studies to look at contributions to reading success were carried out in Scandinavia, by Lundberg and his colleagues (Lundberg, Olofsson, & Wall, 1980) and, in Oxford, by Bradley and Bryant (1983). Lundberg et al. (1980) trained preschool children in Sweden on a wide range of tasks involving phonological knowledge. These included recognition of rhymes, finding the initial phoneme in a word, and segmenting words into their constituent syllables. Lundberg et al. found that children who were trained in these tasks made better reading progress than comparable children who had not received this training.

Since Swedish is an orthographically irregular language, it is possible to compare Lundberg's findings with those of Bradley and Bryant (1983). They investigated pre-reading children's sensitivity to rhyme and alliteration by presenting them with sets of monosyllabic words (such as "hill", "pig", and "pin") and asking them to say which was the odd one out. (The correct answer is "hill" because the other two words both begin with the sound "pi".) Words either had their first sound in common, their middle sound or their final sound. When the children's subsequent reading performance was measured after three years of schooling, those children who had initially been good at judging the odd word out were better readers than those children who had been less good at this task.

In a second study, Bradley and Bryant randomly allocated children to one of three training conditions: (1) sorting words by meaning; (2) sorting words according to their initial and final sounds (phonological analysis); (3) phonological analysis plus training in identification of letters of the alphabet. The children who were given training in phonological analysis alone learned to read more successfully than the group who had been trained to classify words by meaning. However, the third group, who had received training in phonological analysis and had also been taught about letter–sound relations, made even greater progress.

Bradley and Bryant's study was taken as strong evidence that preschool children, who have a high level of phonological awareness and are good at making judgements about similarities in rhyme and initial sound (i.e. rime and onset), have a head start when they begin learning to read. This general conclusion was confirmed by many later studies, including Hoien and Lundberg (1988), Lundberg, Frost, and Petersen (1988), and Stuart and Coltheart (1988). However, as more and more studies were completed, it also became clear that the relation between phonological awareness and learning to read is a complex one involving several distinct skills.

One important distinction can be drawn between two main types of phonological awareness, each of which has a rather different relation to learning to read. The first type is **syllabic awareness**. This is the ability to analyse words into their constituent sounds at the level of the syllable or

KEY TERM
Syllabic awareness: The ability to analyse the sounds within words.

sub-syllabic unit. The kind of tasks used by Bradley and Bryant in their training study—making judgements about the similarity of initial sounds and rhyme—involve awareness at this level; and as both the studies by Bradley and Bryant (1983) and Lundberg et al. (1980) demonstrated, children who are good at making judgements about similarities of rhyme and initial sound before they go to school tend to learn to read more quickly than children who are less good at these skills. Another task that assesses syllabic awareness is syllable counting (where children have to count how many syllables there are in a word). One important characteristic of syllabic awareness is that it develops before children start school and it does not require any knowledge of reading or even any exposure to print.

Although preschool syllabic awareness predicts reading success for orthographically irregular languages, this does not seem to be the case for scripts with a high level of orthographic regularity. Wimmer, Landerl, and Schneider (1994) found that, for German, performance on a rhyme judgement task predicted only later success in reading and spelling. Wimmer et al. argue that syllabic awareness is not predictive of early success in learning to read a regular orthography because children are able to develop an alphabetic reading strategy very rapidly; and this reading strategy is related to the development of phonemic awareness rather than to rhyme awareness. They argue that this contrasts with irregular orthographies where early reading makes greater use of units larger than the phoneme in the initial stages of reading.

Phonemic awareness is the ability to detect and manipulate phonemes within words. It is measured by performance in such tasks as phoneme counting (in which a child counts the number of phonemes in a word) and vowel substitution (where the child substitutes one vowel in a word with another). Phonemic awareness is important for learning to read because, once children can detect the individual phonemes in a word, it becomes possible for them to learn about correspondences between graphemes and phonemes. Several studies (e.g. Lundberg et al., 1980; Stuart & Coltheart, 1988; Wimmer et al., 1994) have shown that phonemic awareness develops as children learn to read. Several authors (e.g. Ehri & Wilce, 1987; Stuart & Coltheart, 1988; Stuart & Masterson, 1992) have found that children's level of phonemic awareness is the strongest predictor of reading age when IQ is equated.

The predictive relation between phonemic awareness and reading that has been found for English has been also shown in studies of other alphabetic scripts including German, Italian, Spanish, and Swedish. The common finding of these studies (Carrillo, 1994; Cossu, Shankweiler, Liberman, Tola, & Katz, 1988; Hoien & Lundberg, 1988; Lundberg et al., 1980; Thorstad, 1991; Wimmer & Hummer, 1990) has been that phonemic awareness—regardless of the method being employed for its assessment—is not only positively correlated with children's subsequent reading and spelling achievement but also plays a central role in learning to read. Despite qualitative differences in learning to read alphabetic scripts with differing levels of orthographic regularity, phonemic awareness tends to be a strong—if not the strongest—predictor of children's reading age after IQ.

Although phonemic awareness develops in the course of learning to read, and as a result of exposure to print, some recent work suggests that letter knowledge may be an important precursor to this skill. Ehri (1987) has argued that letter knowledge directly paves the way for the development of an

KEY TERM
Phonemic awareness: The ability to detect and manipulate phonemes within words.

alphabetic strategy in which children recognise individual graphemes and sound out the corresponding phonemes. According to Ehri, pre-readers use visual or contextual cues to recognise a small number of environmental words but then, as soon as they begin learning to read at school, they rapidly shift to letter–sound cues. Although other authors have disagreed with Ehri's view of the speed with which children move on to an alphabetic strategy, there is evidence from other studies that knowledge of letter names and sounds does underpin phonemic awareness.

Studies by Johnston, Anderson, and Holligan (1996) and Stuart and Coltheart (1988) have found that children's knowledge of letters is a significant predictor of reading success for English; and similar results have been found for German by Wimmer, Landerl, Linortner, and Hummer (1991) and for Greek by Harris and Giannouli (1999). Harris and Giannouli also found that there was a strong association between letter knowledge and phonemic awareness (as measured by vowel substitution and phoneme counting) suggesting that these are, indeed, related skills. In the Bradley and Bryant (1983) training study we described earlier, the children who learned to read most successfully were the ones who had been taught to sort words by sound and also learned letter–sound names. All of these findings point to the importance of letter knowledge for learning to read.

It is easy to see why learning the sound most commonly associated with each letter could pave the way for both phonemic awareness and the development of alphabetic reading. The child who has a high level of syllabic awareness can divide a monosyllabic word into its onset (initial sound) and rime as in CH/AIR or SH/IP. However, in order to carry out a phonemic analysis, the child has to know that there are smaller units contained within the rime and onset which are based on letter sounds. Training in letter names and sounds can provide the child with an essential part of the knowledge required for this level of analysis.

Harris and Giannouli (1999) found that Greek children showed a dramatic improvement both in letter knowledge and phonemic awareness from the end of nursery school to first grade entry at the beginning of the new school year. They attributed this dramatic improvement to Greek parents teaching their children the names of letters in order to prepare them for entry into the first grade of school—the point at which they are first given formal reading instruction. The success of this home teaching was evidenced by the finding that children entering the first grade knew almost all the letters of the Greek alphabet whereas children at the end of the nursery year—only four months earlier—knew very few.

Learning to spell

As for reading, the relative difficulty of learning to spell depends on the level of orthographic regularity in a given script. As we saw, where there is high regularity for both reading and spelling, as in Italian, the two will tend to develop in tandem. Where there is higher regularity for reading than for spelling then spelling will tend to lag considerably behind reading, as in the case of Greek.

Spelling typically lags behind reading in English. This is because there is considerably greater ambiguity about the spelling of an unfamiliar word than there is about its pronunciation. In other words, sound-to-spelling correspondences are considerably more inconsistent than spelling-to-sound relations (Barry, 1994). As in the case of Greek, the main reason for this asymmetry in English lies in the spelling of vowels. As we saw earlier in this chapter (see Orthographic Regularity), there are one to many spelling-to-sound correspondences but, in most cases, one particular pattern is more common than the others. For example, the sequence EA is most commonly pronounced as /iː/ as in EAT or READ. Words in which EA is pronounced in a different way (such as SWEAT or GREAT) are much less common. This means that, when an unfamiliar word containing EA is encountered for the first time, a good reader can make a plausible guess that it is pronounced /iː/.

When we turn to spelling, however, there is a clear difference. Here there are from one to very many mappings. The greatest complexity exists for vowels (as it does for Greek). A striking example is the spelling of the sound /ou/ which, according to Barry (1994), can be spelled in at least 13 different ways including DOLE, BOWL, COAT, FOLK, SEW, and BROOCH. The most common spelling pattern for the /ou/ sound is O-E (as in DOLE, MOLE, HOLE, HOSE, etc.) but this occurs in only 32% of words. The next most common spelling is O which appears in 26% of words, and OW and OA which both occur in about 15% of words. Given that all of these spelling patterns are relatively common, it makes it very difficult to guess how an unfamiliar word with an /ou/ sound might be spelled.

One reason for the complexity of English spelling is that it has changed very considerably over the centuries (see the following box). Another reason is that there are may cases in which spelling captures relations between the meanings of words by preserving the spelling of the root morpheme, that is, the basic word from which other, related, words are derived. Consider, for example, the root morpheme CHILD as it appears in the plural form CHILDREN. Although the pronunciation of the vowel is changed this is not reflected in the spelling which preserves the common morphological root of the two forms.

Children who learn English not only have to acquire phonological and orthographic knowledge to become proficient spellers, they also have to acquire extensive morphological knowledge. This is why learning to spell a script with a deep orthography, that represents the morphological roots of words, takes many years compared with a shallow orthography such as Italian where sound is the main determinant of spelling. The significance of morphological knowledge in the acquisition of English spelling has recently been investigated by Bryant and Nunes (1999).

The development of English orthography

Before the Norman Conquest in 1066, Old English was used. There was almost perfect one-to-one correspondence between graphemes and phonemes and little orthographic irregularity (Scholfield, 1994). The spelling of words directly reflected the way they were spoken so that words that sounded the same were written the same, even though they were quite unrelated in meaning, and words that were related in meaning were spelled differently. Thus, in Old English, the spelling of the singular form of the word for small was SMAEL while the plural form was SMALU. This is quite different from modern English spelling which tends to preserve meaning relations at the expense of guiding pronunciation as in the case of CHILD and CHILDREN or PHOTOGRAPH and PHOTOGRAPHY.

With the Norman Conquest, the sound of many words changed. At first spelling also changed to reflect new pronunciations but, as new words were introduced from Norman French, the close link between spelling and pronunciation weakened. Many spellings were adopted unchanged from the French and, at the same time, new letters were introduced into English spelling from Latin, French, and elsewhere. For example, the sound /kw/ was written in Old English as CW but this was replaced with the French spelling QU as in QUICK. The introduction of new ways of representing sounds meant that, gradually, the consistency in spelling that had characterised Old English began to disappear. Often there were alternative ways to spell the same word and writers chose their preferred spelling. Most notably regional spelling differences began to appear.

In the Tudor and Stuart period, when English once again became the language of government, there were attempts to standardise spelling. Unfortunately these attempts often resulted in greater complexity because of the introduction of spellings from Greek and Latin and attempts to "correct" words by returning to what was assumed to be their original spelling. For example, the spelling of the word DEBT was introduced to replace the original DET and DETTE because scholars showed that is was originally derived from the Latin word "debitum". Sometimes there was a misunderstanding of the derivation of a word as in the case of SCISSORS which, reflecting the assumed Latin origin of "sciere", replaced the old English spelling of SISOURES. It later turned out that the Old English word had not been derived from Latin at all. At the same time that these spelling reforms were occurring, there were important changes in the pronunciation of vowels. These were not, however, reflected in the spelling and so a greater and greater distance developed between the sound and spelling of words.

As in the case of reading, children adopt different strategies for English spelling as they become more proficient. Gentry (1978) suggests that there are five stages. Initially, children spontaneously write words using a letter sequence that bears no relation to the target word, suggesting that they have no awareness of the relation between letters and sounds. In the next stage, children begin to take some account of this relationship and they begin to include some letters that reflect the sounds in a word (e.g. LEFT for *elephant*). Gentry call this the pre-phonetic stage.

Gradually spelling becomes phonetic until the point where all the sounds in a word are represented by letters. However, phonetic spelling will often be incorrect in English because of the many possible ways in which particular sounds—especially vowels—may be spelled. Thus *come* might be spelled as KOM, *type* as TIP, or *eagle* as EGL. In the next—transitional—stage, children begin to take account of English spelling patterns. They start to include a vowel in every syllable (e.g. *eagle* is now spelled as EGUL) and to incorporate common English letter sequences such as AI, EA, and EE and the silent E at the end of words into their spellings. Finally children move towards correct spelling where they are able to take account of the many different rules that are reflected in English spelling including the use of silent and double consonants.

Since both learning to read and learning to spell go through different phases, it makes sense to ask what the relation is between these two processes:

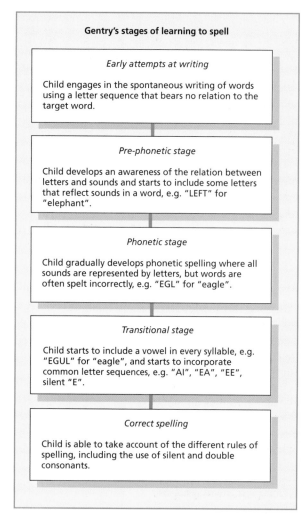

Gentry's stages of learning to spell

Early attempts at writing

Child engages in the spontaneous writing of words using a letter sequence that bears no relation to the target word.

Pre-phonetic stage

Child develops an awareness of the relation between letters and sounds and starts to include some letters that reflect sounds in a word, e.g. "LEFT" for "elephant".

Phonetic stage

Child gradually develops phonetic spelling where all sounds are represented by letters, but words are often spelt incorrectly, e.g. "EGL" for "eagle".

Transitional stage

Child starts to include a vowel in every syllable, e.g. "EGUL" for "eagle", and starts to incorporate common letter sequences, e.g. "AI", "EA", "EE", silent "E".

Correct spelling

Child is able to take account of the different rules of spelling, including the use of silent and double consonants.

Do children use common strategies for reading and spelling? The most obvious point of comparison is between phonetic spelling and alphabetic reading since both make use of relations between letters and sounds. In the case of English, children seem to find it much easier to break words into phonemes when they spell them than they do to identify phonemes in reading. Indeed, children first appear to gain an insight into the alphabetic code through spelling and several authors (including Ehri, 1987; Frith, 1985; Goswami & Bryant, 1990) have argued that children move towards an alphabetic strategy in reading as a result of developing an analogous strategy for spelling. In other words, children learn to read alphabetically as a result of learning about sound–letter patterns in spelling.

The evidence for this claim comes from both observational and training studies. These show that syllabic awareness has an earlier and more significant effect on learning to spell than on learning to read (see Ellis, 1994 for a review). For example, Ehri and Wilce (1987) found that preschool children who were trained to spell words by attending to letter–sound sequences learned to read better than children who were merely taught letter–sound relations; and Lundberg et al. (1988) showed that training preschool children in phonetic awareness greatly improved their ability to divide a word into its constituent phonemes. These improvements, in turn, resulted in greatly enhanced spelling ability at the end of grade 1 but only had a small effect on reading at the same point. However, after another year at school, the initial training was still having a strong effect on spelling ability but there was also a knock-on effect on reading.

Learning to read and write braille

So far in this chapter we have considered reading and spelling of print. However, children who have severe visual impairment may not be able to access print and so they are taught braille which is read by touch.

All braille letters are represented using a 2 x 3 matrix of dots (see the box on pages 264–265) and so they differ in form very considerably from print letters. Typically it takes blind children over a year to learn the braille alphabet in its entirety (Barlow-Brown, 1996; Harris & Barlow-Brown, 1997; Pring, 1994) which is considerably longer than the time taken by a sighted child to learn letters. There are various possible reasons why learning braille letters is relatively difficult. One is that the letters are more similar to each other than print letters and more easily confused. Another possibility is that discriminating by touch is more difficult than

The six dots of the
braille cell are
arranged and numbered:

1 ● ● 4
2 ● ● 5
3 ● ● 6

	a	b	c	d	e	f	g	h	i	j
	k	l	m	n	o	p	q	r	s	t

The capital sign, dot 6
placed before a letter
makes a capital letter.

1   4
2   5
3 ● 6

	u	v	w	x	y	z

The number sign, dots 3,
4, 5, 6, placed before the
characters a through j, makes
the numbers 1 through 0.
For example: a preceded by
the number sign is 1, b is 2, etc.

1 ● 4
2 ● 5
3 ● ● 6

Capital sign	Number sign	Period	Comma	Question mark	Semi-colon	Exclamation mark	Opening quote	Closing quote

making a visual discrimination. A third possibility is that the early reading experience of blind and sighted children is very different.

To begin with the last of these—one striking difference between young blind and sighted children when they are first taught to read is that the latter group already has a great deal of experience of print. Sighted children's knowledge comes from their experience of the written language, which they will have gained through exposure to books as well as to environmental print. On school entry, many sighted children are able to recognise some words, such as their own name, and they have often learned the names and/or sounds of some letters of the alphabet. In comparison, most blind children know little or nothing about braille until they are introduced to it at school and they are unlikely to be able to recognise any braille letters or words. Blind children thus approach the task of learning to read with very much less relevant experience.

One difficulty with providing appropriate preschool exposure to braille is that young children seem to find detecting the pattern of raised dots in a braille cell difficult. One way in which young children might be able to experience braille in a more easily manageable form would be to enlarge it. For sighted children learning to read print, large letters are often used to provide early exposure to print but surprisingly blind children are not introduced to braille through enlarged characters, since it has been assumed that such experience would not help in the learning of conventionally sized letters. There is, however, some evidence in a study by Barlow-Brown (1996; Harris & Barlow-Brown, 1997) that using a large braille cell can help children to learn braille letters. The same study also compared the learning of braille through touch and sight in order to see whether it is the great similarity of braille letters to one another that poses problems or the fact that they are learned through touch rather than sight.

Barlow-Brown taught braille letters to sighted preschool children who had no experience of braille. There were four conditions. These conditions involved learning braille either through sight (as printed dots) or though touch (as raised dots) and in either standard or enlarged format. In the tactile conditions the sighted children felt the letters but could not see them. In the enlarged tactile condition the braille letters were presented as pegs on a 2 x 3 pegboard.

Children learned letters more quickly in the two visual conditions than the two tactile conditions, which suggests that children find it more difficult to learn through touch than vision. However, there was an important difference between the two tactile conditions, with children who were given large braille (that is, the pegboard) learning significantly more letters in a shorter space of time than the children who were presented with standard braille.

After the first part of the study, all the children were presented with the letters that they had been previously taught but this time in standard sized braille. Children who had learned braille visually were able to transfer the knowledge gained during the training sessions directly to standard braille but the most complete transfer was shown by the children who had originally been taught large tactual braille using the pegboard. These children could transfer 100% of the letters that they had learnt to the smaller sized braille. In another study, Barlow-Brown (1996) also found that, like their sighted peers, two young blind children were able to learn braille letters very quickly using the pegboard and then to successfully transfer this knowledge to standard braille. A group of older blind children, who already knew some braille letters, could immediately recognise and produce familiar braille letters using the pegboard and they were also able to learn new letters.

Barlow-Brown argues that experience with a large braille cell allows children to gain important information about the nature of braille which they normally realise only with a lot of time and braille experience. Millar (1997) has shown that braille characters impose a great load on memory until they can be recoded. However, if children can discover that there is a relation among the form of all braille letters in that they all map onto a 2 x 3 braille matrix then the memory load may be decreased. The other advantage in the use of a braille pegboard is that it would make it possible for preschool children to gain experience of braille without having to wait until they develop fine tactile discrimination.

Braille

All braille characters are formed from dots in a 2 x 3 matrix. They are typed using a Perkins Brailler which has six keys. The relation between the keys on the brailler and the array of dots in the braille cell is illustrated below.

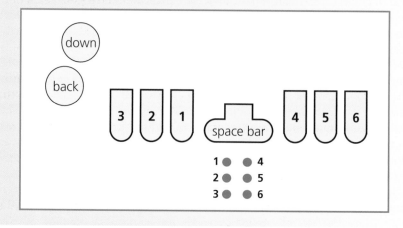

Children who are taught braille in the United Kingdom follow the Royal National Institute for the Blind (RNIB) braille reading scheme. The first five letters introduced to children are B, A, G, L, and I, and all words that they are taught are initially made up only of these letters. At the outset of learning to read, blind children are more or less restricted to the RNIB reading scheme books from which they learn these letters and a small number of words that can be formed from them (such as I, BAG, BALL, BILL, and BIG).

Difficulties with learning to read and spell

Probably the most well-known cause of difficulties with reading and spelling is **developmental dyslexia**. The general characteristic of children with developmental dyslexia is that they have a specific difficulty with reading and spelling that cannot be explained as a more general learning difficulty. Children with developmental dyslexia thus have IQ scores within the normal range and their other abilities—such as mathematics and spoken language—are at an age-appropriate level. Developmental dyslexia is different from acquired dyslexia. As its name implies, the former is a developmental disorder in which children have difficulty in learning to read and spell whereas acquired dyslexia occurs in adults and older children and it follows some kind of brain trauma, typically closed head injury. Adults with acquired dyslexia lose all or some of their ability to read and spell.

Although it is easy to define developmental dyslexia at a simple level it is much more difficult to understand why it occurs. What can be said with certainty is that it has many different causes (see Snowling, 2000, for a detailed review).

Some children with specific reading difficulties have had a history of speech and language problems. Stackhouse (2000) carried out a longitudinal study of children referred to speech and language therapists with speech difficulties. The sample was very carefully chosen so that children whose speech difficulties had a physical cause (such as a cleft palate, or a hearing loss) were excluded. All the children had non-verbal IQ within normal limits and were monolingual English speakers. The children with speech problems were first tested at the age of four and compared with control children who did not have speech problems. Stackhouse used a wide range of tests including assessment of language comprehension, auditory discrimination (distinguishing between words or sounds that are similar, e.g. VOS/VOT, LOST/LOTS, PATE/PLATE), and repetition of words and nonwords. She found that the children's reading ability at age five was predicted by their performance in the auditory discrimination task, their ability to repeat both real words and nonwords, their knowledge of letter names, and their understanding of grammar. One year later the pattern was generally similar with the predictors of reading ability at age six being word repetition, phoneme deletion and completion (tested at age five), understanding grammar, and knowledge of letter names.

Some aspects of these findings are very similar to the pattern that we saw earlier in studies of predictors of reading success within the normal population. Phonemic awareness—the ability to detect and manipulate phonemes within

KEY TERM
Developmental dyslexia: A syndrome causing problems with learning to read and spell, despite normal intelligence. Also known as word blindness.

words—is a strong marker of reading progress and knowledge of letter names is also crucial for early reading success. Problems with word and nonword repetition have also been shown in many dyslexic children (Gathercole & Baddeley, 1990).

The wider significance of the Stackhouse (2000) study is that it points to the conclusion that many dyslexic children have a history of speech difficulties. Often these difficulties are remediated by appropriate speech and language therapy but they reappear when children begin to read. Stackhouse suggests that children with a phonological disorder rather than a phonological delay are those most at risk, and she notes that adults with persistent developmental dyslexia are below average on tests of articulation, even though they have no apparent speech problems.

Given the importance of phonological awareness for learning to read, it is not surprising to find that many children with developmental dyslexia have difficulties with phonological encoding and, in addition, poor phonological awareness is the best single predictor of dyslexia (Rack, Snowling, & Olson, 1992). This difficulty with phonological encoding appears to be related to the poor short-term memory for spoken material that many children with developmental dyslexia experience (McDougall & Hulme, 1994).

The orthographic irregularity of English places high demands on short-term memory, and recent comparisons between German and English children show that comparable problems in short-term memory can have rather different consequences in the two countries. Wimmer, Landerl, and Frith (1999) compared dyslexic children in England and Germany. The children were twelve years old but they had reading ages between eight and nine years. All had a non-verbal IQ that was within the normal range. Wimmer et al. presented the children with lists of words and nonwords that they had to read. The English children were presented with English words and the German children with German words but the items had similar or identical spelling in the two languages, e.g. *milk–Milch* and *butter–Butter*. Nonwords were constructed by changing one or more letters so that *milk* became *bilk* and *Milch* became *Bilch*. The point of choosing words that were so similar across the languages was to make the tasks essentially identical for the two groups of children.

Wimmer et al. found that both groups of dyslexic children were very accurate at reading number words and short high frequency (i.e. very common) real words. On the nonwords, however, and longer low frequency real words, the German dyslexics were faster and more accurate than the English children. The explanation that Wimmer et al. provide for the superior performance of the German dyslexics lies in the different experience of reading that the children had. Reading nonwords and long unfamiliar words requires phonological coding, i.e. sounding out and blending individual phonemes. The high orthographic regularity of German means that the first attempt at pronouncing an unfamiliar word sound-by-sound will be correct. Thus, for German, the online assembly of pronunciation syllable-by-syllable places a low demand on short-term memory and so even a child with a poor short-term memory will usually succeed.

Wimmer et al. argue that dyslexic children who learn to read German will have developed a relatively good ability to read phonologically compared to their English counterparts who have consistently encountered problems with this approach. The low orthographic regularity of English means that a child's first attempt to pronounce an unfamiliar word will very often be incorrect so individual phonemes must be held in short-term memory and recombined until a correct pronunciation is achieved. What this suggests is that the incidence of dyslexia arising from problems in phonological processing will be much lower when children are learning to read a regular orthography. This is what has been found. The incidence of developmental dyslexia is lower in countries like Germany, Italy, or Japan, where children are learning to read a regular orthography.

While children with developmental dyslexia show a general difficulty with reading and spelling, another group of children have a more specific problem with reading. These are children with poor reading comprehension and they are identified by the fact that they can read aloud, that is pronounce words, at an age-appropriate level but their ability to understand a text is comparatively poor. Thus children with poor reading comprehension will have a much higher reading age on a single word reading test (such as the Schonell test or the single word reading test from the British Ability Scales) than they will on a text comprehension test such as the Neale test. The profile of poor comprehenders is very different from that of dyslexic children in that their main problems seem to lie in the area of text processing. Oakhill and Yuill (1996) suggest that three different aspects of text comprehension may be particularly problematic. The first of these is the ability to draw inferences, that is, to link together related ideas and to draw on more general knowledge to interpret what is being read. The second is the ability to understand the structure of what is being read. In the case of stories, which children frequently encounter in their early reading, this may require identification of main characters and their motives and understanding of key components of the plot, being able to understand why something happened, and being able to predict what will happen next. The third problem that poor comprehenders may show is in "comprehension monitoring". This is, the ability to keep track of what has been understood or not understood as reading proceeds. Oakhill and Yuill argue that poor comprehenders typically have problems in all three areas.

A third group of children who experience great difficulty in learning to read are those who have profound prelingual deafness. Such children, who are born with little or no hearing or become profoundly deaf within the first year of life, generally have great difficulty in learning to read (Marschark & Harris, 1996). In one study, Gaines, Mandler, and Bryant (1981) found that only just over 1% of deaf children read at a level appropriate for their age by the time they leave school. Two decades later the picture is much the same.

One major reason for the difficulty that deaf children experience in learning to read is that they often have a very poor understanding of the relation among speech sounds and, in particular, they find it almost impossible to understand the nature of rhyming. Harris and Beech (1994) gave a group of preschool deaf children a version of the Bradley and Bryant (1983) test that measures sensitivity to rime and onset. Overall the deaf children performed much worse than a comparison group of hearing children, although there was considerable variation, with some of the deaf children performing as well as hearing children. When the deaf children were followed up over their first year at school it turned out that the children who had performed best on the rime–onset test generally made faster reading progress than the children who had performed poorly. Reading level was also positively correlated with the children's language ability—a point to which we shall return.

Given that young deaf children have poor syllabic awareness it is not surprising to find that they do not appear to read alphabetically. Several studies (Beech & Harris, 1997; Harris & Beech, 1994; Merrills, Underwood, & Wood, 1994; Waters & Doehring, 1990), using lexical decision tasks, have shown that deaf children with reading ages of between seven and nine years are not subject to the regularity or pseudohomophone effects (reading a nonword, e.g. HOAM, as a word because of its sounds) that are characteristic of alphabetic reading in hearing children of the same reading age. Merrills et al. (1994) also found that deaf readers placed greater reliance on visual word features than hearing readers of either the same chronological or reading age.

Studies with deaf college students, however, have provided some evidence for phonological coding (see Marschark & Harris, 1996), suggesting that reading strategies change with age and experience (at least in the case of those children who become successful readers). Leybaert and Alegria (1995) compared the spelling strategies of 11-year-old and 13-year-old deaf French children. They found that the older children were sensitive to sound-to-spelling regularities whereas the younger group were not. Significantly, though, this development was limited to children with intelligible speech which is in line with an earlier study by Hanson, Schankweiler, and Fischer (1983) in which only deaf students with better speech skills showed orthographic regularity effects in their reading.

One possible explanation for these results is that deaf children begin reading with little syllabic awareness—or letter knowledge—and so they do not initially develop phonemic encoding skills. Thus, when they are assessed in primary school, they will typically show little evidence of reliance upon phonological recoding in either reading or spelling. However, some deaf children—perhaps those with more intelligible speech—go on to develop phonemic awareness and so show evidence of phonological effects in reading and also phonological similarity effects in short-term memory (Campbell, 1992), where the accuracy of recall is lower for similar sounding words than for words that do not sound the same.

Deaf children also have problems with reading that stem from more general difficulties with language. Many deaf children have a lower level of language ability than their hearing peers and so they are less able to use top-down skills in reading, that is, to use their general linguistic knowledge to interpret unfamiliar words when they occur in context. Studies by Campbell and Burden (1994) and Harris (1994) have shown that profoundly deaf children with reading ages of seven–ten years not only had a lower reading vocabulary than their hearing peers but also additional difficulties at the text level that could not be not explained by limited vocabulary. In the Harris (1994) study, deaf children had a lower score on the Neale test—which assesses children's ability to read and understand text—than would be predicted by their ability to read single words. They also had great difficulty in carrying out the Oakhill instantiation task, suggesting that, in general, deaf children are poor comprehenders.

Conclusion and summary

The speed with which children learn to read and spell depends on many factors. An alphabetic script with high orthographic regularity, such as Italian, or a script that uses a syllabary, like Japanese, can be mastered much more easily than English which has considerable irregularity. Progress in learning to read and spell is also affected by pre-reading experience in the form of sound and letter knowledge. Children who begin formal reading instruction with good knowledge typically make better progress in reading and spelling although the precise skills that are useful appear to vary as a function of the orthographic regularity of the script.

The strategies that underpin success in reading and spelling also vary as a function of the script that children are being taught. In English, visual, alphabetic, and orthographic strategies all seem to be important, whereas, with an orthographically regular script, alphabetic reading may be the only strategy that is necessary. However, difficulties in developing a successful alphabetic reading strategy appear to have a severe effect on success in learning to read even in English. Many dyslexic children have difficulty in converting a string of graphemes into its corresponding phoneme string and the serious problems that many deaf children encounter in learning to read appear to have a similar origin.

Further reading

- Brown, D.A., & Ellis, N.C. (1994). *A handbook of spelling*. Chichester, UK: Wiley. This edited book provides a series of excellent chapters on spelling in children and adults. It is suitable for advanced undergraduates.
- Harris, M., & Hatano, G. (1999). *Learning to read and write: A cross-linguistic perspective*. Cambridge, UK: Cambridge University Press. This edited book contains chapters on learning to read in many different scripts including Italian, German, Portuguese, Greek, Hebrew, Chinese, and Japanese. It is suitable for advanced undergraduates.
- Marschark, M., & Harris, M. (1996). Success and failure in learning to read: The special (?) case of deaf children. In C. Cornoldi & J. Oakhill (Eds.), *Reading comprehension difficulties: Processes and intervention* (pp. 279–300). Hillsdale, NJ: Lawrence Erlbaum Associates Inc. This chapter reviews studies of the many problems that deaf children experience in learning to read. It is suitable for first- and second-year undergraduates.
- Snowling, M.J. (2000). *Dyslexia* (2nd ed.). Oxford, UK: Blackwell. This book provides a detailed account of dyslexia as well as explaining the normal processes involved in learning to read and spell. It is suitable as an introduction to this topic.

CONTENTS

Learning to do mathematics

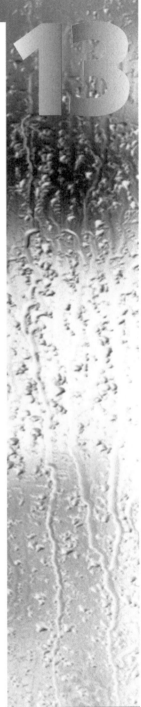

Formal instruction in mathematics does not normally begin until children start school, but many of the skills that are important for early mathematical understanding develop in the preschool years. These skills include learning to count and to recognise spoken and written numbers.

Early knowledge of number

Even young babies know something about number although they do not, of course, know anything about counting. Wynn (1992a) has shown that young babies understand that when one object is added to another object there are two objects and when one object is removed from two objects only one remains. Wynn tested babies aged five months and presented them with one of two conditions. In the first, the babies were shown one toy figure that was then occluded by a screen; a mechanical arm then placed another figure behind the screen. In the second condition, babies initially saw two figures that were then occluded by a screen; then the mechanical arm moved behind the screen and came out holding one of the figures. The screen was then lowered and each group of babies was shown one of two test conditions, either two figures or only one figure (see Figure 13.1). Babies looked longest when the test condition was not in accordance with the rules of addition and subtraction. Thus babies in the first condition (1 + 1 = 2) looked longer when they saw only one figure after the screen was removed, whereas babies in the second condition (2 − 1 = 1) looked longer when there were two figures.

Babies can also tell the difference between small numbers of objects. Antell and Keating (1983) showed that newborns could discriminate two objects from three and, less reliably, three objects from four. Like Wynn, they used an **habituation** paradigm (see the box on pages 107–108) in which the baby was repeatedly presented with a picture showing a number of objects and then, once habituation had occurred, with another picture that depicted either the same number of objects or a different number. Babies tended to look significantly longer at the new picture if it depicted a different number of objects than if the number of objects was the same.

Starkey, Spelke, and Gelman (1983) showed that infants' ability to distinguish numbers of items up to four is not restricted to visual perception. Infants could also detect correspondences between the number of items that

FIG. 13.1 The addition events used in Wynn's (1992b) study. Reproduced with permission from K. Wynn (1992b), Addition and subtraction by human infants. *Nature, 358,* 749–750. Copyright © 1992 Macmillan Magazines Limited.

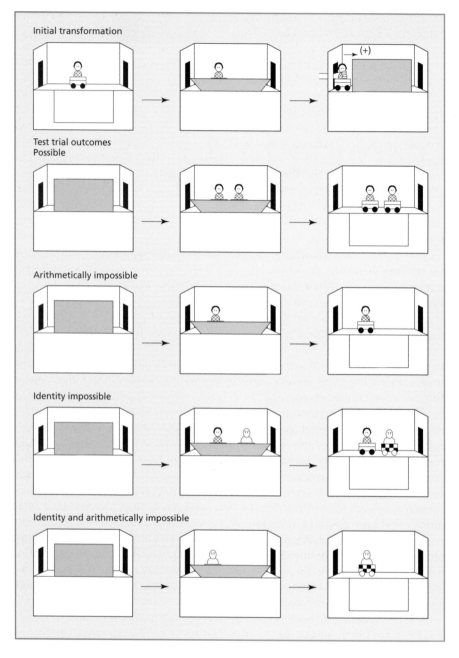

they saw and the number of sounds that they heard. In one study, infants aged between six and nine months heard a tape of either two or three drumbeats and were then shown two pictures, one with two items and the other with three. The babies preferred to look at the picture with the number of objects that corresponded to the number of drum beats.

There has been considerable speculation about the basis of infants' numerical abilities and whether they are based on counting. Gallistel and Gelman (1992) have argued that these early abilities are based on a kind of non-verbal counting using a mechanism called the accumulator—a mechanism that was originally proposed to account for the sensitivity of rats to time intervals (Meck & Church, 1983). The proposed workings of this accumulator are complex but, in essence, the idea is that impulses, which are generated at a steady rate, are accumulated according to the total number of items that are counted (see Sophian, 1998 for a detailed account).

An alternative view of the basis for infants' numerical abilities is that they stem from the ability to **subitise**. Subitising is well-established in adults who are able to estimate small numbers of objects (usually up to three or four) without counting. Subitising has been distinguished from counting mainly because of a difference in the relation between the time taken to determine the total number of items and the number of items in the array. For small numbers (where it is assumed that subitising operates) there is only a very small increase in the time taken to state the number of items with each increase in display size. However, for larger displays (where it is assumed that counting takes place), there is a relatively large increase in the time taken as the number of objects increases. For example, adults take around 40 ms longer to assess three items rather than two, whereas it takes an additional 380 ms to determine the size of a set of seven rather than six objects or six rather than five (Mandler & Shebo, 1982).

The finding that the limits of infants' number judgements are identical to the limits of adult subitising suggests that these two abilties are very closely related. However, the accumulator theory of Gallistel and Gelman could also explain the limitations of infant ability by arguing that there is a developmental increase in the capacity of the accumulator (see Sophian, 1998) that is most limited in infancy.

A study by Starkey and Cooper (1995) compared the subitising and accumulator accounts of early numerical ability. They asked two and a half year-old children to judge whether the number of items in two displays was the same or not. All displays were linear and contained from one to six items. The children were not yet able to count but they were able to make reliable (i.e. better than chance) judgements about two displays containing up to three items. However, their performance was at chance level for displays with four or more items. This level of ability was very similar to the findings reported for infants. Three and a half year-old children were able to make reliable comparisons of displays with up to four items (one more than the younger group) but there was no further improvement for children up to five and a half years. Across all the age groups, children were more accurate in their comparative judgements when the larger array was also longer, supporting Piaget's original claims about the use of length in number conservation tasks (see Chapter 9, Cognitive Development in the Preschool Years). However, neither errors nor response time increased with the size of displays, which suggests that a preverbal counting mechanism of the sort proposed by Gallistel and Gelman was not being used in the comparison tasks.

Starkey and Cooper conclude that subitising is present in young children before the development of verbal counting. More controversially they argue that counting skills grow out of the ability to subitise. They suggest that young children see the result (via subitising) when objects are added or taken away from small sets and in this way they may come to realise, for example, that three is greater than two.

KEY TERM

Subitise: To perceive the number of a group of items at a glance and without counting.

Learning to count

Although the basis of numerical knowledge in infancy remains controversial, there is general agreement about the importance of verbal counting as a basis for the development of mathematical skills. Gelman and Gallistel (1978) describe three principles that children have to master in order to count objects correctly. These are the **one-to-one correspondence**, **stable order**, and **cardinality** principles.

One-to-one correspondence requires children to understand that, when they count, they must count each object only once but also count all the objects. Stable order requires that number words be produced in their canonical sequence. If children do not use the correct sequence of number words when they count—saying, for example, 1 2 3 5 4 when counting five items—then they will arrive at an incorrect answer even if they respect the one-to-one principle. The third of Gelman and Gallistel's principles, cardinality, refers to the fact that, in counting, the final number word reached is equal to the total number of items that have been counted. Thus, if the final number that is counted is seven, this means that there are seven items. Of course, this will only be the case if both the one-to-one and stable order principles have been respected.

As Nunes and Bryant (1996) point out, when children apply their counting skills to formal mathematics, they have to move on from counting objects and master additional principles concerning written numbers. However, most children first experience the concepts of addition and subtraction through the counting of objects so it is important to understand how children's ability to count objects develops.

Preschool children often first become aware of the number sequence through counting games. A longitudinal study by Durkin, Shire, Riem, Crowther, and Rutter (1986) found that the first number word of English-speaking children was "two", which usually appeared a few months after the first birthday. Children below the age of two years mainly produced number words either singly or as part of an expression such as "one, two, buckle my shoe". Towards the end of the second year, children began to produce number sequences in a turn-taking context with their parents but, by their third birthday, they were often producing number sequences on their own.

The learning of the number name sequence is further helped by number games that form an important part of the preschool curriculum. However, learning about the number sequence does not teach children to apply this knowledge to object counting. Thus young children may be able to count up to ten without understanding that the number 10 can be related to 10 objects in a set. One of the most extensive studies of how the principles of counting come together when counting objects was carried out by Fuson (1988).

Fuson found that counting is initially easier if objects are lined up in a row. In Fuson's study, five-year-old children were able to count large linear arrays (containing up to 40 items) accurately. However, when objects were not presented in a straight line, and especially when they occurred in random order, the children were much less accurate. Nunes and Bryant (1996) suggest two possible reasons why young children can count objects in linear arrays more accurately than those in non-linear

KEY TERMS
One-to-one correspondence: Counting each object only once.
Stable order: Counting using the standard number sequence.
Cardinality: When counting the final number reached is the total.

arrays. One possibility is that five-year-old children are aware of the principle of one-to-one correspondence and the linear array allows them to apply this principle by accurately monitoring which objects they have counted. The other explanation is that the structure of the linear array pushes children towards an apparently correct counting strategy and so makes them appear more competent than they really are. In other words, the regular pattern of a linear display might induce children to move their finger from one item to the next in rhythm with their counting. Linear displays also have a clearly identifiable beginning and end which is another important feature that helps children when they count objects. This means that, when a set of objects is placed in a straight line, children will be encouraged to point at each item in turn and also to point at each item only once beginning with the first and ending with the last. In this way children will apparently respect the rule of one-to-one correspondence even though they do not really understand it.

Pointing at each object in turn does not always provide an accurate way of keeping track of which items have already been counted. If objects are not in a straight line it is much more difficult to keep track of counting through pointing alone. A more reliable strategy, which does not rely on the position of objects, is to move each object as it is counted. (This is the strategy that bank tellers use when they are counting money.) One way of looking at whether children really understand the one-to-one principle is to see whether they attempt to use such a strategy. Fuson (1988) found that the majority of children did not adopt this strategy of moving objects until they were over five years old. This suggests that the younger children were not aware of the need to count in a way that ensured one-to-one correspondence, a conclusion that is supported by the fact that children under five often made errors even when counting objects in rows.

Further evidence that children under five do not understand the importance of one-to-one correspondence in counting comes from another of Fuson's studies. She presented children with an array of dots arranged in a circle. As we have already seen, young children find it very difficult to count dots when they are not in a straight line. In the case of a circular array, the main difficulty is to keep track of the starting and ending point of the count so that each dot is counted once. To make this aspect of the task easier, Fuson used a display with green dots and one red dot which could be used as a starting and end point for counting. She first taught the children to use the red dot as the starting point and found that more than half the three-year-old children were able to do this. Fuson then taught the children to use the red dot to stop counting and the majority of children were now able to count correctly. However, not all the children were able to apply this strategy consistently over three trials and, overall, only 12/19 were correct.

Clearly, there seems to be some doubt about how early children really understand the important principle of one-to-one correspondence. Nunes and Bryant conclude that four-year-old children can often count accurately when they have someone to help them but when they have to count unaided they often make mistakes. By the age of five, however, most children have robust knowledge of the one-to-one principle and can count sets of objects accurately regardless of their spatial arrangement.

How Oksapmin children learn to count

Systems for representing number can be divided into formal systems that use written numerals, and more informal systems that make use of objects or body parts to represent numbers. The most widely used formal system employs Arabic numerals in which the underlying base of the counting system—10—is explicitly represented. This contrasts with the Roman numeral system in which the counting base is not explicitly represented.

In the Roman system the number 10 is represented by the letter X and the number 100 by C. The use of these letters does not reveal anything about the numerical relationship between the two numbers, notably that the second (C) is ten times as big as the first (X). By contrast, the equivalent Arabic numerals tell you a great deal about the relationship between the two numbers once you understand the convention that the first column represents units (the numbers from 0–9), the second, tens, and the third, hundreds. The transparency of number representation in the Arabic numeral system facilitates simple mathematical operations and also allows complex operations with large numbers to be carried out.

In some societies more informal systems for representing number are used. These do not have a corresponding written form but they may, nevertheless, allow simple arithmetic calculations to be carried out. The Oksapmin, who live in a remote part of New Guinea, use body locations to represent numbers (Saxe, 1981). They start counting on the thumb and fingers of the right hand, work up the right arm and round the head and finishing by working down the left arm and finally using the fingers of the left hand. In this way the Oksapmin are able to represent numbers up to 27 in sequential order ending with the little finger of the left hand. Numbers greater than 27 are represented by continuing down the left wrist and then ascending back up the body. A similar system is used by the native people of the Torres Strait. (See Figure 13.2.)

The names of the numbers are the names of the body parts. For example, the number 14—the middle of the sequence—is called "aruma" as it is located on the nose. In order to distinguish a number from its symmetrical counterpart on the other side of the body a prefix—"tan"—is attached to the higher numbers. Thus the 12th number is called "nata" and is located on the right ear, whereas the 16th number, located on the other ear, is called "tan-nata".

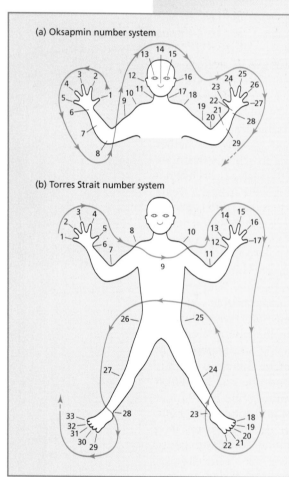

FIG. 13.2 Two alternatives to our number system; (a) shows the Oksapmin number system, and (b) shows the number system used by Torres Strait islanders. (a) Reproduced with permission from G.B. Saxe (1981), Body parts as numerals: A developmental analysis of numeration among the Oksapmin in Papua New Guinea. *Child Development, 52,* 306–316. Copyright © The Society for Research in Child Development. (b) Reproduced with permission from G. Ifrah (1985), *From one to zero: A universal history of numbers.* New York: John Wiley & Sons, Inc. Copyright © 1985 John Wiley & Sons Inc.

Saxe (1981) found that Oksapmin children's understanding of numerosity was influenced by their number system. He tested children aged between seven and sixteen and found that the younger children tended to treat different numbers that were located on the same body part as being equivalent. It was not until the children were more than nine years old that they were able to treat numbers as independent of their physical location on the body. Another confusion that some of the younger Oksapmin children exhibited was to start counting from the left side of the body rather than the right side. Even when it was explained that counting always started on the right some children remained confused.

Other informal systems that use objects as the basis of counting can be used to carry out arithmetic operations (at least addition and subtraction) on larger numbers. Cole and Cole (2001) report that West Africans, who used cowrie shells as counters, could calculate sums running into tens of thousands when trading with Portuguese merchants. It is interesting to compare a system of number representation using counters with one, like that of the Oksapmin, that uses body parts. The use of counters provides the basis by which large numbers can be represented and manipulated and allows the development of a number system that is closer to a formal system.

Adding and subtracting objects

Once children are able to count reliably, they are ready to begin the long process of mastering arithmetic skills. Formal mathematics requires children to understand written numbers but their first exposure to the arithmetic operations of addition and subtraction usually relies on oral counting and often makes use of objects. In this way early experience of addition and subtraction becomes a natural extension of counting.

The most straightforward way to use counting for simple addition and subtraction is to use a **counting all strategy**. For example, if children are shown two sets of sweets and asked to find out how many sweets there are altogether, they can do this by counting all the sweets in the first set (e.g. 1, 2, 3, 4) and then continuing the count for the sweets in the other set (e.g. 5, 6, 7). Studies of five-year-old children show that this is the strategy they most often apply when asked to add up two sets of objects (Nunes & Bryant, 1996).

A counting all strategy can also be used for subtraction problems using objects. Riley, Greeno, and Heller (1983) gave simple addition and subtraction problems to six-year-old American children. The subtraction problems were of the kind: "Joe had eight marbles. Then he gave five marbles to Tom. How many does he have now?" The children proved to be successful at both kinds of problem providing that they were able to use blocks to represent the numbers involved and providing that the numbers were small.

The importance of physically present items for early success in addition and subtraction was highlighted in a study by Hughes (1986) of preschool children aged from three to five. He used only small numbers in his problems so that the children would be able to find the answer if they understood what was required to do this. In one condition children counted the number of bricks inside a box (e.g. two) and then saw how many Hughes added (e.g. one) or took

KEY TERM
Counting all strategy: Early strategy for simple addition involving the counting of all the items in both sets.

away. They were then asked how many bricks there were in all but they were not allowed to look in the box. A second condition was similar except that, this time, the children were asked to imagine the box and the bricks. In a third condition, children were asked about the number of children in an imaginary shop while, in a fourth condition, they were asked to make an identical calculation using numbers (e.g. What is 2 and 1 more?).

Although none of the conditions allowed the children to count the total number of objects remaining after the addition or subtraction the different conditions did not produce identical performance. The easiest condition was the first one with the real box. The second and third conditions produced rather similar but less good performance. The fourth condition, which used only numbers, was the most difficult. Perhaps the most surprising aspect of the results is that asking children to imagine countable objects (bricks or people) made the task much easier than asking directly about numbers. This suggests that, for preschool children, ideas about adding and subtracting are so rooted in the counting of objects that even imaginary objects provide support for their calculations.

Training mathematical skill

Many studies have now established that providing preschool children with suitable training in pre-reading skills can improve their later success in learning to read (see Chapter 10, Social Development in the Preschool Years). It is natural to ask whether young children's mathematical skills can be facilitated in a similar way through appropriate training.

We saw in Learning to Count, earlier in this chapter, that understanding one-to-one correspondence is essential for the successful application of counting in early addition and subtraction. This suggests that training in the application of one-to-one correspondence to simple addition and subtraction problems with objects could improve children's performance. This hypothesis was tested by Nunes and Bryant (1991, reported in Nunes & Bryant, 1996) who carried out a training study with 180 Brazilian children aged from five to seven. The younger children (five/six years) were attending preschool and the seven-year-olds were in their first year at school.

The first stage in the study was to test all the children to see if they had a basic understanding of one-to-one correspondence. This was done by asking each of the children to share 16 pretend sweets equally between themselves and the experimenter. Then the children counted their own sweets and were asked how many sweets the experimenter had. They were not able to count the experimenter's sweets, which were hidden from view, and so they had to draw an inference from one-to-one correspondence to work out the answer. Almost all the children were able to draw the correct inference and those who were not were excluded from the study.

All the children were then tested on four comparison problems to provide a pretest baseline. Two were of the form "Joe has eight marbles. Tom has three. How many more marbles does Joe have than Tom?", while the other two had the slightly different form, "Tom has three marbles. Joe has five more marbles than Tom. How may marbles does Joe have?" Next the children took part in the training phase of the study. They were given a series of problems that were similar to the first set used in the pretest. These involved comparisons between the number of pretend sweets allocated to the child and to the experimenter. While they were solving these problems one group of children was given only feedback and two groups received training. In the *feedback only* condition, the children were encouraged to use blocks to represent the numbers of sweets and they were told whether their answer was correct after each trial. The two *training* conditions initially involved the creation of equal sets of sweets for the child and experimenter and then the addition or subtraction of sweets to one set. The training varied in the way that the initial equality of the sets was established. In the *spatial one-to-one correspondence* condition, the children set aside one set of sweets for themselves and were then asked to set aside an equal set for the experimenter by placing their own sweets in a straight line and matching each with a sweet for the experimenter. In the *temporal one-to-one correspondence* condition, the experimenter placed sweets one-by-one in a box and the children placed sweets in their box at the same time as the experimenter. Then, in both training conditions sweets were added or taken away from the child's set and the child was asked about the total number he or she now had. As in the feedback condition, children were told whether they were correct and were given the right answer if necessary.

At the end of the training phase all children were retested on the two types of comparison problem presented in the pretest. All three groups improved significantly from pretest to post-test showing the practice and feedback alone had improved performance. However, children who had received training in spatial one-to-one correspondence improved significantly more than the other two groups. The younger children who had received this training performed as well as the first graders in the other two groups, while the older children solved three of the four problems correctly, A detailed look at these children's performance showed that this was because they had improved both on the problems that were similar to the ones in the training phase and also on the other problems for which they had not received specific training. These required the children to work out how many marbles one person had, given knowledge of the number possessed by the other person and the difference between the two: "Tom has three marbles. Joe has five more marbles than Tom. How may marbles does Joe have?" The fact that the older children, who had received training in spatial one-to-one correspondence, were able to succeed in a task on which they had not been trained supports the idea that training in one-to-one correspondence can provide children with improved understanding of the logic of addition and subtraction.

Adding and subtracting numbers

The use of physical markers to assist in addition and subtraction continues once children move on to formal operations involving written numbers. The counting all strategy can be applied to fingers just as to objects and this is often how children first solve simple addition problems using numbers. Thus, to add 3 + 4 children hold up three fingers and then, while still holding up the first set of fingers, they hold up another four fingers (often on the other hand). The total number of fingers is then counted to give the answer, 7.

The counting all strategy cannot easily be applied to addition where the sum is greater than 10. Children thus move on to a **counting on strategy** in which they can still use their fingers but now they count upwards from one of the addends. Now, to add 3 + 4 the child would start from three, hold up four fingers and count 4, 5, 6, 7. In the counting on strategy, it is more efficient to count on from the larger number rather than the smaller as it involves less counting. Groen and Parkman (1972) found that primary school children naturally do count on from the larger number, for example, counting on from 7 rather than 2 in 7 + 2. However, it is possible that when children first employ the counting on procedure they always start with the first number in an addition and count on according to the size of the second number. Selecting the larger number as the starting point requires the child to realise the numerical equivalence of, say, 15 + 7 and 7 + 15. Although this equivalence is obvious to someone who is familiar with arithmetic it is not immediately apparent to a child.

Counting aloud is usually replaced by subvocal (silent) counting as children reach the end of primary school. It is more difficult to study the use of subvocal counting in the solution of arithmetic problems but reaction time studies, comparing the time taken to solve addition problems involving numbers of different magnitudes, show that subvocal counting continues to be used to solve arithmetic problems throughout the early school years (Gallistel & Gelman, 1991). This method is later supplemented by the **retrieval of number facts** from memory in which the addition of numbers is carried out by recalling the answer from previous additions.

Methods for adding numbers

"Counting all" strategy is used to solve simple addition problems. Fingers are held up and counted and this is effective up to a total of 10.

Where the sum is greater than 10, children use the "counting on" strategy. Fingers are still used, but now the child counts upwards from one of the addends. It is more efficient if the child counts on from the largest number, but initially children tend to follow the order of the sum and count on from the first number.

Counting aloud is replaced by subvocal counting, and this strategy is employed throughout the early school years.

Subvocal counting is later supplemented by the retrieval of number facts from memory in which the addition of numbers is carried out by recalling the answer from previous additions.

For *subtraction* the most common method used by primary school children is the **choice algorithm** (Woods, Resnick, & Groen, 1975) which can be seen as analogous to the counting on method used for addition. There are two ways of employing the choice algorithm. The first involves counting the number of steps required to get from the subtrahend (the number to be subtracted) to the minuend (the number from which the subtraction is to take place). For example, the solution to the sum 8 – 6 is obtained by counting up from 6 to 8 (7, 8) and seeing how many steps are involved (2). In the second method the child counts down from the minuend the number of steps specified by the subtrahend. The answer to 8 – 2 is obtained by counting down from 8 two steps, thus 7, 6 (6 being the correct answer). The use of the choice method is demonstrated both by reaction time data (which show that reaction time increases with the difference in size between the minuend and the subtrahend) and by interviews with children in which use of these methods is spontaneously reported (Gallistel & Gelman, 1991). As in the case of addition, these counting methods are finally replaced by the use of retrieval of number information.

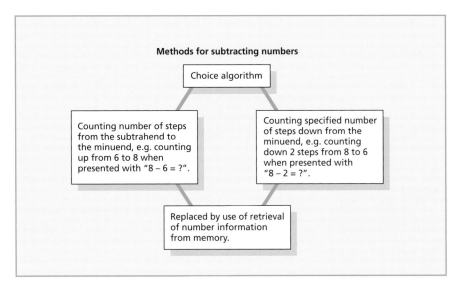

Success in addition and subtraction, as well as the more complex operations of multiplication and division, requires children to understand the basis of written number representation. The key to this is understanding the relation between the columns in multi-digit numbers and how these relations are maintained in arithmetic operations. In the first instance, children have to learn about **place value** which is an important convention in the Hindu-Arabic system for writing numbers. They must learn that the rightmost column represents numbers from 0 to 9 (units), the column to the immediate left represents tens, the next left hundreds, and so on. For example, in a number such as 254, children must learn that the 2 stands for two hundreds, the 5 for five tens while the 4 represents four ones. One important aspect of place values that can be especially difficult to grasp is the significance of 0. Zero is used as a **place holder**, that is, it indicates the presence of an empty column. For example, in 204 the 0 indicates that there are no tens. If the 0 were omitted, giving 24, a very different value would be indicated.

Having understood place values and the importance of zeros, the next step is for children to learn how these are maintained when multi-digit numbers are added, subtracted, multiplied, and divided. This is a complex problem and many of the difficulties that children experience in mastering formal arithmetic stem from failures to understand the maintenance of place values, especially the significance of zeros. The next box describes some of the difficulties that Brazilian children experience with place values and place holding.

Sinclair (1988) found that six- and seven-year-old French children did not understand place value even for two-digit numbers and were not aware that in a number such as 16 the first digit stood for one ten (i.e. 10) rather than one one. Nunes and Bryant (1996) gave five- and six-year-old children in England a series of tasks that assessed understanding of place value. These included reading and writing numbers containing from one to four digits as well as round numbers (10, 60, 100, 200, 1000). The children found it relatively easier to read and write the round numbers than other numbers with the same number of digits. Thus 200 was easier than 202 and 1000 than 1237. Nunes and Bryant suggest that this is because of the relatively greater familiarity of the round numbers.

Problems with writing numbers again reflected confusions in understanding the value of 0 as a place holder. Some children added additional zeros as in two examples reported by Nunes and Bryant of children who wrote 108 as 1008 and, even more dramatically, 2569 as 200050069. The logic of such a representation is clear: Thousands and hundreds are each followed by the correct number of zeros to act as place holders. What had confused the children is that place holders are only necessary when lower place values are empty. In all, 40% of the five- and six-year-old children described by Nunes and Bryant used an incorrect number of noughts (either too many or too few) to write the numbers 108 and 2569.

Overall, there was an interesting difference between the children who were good at writing numbers and those who were not. Children in the former group were generally better at understanding how numbers could be decomposed and added. This was tested in a task where children were given pretend coins of different values which they were required to give to a shopkeeper to pay for a particular item. Both single denomination (1p) and multiple denomination (10p and 20p) coins were used and the children were required to use combinations of these. Thus to pay for an item that cost 11p a child would require one 10p and one 1p coin. In order to select the correct coins, children had to realise the relation between single and multiple denomination coins and understand how a combination of coins could produce the correct amount. Additive composition—as this ability is called—clearly has a great deal in common with place values and Nunes and Bryant suggest that understanding the additive composition of numbers provides a basis for subsequent understanding of place values in written numbers. Evidence from studies of the informal maths used in buying and selling on the streets of Brazil (see the following box) shows that children may have a very good understanding of additive composition but not understand how place values operate in formal written mathematics.

Difficulties with place values and place holders are a major factor in children's problems with multi-digit arithmetic. Dockrell and McShane (1992) summarise the findings of Brown and Burton (1978), who analysed nearly 20,000 multi-digit additions and subtractions carried out by schoolchildren. Brown and Burton found that 40% of children made procedural errors with subtraction. The most common errors occurred when children had to deal with zeros, for example, borrowing from zero in order to subtract a larger number from a smaller but failing to carry the borrowing over to the next column; or writing the bottom digit in a column as the answer whenever the top digit was zero. Another common error was to subtract the smaller from the larger digit regardless of which was on the top line and which on the bottom.

Mathematical skills in the street children of Brazil

Several studies have shown that many children find the abstract nature of formal arithmetic to be difficult to deal with. Such children can often demonstrate understanding of basic mathematical principles when asked to solve a concrete problem, even though they cannot solve an identical problem when it is presented as formal arithmetic. The most striking example of this difference between knowledge of mathematical principles in a practical context and the ability to carry out formal arithmetic in a school setting comes from studies of the Brazilian street children.

Carraher, Schliemann, and Carraher (1988) carried out a study of children in Brazil who made a living from working in street markets, selling fruit, drinks, and popcorn. In the course of these activities the children had to carry out quite complex additions, subtractions, and multiplications in their head in order to work out the cost of the goods that they were selling and the change that they had to give their customers. The children also attended school where they carried out addition, subtraction, and multiplication of equal complexity using formal mathematical notation and working with pencil and paper.

The children were fast and accurate at working out the answers to mathematical problems when selling goods. For example, when asked to work out the total cost of two coconuts each costing 40 cruzeiros and the change that a customer would be due from a 500 cruzeiros note, a child replied unhesitatingly "Eighty, ninety, one hundred, four hundred and twenty". This correct answer was obtained by adding on from 80 up to 500 in a way that is rather similar to the choice algorithm. The same child was unable to solve a similar formal addition problem. When asked "What is $420 + 80$?" the child wrote down the sum and obtained the answer 130. (This answer was arrived at by adding $0 + 0$ to get 0 then adding $2 + 8$, carrying 1 and adding this to the 4 and finally adding $8 + 5$ to get 13!)

Carraher et al. give many other examples which show that the children used different methods for arithmetic calculations in the street and classroom context. One of the most common methods used for mental calculations in the street markets was decomposition in which numbers were broken down into parts and each part dealt with in turn. For example when asked to find the answer to $200 - 35$ one girl solved this in her head as follows: "If it were 30, then the result would be 70. But it is 35. So it is 65, 165." The steps involved in this calculation were, first, to split 200 into $100 + 100$ then to split 35 into $30 + 5$ and to subtract these sequentially from 100 ($100 - 30 = 70$: $70 - 5 = 65$). The 100 which had been "set aside" was then added back on to give the correct answer of 165.

The formal subtraction method used in school involved "borrowing" from each column as appropriate and "paying back" in the next column, a procedure that often led to the kind of mistakes noted by Brown and Burton (1978). Another difference between the methods used in mental calculation and those adopted with pencil and paper was that, in the former case, children worked from hundreds to tens and then units while the formal procedure worked in the opposite direction from units to tens then hundreds. Carraher et al. suggest that this is one reason why, in using the formal procedures, children tended to lose track of the sort of answer that they should obtain. Their other difficulty was that they looked upon the school procedures merely as rules to be followed and they often had little or no understanding of why the procedures would, if correctly applied, produce the right answer.

Cross-cultural differences in mathematical ability

Many studies have shown that children in Asian countries (China, Japan, Korea, and Taiwan) perform at a consistently higher level on tests of mathematical ability than their contemporaries in the West. One of the most extensive comparative studies was carried out by Stevenson and his colleagues who tested over 4000 primary school children in Taiwan, Japan, and the United States (Stevenson, Lee, Chen, Stigler, Hsu, & Kitamura, 1990). All the children in the three countries came from large cities and attended schools that were representative of their local area. Half the children were in grade 1 (age six years) and the others were in grade 5 (age eleven years). All children were given a wide range of tests to assess different aspects of mathematical ability and also reading. There was no overall difference between the three groups on the reading tests although more American fifth-graders performed at the extremes (i.e. reading well above or well below their chronological age) than their peers in Taiwan and Japan. (This could be explained by differences in reading strategies for English and the other two scripts—see Learning to Read Alphabetic Scripts, and Learning to Read Non-alphabetic Scripts, in Chapter 12). However, for maths, there was a clear overall difference, with the Japanese and Taiwanese children having significantly higher scores on almost all of the tests.

One clear indication of the extent of the superiority of the Japanese and Taiwanese children over their peers in the United States came from a comparison of the highest and lowest scorers across the entire sample. In the first grade, only 14 children from the US were in the top 100 while 56 were in the bottom 100. By the fifth grade, only one American child was in the top 100 while 67 were in the bottom 100. Had the ability of the children in the three countries been the same, there should have been around 33 American children in both the top and bottom 100 since an equal number from each country were tested. However, Stevenson's data show that, particularly in fifth grade, the American children were significantly underrepresented in the group of high achievers and significantly overrepresented in the group of low achievers.

Accounting for the mathematical superiority of the Asian children has proved difficult because there are many possible factors that could contribute to this difference (see Towse & Saxton, 1998 for a review). We have already seen in this chapter that early experience and specific training can improve children's mathematical skills, so an obvious starting point is to consider whether there are differences in the educational experiences of the children. So far there is little direct evidence about differences in preschool experience, although this clearly would be a fruitful area for future investigation. There have, however, been a number of studies looking at the way that mathematical concepts are taught in school. Perry, Van der Stoep, and Yu (1993) compared the methods used in Taiwan, Japan, and the United States for teaching addition and subtraction. One difference in approach stood out. Teachers in Japan and Taiwan were more likely to ask the children conceptual questions that required them to integrate information and draw inferences. For example, Japanese and Taiwanese children were often asked to compare solutions across different problems. A similar difference in approach was evident in a comparison of mathematics textbooks. Mayer, Sims, and Tajika (1995) found that American textbooks devoted a great deal of space to series of exercises that the children were expected to work through, whereas Japanese textbooks spent more time in explaining underlying concepts and providing worked-out examples for the children to follow.

There are also striking differences between American and Asian children in the amount of time spent on mathematics education. Considerably more class time is spent on mathematics in Japan and Taiwan, and many children have additional private tuition to supplement school teaching. Stevenson et al. (1990) found that, in grade 1, Japanese children spent an average of 5.8 hours per week on mathematics, Taiwanese children spent 4.0 hours, and American children only 2.7 hours. By grade 5, these figures had increased to 7.8, 11.7, and 3.4 hours. Older pupils were also given more mathematics homework than their American peers (Fuligni & Stevenson, 1995). This greater emphasis on mathematics reflected a finding from the Stevenson et al. (1990) study that Taiwanese and Japanese children and their families saw success in mathematics as closely related to hard work and effort, whereas American children and their families were more likely to attribute success to natural ability rather than hard work. This difference in attitude has also been highlighted by Hatano, who notes: "Japanese people think that effort makes a difference everywhere (i.e., even when one lacks ability)" (Hatano, 1990, p. 112).

Another factor that has been identified as a possible source of the mathematical superiority of Asian children is their number system. We have already seen that the spoken names given to numbers can have an effect on the way that children count (see the box on page 276). It has also been suggested that number names can affect children's understanding of the number system itself, particularly the concept of place value (see the previous section in this chapter). As we saw, understanding place value is essential for success in multi-digit arithmetic and so it has been suggested that spoken numbers that consistently reflect place value assist children in mastering this concept. English is not consistent in its number names (see Towse & Saxton, 1998) especially for numbers between 11 and 19 where some, but not all, numbers end with the suffix "teen" and some numbers have their unit value expressed in full (as in fourteen) while others have a reduced form of their unit value (as in fifteen rather than fiveteen). Similar inconsistencies exist with the use of full and modified forms to describe the tens in numbers from 20 to 100. Thus we have "fifty" rather than "fivety" and the suffix "teen" becomes "ty". Even greater irregularities have been noted in French number names, which has "quatre-vingts" for 80 and "dix sept" for 17.

The Asian countries where mathematical superiority has been documented all have Chinese-based number names. These are highly regular for numbers up to 100 and, importantly for the concept of place value, the number of tens is made explicit. For example, in Japanese, 2 is "ni", 10 is "juu", and 20 is "ni-juu" (i.e. two-ten). The number of units is stated after the number of tens so 21 is "ni-juu-ichi" (i.e. two-ten-one). More comparisons between number names in English, French, and Japanese are shown in the table on the right. This explicit

Comparisons between number names

English	French	Japanese
one	un (or une)	ichi
two	deux	ni
three	trois	san
four	quatre	shi
ten	dix	juu
eleven	onze	juu-ichi
twelve	douze	juu-ni
twenty	vingt	ni-juu
twenty-one	vingt-et-un	ni-juu-ichi

representation of the number of tens and units in numbers up to 100 has led to the suggestion that Japanese children develop a more precocious understanding of place value and additive composition. This hypothesis was tested by Miura et al. (1994), who asked children in China, Japan, and Korea, and in three Western countries (Sweden, France, and the United States) to represent written numbers using single unit and multiple units blocks which represented ten units. This task was very similar in rationale to the Nunes and Bryant (1996) task in which the child had to pay a shopkeeper with single and multiple denomination coins (see the previous section in this chapter, Adding and Subtracting Numbers). As in the shop task, the important issue in the Miura paradigm was whether children would represent numbers through single units only or through a combination of multiple and single units.

Miura et al. found that six- and seven-year-old Chinese, Korean and Japanese children produced significantly more responses in which they correctly used a combination of single and ten unit blocks. The Western children mainly used only single unit blocks to represent numbers. Miura et al. claim that this reflects a more sophisticated understanding of number by the Asian children which stems from differences in the explicitness of number names. The problem with this conclusion is that all that has been demonstrated is a correlation rather than a causal link between number names and the understanding of additive composition; and, as we have seen, there are other important differences in the mathematics education of the West and Asia. Furthermore, Towse and Saxton (1998) have shown that performance in the Miura task can be significantly affected by relatively small changes in procedure. In one study, a group of English children was given blocks that represented 20 units and single units, and another group of the same age was given 10 unit and single unit blocks as in the original Miura task. The 20-unit condition produced many more composite responses in which the children represented numbers through a combination of multiple and single unit blocks. In the study, Towse and Saxton found that the performance of both Japanese and English children was affected by the examples given to them at the start of the study. Both groups used the 10-unit block more often if they had received an example of its use from the experimenter at the start of the study. These findings suggest that differences in the representation of number by Japanese and English children may not be as profound as Miura has argued.

Conclusion and summary

As with reading, children begin to acquire the skills that are necessary for the development of mathematical understanding long before they begin formal instruction. Some awareness of number is present even in infancy, when distinctions between one, two, and three items can be made. However, the real beginning of mathematical skills comes about when, during the preschool period, children begin to embark on the complex process of learning to count. This process is usually well established by the age of five years when the principle of one-to-one correspondence has been mastered.

Having learned how to count sets of objects children are then in a position to begin adding and subtracting. Initially addition and subtraction also centres on objects but gradually children learn how to carry out these operations using written symbols. Counting on the fingers usually acts as a bridge between addition and subtraction of objects and the use of written forms; and counting, first aloud and later subvocally, continues to be an important part of addition and subtraction until the end of the primary school years when the retrieval of number facts becomes increasingly important.

Understanding the representation of written numbers is another essential component in learning to do formal mathematics. Here, developing an understanding of the concept of place value and of the role of place holders is crucial. Understanding how numbers can be broken down into their component parts appears to be an integral part of understanding place value and knowing what zero means is essential for getting to grips with the notion of place holding. Zero is a particularly difficult concept for many children because it stands for nothing as well as acting as a place holder. The history of mathematics shows that the use of zero was a relatively recent introduction into numerical notation, so it is not surprising that it such a challenging concept for children.

Many difficulties with primary school mathematics can be traced back to problems that children encounter in understanding how multi-digit numbers are represented in written form and how such numbers can be added, subtracted, multiplied, and divided. There are interesting cross-cultural differences in children's mathematical ability and it has been suggested that the regularity with which number names are formed in a given language has an impact on children's understanding of multi-digit numbers. However, although differences in the regularity of number names may account for some of the performance superiority of children from Asian countries, it is clear that the amount and style of teaching, as well as cultural differences in attitudes to mathematical ability, are at least equally important in explaining cross-cultural differences in ability. Comparisons between countries show that there is considerable variation in the amount of time that children are expected to spend on mathematics outside the classroom and it is clear that success in mathematics is usually the result of sustained effort and practice.

Further reading

- Dehaene, S. (1997). *The number sense*. London: Penguin Books. This book is written for a lay audience but it provides both a clear account of the development of mathematical abilities from infancy onwards and a historical and cross-cultural perspective on adult skills in mathematics. There is an excellent discussion of number systems.
- Donlan, C. (Ed.). (1998). *The development of mathematical skills*. Hove, UK: Psychology Press. This edited book provides chapters summarising recent research on the development of mathematical abilities. It is mainly intended for advanced undergraduates.
- Nunes, T., & Bryant, P. (1996). *Children doing mathematics*. Oxford, UK: Blackwell. This book, which is suitable for first- and second-year undergraduates, provides a comprehensive overview of the development of mathematical skills through the school years.

CONTENTS

Social development in the school years

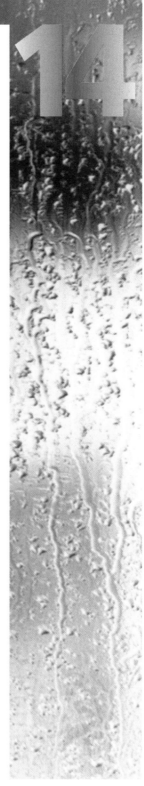

Children's entry into school not only marks the beginning of important changes in cognitive skills, it also has a profound effect on children's social development. The school environment brings children into daily contact with their peers and, as the school years progress, peer relationships become increasingly important. In this chapter we consider how children relate to their peers and develop friendships. We also look at their developing understanding of the complexity of moral judgements and their growing notions of distributive justice. In the final part of the chapter we turn to children's increasingly sophisticated understanding of their own emotions and those of other people.

Interactions with other children

One way of viewing the increasing significance of children's interactions with other children is to compare the relative amount of time devoted to peer interactions (Higgins & Parsons, 1983). At two, children spend around 10% of their time with peers (though this will vary depending on their childcare regime). When children start school, more than 30% of their time is spent with peers. Entry into school brings children into contact with many more children so the peer reference group is widened. At the same time, although parents continue to monitor their children's activities, much of the time children's interactions with peers are carried out unsupervised. So, while preschoolers usually play with other children under the close scrutiny of an adult, children's interactions with their peers in the classroom, playground, and in the neighbourhood are much less closely observed.

Hinde (1987) has outlined three successive levels of complexity that can be distinguished in children's experiences with their peers. These are *interactions*, *relationships*, and *groups*. Interactions are defined as "dyadic behaviour in which the participants' actions are interdependent such that each actor's behaviour is both a response to and a stimulus for the other participant's behaviour" (Rubin et al., 1998, p. 624). The important point here is that, in an interaction, participants are mutually engaged. If two children are merely sitting next to each other while carrying out independent activities this is not an interaction.

Interactions during the school years may take many forms. A great many interactions involve conversation: Children may gossip, argue, provide comfort, or tell jokes. They may also engage in a wide range of behaviours that extend from very physical play to highly complex and extended fantasies. As Rubin et al. (1998) note, the wide range of interactions in which school-aged children engage makes description and classification difficult. Hence, researchers have tended to concentrate on aspects of relationships that are in common across these diverse situations. These are: moving towards another child, moving away from another child, and moving against another child, i.e. showing aggression. Most children show all of these three patterns at different times and in different situations, although individual children often favour particular patterns of response. Also, in a particular relationship, one of these general patterns of behaviour may predominate. For example, children who are friends will attempt to resolve conflicts so that they do not have to move away, whereas the motivation for resolution will be much weaker in the case of someone who is not a friend (Hartup & Laursen, 1992).

The amount of negative behaviour that children show in their interactions does not appear to change over the school years but there are noticeable changes in the form that aggressive behaviour takes. Direct physical aggression is replaced by verbal aggression that includes insults, derogatory remarks, and threats. Aggressive behaviour in six- to twelve-year-olds is also more directed towards individuals rather than being concerned with possessing particular objects or occupying a particular territory. Thus, preschoolers will fight about whose turn it is to play on the slide, whereas school-aged children are more likely to direct aggression towards children that they do not like (Coie & Dodge, 1998).

Children become increasingly concerned about their acceptance in their peer group during middle childhood. There is much discussion—gossip— about other children and being the subject of gossip can occasion anxiety. A study of gossip in school-aged children (Teasley & Parker, 1995, cited in Rubin et al., 1998) has revealed that much gossip involves making negative and critical remarks about other children. A more positive aspect of gossip is that children discuss relationships and behaviour within the peer group. Much time is spent in discussing the kind of activities that others engage in and deciding whether other children are friends or enemies. This reflects the fact that children of this age are very interested in "social maps"—knowing the patterns of friendship and enmity that exist in their peer group (Rubin et al., 1998).

Relationships bring a higher order complexity to children's peer interactions. A relationship can be thought of as a series of interactions between two children who know each other. The important, additional feature of a relationship is that the past history of the relationship will have an impact on new interactions. Hinde (1987) has suggested that relationships contain an essential element of commitment. In other words, the two partners in a relationship accept that it will continue and they will behave in ways that support this, as in the case of friends attempting to resolve disputes.

Relationships are dyadic (that is they involve two people) but many relationships exist within the wider context of a group. This is particularly true of children's relationships at school and, often, with children in the local neighbourhood. The peer group is an important point of reference for children since it manifest both *cohesiveness*—the degree of unity and inclusiveness within the group—and *hierarchy*—the ordering of individuals within the group (Hinde, 1979). School-age children are very aware of group norms in dress, speech, and behaviour and most children strive to conform to these. They are also very aware of their status within the group, particularly at school. Children readily compare themselves with their peers in performance in reading, maths, physical activities, and so on. They are also very interested in physical attributes such as height, weight, and even shoe size. At the same time, children's appreciation both of their own popularity and that of peers increases sharply during the school years.

These changes in middle childhood are indicative of the fact that children use social comparison as an important metric. Preschool children are likely to evaluate their own performance and characteristics against a set of absolute standards, whereas school-aged children will adopt a more relative view that involves social comparison. They also place considerable weight on being part of an in-group or clique.

Cliques are a characteristic feature of interactions at school. They are small groups of children of the same sex (and usually race) that typically contain three to nine members. By 11 years of age, most children report that their peer interaction takes place within a clique and nearly all children report being a member of a clique. It is perhaps unfortunate that, during this same period, children's membership of such groups is very labile. Kanner, Feldman, Weinberg, and Ford (1987, cited in Rubin et al., 1998) found that around one-third of 11-year-olds reported recently losing a friend or being picked last to take part in an activity; and almost two-thirds reported being teased by peers within the preceding month.

Hinde's levels of complexity in peer relationships

Interactions
- Participants are mutually engaged.
- Actions are interdependent so each action is both a response and a stimulus.

Relationships
- Series of interactions between two children who know each other.
- Past history will have an impact on new interactions.
- There is an element of commitment.

Groups
- Provide both cohesiveness and hierarchy.
- Social comparison becomes an important metric.
- Importance is given to membership of a clique.

Friendships

During middle childhood and early adolescence, children show an increasing sophistication in their understanding of friendship. Bigelow (1977) asked children "What do you expect from a best friend?" Their answers reveal that preschool children's ideas about friendship are anchored in the here-and-now and are typically tied to particular social situations such as attending playgroup or nursery or attending swimming classes. By school age, however, children have developed friendships that transcend time and activity but Bigelow found that, even at seven or eight, children still have a fairly pragmatic view about the nature of friendship. They see friends as children who are rewarding to be with in comparison to non-friends who are unrewarding or uninteresting to be with. A friend is someone convenient in the sense of being available (typically living nearby or attending the same school) who has interesting toys and possessions and compatible views about play. By 10 or 11 years, there is a significant development in that friends are expected to share values and rules and to show public loyalty. Later still, at 11 to 13 years, friends are seen as sharing similar interests and engaging in attempts to understand each other. Self-disclosure becomes an increasingly important aspect of friendship at this stage and continues into adolescence.

Selman and Schutlz (1990) have argued that changes in perspective-taking ability underlie children's evolving views about the nature of friendship. We saw in Chapter 10, Social Development in the Preschool Years, that preschoolers typically acquire a theory of mind between the ages of three and four (see Social Cognition and Theory of Mind in that chapter). Thus, they are able to realise that different people may have different beliefs about a situation. However, it takes greater developmental maturity to appreciate that common beliefs and attitudes can consolidate or destroy friendships, and it is significant that an adult-like view of friendship does not emerge until 11 to 13 when children become capable of abstract thinking and can see that friendships transcend time, distance, and events.

We saw in The Formation of Friendships in Chapter 10 that preschool children tend to form friendships with children of similar age and sex. Similarity of behaviour is also important among school-aged children. Hartup and his colleagues (see Hartup, 1998) obtained peer rating from 11-year-olds on three constructs: prosocial behaviour (see Chapter 10), antisocial behaviour, and shyness. Friends were rated as more similar to each other on all three constructs compared with non-friends. The similarity of antisocial behaviour in friends (fighting, disruption, and bullying) was higher than either prosocial behaviour or shyness; and for both, prosocial and antisocial behavioural similarity between friends was higher for girls than for boys, whereas boys were more similar in shyness. Hartup argues that these gender differences can be attributed to differences in **reputational salience** for boys and girls. Reputational salience is the importance of a particular attribute in determining a child's social reputation. The idea is that, for girls, being judged as kind or unkind is very important in determining social reputation, whereas, for boys, shyness is more important.

Bullying

Having discussed the importance of friendships in the school years we now turn to another aspect of social interaction that emerges in middle childhood. Bullying refers to acts of physical and verbal aggression on the part of the bully that are directed towards particular peers (i.e. victims). According to Rubin et al. (1998), bullying makes up a large proportion of the aggression that occurs in the peer group during the school years. Bullying can be distinguished from other aggressive behaviour because it is directed only towards certain peers. It has been estimated that around 10% of the school population is subject to persistent bullying, although the majority of children are subject to occasional hostile acts from other children. Indeed, for most children, physical and verbal abuse is a normal part of social interactions with peers during primary school— the difference in the case of bullying is that particular individuals are singled out for sustained verbal and physical assaults.

Research on bullying suggests that bullies tend to show a strong tendency towards aggressive

Copyright © Photofusion/Sam Scott Hunter.

Gender differences in displaying emotions

Evidence that girls are often better than boys at concealing negative emotions comes from a study by Davis (1995) of American children. Her study was well designed in that the children who took part were highly motivated to conceal their true emotions. This was achieved by asking the children to play a game in which there were two possible prizes. One was highly desirable but the other was not. Each prize was placed in a box that allowed the child, but not the experimenter, to see what was inside. Before the game started, the children were told that if they were able to trick the experimenter into believing that they liked both prizes then they would be allowed to keep both. However, if they failed, they would not receive either prize.

Davis found that girls were better than boys at masking their negative emotions about the undesirable prize. The girls also engaged in more social monitoring than the boys—glancing at the experimenter to gauge her reaction. Davis concluded from her study that girls are better at managing the expression of negative emotions. However, there may well be cultural norms at work here, because a study by Joshi and MacLean (1994) found that Indian girls were three times more likely than their English peers to acknowledge that children might conceal a negative emotion from an adult. The same study found no differences between Indian and English boys. Joshi and MacLean argue that these differences reflect the fact that Indian girls experience strong cultural pressure to adopt a deferential attitude to adults in which negative emotions are suppressed.

Conclusion and summary

Entry into school brings children into contact with a large peer group with whom they spend a considerable—and increasing—amount of time. The peer group serves as an important reference point for children's own assessments of themselves; and much attention is given to the interactions of individuals within the group. Over the school years, children develop increasingly sophisticated ideas about the nature of friendship and they begin to make friends less on the basis of convenience and availability and more on the basis of shared values and beliefs. Friends tend to behave in similar ways but there appear to be differences between girls and boys in the aspects of behaviour that are most similar. Entry into school brings children into contact with a large peer group with whom they spend a considerable—and increasing—amount of time. While family members still continue to act as an important source of emotional support, contact with the peer group provides an opportunity for children to compare themselves with others and, as the school years continue, the peer group becomes the key reference group for children's own assessment of themselves. Children acquire detailed knowledge of what other children at school wear and like to do and how they behave both in and out of school. Considerable attention is given to the interactions of individuals within the group as children discover which children are friends and which ones do not like each other. In this way they build up social maps within which they can locate themselves.

Over the school years, children develop increasingly sophisticated ideas about the nature of friendship. In the early years children often make friends on the basis of convenience and will play with any nearby child who can play the same games as them. As children grow older and begin to approach adolescence, friendships become more specific and are made on the basis of shared values and beliefs. Friends tend to behave in similar ways but there appear to be differences between girls and boys in the aspects of behaviour that are most similar. However, one should be cautious about simplistic views of similarity because children tend to choose their friends on the basis of what matters to them. This is an issue that we explore further in the final chapter when we consider development during adolescence.

The increasing sophistication of notions of friendship is mirrored in an increasing understanding of moral issues. Piaget and Kohlberg outlined three main stages in moral reasoning—preconventional, conventional, and postconventional stages. Their method of studying moral reasoning involved asking children to offer solutions to various moral dilemmas and to justify these solutions. More naturalistic methods can reveal higher levels of moral understanding than are evident in these very formal tasks. Dunn used naturalistic observation of children with family members, whereas Damon presented children with real-life dilemmas. Both methods reveal much greater complexity in children's understanding of morality than performance in the moral reasoning tasks of Piaget and Kohlberg might suggest. This greater complexity is also reflected in Turiel's important distinction between judgements about "moral" and "socio-conventional" issues, which children begin to distinguish as young as five.

During the school years children also learn to disguise their emotions as they gain an explicit understanding of the difference between feeling an emotion and displaying it. Interestingly, girls appear to be better than boys at masking negative emotions.

Further reading

- Bukowski, W.M., Newcomb, A.F., & Hartup, W.W. (Eds.). (1996). *The company they keep: Friendship in childhood and adolescence*. Cambridge, UK: Cambridge University Press. This edited book contains a number of useful chapters on the development of friendships through the school years. It is suitable for all undergraduates.
- Campbell, A., & Muncer, S. (Eds.). (1998). *The social child*. Hove, UK: Psychology Press. This edited book is aimed at undergraduates and covers many aspects of social development including families, friendships, and the understanding of emotion and morality.
- Olweus, D. (1993). *Bullying at school: What we know and what we can do*. Oxford, UK: Blackwell. This book provides a detailed account of bullying which is suitable for undergraduates. There is emphasis on programmes that reduce bullying in schools as well as research into the characteristics of bullies and victims.
- Rubin, K.H., Bukowski, W.M., & Parker, J.G. (1998). Peer interactions, relationships, and groups. In N. Eisenberg (Ed.), *Handbook of child psychology: Vol. 3. Social, emotional, and personality development*

(W. Damon, Gen. Ed.; pp. 619–700). New York: Wiley. This excellent chapter summarises recent research on the changing nature of children's social interactions with other children. It is intended for advanced undergraduates.

- Saarni, C.S., Mumme, D.L., & Campos, J.J. (1998). Emotional development: Action, communication and understanding. In N. Eisenberg (Ed.), *Handbook of child psychology: Vol. 3. Social, emotional, and personality development* (W. Damon, Gen. Ed.; pp. 237–309). This authoritative chapter provides a comprehensive overview of research on the development of emotional expression and emotional understanding. It is intended for advanced undergraduates.

CHAPTER 15

CONTENTS

Adolescence

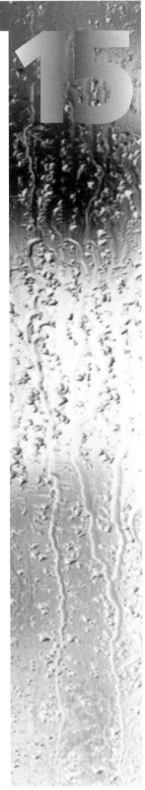

In this final chapter we consider the main changes that occur as children move towards adulthood. We begin by discussing Piaget's account of adolescent thinking and then move on to consider some more recent work in this area. Moshman (1998) notes that the psychological study of adolescence remained "relatively sparse and atheoretical" until the publication of *The Growth of Logical Thinking from Childhood to Adolescence* by Inhelder and Piaget in 1955. Moshman contrasts the richness of this account with that of Horrocks (1954) who wrote, what was for the time, a comprehensive account of adolescence in which he devoted barely one page to mental growth. Piaget and Inhelder's account of adolescence as structurally distinct from childhood cognition can thus be seen as the starting point for a revolution in the study of cognitive development beyond the primary school years.

Social and biological markers of adolescence

The onset of adolescence is signalled by both biological and cultural markers. The main biological marker, reproductive maturity at puberty, universally signals the biological transition from childhood. However, there is wide cultural variation in the recognition of this important biological transition.

Other obvious biological markers of adolescence are the rapid changes in physical development that comprise the "growth spurt" typically correlated with the onset of puberty. The growth spurt refers to the accelerated rate of increase in height and weight that occurs in adolescence. This physical change has many of the features of stage transition predicted by the epigenetic landscape model (see Figure 3.1 on page 38). There is a wide variation, both between and within the sexes, in the onset and rate of change during the transition to adolescence. In boys, the growth spurt may begin as early as 10 years, or as late as 16 years. In girls, the same process may begin as early as 8 years or not until 12 or 13 years. Other physical changes include increases in strength, a doubling in the size of the heart, greatly increased lung capacity, and the release of sex hormones by the pituitary gland of the brain, including testosterone in males and oestrogen in females.

Biological growth continues into young adulthood. For example, between 17 and 30 years the long bones of the skeleton and the vertebral column continue to grow and this may add up to a quarter of an inch to men's height (less for women). Some bones of the skull continue to grow throughout life (Tanner, 1978). Visual and auditory acuity are usually at their peak in young adults (20 years for vision and 13 years for hearing), with changes in vision and hearing being well documented from 25 to 70 years.

There have been marked increases in average adult height over time. Mediaeval European armour would fit the average 10- to 12-year-old boy today. The average male today wears a size 9–10 shoe, whereas the shoe worn by his grandfather was a size 7. There have also been dramatic increases in average height over the course of the 20th century. For example, in 1900 the average height of a marine was only 5' 9", whereas it is over 6' 0" today. Another significant change during the 20th century has been in the average age at which girls enter puberty. This has fallen by around two years. All these statistics show how the rate and course of development can be significantly altered, within biological limits, by circumstances such as improvements in health care and living conditions.

Physical strength increases to peak efficiency at between 25 and 30 years. Rutter and Rutter (1992) give two examples from athletics; the 10,000 metre runner, Paavo Nurmi, ran his fastest race at the age of 27 and the hammer thrower, Karl Hein, reached his peak at 30. However, both athletes showed less than a 5% decline in performance over the next 20 years, possibly because they continued to take vigorous physical exercise

On average, sexual maturity is reached 18–24 months earlier in girls than in boys. In girls, rapid change in height usually precedes the development of secondary sexual characteristics, whereas in boys, the height spurt generally occurs after the genitals have begun to grow (Coleman, 1980). These biological differences between males and females may have important consequences for psychological development, especially for aspects of identity formation, such as the body image, which are differentiated between the sexes (Brooks-Gunn & Warren, 1988).

In traditional societies, there may be virtually no gap between sexual maturity and adulthood. Cole and Cole (2001) point out that, among the !Kung San people of the Kalahari desert, the children learn hunting and gathering skills in middle childhood, so that they are self-sufficient by the time of puberty. Consequently, there is no direct equivalent to the stage of adolescence since, by the time of puberty, the !Kung San are economically independent. The period of adolescence varies from culture to culture and, indeed, from one period to another within the same culture. At least in part, the adolescent transition may therefore be a reflection of the requirement, in industrialised societies, for prolonged education to train towards non-traditional occupational roles.

Adolescence is also marked by new forms of thinking, with special sensitivity to received wisdom and moral and ethical ideals. Many of the preoccupations of adolescence arise as a consequence of the systematic thinking that becomes possible and the new capacity for more abstract thought. Indeed, many of the developments that are observable in adolescence, including the nature of friendships and moral reasoning, should be understood against the backdrop of cognitive change.

Piaget's theory of formal operational reasoning

The idea that cognition progresses to an advanced stage, beyond childhood, was first advanced by James Mark Baldwin who postulated a "hyper-logical" stage of mental development. Following on from this idea, Piaget argued that "formal reasoning" begins to be seen around the age of 10 or 11. For Piaget, the term "formal reasoning" was synonymous with "formal deduction", by which he meant:

> *Drawing conclusions, not from a fact given in immediate observation ... but in a judgement which one assumes, i.e. which one admits without believing it, just to see what it will lead to.*
> (Piaget, 1924/1972, p. 69, cited in Moshman, 1998)

Piaget defined this new stage in development by the systematic way in which the child becomes able to consider all possible combinations in relation to the whole problem and to reason about an entirely hypothetical situation. By contrast, the concrete operational child has acquired some organised systems of thought but proceeds only from one concrete link to the next.

Moshman (1998) points out that all of the 15 studies reported in Inhelder and Piaget (1955) revolve around some kind of physical apparatus—flexible rods, a pendulum, an inclined plane, communicating vessels, a hydraulic press, and a balance beam. (It is evident from this list that many of the tasks that are indispensable in the psychological study of children's thinking were originally used by Piaget and Inhelder.) Children from the ages of five to sixteen were asked to manipulate the apparatus, and to derive an understanding of the underlying physical phenomena that determined the behaviour of the apparatus. For example, in the case of the pendulum, children could determine how oscillation of the weight was affected by the length of the rod holding it. Children were interviewed individually and records were made of the experiments that they carried out with the apparatus and the conclusions that they drew. Their responses were interpreted as revealing patterns of thinking that were not observable in middle childhood—the period of concrete operations—but were common after the age of 11. Concrete operational children, operating on only one variable at a time, had great difficulty in determining the general principles that governed the operation of the apparatus, whereas children who were capable of formal operational thinking treated the problem as a whole and carried out systematic variation of the relevant parameters (see the box on pages 308–309).

A clear example of the difference between formal and concrete operations can be seen in the logical process called transitive inference which we discussed in Chapter 11, Cognitive Development in Middle Childhood. Children, who are in the stage of concrete operations, can infer that if A=B and B=C then A=C. This type of logic enables measurement, for example, where one concrete object, a ruler, is used to measure the relative lengths of two rods (see Piaget's Theory of Concrete Operational Reasoning, in Chapter 11). However, children who function at the concrete operational stage cannot solve the transitive inference problem if it is placed on a purely verbal and hypothetical plane, e.g. "John is taller than Mary, Mary is taller than Jane. Who is the tallest?" They are unable to consider all the possible combinations in relation to the whole problem. Progressing to the stage of formal operational reasoning removes these limitations and enables children to deal with hypothetical problems.

Other examples of stage-like transitions come from systematic experiments in scientific reasoning, carried out by Inhelder and Piaget (1958). Children were asked to explain physics problems such as working out how a pendulum operates, or how a balance beam works (see the following box).

Formal operational thinking

Having proposed a set of operations that are acquired during the stage of concrete operations, Piaget explained the transition from concrete to formal operations as involving the construction of second-order operations that involved the transformation of first-order (i.e. concrete) operations. This is the most technically complex part of Piaget's theory so we will focus on the key ideas. For a more detailed overview see Moshman (1998).

There are two forms of reversibility—inversion and reciprocity. These operations are hierarchically integrated into a totally internally coherent logical structure known as the Identity–Negation–Reciprocity–Correlative (INRC) group. This advance enables the child to take into account two frames of reference at the same time. Smith (1987) has shown that, in effect, Piaget was postulating a version of propositional logic.

An example of the quality of thinking that this new co-ordination allows comes from Einstein's theory of relativity. According to Einstein, motion is always relative to two frames of reference; the speed of a particular object and the speed of the observer. Imagine a satellite in orbit around the earth so that relative to the earth it is always above the same point in geostationary orbit. An astronaut sent up to repair a fault in the satellite is also rotating around the earth at the same speed as the satellite, yet relative to the astronaut (and relative to a particular position on the earth) the astronaut and satellite are stationary: If you were standing on the moon it would be readily apparent that we are all moving at a speed that can be defined relative to the motion of the moon with respect to the earth.

Following Piaget's theory is difficult in the abstract so let us take a more concrete example. The height of water in jars in the conservation of liquid volume task will serve. The task begins with two identical jars with identical levels of water of—self-evidently—identical volumes. When the contents of one tall, thin jar are poured into a second, short, fat jar the level of water drops. Children are asked, "Does the water in each jar take up the same amount of room?" Concrete operational children will say "yes".

Then children are given a new test in which a ball of clay is dropped into the water and they observe how the water level rises. The new, higher, level of water is marked on the side of the glass. Then the clay ball is taken out and flattened into a pancake. Children are asked to predict where the water level will be when the pancake-shaped clay is put back. Children are not able to predict this until the age of 11 or 12. Piaget argues that it is only when children can co-ordinate information from two sub-problems (conservation of the volume of the liquid and conservation of the volume of the clay) that they can draw the correct conclusion that the change in the height of liquid must be proportionate to the volume of clay dropped into the water.

Children's performance on balance beam problems follows a similar pattern as we saw in Chapter 11, Cognitive Development in Middle Childhood. Understanding of the relationship between weight and distance from the fulcrum does not come about until age 13 when most children tested by Siegler (1976) used rule 3. Siegler found that very few adolescents used rule 4 even if they had had explicit training on very similar tasks. This shows that, as Piaget himself found, not everyone manages to master the more complex relations that form part of formal operational thinking.

Criticisms of Piaget's theory

Piaget makes two claims about thinking in the period after concrete operations. The first is that developmental changes continue through early adolescence and the second is that formal operational thinking is the final stage of development. Both of these claims have been challenged (Moshman, 1998).

As we have seen in earlier chapters, there is considerable evidence that many important cognitive skills emerge rather earlier than Piaget proposed. Some authors (including DeLoache et al., 1998; Wellman & Gelman, 1998) have suggested that the fundamental aspects of cognition are acquired before adolescence and, thus, later changes are not developmental in nature. The idea here is that adolescent thinking changes *quantitatively* but not *qualitatively*. That is, children may simply become able to process more information, perhaps as a result of biological growth of the brain. Along with more information-processing capacity they tend to develop better memory, and hence become able to relate more elements of a problem to each other. This general type of explanation is similar to the maturationalist theories of the turn of the nineteenth century (see Chapter 1, A Brief History of Developmental Psychology) and it is subject to the same criticism that the notion of maturation may describe, but fails to explain why changes that are merely the result of growth should occur.

The other way of refuting a quantitative—non-developmental—explanation is to look at the nature of the changes associate with puberty (Moshman, 1998). We have already described some of these changes in the introduction to this chapter but it is useful to note that the biological changes occurring in puberty are qualitative, progressive, and internally directed. The changes are qualitative because they involve a co-ordinated transformation of anatomical and physiological systems that result in a distinct state of maturity. Change in puberty is progressive because it has a natural direction—a progression towards the clearly defined endstate of maturity. Puberty is an internally directed change because, although it requires environmental support in the form of adequate nutrition, it is not caused by any environmental effects. Interestingly Chomsky drew an analogy between puberty and the acquisition of language but, in fact, the role of the environment in these two developmental changes is rather different (see Chapter 8, Language Development in the Preschool Years).

The strong evidence for the developmental nature of the biological change that occurs in puberty supports Piaget's claim that there is a stage transition around the age of 11 or 12. It is not entirely clear, however, that the three characteristics of biological change in puberty apply equally to the cognitive changes. For example, education and culture have a large influence on the extent to which formal operational thinking is acquired. We discuss this later in the chapter.

Piaget's other claim, that the attainment of formal operations is the final stage of cognitive development, has been challenged by those who argue for later advances in cognition that occur towards the end of adolescence and into adulthood. There is now a growing body of research that has charted the developments in cognition occurring in late adolescence and adulthood (see Moshman, 1998 for a review). Cole and Cole (2001) discuss a study by Adelson (1972) of social and political reasoning in adolescents. When Adelson asked, "What is the purpose of laws?", 12- and 13-year-olds said, "If we had no laws, people could go around killing people". At this age, Cole and Cole argue, the children respond in terms of concrete people and events. However, 15- to 16-year-olds replied, "To ensure safety and enforce the government", "To limit what people can do". Older adolescents can reason hypothetically and take many facets into account and Cole and Cole suggest that they respond in terms of abstract principles based on hypothetical reasoning.

The search for inconsistency among belief systems—an awareness of contradictions in the behaviour of adults or in the rules governing behaviour—is also revealed by the ability to think hypothetically. The idealism of (some) adolescents can also be explained by an ability to reason hypothetically. What is to replace the imperfect institutions the adolescent observes? Such questions may lead to an ideal or utopian project.

Another example that illustrates developments in reasoning through adolescence is that of correlational reasoning. In one study, Inhelder and Piaget (1958) asked children and young adults to make a judgement about the co-variation of two variables. For example, if there are four combinations of hair and eye colour—dark hair/dark eyes; dark hair/light eyes; light hair/dark eyes; light hair/light eyes—it is possible to determine whether occurrence of the colour of hair and eyes is correlated. Inhelder and Piaget found evidence that the ability to understand co-variation continued to develop through adolescence but subsequent research has found that there is considerable variation among adults (Shaklee, Holt, Elek, & Hall, 1988). Indeed, formal operational reasoning is far from universal and adults often have great difficulties with problems such as the balance beam (see Girotto & Light, 1992). Piaget had difficulty in explaining the non-universal nature of formal operations.

Culture and context specificity in adult thinking

Some of the most interesting information about the forms of adult thinking comes from studies in which people in different cultures are compared. Whereas Piaget emphasised the new logical form of adult thought that appears in adolescence, the cross-cultural approach emphasises the contribution of the context to thought processes. That is, the life setting may require different degrees of systematic thought. Cultural differences in important variables such as how available schooling is, or levels of literacy, may have a profound impact on whether or not one observes formal operational reasoning in particular societies or whether concrete operational problem solving is sufficient for everyday needs. Furthermore, life settings may create specific opportunities for problem solving. The next box illustrates the complex reasoning involved in navigation by South Pacific island natives. This is a striking example of how the need to develop a reliable way of determining position at sea led to the development of a sophisticated method of calculation—requiring formal operational reasoning—that was based on the position of the stars.

Pulawat navigators

In the Polynesian islands natives would sail from one island to another in small outrigger canoes using a compass based on 14 distinctive star paths (see Figure 15.1). These are sets of stars that always rise at the same place on the eastern horizon and set at the same place in the west. The navigator, who is trained from adolescence, also has a "reference island", which may actually be purely hypothetical but whose bearing on the

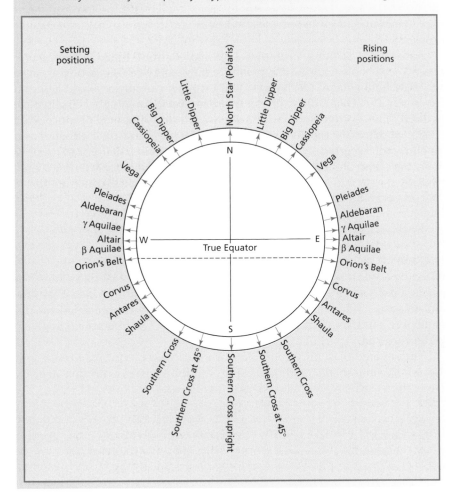

FIG. 15.1 The Pulawat star chart. Adapted from Goodenough (1953).

compass is known for any starting position. For the Polynesian islanders, navigation involves mentally combining star paths with the location of the reference island and with information about speed.

The investigator, Gladwin (1970), found that the Polynesian islanders seemed not to talk logically about how they solved the navigation problem. It was obvious to Gladwin that the canoe moved across the water while the islands remained still. However, the natives' system depended on imagining that the reference island moved while the boat stayed still. That is, they demonstrated formal operational reasoning within the frame of reference that was culturally specific for the purpose. Gladwin found that, unless they had attended high school, the same expert navigators were unable to solve a simple Piagetian problem in which all combinations of sets of colours in a pile of poker chips had to be worked out (Gladwin, 1970).

The example of reasoning among the Pulawat navigators illustrates very nicely a principle that is beginning to emerge in recent studies. This is that reasoning in everyday situations may be quite different from that in formal testing situations—an issue that has already arisen in earlier chapters. In everyday situations it is not always necessary to consider all possible combinations of hypotheses and often people develop heuristic devices to solve particular problems.

Some very striking examples have come from Brazil where many unschooled people carry out complex reasoning tasks (see also the box on pages 282–283). Schliemann and Nunes (1990) studied proportional reasoning in fishermen. These fishermen catch and store shrimp that may either be sold fresh or dried. They need to know what weight of fresh shrimp will produce what weight of dried shrimp. When working out the price of their product as a function of its weight they also have to allow for inflation, so they can't simply apply the same solution to repeated transactions but must work out each time what the cost should be. Schliemann and Nunes tested the fishermen on simple proportion problems: For example:

How much shrimp needs to be caught for a customer who wants 2 kilos of processed shrimps when 18 kilos yield 3 kilos of processed food?

Without pencil and paper the problem is solved as follows: One and a half kilos processed would be 9 kilos fresh (i.e. halves the initial values) … and a half kilo processed is 3 kilos unprocessed (i.e. finds the proportion needed for the remaining half kilo) … then it would be 9 plus 3 is 12 (unprocessed) to give 2 kilos processed.

The situated reasoning about proportionality proceeds by decomposing the problem into smaller units and using addition to arrive at the final answer. These steps can be represented formally as follows:

$$a/b = c/?$$
$$a \times ? = b \times c$$
$$? = (b \times c)/a$$
$$? = 18 \times 2/3$$
$$? = 12$$

Most of the fishermen have had little or no schooling. They cannot solve the problem using the written arithmetic method. The implication is that intuitive schemas of proportionality may actually conflict with algorithms used for teaching proportionality in schools. When the authors went on to study students from the same town, who were familiar with many of the commercial transactions in fishing, the students themselves scored better when using the intuitive methods they had learned in the market place than when using the formal notation.

When we compare individuals from different cultures we gain the impression that perhaps Piaget's theory of formal operational reasoning is in a way far too formal—it is overly abstracted from what people actually do. As Margaret Donaldson complained with respect to early development, disembedded thinking, as exemplified by Piaget's account, may underestimate the cognitive capabilities of adolescents and adults.

Moral reasoning

One important trend in thinking that occurs as children move into adolescence and adulthood is a change from the use of implicit principles to the deliberate application of explicit principles (Moshman, 1998). Kohlberg (1982) argued that principled reasoning is central to higher levels of moral development since, in his view, the moral reasoner construes morality as a matter of acting in accordance with justifiable principles. Rules differ from principles because the former are to be followed under all circumstances and so give an absolute solution to any moral dilemma. By contrast, principles give guidelines about what should be considered in arriving at a solution—and hence they offer a range of acceptable solutions rather than a single solution.

Kohlberg set stringent structural criteria for principled moral reasoning. Arguably these criteria are too stringent because most people to do not develop a level of moral reasoning that satisfies these criteria. Moshman (1995) proposed a less stringent conception of moral principles in which there is a set of metalaws that justifies a range of moral rules. He has suggested that young children use such principles implicitly but, as children become adolescents and move on into adulthood, these principles become the object of reflection. This can explain why many adolescents in Western society become very concerned about such issues as animal rights and third world debt. Studies of the development of principles relating to the essential freedoms of expression and religion show that adolescents and adults engage in forms of principled reasoning that are qualitatively different from the rule-based inferences that characterise younger children's thinking about these issues.

Another aspect of Kohlberg's theory that has been criticised is his view of gender differences in moral reasoning. As we saw in Chapter 14, Social Development in the School Years, Kohlberg interviewed only males and he found differences between males and females of college age with females scoring at stage 3 and males at stage 5. In stage 3 morality, people consider that whatever pleases or helps others is good and they are able to take into account the points of view and intentions of other people. In stage 5 morality, what is morally correct is determined by values agreed upon by society, including individual rights. In this stage, laws are no longer viewed as fixed but as relative.

Gilligan (1982) has argued that men and women focus on different aspects of moral dilemmas and so, on Kohlberg's male-orientated scale, men score higher than women. Men tend to focus on justice while women tend to focus on caring and responsibility. She claims that these different emphases reflect an underlying difference in the way that men and women see the relationship among people in society. Thinking of people as separate beings who are in continual conflict with one another requires an ethic of justice in which there are rules and contracts. An ethic of caring and responsibility—which Gilligan sees as characteristically female—stems from a view of the interconnectedness of people.

Gilligan's criticisms of Kohlberg have not gone unchallenged (see Haste, Helkama, & Markoulis, 1998 for a review). Johnson (1998) has shown that men and women are both capable of using either a justice orientation or a caring orientation if pressed, although there are clear gender-linked preferences in line with Gilligan. Differences in orientation also emerge when people are asked about real-life dilemmas that they have faced. Walker, de Vries, and Trevethen (1987) found that women were more likely than men to report moral dilemmas that concerned relationships with other people, whereas men were more likely to report impersonal dilemmas. Personal dilemmas were more likely to involve the care dimension and impersonal dilemmas a justice or rights orientation but, within the type of dilemma, there was no difference between men and women. This confirms the view that men and women—at least in Western society—place different emphases on the importance of relationships but it does not support the view that they have inherently different orientations. As Haste et al. (1998) conclude, there is support for Gilligan's claim that there is more than one moral "voice" but not for her claim that women typically adopt a caring voice.

Kohlberg's theory has also been criticised for its Western orientation. Cultural psychologists argue that we should not look for universal moral stages but, rather, we should attempt to understand moral diversity. For example, reasoning about justice may not be an appropriate concept to investigate in many cultures: South East Asian culture places family loyalty at the centre of their ethical system and reasoning has to be understood in these terms. Some examples of cultural variation in the rationale underlying moral judgements are shown in the box below.

Cultural variations in moral reasoning (adapted from Haste et al., 1998)

Indian Hindus

Shweder (1990) presented a number of "moral" and "conventional" examples of behaviour to children and adults in Chicago and India. The Indian participants were Hindus. The behaviours concerned eating, forms of punishment, dealing with members of the family, sex roles, and the way one should behave following the death of a relative. Shweder found some striking cultural differences as well as some similarities. Hindus saw certain behaviours as moral and binding because of the need to avoid pollution and to seek salvation for oneself and one's relatives. The need to avoid pollution means that there are tight constraints on the behaviour of menstruating women—as there are in many other cultures—and the search for salvation governs a number of prohibitions that follow the death of a relative. These include cutting one's hair and eating chicken or fish. American participants considered violation of the prohibitions to be trivial but the Hindu participants considered them to be a "great sin" since they jeopardised the chances of salvation. Some American children, by contrast, considered sexual inequality to be a moral issue because it contravened their ideas of justice.

Southern India

Miller and Bersoff (1995) explored different moral perspectives on family relationships amongst adults in the United States and Southern India. Americans saw family life as existing primarily to meet the needs of every individual member and they resolved dilemmas about conflicting needs in these terms. Indian participants saw the family units as having value over and above the needs of its individual members so dilemmas were resolved in terms of the overall need of the family rather than of individuals. American adults were found to place great value on psychological support and enhancing family relationships, whereas Indian adults valued selfless behaviour and enhancing the well-being of other family members.

Japan

Isawa (1992) compared responses to one of Kohlberg's dilemmas in Japan and the United States. The dilemma, which we described on page 294, concerns a man who breaks into a chemist's shop to steal a cancer treatment drug for his wife that he cannot afford to buy. While there was no difference in the moral stage of the participants' responses, there were interesting qualitative differences in why human life was valued. Americans were concerned to prolong the length of life and so thought that the man should steal the drug: Japanese participants were concerned to make life purer and cleaner and so typically thought that the man should not steal the drug.

Relationships

Within Western society there are significant changes in relationships over the lifespan (see van Lieshout & Doise, 1998 for a review). Mothers and fathers are seen as the most frequent providers of emotional support in middle childhood. Same-sex friends are perceived to be just as supportive as parents in early adolescence and, by middle adolescence, they provide the main sources of support. In late adolescence romantic partners become a very important source of emotional support along with friends and mothers but there is an interesting sex difference. Males experience romantic relationships as most supportive, while females receive equal support from a wider range of people—mothers, friends, and siblings as well as romantic partners (Furman & Buhrmester, 1992). There are also age-related changes in perceived conflict, punishment, and power. Tension in parent–child relationships and sibling relationships peaks in early and middle adolescence.

One way of illustrating these developmental changes in the relative importance of friends and family members is to look at the pattern of self-disclosure. Buhrmester (1996) reviews a number of studies of intimate

As individuals move through adolescence, their main source of emotional support changes from their same-sex friends to their romantic partners. Copyright © Popperfoto (left); Copyright © TRIP/H. Rogers (right).

self-disclosure, which he summarises in a graph (see Figure 15.2). This shows that American second-graders (age seven) and fifth-graders (age ten) are most likely to tell their parents intimate personal information. However, by the 10th grade (age 15) there is marked change, with intimate self-disclosure being highest to a friend and least to a parent. Disclosure to a romantic partner is greater than to parents. By college age romantic partners and friends are of equal importance but, interestingly, the importance of parents has begun to increase again.

Furman and Buhrmester (1992) suggest that a number of factors may contribute to developmental shifts in perceived support from different members of a personal network. Adolescents typically distance themselves from their families and invest more time in peer relationships than they did as children. Initially these relationships are friendships with same-sex peers but, in adolescence, romantic relationships become increasingly important, as Figure 15.2 illustrates. Advances in cognitive abilities in adolescence—which we described earlier in this chapter—can facilitate self-exploration and validation of the adolescent's self concept; and the adolescent's search for independence will lead to an increasing interest in issues and relationships outside the home.

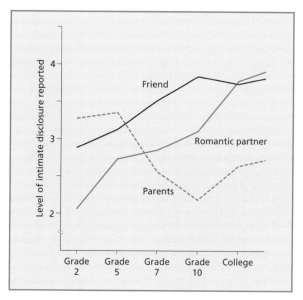

Most individuals are involved in friendships throughout their lives; and many friendships are long lasting. Mutuality is an essential prerequisite for friendship (van Lieshout & Doise, 1998). Unilateral friendships that are one-way are rather different from mutual friendships in which both parties recognise the other as a friend. Mutual friendships take a great variety of different forms at different ages and stages of friendship and with different partners. However, there are certain stable characteristics that underlie all friendships. Hartup (1996, cited in van Lieshout & Doise, 1998) posits four features that distinguish friendships from other relationships. First, friends know one another

FIG. 15.2 Graph showing how a child's closest confidante changes from parents to friends and romantic partners over time. Reproduced with permission from D. Buhrmester (1996), Need fulfilment, interpersonal competence, and the developmental context of early adolescent friendship. In W.M. Bukowski, A.F. Newcomb, and W.W. Hartup (Eds.), *The company they keep: Friendship in childhood and adolescence*. Cambridge, UK: Cambridge University Press.

better than non-friends and they share joint domains of interest. This enables them to communicate effectively and to share common expertise. Second, friends have common expectations about assistance and support. Equality and similarity are more evident than dominance and power assertion. The third feature of friendship is that the affective climate that exists between friends provides a positive environment for exploration of solutions to problems. Finally, the friends have common goals and convergent goal orientations, and these help to make the friendship stable. A serious opposition of goals can be very disruptive in a friendship.

Similarities between friends are the norm throughout development, as we have seen in preceding chapters, although there are interesting variations among groups in the way that friends are selected during adolescence (see the box below). Hartup (1998), summarising research on adolescent friendships, notes that friends are more similar to one another than non-friends in two main areas. These are: attitudes to school and levels of achievement; and normative behaviours such as smoking, drinking, drug use, and antisocial behaviour. Friends also like the same kinds of activities. There is an interesting difference between girls and boys in the similarity of sexual behaviour. Adolescent girls of similar age in the United States—both white and African-American—have been shown to have very similar attitudes towards sexual activity and to have similar sexual behaviour. However there was less similarity among boys, especially in the level of sexual activity. Hartup takes this as further evidence for the idea of reputational salience that was evident in the friendship patterns of school-aged children (see Friendships, in Chapter 14). He argues that sexual activity is more significant for the social reputation of girls than for boys and, hence, it will be more similar among female friends than among male friends in adolescence.

How similar are friends to each other?

Although friends tend to be similar to one another, recent research has suggested that the extent and nature of this similarity is not the same for all adolescents. Hamm (2000) has investigated the complex interplay of factors that determine how friends are selected. She argues that adolescents select their friends mainly within the confines of their school. Thus, features of the schools, such as ethnic diversity and academic orientation, will have an important role in shaping friendships. She reports that, within American schools, shared ethnic background is often a crucial factor in choosing friends. However, what is particularly interesting in her study is the differences that she has found among different ethnic groups.

The participants in Hamm's study came from seven ethnically diverse high schools. They were aged between fourteen and eighteen years and came from one of three ethnically defined groups—African-American, Asian-American, and European-American. The seven schools varied in the proportion of pupils coming from each of these three groups although, in five of the schools, the majority of pupils were from a European-American family. Hamm assessed the pupils on their academic attitudes and behaviour as well as gathering information on academic achievement, substance use (i.e. the use of controlled drugs) and ethnic identity (i.e. sense of belonging to a particular ethnic group and the attitude towards one's own group). Later in the same year she asked the participants to nominate their closest friends.

Hamm found that 80% of the African- and European-American participants had a best friend who came from the same ethnic background. This figure was just under 60% for the Asian-Americans. When other similarities between friends were determined, the highest similarity for all three groups was in substance use, consistent with the findings of earlier studies. Significant (though less) similarity was found for academic orientation (i.e. attitude to schooling and academic aspirations) in pupils from an Asian or European background, but the similarity of this measure was very low in the African-American group. Ethnic identity—as distinct from ethnic background—proved to have low similarity between friends for all three groups, although the level of similarity was highest for the pupils from an African-American background.

In addition to demonstrating ethnic differences in the dimensions on which adolescents choose their friends, Hamm's study also highlighted the variable nature of similarity. In essence, she found that adolescents selected more similar friends on a dimension that was particularly significant to them. Thus, among pupils who had a positive attitude to schooling and high academic aspirations, there was typically a high similarity on academic orientation; and similarities in substance use were highest among pupils with low levels of use who, presumably, had taken a decision *not* to use illegal drugs. Interestingly, similar patterns of substance use were more evident in cross-ethnic friendships than in friendships between pupils from the same ethnic background. Hamm suggests that the search for a friend with a shared attitude to substance use may have been an initial point of attraction for adolescents from different and diverse ethnic backgrounds.

Friendship throughout life provides a context for social and emotional growth (van Lieshout & Doise, 1998). Between 80% and 90% of people have a mutual friendship, although the nature of the friendship will depend on such factors as age, gender, living conditions, and whether or not the person is employed. Friends provide security and emotional support in the face of stress. For children this might be the stress of parental divorce, parental maltreatment, or pressure of school. For adolescents, and adults, friendship also provides emotional support for work-related problems and difficulties in relationships. Friends also provide security and support when young children first go to school and when older children change schools. Troubled children or those referred to clinics are more likely to have no friends than non-troubled children.

While people can choose their friends they cannot choose their families. Each family member has a unique role within the family as mother, father, son, daughter, brother, sister, grandfather, or grandmother, or as a step-parent or step-child. Amongst the children within a family each occupies a unique position by virtue of birth order so, for example, the youngest child and the oldest child have a different role within the family. Each family member's behaviour depends, in part, on the behaviour of other family members and it involves a unique set of relationships with a known history.

Families take a wide variety of forms both across time and across cultures. Since the Second World War the multi-generational extended family—

consisting of parents, children, and older family members such as grandparents—has largely been replaced by a nuclear family consisting of two biological parents and their children. In more recent years the family unit has become even more diverse with single-parent families becoming increasingly common and more adults living alone. The number of unmarried teenage mothers has rapidly increased in the United States and their incidence is far higher than in Europe.

The quality of relationships between family members can affect other members of the same family. Erel and Burman (1995) carried out a meta-analysis of 68 previous studies in order to determine the inter-relatedness of the parents' relationship with each other and parent–child relationships. The interparental relationship was measured according to global quality, marital satisfaction, and absence of overt conflicts. The parent–child relationship was measured in terms of global quality, but measures were also taken of consistency between and within parental behaviour, satisfaction, and absence of negative control and harsh punishments. Erel and Burman found strong support for a "spillover hypothesis" in which the quality of marital relationships and the quality of parent–child relationships was strongly linked. Parents who had a strong and supportive relationship with each other responded more sensitively to their children; parents who had a negative or conflict-filled relationship with each other appeared to be less attentive and sensitive to their children—perhaps because they were emotionally drained by the negative relationship with their partner. Many studies have demonstrated a causal relationship between increased marital conflict and increased behavioural and emotional problems in children (Grych & Fincham, 1990). There are also links between psychiatric disorders in mothers and daughters (see the box below).

Intergenerational effects in mental disorders

Genetic factors make a major contribution to the recurring incidence within families of severe mental disorders such as schizophrenia. There are also familial patterns in the incidence of less severe conditions but, here, psychosocial factors appear to be particularly important. Evidence suggests that early environmental factors, especially the lack of adequate parenting, lead to an increased risk of depressive disorder in adult life (Bifulco, Brown, & Harris, 1987). Children who are exposed to aggression and hostility at home are more likely to be disturbed than children who have a more supportive family environment, regardless of whether or not they have a parent with a mental disorder (Rutter & Quinton, 1984).

Andrews, Brown, and Creasey (1990) carried out a study that was designed to investigate the role of parenting in links between mental disorders in mothers and daughters. The mothers in the study were classified as working class. Mothers and daughters were interviewed to determine whether they had experienced psychiatric symptoms in the previous 12 months and, in the case of mothers, over the period of their daughter's childhood. Daughters were also interviewed about their early family experiences and asked about the quality of care they had received, their attitude to their mother, and physical and sexual abuse.

Mothers who had significant psychiatric symptoms fell into two categories—those who had had only one depressive episode of less than one year in their daughter's lifetime and those who had a chronic or recurrent disorder. Mothers in the former group were no more likely to have a daughter with a disorder than those who had not experienced an episode of depression—the incidence in the daughters was 5%. However, where mothers had experienced a chronic or recurrent disorder, there was a 25% chance that their daughter also suffered from a disorder. However, Andrews et al. found that early family experience was also important as a predictor of the daughters' mental health: 89% of the daughters with a mental disorder reported adverse early family experiences, compared with only 27% of those with no disorder. Some of this difference may have arisen because the daughters who were depressed gave a more negative report of their childhood experiences but an even more stringent interpretation of the reports showed clear differences between the clinical and non-clinical groups. The precise pattern of cause and effect in this study is difficult to determine since both mothers and fathers contributed to adverse early effects. It is possible, for example, that the mother's depression had a negative influence on the marriage and so an indirect effect on the father's behaviour or that the father, as well as the mother, was subject to a psychiatric disorder. However, it is clear from the study that the relationship between persistent maternal disorders and disorders in the daughters was mediated by the daughter's early experience within the family.

One final point of interest about this study lies in the nature of the psychiatric disorders of the daughters. Daughters were less likely to have been clinically depressed in the year preceding the interview than their mothers, but the overall incidence of psychiatric disorder was very similar in the two groups. This was because, among the daughters, there were cases of eating disorders and alcohol abuse as well as anxiety. Anxiety in the mothers—and adverse family experiences—thus gave rise not only to depression in the daughters but also to other mental disorders.

Gender differences in adolescent friendships

We have already hinted that there are some notable differences in the friendship patterns of male and female adolescents. This is an issue that has been explored in a number of recent studies that have argued for the existence of different "cultures" in the peer relationships of girls and boys.

Maccoby (1990a) notes that female–female interactions typically focus on the building of interpersonal connections, whereas male–male interactions are more directed towards the development of individual status. She sees this difference as exerting a strong influence on the development of gender-specific behaviour patterns. Her argument is that children actively shape their own behaviour—for example, their clothes and manner of speech—to conform to the perceived gender norm. As we noted, the influence of same-sex peers is very powerful in adolescence and this may run counter to the efforts of parents to instil either traditional or non-traditional gender norms.

Empirical support for Maccoby's claims about differences in male and female same-sex friendships comes from a number of studies. Buhrmester and

Carbery (1992, cited in Buhrmester, 1996) interviewed two hundred 12- to 15-year-old American adolescents over five consecutive evenings. They asked about the social interactions of the preceding day, which the participants had been asked to record, noting the type of partners that had been present (i.e. same-sex friends, parents, siblings). For each recorded interaction, participants rated the extent of self-disclosure and emotional support that had occurred.

The findings of the Buhrmester and Carbery study were consistent with the view that female friendships provide greater opportunity for socio-emotional support than male friendships. For example, females reported a higher number of interactions with same-sex friends than males, and they also reported substantially higher levels of self-disclosure and emotional support than males did in their daily interactions. This pattern is consistent with the image of female–female friendships as "face to face" and having an emphasis on talking, in contrast to the image of male–male friendships as being "side by side" with a focus on doing things together, notably sports and competitive games. Buhrmester (1996) notes that, when male friends talk, their discussions often focus on what are described as "agentically oriented" issues such as the achievements of sporting teams and individuals and the evaluation of the academic and sporting prowess of peers. These gender differences in the patterns of friendship support Maccoby's argument that there are different processes of socialisation at work for boys and girls, particularly in adolescence. The typical pattern of male friendships will often put adolescent boys into situations that reinforce the need for achievement, recognition, and power.

Differences in the patterns of typical male and female friendships are also evident in the specific norms that they encourage. Brown and Gilligan (1992) and Maccoby (1990a) point out that the norms for girls' friendships seem to actively reward intimate self-disclosure and the provision of emotional support and also actively discourage open competition and the discussion of status differences. In contrast, as Maccoby (1990a) notes, the agentic style fostered by

Female–female friendships tend to involve more social interaction; whereas male–male friendships tend to be based more on doing things together. Copyright © TRIP/H. Rogers (left); Copyright © Photofusion/David Montford (right).

boys' friendships often precludes the building of intimate connections. Indeed, there is evidence that male–male friendships actively discourage the expression of socio-emotional needs through a strong prohibition of "mushy" sentimentality and the open expression of "love" for a male friend (Parker & Gottman, 1989, cited in Buhrmester, 1996).

In contrast to female–female friendships, the norms of male–male friendship contribute to the socialisation of agentic needs, that is, success in attaining a goal. Most Western societies value individual achievement and a clear sense of identity and purpose—values that are supported and developed within the norms of male–male friendships with their emphasis on doing and achieving things together and being individually successful. Boys' friendships with each other thus typically provide more opportunities than girls' friendships to learn to thrive in an environment where there is an emphasis on playing complex games in which success and failure are deemed to be very important. Many discussions of the socialising effects of peers (notably Maccoby, 1990a) have tended to emphasise the negative aspects of boys' friendships. However, it is probably too simple to argue that male–male friendships have a negative influence in contrast to the values of mutual support that are promulgated in female–female friendships. Learning to work as a team and to succeed can also be seen in a positive light and, arguably, both male and female friendships can be seen as developing skills that are important for the successful functioning of a community.

Conflict and aggression in adolescence

Throughout adolescence, family members are the most likely source of conflict. In the Furman and Buhrmester (1992) study described earlier, adolescents of various ages reported that conflict (i.e. quarrelling, arguing, getting mad)

Laursen (1996) demonstrated that adolescents are more likely to compromise and negotiate with close peers and romantic partners than with family members. Copyright © TRIP/ H. Rogers.

occurred most often with parents and siblings and least with teachers and grandparents. Conflict with friends and romantic partners was reported as occurring at an intermediate level. The level of conflict with mothers and siblings tends to remain at a rather similar level across adolescence but relative rates of disagreement with peers change with age. There is a decline in conflict with same-sex friends and, typically, an increase in conflict with romantic partners.

One reason why there are fewer conflicts with peers is that adolescents are more likely to compromise and negotiate with close peers, and especially romantic partners, than with family members (Laursen, 1996). In contrast, coercion tends to dominate conflicts with non-friends and siblings, whereas this is rare for conflicts between close friends or romantic partners. Adolescents are very aware of the potential consequences of conflict although, as one might expect, females tend to place more emphasis on the importance of resolving disagreements through compromise.

This gender difference becomes more pronounced with age so that a significant minority of adolescent males have yet to develop a mature understanding of the potential costs of conflict and to learn appropriate behaviour for preserving friendships and romantic relationships.

Most longitudinal studies show a general decrease in physical aggression as children enter adolescence. However, adolescence is also the period in which serious violent behaviour increases among a small section of the population (see Coie & Dodge, 1998 for a review). Such behaviour is most common in encounters between males. Data from a large longitudinal survey of adolescent behaviour in the United States (The National Youth Survey, reported by Elliott, 1994, cited in Coie & Dodge, 1998) has shown that violent offending almost invariably begins in the adolescent years. Self-reports of serious violent offences (aggravated assault, robbery, or rape) rise sharply from the ages of 12 to 20 and fewer than 1% of first offences occur after the age of 20.

Gender differences in violent behaviour are very striking. In the United States eight times as many adolescent boys as girls are arrested for violent crime, although Coie and Dodge (1998) note that there is a slight trend for this ratio to decrease over time as more girls are involved in serious violence. In the National Youth Survey data reported by Elliott (1994), 42% of males reported committing a serious violent offence at some time in their youth compared with 16% for females. There was also a notable difference in the peak age of first offences for boys (16 years) and girls (14 years).

The National Youth Survey data paint a depressing picture of the developmental precursors of violent crime. Children begin with minor aggressive acts and delinquent behaviour in the early school years and progress to serious and frequent offending by the age of 17. The beginning of substance use and sexual activity add incrementally to the risk of aggressive behaviour during adolescence. Minor forms of delinquent behaviour and alcohol use typically precede more serious forms of violence; aggravated assault precedes robbery in 85% of cases, and robbery precedes rape in 72% of cases. Thus, as Coie and Dodge (1998) note, there is a chilling inevitability about the developmental path taken by a small proportion of the population in which behaviours become more serious and more violent with age. Fortunately, however, the picture changes after adolescence with self-reported aggressive behaviour declining significantly between the ages of 18 and 25; and, as the National Youth Survey data suggest, virtually no new cases of antisocial behaviour begin in adulthood.

Conclusion and summary

The transition to adulthood generates a need to come to terms with sexual maturity and to adopt adult roles but this transition will be experienced differently in different cultures. There are also important differences in the transitions that take place for males and females, although, here too, cultural differentiation on the basis of gender varies widely.

The study of cognition in adolescence was revolutionised by Piaget and Inhelder's account of formal operational thinking, which has had a great influence on subsequent research. Their claim was that, as children move into adolescence, they become capable of reasoning in a new way that is not evident during the preceding stage of concrete operations. In the stage of formal operations, adolescents are able to reason about entirely hypothetical situations and they can consider all possible combinations of relevant variables. As with the previous stages of Piaget's theory that we have discussed in earlier chapters, the notion of formal operational thinking has not gone unchallenged. One view has been adolescent thinking changes quantitatively but not qualitatively—a claim that stems from consistent findings of more precocious abilities in the stage of concrete operations than Piaget proposed. Other researchers have argued that the ability to reason continues to develop throughout adolescence and into adulthood. A final criticism has been that formal operational reasoning is far from universal. At some level all of these claims can be supported but perhaps the most important conclusion to be drawn is that culture and education have a particularly important role in the level of thinking that an individual finally attains.

The ability to use abstract thinking in adolescence gives rise to important and significant advances in moral reasoning. As with cognition, there are important cultural differences in moral reasoning. There are also differences in the way the moral principles are applied to hypothetical and real-life situations. This implies that in order to understand the development and implementation of moral reasoning in an individual we have to identify the appropriate cultural context. Recent research has also suggested that there is a variety of moral voices rather than the single voice that Kohlberg describes in his last stage of moral reasoning.

Throughout adolescence, relationships between an individual and family members and friends continue to be important. Relationships outside the family become increasingly significant, whereas relationships within the family may become less important. As adolescents enter adulthood, new family relationships are often formed as people set up home with a partner. In spite of these significant changes in the support network, the need for emotional support continues and, as in earlier stages of development, those who have stable emotional support are less vulnerable to mental disorders than those who do not.

Adolescence is also a period in which social negotiation skills become increasingly sophisticated as peer conflicts are resolved through compromise. Clear differences between males and females are evident in patterns of friendship and these serve to support the differences in emphasis that are evident in the values of adolescent girls and boys. For a small minority, adolescence is the period in which a pattern of violent behaviour is established and, here again, there are marked gender differences in behaviour with violence being more common between males.

We began this book with the claim that any satisfactory account of human development requires us not only to understand the way that children's abilities change and expand over time but also to consider the diverse effects that are brought about by the experience of growing up in a particular society and a particular family at a particular point in history. We argued that development is as much a matter of the child acquiring a culture as it is a process of biological growth. This has been evident in all the stages of development—infancy, preschool, the school years, and adolescence—that we have considered. One final conclusion to draw is that the impact of the culture increases with age and we can view adolescence as the period that most flexibly combines biological, social, and historical factors. The study of adolescence thus confirms the view that developmental change is a multi-faceted phenomenon.

Further reading

- Bukowski, W.M., Newcomb, A.F., & Hartup, W.W. (Eds.). (1996). *The company they keep: Friendship in childhood and adolescence*. Cambridge, UK: Cambridge University Press. This edited book has chapters spanning the school years and adolescence. It is suitable for all undergraduates.
- Haste, H., Helkama, K., & Markoulis, D. (1998). Morality, wisdom and the life-span. In A. Demetriou, W. Doise, & C.F.M. van Lieshout (Eds.), *Life-span developmental psychology*. Chichester, UK: Wiley. This is a clear chapter on moral development, with particular emphasis on alternative theoretical accounts and cross-cultural issues. It is suitable for first- and second-year undergraduates.
- Moshman, D. (1998). Cognitive development beyond childhood. In D. Kuhn & R.S. Siegler (Eds.), *Handbook of child psychology: Vol. 2. Cognition, perception, and language* (W. Damon, Gen. Ed.). New York: Wiley. This is an excellent chapter on cognitive development in adolescence that provides both an historical overview and a thorough account of recent research. It is intended for advanced undergraduates.
- van Lieshout, C.F.M., & Doise, W. (1998). Social development. In A. Demetriou, W. Doise, & C.F.M. van Lieshout (Eds.), *Life-span developmental psychology*. Chichester, UK: Wiley. This chapter provides a clear account of social development—especially relationships—with an emphasis on friendships and bullying. It is suitable for all undergraduates.

References

Abranavel, E., & Sigafoos, A.D. (1984). Explaining the presence of imitation in early infancy. *Child Development, 55,* 381–392.

Adelson, J. (1972). The political imagination of the young adolescent. In J. Kagan & R. Coles (Eds.), *Twelve to sixteen: Early adolescence.* New York: Norton.

Ahmed, A., & Ruffman, T. (1998). Why do infants make A not B errors in a search task, yet show memory for the location of hidden objects in a nonsearch task? *Developmental Psychology, 34,* 441–453.

Ahrens, R. (1954). Beitrage zur entwicklung des physiognomie- und mimerkennes. *Zeitschrift für Experimentelle und Angewandte Psychologie,* 412–454.

Ainsworth, M., & Bell, S. (1970). Attachment, exploration and separation: Illustrated by the behaviour of one-year-olds in a strange situation. *Child Development, 41,* 49–67.

Ainsworth, M.D.S. (1973). The development of infant–mother attachment. In B. Caldwell & H. Ricciuti (Eds.), *Review of child development research* (Vol. 3, pp. 1–94). Chicago: University of Chicago Press.

Akita, K., & Hatano, G. (1999). Learning to read and write in Japanese. In M. Harris & G. Hatano (Eds.), *Learning to read and write: A cross-linguistic perspective* (pp. 214–234). Cambridge, UK: Cambridge University Press.

Amiel-Tison, C., & Grenier, A. (1985). *La surveillance neurologique au cours de la premiere annee de la vie.* Paris: Masson.

Andrews, B., Brown, G.W., & Creasey, L. (1990). Intergenerational links between psychiatric disorder in mothers and daughters: The role of parenting experiences. *Journal of Child Psychology and Psychiatry and Allied Disciplines, 31,* 1115–1129.

Anglin, J.M. (1993). Vocabulary development: A morphological analysis. *Monographs of the Society for Research in Child Development, 58*(10, Serial No. 238). Chicago: University of Chicago Press.

Anisfeld, M. (1991). Neonatal imitation. *Developmental Review, 11,* 60–97.

Antell, S.E., & Keating, D.P. (1983). Perception of numerical invariance in neonates. *Child Development, 54,* 695–701.

Archer, J. (1993). *Ethology and human development.* Hemel Hempstead, UK: Harvester.

Aslin, R. (1985). Effects of experience on sensory and perceptual development. In J. Mehier & R. Fox (Eds.), *Neonatal cognition: Beyond the buzzing, blooming confusion.* Hillsdale, NJ: Lawrence Erlbaum Associates Inc.

Atkinson, J., & Braddick, O.L. (1989). Development of basic visual functions. In A. Slater & G. Bremner (Eds.), *Infant development.* Hove, UK: Psychology Press.

Baillargeon, R. (1991). The object concept revisited: New directions in the investigation of the infant's physical knowledge. In C.E. Granrud (Ed.), *Visual perception and cognition in infancy* (Carnegie-Mellon Symposia on Cognition, Vol. 23). Hillsdale, NJ: Lawrence Erlbaum Associates Inc.

Baillargeon, R. (1999). Young infants' expectations about hidden objects: A reply to three challenges. *Developmental Science, 2*(2), 115–163.

Baillargeon, R., & Graber, M. (1987). Where's the rabbit? 5.5-month-old infants' representation of the height of a hidden object. *Cognitive Development, 2*(4), 375–392.

Baillargeon, R., Spelke, E.S., & Wasserman, S. (1985). Object permanence in five-month-old infants. *Cognition, 20,* 191–208.

Baldwin, D.A., & Markman, E.M. (1989). Establishing word–object relations: A first step. *Child Development, 60,* 381–398.

Baldwin, J.M. (1894). Imitation, a chapter in the natural history of consciousness. *Mind, 3,* 26–55.

Baldwin, J.M. (1905). *Dictionary of philosophy and psychology.* London: Macmillan.

Baldwin, J.M. (1915). *Genetic theory of reality, being the outcome of genetic logic, as issuing in the aesthetic theory of reality called pancalism.* New York: Putnam.

Bandura, A. (1973). *Aggression: A social learning analysis.* New York: Prentice-Hall.

Bandura, A. (1977). *Social learning theory.* New York: Prentice-Hall.

Bandura, A. (1986). *Social foundations of thought and action: A social cognitive theory.* Upper Saddle River, NJ: Prentice-Hall.

Bandura, A., & Walters, R. (1963). *Social learning and personality development.* New York: Holt.

Barker, J. (1994). *The Brontës.* London: Phoenix.

Barlow-Brown, F. (1996). *Early developmental strategies used by blind children learning to read braille.* Unpublished PhD thesis, University of London.

Baron-Cohen, S., Leslie, A.M., & Frith, U. (1985). Does the autistic child have a theory of mind? *Cognition, 21,* 37–46.

Barrett, M. (1986). Early semantic representations and early semantic development. In S.A. Kuczaj & M. Barrett (Eds.), *The development of word meaning.* New York: Springer-Verlag.

Barrett, M., Harris, M., & Chasin, J. (1991). Early lexical development and maternal speech: A comparison of children's initial and subsequent uses. *Journal of Child Language, 18,* 21–40.

Barry, C. (1994). Spelling routes (or roots or rutes). In G.D.A. Brown & N.C. Ellis (Eds.), *Handbook of spelling* (pp. 27–50). Chichester, UK: Wiley.

Bates, E. (1993). Comprehension and production in early language development. *Monographs of the Society for Research in Child Development, 58*(3–4, Serial No. 233), 222–242.

Bates, E., Benigni, L., Bretherton, I., Camaloni, L., & Volterra, V. (1979). *The emergence of symbols: Cognition and communication in infancy.* New York: Academic Press.

Bates, E., Bretherton, I., & Snyder, L. (1988). *From first words to grammar: Individual differences and dissociable mechanisms.* Cambridge, UK: Cambridge University Press.

Bates, E., Dale, P.S., & Thal, D. (1994). Individual differences and their implications for theories of language development. In P. Fletcher & B. MacWhinney (Eds.), *Handbook of child language.* Oxford, UK: Basil Blackwell.

Bates, E., & MacWhinney, B. (1989). Functionalism and the competition model. In B. MacWhinney & E. Bates (Eds.), *The crosslinguistic study of sentence processing.* Cambridge, UK: Cambridge University Press.

Beech, J.R. (1989). The componential approach to learning reading skills. In A.M. Colley & J.R. Beech (Eds.), *Acquisition and performance of cognitive skills.* New York: Wiley.

Beech, J.R., & Harris, M. (1997). The prelingually deaf young reader: A case of reliance on direct lexical access. *Journal of Research in Reading, 20,* 105–121.

Bell, S.M.V. (1970). The development of the concept of object as related to infant–mother attachment. *Child Development, 41,* 291–311.

Belsky, J., & Most, R.K. (1981). From exploration to play: A cross-sectional study of infant free play behavior. *Developmental Psychology, 17,* 630–639.

Bergenn, V.W., Dalton, T.C., & Lipsitt, L.P. (1994). Myrtle B. McGraw: A growth scientist. In R.D. Parke, P.A. Ornstein, J. Reiser, & C. Zahn-Waxler (Eds.), *A century of developmental psychology* (pp. 389–426). Washington DC: American Psychological Association.

Bertenthal, B.I., & Fischer, K.W. (1978). Development of self-recognition in the infant. *Developmental Psychology, 14,* 44–50.

Bertoncini, J., Bijeljac, R., McAdams, S., Peretz, I., & Mehler, J. (1989). Dichotic perception of laterality in neonates. *Brain and Language, 37,* 591–605.

Best, C.T., McRoberts, G.W., & Sithole, N.M. (1988). Examination of perceptual reorganization for nonnative speech contrasts: Zulu click discrimination by English-speaking adults and infants. *Journal of Experimental Psychology: Human Perception and Performance, 14,* 345–360.

Bifulco, A.T., Brown, G.W., & Harris, T.O. (1987). Childhood loss of parent, lack of adequate parental care and adult depression: A replication. *Journal of Affective Disorders, 12,* 115–128.

Bigelow, A.E. (1977). The development of self recognition in young children. *Dissertation Abstracts International, 37*(12B), 6360–6361.

Boden, M. (1994). *Dimensions of creativity.* Cambridge, MA: MIT Press.

Bogartz, R.S., Shinskey, J.L., & Speaker, C.J. (1997). Interpreting infant looking: The event set x event set design. *Developmental Psychology, 33,* 408–122.

Bornstein, M.H., Kessen, W., & Weiskopf, S. (1976). The categories of hue in infancy. *Science, 191,* 201–202.

Bouchard, T.J., Lykken, D.T., McGue, M., Segal, N.L., & Tellegen, A. (1990). Sources of human psychological differences: The Minnesota study of twins reared apart. *Science, 250,* 223–250.

Bower, T.G.R. (1971). The object in the world of the infant. *Scientific American, 225,* 31–38.

Bower, T.G.R. (1982). *Development in infancy* (2nd ed.). San Francisco: Freeman.

Bower, T.G.R., & Wishart, J.G. (1972). The effects of motor skill on object permanence. *Cognition, 1,* 165–172.

Bowlby, J. (1969). *Attachment and loss, Vol. 1.* Harmondsworth, UK: Pelican Books.

Bradley, L., & Bryant, P.E. (1983). Categorising sounds and learning to read—a causal connection. *Nature, 301,* 419–521.

Brainerd, C.J. (1978). *Piaget's theory of intelligence.* Englewood Cliffs, NJ: Prentice-Hall.

Bray, N.W., Reilly, K.D., Villa, M.F., & Grupe, L.A. (1997). Neural network models and mechanisms of strategy development. *Developmental Review, 17,* 525–566.

Bremner, J.G. (1994). *Infancy* (2nd ed.). Oxford, UK: Blackwell.

Bretherton, I. (1994). Infants' subjective world of relatedness: Moments, feeling shapes, protonarrative envelopes, and internal working models. *Infant Mental Health Journal, 15,* 36–41.

Bretherton, I., & Waters, E. (1990). Growing points of attachment theory and research. *Monographs of the Society for Research in Child Development, 209,* 1–2.

Brooks-Gunn, J., & Warren, M.P. (1988). The psychological significance of secondary sexual characteristics in nine- to eleven-year-old girls. *Child Development, 59,* 1061–1069.

Broughton, J.M., & Freeman-Moir, D.J. (1982). *The cognitive developmental psychology of James Mark Baldwin.* Norwood, NJ: Ablex.

Brown, A.L., Kane, M.J., & Long, C. (1989). Analogical transfer in young children: Analogies as tools for communication and exposition. *Applied Cognitive Psychology, 3,* 275–293.

Brown, G., & Harris, T. (1980). *The social origins of depression.* London: Tavistock.

Brown, J.S., & Burton, R.R. (1978). Diagnostic models for procedural bugs in basic mathematical skills. *Cognitive Science, 2,* 155–192.

Brown, L.M., & Gilligan, C. (1992). *Meeting at the crossroads: Women's psychology and girls' development.* Cambridge, MA: Harvard University Press.

Brown, R.W. (1973). *A first language: The early stages.* London: George Allen & Unwin.

Brown, R.W., & Hanlon, C. (1970). Derivational complexity and order of acquisition in child speech. In R. Brown (Ed.), *Psycholinguistics.* New York: Free Press.

Bruner, J.S. (1974). The organisation of early skilled action. In M.P.M. Richards (Ed.), *The integration of a child into a social world.* Cambridge, UK: Cambridge University Press.

Bruner, J.S. (1975). The ontogenesis of speech acts. *Journal of Child Language, 2,* 1–19.

Bruner, J.S. (1983). The acquisition of pragmatic commitments. In R.M. Golinkoff (Ed.), *The transition from prelinguistic to linguistic communication.* Hillsdale, NJ: Lawrence Erlbaum Associates Inc.

Bruner, J.S. (1990). *Acts of meaning.* Cambridge, MA: Harvard University Press.

Bruner, J.S., Olver, R.R., & Greenfield, P.M. (1966). *Studies in cognitive growth.* New York: John Wiley.

Bryant, P.E. (1974). *Perception and understanding in young children.* London: Methuen.

Bryant, P.E., & Koptynskya, H. (1976). Spontaneous measurement by young children. *Nature, 260,* 773–774.

Bryant, P.E., & Nunes, T. (1999). Different morphemes, same spelling problems: Cross-linguistic developmental studies. In M. Harris & G. Hatano (Eds.), *Learning to read and write: A cross-linguistic perspective* (pp. 112–133). Cambridge, UK: Cambridge University Press.

Bryant, P.E., & Trabasso, T. (1971). Transitive inferences and memory in young children. *Nature, 232,* 456–458.

Buhler, C. (1935). *From birth to maturity: An outline of the psychological development of the child.* London: Routledge & Kegan Paul.

Buhrmester, D. (1996). Need fulfilment, interpersonal competence, and the developmental context of early adolescent friendship. In W.M. Bukowski, A.F. Newcomb, & W.W. Hartup (Eds.), *The company they keep: Friendship in childhood and adolescence.* Cambridge, UK: Cambridge University Press.

Buhrmester, D., & Carbery, J. (1992). *Daily patterns of self-disclosure and adolescent adjustment*. Paper presented at the biennial meeting of the Society for Research on Adolescence, Washington DC.

Bullock, M., & Luetkenhaus, P. (1988). The development of volitional behavior in the toddler years. *Child Development, 59*, 664–674.

Bushnell, I.W.R. (1998). The origins of face perception. In F. Simion & G. Butterworth (Eds.), *The development of sensory, motor and cognitive capacities in early infancy* (pp. 69–86). Hove, UK: Psychology Press.

Bushnell, I.W.R., Sai, F., & Mullin, J.T. (1989). Neonatal recognition of the mother's face. *British Journal of Developmental Psychology, 7*, 3–15.

Butterworth, G.E. (1989). Events and encounters in infant perception. In A. Slater & G. Bremner (Eds.), *Infant development* (pp. 73–83). Hillsdale, NJ: Lawrence Erlbaum Associates Inc.

Butterworth, G.E. (1994). Infant perception and the explanation of intelligence. In F. Khalfa (Ed.), *Intelligence*. Cambridge, UK: Cambridge University Press.

Butterworth, G.E. (1998a). Origins of joint visual attention in human infancy. Commentary on Carpenter, Nagell & Tomasello, *Social cognition, joint attention and communicative competence in babies from 9 to 15 months of age. Monographs of the Society for Research in Child Development, 63*, No. 4, (Serial number 255), 144–166.

Butterworth, G. (1998b). What is special about pointing in babies? In F. Simion & G. Butterworth (Eds.), *The development of sensory, motor, and cognitive capacities in infancy*. Hove, UK: Psychology Press.

Butterworth, G.E. (1999). Neonatal imitation: Existence, mechanisms and motives. In J. Nadel & G. Butterworth (Eds.) *Imitation in infancy* (pp. 63–88). Cambridge, UK: Cambridge University Press.

Butterworth, G.E., & Castillo, M. (1976). Coordination of auditory and visual space in newborn human infants. *Perception, 7*, 513–525.

Butterworth, G.E., & Franco, F. (1990). Motor development: Communication and cognition. In L. Kalverboer, B. Hopkins, & R.H. Gueze (Eds.), *A longitudinal approach to the study of motor development in early and later childhood.* Cambridge, UK: Cambridge University Press.

Butterworth, G.E., & Harris, M. (1994). *Principles of Developmental Psychology*. Hove, UK: Psychology Press.

Butterworth, G.E., & Hopkins, B.N. (1988). Hand–mouth coordination in the new-born baby. *British Journal of Developmental Psychology, 6*, 303–314.

Butterworth, G.E., & Hopkins, B.N. (1993). Origins of handedness in human infancy. *Developmental Medicine and Child Neurology, 35*, 177–184.

Butterworth, G.E., & Itakura, S. (1998). Development of precision grips in chimpanzees. *Developmental Science, 11*, 39–44.

Butterworth, G.E., & Jarrett, N. (1991). What minds have in common is space: Spatial mechanisms serving joint attention in infancy. *British Journal of Developmental Psychology, 9*, 55–72.

Butterworth, G.E., Jarrett, N.L.M., & Hicks, L. (1982). Spatio-temporal identity in infancy: Perceptual competence or conceptual deficit? *Developmental Psychology, 18*, 435–449.

Butterworth, G.E., Rutkowska, J., & Scaife, M. (1985). *Evolution and developmental psychology.* Brighton, UK: Harvester.

Butterworth, G.E., Verweij, E., & Hopkins, B. (1997). The development of prehension in infants: Halverson revisited. *British Journal of Developmental Psychology, 15*, 223–236.

Cairns, R.B. (1979). *Social development: The origins and plasticity of social interchanges.* San Francisco: Freeman.

Cairns, R.B. (1992). The makings of a developmental science: The contributions of James Mark Baldwin. *Developmental Psychology, 28*, 17–24.

Cairns, R.B. (1998). The making of developmental psychology. In R.M. Lerner (Eds.), *Handbook of child psychology: Vol. 1. Theoretical models of human development*, pp. 25–105, W. Damon, Gen. Ed.). New York: Wiley.

Campbell, R. (1992). Speech in the head? In D. Reisberg (Ed.), *Auditory imagery*. Hillsdale, NJ: Lawrence Erlbaum Associates Inc.

Campbell, R., & Burden, V. (1994). The development of word-coding skills in the born deaf: An experimental study of deaf school leavers. *British Journal of Developmental Psychology, 24*, 331–350.

Campbell, R.N., & Harrison, A. (1990). *The representational status of early child drawings.* Poster presented at the fourth European Conference on Developmental Psychology, Stirling, UK.

Campos, J., Bertenthal, B., & Kermoian, R. (1981). Early experience and emotional development: The emergence of wariness of heights. *Psychological Science, 3*, 61–64.

Campos, J., & Stenberg, C.R. (1981). Perception, appraisal and emotion: The onset of social referencing. In M.E. Lamb & L.R. Sherrod (Eds.), *Infant social cognition: Empirical and theoretical considerations* (pp. 274–313). Hillsdale, NJ: Lawrence Erlbaum Associates Inc.

Camras, L.A., & Sachs, V.B. (1991). Social referencing and caretaker expressive behavior in a day care setting. *Infant Behavior and Development, 14,* 27–36.

Candland, D.K. (1994). *Feral children and clever animals: Reflections on human nature.* Oxford, UK: Oxford University Press.

Carey, S. (1985). *Conceptual change in childhood.* Cambridge, MA: MIT Press.

Carraher, T.N., Schliemann, A.D., & Carraher, D.W. (1988). Mathematical concepts in everyday life. In G.B. Saxe & M. Gearhart (Eds.), *Children's mathematics.* San Francisco: Jossey-Bass.

Carrillo, M. (1994). Development of phonological awareness and reading acquisition: A study in Spanish language. *Reading and Writing, 6,* 279–298.

Case, R. (1998). The development of conceptual structures. In D. Kuhn & R.S. Siegler (Eds.), *Handbook of child psychology: Vol. 2. Cognition, perception, and language* (pp. 745–800, W. Damon, Gen. Ed.). New York: Wiley.

Castillo, M., & Butterworth, G.E. (1981). Neonatal localisation of a sound in visual space. *Perception, 10,* 331–338.

Charlesworth, W.R. (1992). Charles Darwin and developmental psychology: Past and present. *Developmental Psychology, 28,* 5–16.

Chi, M.T.H. (1978). Knowledge structures and memory development. In R.S. Siegler (Ed.), *Children's thinking: What develops?* Hillsdale, NJ: Lawrence Erlbaum Associates Inc.

Chi, M.T.H., & Koeske, R.D. (1983). Network representation of a child's dinosaur knowledge. *Developmental Psychology, 19,* 29–39.

Chomsky, N. (1959). Review of *Verbal Behavior* by B.F. Skinner. *Language, 35,* 26–58.

Chomsky, N. (1965). *Aspects of the theory of syntax.* Cambridge, MA: MIT Press.

Chomsky, N. (1979). Interview with Brian McGee. In B. McGee (Ed.), *Men of ideas.* London: BBC Publications.

Chomsky, N. (1981). *Lectures on government and binding.* Dordrecht, The Netherlands: Foris.

Chomsky, N. (1986). *Knowledge of language: Its nature, origins and use.* New York: Praeger.

Christophe, A., & Morton, J. (1998). Is Dutch native English? Linguistic analysis by 2-month-olds. *Developmental Science, 1,* 215–219.

Clark, E.V. (1995). Later lexical development and word formation. In P. Fletcher & B. MacWhinney (Eds.), *The handbook of child language.* Oxford, UK: Blackwell.

Clarke-Stewart, A., & Koch, J.B. (1983). *Children: Development through adolescence.* New York: John Wiley & Sons Inc.

Cohen, D., & MacKeith, S.A. (1991). *The development of imagination: The private worlds of childhood.* London: Routledge.

Coie, J.D., & Dodge, K.A. (1998). Aggression and antisocial behavior. In N. Eisenberg (Ed.), *Handbook of child psychology: Vol. 3. Social, emotional, and personality development* (pp. 779–862, W. Damon, Gen. Ed.). New York: Wiley.

Coie, J.D., Terry, R., Lennox, K., Lochman, J.E., & Hyman, C. (1995). Childhood peer rejection and aggression as predictors of stable patterns of adolescent disorder. *Development and Psychopathology, 7,* 697–713.

Cole, M., & Cole, S.R. (2001). *The development of children* (4th ed.). New York: Freeman.

Cole, P. (1986). Children's spontaneous control of facial expressions. *Child Development, 57,* 1309–1321.

Coleman, J. (1980). *The nature of adolescence.* London: Methuen.

Collis, G.M. (1977). Visual coorientation and maternal speech. In H.R. Schaffer (Ed.), *Studies of mother–infant interaction.* London: Academic Press.

Collis, G.M., & Schaffer, H.R. (1975). Synchronization of visual attention in mother–infant pairs. *Journal of Child Psychology and Child Psychiatry, 16,* 315–320.

Connelly, V., Johnston, R., & Thompson, G.B. (2001). The effect of phonics instruction on the reading comprehension of beginning readers. *Reading and Writing, 14,* 423–457.

Cossu, G. (1999). The acquisition of Italian orthography. In M. Harris & G. Hatano (Eds.), *Learning to read and write: A cross-linguistic perspective* (pp. 10–33). Cambridge, UK: Cambridge University Press.

Cossu, G., Shankweiler, D., Liberman, I.Y., Tola, G., & Katz, L. (1988). Awareness of phonological segments and reading ability in Italian children. *Applied Psycholinguistics, 9,* 1–16.

Cox, M.V. (1991). *The child's point of view* (2nd ed.). Hemel Hempstead, UK: Harvester.

Curcio, F. (1978). Sensori-motor functioning and communication in mute autistic children. *Journal of Autism and Childhood Schizophrenia, 8,* 281–292.

Cutting, A.L., & Dunn, J. (1999). Theory of mind, emotion understanding, language, and family background: Individual differences and interrelations. *Child Development, 70,* 853–865.

Damon, W. (1977). *The social world of the child.* San Francisco: Jossey-Bass.

Damon, W. (1980). Patterns of change in children's social reasoning: A two-year longitudinal study. *Child Development, 51,* 1010–1017.

Damon, W., & Phelps, E. (1988). Strategic uses of peer learning in children's education. In T. Berndt & G. Ladd (Eds.), *Children's peer relations.* New York: Wiley.

Darwin, C. (1859). *The origin of species.* London: John Murray.

Darwin, C. (1871). *The descent of man: Selection in relation to sex.* London: John Murray.

Darwin, C. (1872). *The expression of emotions in men and animals.* London: John Murray.

Darwin, C. (1967). The provisional hypothesis of pangenesis. Reprinted in R.E. Grinder, *A history of genetic psychology: The first science of human development* (pp. 78–88). New York: Wiley. (Original work published 1896)

Dasen, P. (1972). Cross-cultural Piagetian research: A summary. *Journal of Cross Cultural Psychology, 3,* 29–39.

Davis, T. (1995). Gender differences in masking negative emotions: Ability or motivation? *Developmental Psychology, 31,* 660–667.

De Boysson-Bardies, B., Halle, P., Sagart, L., & Durand, C. (1989). A cross linguistic investigation of vowel formats in babbling. *Journal of Child Language, 16,* 1–18.

DeCarie, T.G. (1969). A study of the mental and emotional development of the thalidomide child. In B.M. Foss (Ed.), *Determinants of infant behaviour, Vol. IV.* London: Methuen.

De Casper, A.J., & Fifer, W. (1980). Of human bonding: Newborns prefer their mothers' voices. *Science, 208,* 1174–1176.

De Casper, A.J., Lecanuet, J.-P., Busnel, M.-C., Granier-Deferre, C., & Maugeais, R. (1994). Fetal reactions to recurrent maternal speech. *Infant Behavior and Development, 17,* 159–164.

De Casper, A.J., & Spence, M.J. (1986). Prenatal maternal speech influences newborns' perception of speech sounds. *Infant Behavior and Development, 9,* 133–150.

DeFrancis, J. (1989). *Visible speech: The diverse oneness of writing systems.* Honolulu, HI: University of Hawaii Press.

DeLoache, J.S., Miller, K.F., & Pierroutsakos, S.L. (1998). Reasoning and problem solving. In D.

Kuhn & R.S. Siegler (Eds.), *Handbook of child psychology: Vol. 2. Cognition, perception, and language* (pp. 801–850, W. Damon, Gen. Ed.). New York: Wiley.

Dennis, W., & Dennis, M.G. (1940). The effect of cradling practice upon the onset of walking in Hopi Indians. *Journal of Genetic Psychology, 56,* 77–86.

Dennis, W., & Najarian, P (1957). Infant development under environmental handicap. *Psychological Monographs, 7,* 1–7.

De Vries, J.I.P., Visser, G.H.A., & Prechtl, H.F.R. (1984). Fetal motility in the first half of pregnancy. In H.F.R. Prechtl (Ed.), *Continuity of neural function from prenatal to postnatal life.* London: Spastics International Medical Publications.

De Vries, R. (1969). Constancy of genetic identity in the years three to six. *Monographs of the Society for Research in Child Development, 34,* 127.

Diamond, A. (1988). Differences between adult and infant cognition: Is the crucial variable presence or absence of language? In L. Weiskrantz (Ed.), *Thought without language.* Oxford, UK: Clarendon Press.

Dias, M., & Harris, P.L. (1990). The influence of the imagination on the reasoning of young children. *British Journal of Developmental Psychology, 8,* 305–318.

Dixon, R.A. (1990). History of research of human development. In R.M. Thomas (Ed.), *The encyclopaedia of human development and education: Theory, research and studies* (pp. 9–17). Oxford, UK: Pergamon Press.

Dockrell, J., & McShane, J. (1992). *Children's learning difficulties: A cognitive approach.* Oxford, UK: Blackwell.

Doctor, E., & Coltheart, M. (1980). Children's use of phonological encoding when reading for meaning. *Memory and Cognition, 8,* 195–209.

Donaldson, M. (1978). *Children's minds.* Glasgow, UK: Fontana.

Dore, J. (1978). Conditions for the acquisition of speech acts. In I. Markova (Ed.), *The social context of language.* New York: John Wiley.

Dore, J. (1985). Holophrases revisited: Their "logical" development from dialogue. In M.D. Barrett (Ed.), *Children's single-word speech.* Chichester, UK: John Wiley.

Dromi, E. (1987). *Early lexical development.* Cambridge, UK: Cambridge University Press.

Dunlea, A. (1989). *Vision and the emergence of meaning.* Cambridge, UK: Cambridge University Press.

Dunn, J. (1984). *Sisters and brothers*. London: Fontana.

Dunn, J. (1987). The beginnings of moral understanding: Development in the second year. In J. Kagan & S. Lamb (Eds.), *The emergence of morality in young children*. Chicago: University of Chicago Press.

Dunn, J., & Kendrick, D. (1982). *Siblings: Love, envy and understanding*. Cambridge, MA: Harvard University Press.

Durkin, K. (1995). *Social psychology*. Oxford, UK: Blackwell.

Durkin, K., Shire, B., Riem, R., Crowther, R.D., & Rutter, D.R. (1986). The social and linguistic context of early number use. *British Journal of Developmental Psychology, 4*, 269–288.

Eckerman, C.O. (1979). Imitation and toddlers' achievement of co-ordinated action with others. In J. Nadel & L. Camaioni (Eds.), *New perspectives in early communicative development* (pp. 116–146). New York: Routledge & Kegan Paul.

Ehri, E.C. (1987). Learning to read and spell words. *Journal of Reading Behavior, 19*, 5–31.

Ehri, L., & Wilce, L.S. (1987). Does learning to spell help beginners to learn to read words. *Reading Research Quarterly, 12*, 47–65.

Ehri, L.C., & Robbins, C. (1992). Beginners need some decoding skills to read words by analogy. *Reading Research Quarterly, 27*, 12–28.

Eibl-Eibesfeldt, L. (1989). *Human ethology*. New York: De Gruyter.

Eimas, P. (1974). Auditory and linguistic cues for place of articulation by infants. *Perception and Psychophysics, 16*, 513–521.

Eimas, P., & Miller, J. (1980). Discrimination of the information for manner of articulation. *Infant Behavior and Development, 3*, 367–375.

Eimas, P.D., Siqueland, E., Jusczyk, P., & Vogorito, J. (1971). Speech perception in infants. *Science, 171*, 303–306.

Eisenberg, N., & Fabes, R.A. (1998). Prosocial development. In N. Eisenberg (Ed.), *Handbook of child psychology: Vol. 3. Social, emotional, and personality development* (pp. 701–778, W. Damon, Gen. Ed.). New York: Wiley.

Eisenberg, N., Wolchik, S., Goldberg, L., & Engel, I. (1992). Parental values, reinforcement, and young children's prosocial behaviour: A longitudinal study. *Journal of Genetic Psychology, 153*, 19–36.

Elliot, C.D. (1996). *British Ability Scales II*. Windsor, UK: NFER.

Elliott, D.S. (1994). Serious violent offenders: Onset, developmental course and termination. *Criminology, 32*, 1–21.

Ellis, N.C. (1994). Longitudinal studies of spelling development. In G.D.A. Brown & N.C. Ellis (Eds.), *Handbook of spelling*. Chichester, UK: Wiley.

Ellis, R., & Wells, G. (1980). Enabling factors in adult–child discourse. *First Language, 1*, 46–62.

Ellis, S., & Schneider, B. (1989). *Collaboration on children's instructions: A Navajo versus Anglo comparison*. Paper presented at the biennial meeting of the Society for Research in Child Development, Kansas City, MO.

Elman, J.L., Bates, E.A., Johnson, M.H., Karmiloff-Smith, A., Parisi, D., & Plunkett, K. (1996). *Rethinking innateness: A connectionist perspective on development*. Cambridge, MA: MIT Press.

Emmerich, W., Goldman, K.S., Kirsh, B., & Sharabany, R. (1977). Evidence for a transitional phase in the development of gender constancy. *Child Development, 48*, 930–936.

Erel, O., & Burman, B. (1995). Interrelatedness of marital relations and parent–child relations: A meta-analytic review. *Psychological Bulletin, 118*, 108–132.

Fabricus, W. (1988). The development of forward search planning in preschoolers. *Child Development, 59*, 1473–1488.

Fantz, R.L. (1961). The origins of form perception. *Scientific American, 204*, 66–72.

Fantz, R.L. (1965). Visual perception from birth as shown by pattern selectivity. *Annals of the New York Academy of Sciences, 118*, 793–814.

Fenson, L., Dale, P., Resnick, S., Bates, E., Thal, D., Reilly, J., & Hartung, J. (1990). *MacArthur communicative development inventories: Technical manual*. San Diego: San Diego State University.

Fenson, L., Dale, P.S., Resnick, J.S., Bates, E., Thal, D.J., & Pethick, S.J. (1994). Variability in early communicative development. *Monographs of the Society for Research in Child Development, 59*, v–173.

Fernald, A., & Morikawa, H. (1993). Common themes and cultural variations in Japanese and American mothers' speech to infants. *Child Development, 64*, 637–656.

Field, T., Healy, B., Goldstein, S., & Guthertz, M. (1990). Behavior state matching and synchrony in mother–infant interaction of non-depressed dyads. *Developmental Psychology, 26*, 7–14.

Field, T.M., Woodson, R.W., Greenberg, R., & Cohen, C. (1982). Discrimination and imitation of facial expressions by neonates. *Science, 218,* 179–181.

Fischer, K., & Lazerson, A. (1984). *Human development from conception to adolescence.* New York: W.H. Freeman.

Fischer, K.W., & Rose, S.P. (1994). Dynamic development of co-ordination of components in brain and behavior: A framework for theory and research. In G. Dawson & K.W. Fischer (Eds.), *Human behavior and the developing brain.* New York: Guilford Press.

Flavell, J.H. (1963). *The developmental psychology of Jean Piaget.* Princeton, NJ: Van Nostrand.

Flavell, J.H., Miller, P.H., & Miller, S.A. (1993). *Cognitive development* (3rd ed.). Englewood Cliffs, NJ: Prentice-Hall.

Fogel, A. (1991). *Infancy.* New York: West Publishing.

Folven, R.J., Bonvillian, J.D., & Orlansky M.D. (1984–85). Communicative gestures and early sign language acquisition. *First Language, 5,* 129–144.

Fox, N.A. (1995). On the way we see: Adult memories about attachment experiences and their role in determining infant–parent relationships: A comment on van Ijzendoorn. *Psychological Bulletin, 113,* 387–403.

Fraiberg, S. (1974). *Insights from the blind.* New York: Basic Books.

Freedman, D. (1974). *Human infancy: An evolutionary perspective.* Hillsdale, NJ: Lawrence Erlbaum Associates Inc.

Freeman, N. (1980). *Strategies of representation in young children: Analysis of spatial skills and drawing processes.* London: Academic Press.

Freeman, N. (1987). Current problems in the development of representational picture-production. *Archives de Psychologie, 55,* 127–152.

Freeman, N., & Janikoun, R. (1972). Intellectual realism in children's drawings of a familiar object with distinctive features. *Child Development, 43,* 1116–1121.

Freud, S. (1938). Three contributions to the theory of sex. In A.A. Brill (Ed.), *The basic writings of Sigmund Freud.* New York: Random House.

Frith, U. (1985). Beneath the surface of developmental dyslexia. In K. Patterson, M. Coltheart, & J. Marshall (Eds.), *Surface dyslexia.* Hove, UK: Psychology Press.

Frith, U. (1989). *Autism: Explaining the enigma.* Oxford, UK: Blackwell

Fuligni, A.J., & Stevenson, H.W. (1995). Time use and mathematics achievement among American, Chinese, and Japanese high school students. *Child Development, 66*(3), 830–842.

Furman, W., & Buhrmester, D. (1992). Age and sex differences in perceptions of networks of personal relationships. *Child Development, 63,* 103–115.

Furth, H.G., & Kane, S.R. (1992). Children constructing society: A new perspective on children at play. In H. McGurk (Ed.), *Childhood social development: Contemporary perspectives* (pp. 149–171). Hove, UK: Psychology Press.

Fuson, K.C. (1988). *Children's counting and concepts of number.* New York: Springer.

Gaines, R., Mandler, J.M., & Bryant, P.E. (1981). Immediate and delayed recall by hearing and deaf children. *Journal of Speech and Hearing Research, 24,* 463–469.

Gallistel, C.R., & Gelman, R. (1991). Preverbal and verbal counting and computation. In S. Dehaene (Ed.), *Numerical cognition.* Oxford, UK: Blackwell.

Gallistel, C.R., & Gelman, R. (1992). Preverbal and verbal counting and computation. *Cognition, 44,* 43–74.

Gallup, G.G., Jr. (1977). Self recognition in primates: A comparative approach to the bi-directional properties of consciousness. *American Psychologist, 32,* 329–338.

Galton, F. (1869). *Hereditary genius: An inquiry into its laws and consequences.* London: Macmillan.

Gardner, B.T., & Gardner, R.A. (1971). Two-way communication with an infant chimpanzee. In A.M. Schrier & F. Stollnitz (Eds.), *Behavior of nonhuman primates, Vol. 4.* New York: Academic Press.

Gardner, R.A., & Gardner, B.T. (1974). A vocabulary test for chimpanzees. *Journal of Comparative Psychology, 98,* 381–404.

Garvey, C. (1977). *Play.* Cambridge, MA: Harvard University Press.

Gathercole, S.E., & Baddeley, A.D. (1990). Phonological memory deficits in language disordered children: Is there a causal connection? *Journal of Memory and Language, 29,* 336–360.

Gauvain, M., & Rogoff, B. (1989). Collaborative problem solving and children's planning skills. *Developmental Psychology, 25,* 139–151.

Gelman, R., & Gallistel, C.R. (1978). *The child's understanding of number.* Cambridge, MA: Harvard University Press.

Gentry, J.R. (1978). Early spelling strategies. *The Elementary School Journal, 79,* 88–92.

Gerson, R., & Damon, W. (1978). Moral understanding and children's conduct. In W. Damon (Ed.), *Moral development: New directions in child development* (pp. 41–60). San Francisco: Jossey-Bass.

Gesell, A. (1941). *A wolf child and a human child*. New York: Harper.

Gesell, A., Ilg, F.L., & Bullis, G.E. (1949). *Vision: Its development in infant and child*. New York: Paul B. Heober.

Gibson, E.J., & Spelke, E.S. (1983). The development of perception. In J.H. Flavell & E.M. Markman (Eds.), *Handbook of child psychology: Vol. III. Cognitive development* (pp. 1–76). Chichester, UK: John Wiley.

Gibson, J.J. (1966). *The senses considered as perceptual systems*. London: George Allen & Unwin.

Gilligan, C. (1982). *In a different voice*. Cambridge, MA: Harvard University Press.

Gilligan, C. (1986). On a different voice: An interdisciplinary forum: Reply. *Signs, 11*, 324–323.

Girotto,V., & Light, P. (1992). The pragmatic bases of children's reasoning. In P. Light & G.E. Butterworth (Eds.), *Context and cognition* (pp. 134–156). Hemel Hempstead, UK: Harvester.

Gladwin, E.T. (1970). *East is a big bird*. Cambridge, MA: Harvard University Press.

Gleitman, L.R. (1990). The structural sources of verb meanings. *Language Acquisition, 1*, 3–55.

Gleitman, L.R., Newport, E.L., & Gleitman, H. (1984). The current status of the motherese hypothesis. *Journal of Child Language, 11*, 43–80.

Gobbo, C., & Chi, M. (1986). How knowledge is structured and used by expert and novice children. *Cognitive Development, 1*, 221–237.

Goldfield, B.A., & Reznick, J.S. (1990). Early lexical acquisition: Rate, content, and the vocabulary spurt. *Journal of Child Language, 17*, 171–183.

Golomb, C. (1992). *The child's creation of a pictorial world*. Oxford, UK: University of California Press.

Goodenough, W.H. (1953). *Native astronomy in the central Carolines*. Museum Monographs. Philadelphia University Museum, University of Philadelphia.

Gopnik, A., & Choi, S. (1995). Names, relational words and cognitive development in English and Korean speakers: Nouns are not always learned before verbs. In M. Tomasello & W.E. Merriman (Eds.), *Beyond names for things: Young children's acquisition of verbs* (pp. 83–90). Hillsdale, NJ: Lawrence Erlbaum Associates Inc.

Goswami, U. (1986). Children's use of analogy in learning to read: A developmental study. *Journal of Experimental Child Psychology, 42*, 73–83.

Goswami, U. (1998). *Cognition in childhood*. Hove, UK: Psychology Press.

Goswami, U., & Brown, A.L. (1990). Higher-order and relational reasoning: Contrasting analogical and thematic relations. *Cognition, 36*, 207–226

Goswami, U., & Bryant, P. (1990). *Phonological skills and learning to read*. Hove, UK: Psychology Press.

Gottlieb, G. (1992). *Individual differences and evolution: The genesis of novel behavior*. New York: Oxford University Press.

Gould, S.J. (1977). *Ontogeny and phylogeny*. Cambridge, MA: Harvard University Press.

Greenough, W.T., Black, J.E., & Wallace, C.S. (1987). Experience and brain development. *Child Development, 58*, 539–559.

Gregory, R.L., & Wallace, J.G. (1963). *Recovery from early blindness: A case study*. Cambridge, UK: Cambridge University Press.

Griffiths, R. (1954). *The abilities of babies*. London: University of London Press.

Groen, G.J., & Parkman, J.M. (1972). A chronometric analysis of simple addition. *Psychological Review, 79*, 329–343.

Grossman, K., Grossman, K.E., Spangler, G., Suess, G., & Unzner, L. (1985). Maternal sensitivity and newborns' orientation responses as related to quality of attachment in Northern Germany. In I. Bretherton & E. Waters (Eds.), Growing points of attachment theory and research. *Monographs of the Society for Research in Child Development, 50*(1/2, Serial No. 209), 233–256.

Grossman, K.E. (1988). Longitudinal and systematic approaches to the study of biological high- and low-risk groups. In M. Rutter (Ed.), *Studies of psychosocial risk: The power of longitudinal data* (pp. 138–157). Cambridge, UK: Cambridge University Press.

Grych, J., & Fincham, F. (1990). Marital conflict and children's adjustment: A cognitive-contextual framework. *Psychological Bulletin, 108*, 267–290.

Haeckel, E. (1906). *The evolution of man*. London: Watts & Co. (Original work published 1874)

Haith, M.M. (1980). *Rules that babies look by: The organisation of newborn visual activity*. Hillsdale, NJ: Lawrence Erlbaum Associates Inc.

Hamm, J.V. (2000). Do birds of a feather flock together? The variable bases for African American, Asian American, and European adolescents' selection of similar friends. *Developmental Psychology, 36*, 209–219.

Hanson, V.L., Shankweiler, D., & Fischer, F.W. (1983). Determinants of spelling ability in deaf and hearing adults: Access to linguistic structure. *Cognition*, *14*, 323–344.

Harlow, H., McGaugh, J.L., & Thompson, R.F. (1971). *Psychology.* San Francisco: Albion Publication Co.

Harris, M. (1994). *Reading comprehension difficulties in deaf children.* Workshop on Comprehension Disabilities, Centro Diagnostico Italiano, Milan.

Harris, M. (1996). *Language development* (Study Guide). Milton Keynes, UK: Open University Press.

Harris, M., & Barlow-Brown, F. (1997). Learning to read in blind and sighted children. In V. Lewis & G.M. Collis (Eds.), *Blindness and psychological development 0–10 years.* Leicester, UK: BPS Books.

Harris, M., Barlow-Brown, F., & Chasin, J. (1995). The emergence of referential understanding: Pointing and the comprehension of object names. *First Language*, *15*, 19–34.

Harris, M., Barrett, M., Jones, D., & Brookes, S. (1988). Linguistic input and early word meaning. *Journal of Child Language*, *15*, 77–94.

Harris, M., & Beech, J. (1994). Reading development in prelingually deaf children. In K. Nelson & Z. Reger (Eds.), *Children's language, Vol. 8.* Hillsdale, NJ: Lawrence Erlbaum Associates Inc.

Harris, M., & Giannouli, V. (1999). Learning to read and spell Greek: The importance of letter knowledge and morphological awareness. In M. Harris & G. Hatano (Eds.), *Learning to read and write: A cross-linguistic perspective* (pp. 51–70). Cambridge, UK: Cambridge University Press.

Harris, M., Jones, D., Brookes, S., & Grant, J. (1986). Relations between the non-verbal context of maternal speech and rate of language development. *British Journal of Developmental Psychology*, *4*, 261–268.

Harris, M., Jones, D., & Grant, J. (1983). The nonverbal context of mothers' speech to children. *First Language*, *4*, 21–30.

Harris, M., Jones, D., & Grant, J. (1984–85). The social-interactional context of maternal speech to children: An explanation for the event-bound nature of early word use? *First Language*, *5*, 89–100.

Harris, M., Yeeles, C., Chasin, J., & Oakley, Y. (1995). Symmetries and asymmetries in early lexical comprehension and production. *Journal of Child Language*, *22*, 1–18.

Harris, P.L. (1989). *Children and emotion.* Oxford, UK: Blackwell.

Harris, P.L. (1992). From simulation to folk psychology: The case for development. *Mind and Language*, *7*, 120–144.

Harris, P.L. (1994). The child's understanding of emotion: The developmental process and the family environment. *Journal of Child Psychology and Psychiatry*, *135*, 3–28.

Harris, P.L. (1997). Piaget in Paris: From "autism" to logic. *Human Development*, *40*, 109–123.

Harris, P.L. (2000). *The work of the imagination.* Oxford, UK: Blackwell.

Harris, P.L., Brown, E., Marriott, C., Whittall, S., & Harmer, S. (1991). Monsters, ghosts and witches: Testing the limits of the fantasy–reality distinction in young children. *British Journal of Developmental Psychology*, *9*, 105–123.

Hart, M. (1991). Input frequency and children's first words. *First Language*, *11*, 289–300.

Hartshorn, K., & Rovee-Collier, C. (1997). Infant learning and long-term memory at 6 months: A confirming analysis. *Developmental Psychobiology*, *30*, 71–85.

Hartshorn, K., Rovee-Collier, C., Gerhardstein, P., Blatt, R.S., Wondolski, T.L., Klein, P., Gilch, J. (1998). The ontogeny of long-term memory over the first year-and-a-half of life. *Developmental Psychobiology*, *32*, 69–89.

Hartup, W.W. (1996). Cooperation, close relationships, and cognitive development. In W.M. Bukowski, A.F. Newcomb, & W.W. Hartup (Eds.), *The company they keep: Friendship in childhood and adolescence* (pp. 213–237). Cambridge, UK: Cambridge University Press.

Hartup, W.W. (1998). The company they keep: Friendships and their developmental significance. In A. Campbell & S. Muncer (Eds.), *The social child* (pp. 143–164). Hove, UK: Psychology Press.

Hartup, W.W., & Laursen, B. (1992). Conflict and context in peer relations. In C.H. Hart (Ed.), *Children on playgrounds: Research perspectives and applications* (pp. 44–84). Albany, NY: State University of New York Press.

Haste, H., Helkama, K., & Markoulis, D. (1998). Morality, wisdom and the life-span. In A. Demetriou, W. Doise, & C.F.M. van Lieshout (Eds.), *Life-span developmental psychology.* Chichester, UK: Wiley.

Hatano, G. (1990). Towards the cultural psychology of mathematical cognition: Commentry on H.W. Stevenson and S.Y. Lee. Contexts of achievement. *Monographs of the Society for Research in Child Development*, *51*, 108–115.

Hay, D.F., Pedersen, J., & Nash, A. (1982). Dyadic interaction in the first year of life. In K.H. Rubin & H.S. Ross (Eds.), *Peer relationships and social skills in childhood* (pp. 11–40). New York: Springer-Verlag.

Hayes, L.A., & Watson, J.S. (1981). Neonatal imitation: Fact or artefact? *Developmental Psychology, 17,* 655–660.

Hepper, P.G., Shahidullah, S., & White, R. (1991). Handedness in the human fetus. *Neuropsychologia, 29,* 1107–1111.

Hespos, S.J., & Baillargeon, R. (1999). Reasoning about containment events in very young infants. *Manuscript submitted for publication.*

Hespos, S.J., & Baillargeon, R. (2001). Infants' knowledge about occlusion and containment events: A surprising discrepancy. *Psychological Science, 121,* 141–147.

Heyes, C., & Galef, B.G. (1996). *Social learning in animals.* New York: Academic Press.

Higgins, E.T., & Parsons, J.E. (1983). Social cognition and the social life of the child: Stages as subcultures. In E.T. Higgins, D.N. Ruble, & W.W. Hartup (Eds.), *Social cognition and social development* (pp. 15–62). Cambridge, UK: Cambridge University Press.

Hinde, R.A. (1979). On describing relationships. *Journal of Child Psychology and Child Psychiatry, 17,* 1–19.

Hinde, R.A. (1982). Attachment: Some conceptual and biological issues. In J. Stephenson-Hinde & C. Murray Parkes (Eds.), *The place of attachment in human behavior* (pp. 60–76). New York: Basic Books.

Hinde, R.A. (1987). *Individuals, relationships and culture.* Cambridge, UK: Cambridge University Press.

Hinde, R.A. (1995). A suggested structure for a science of relationships. *Personal Relationships, 2,* 1–15.

Hinde, R.A., Titmus, G., Easton, D., & Tamplin, A. (1985). Incidence of "friendship" and behaviour with strong associates versus non-associates in preschoolers. *Child Development, 56,* 234–245.

Hirsh-Pasek, K., & Golinkoff, R.M. (1996). *The origins of grammar: Evidence from early language comprehension.* Cambridge, MA: MIT Press.

Hitch, G.J., & Towse, J.N. (1995). Working memory: What develops? In F.E. Wienert & W. Schneider (Eds.), *Memory performance and competencies: Issues in growth and development.* Mahwah, NJ: Lawrence Erlbaum Associates Inc.

Hobson, R.P. (1993). *Autism and the development of mind.* Hove, UK: Psychology Press.

Hoien, T., & Lundberg, I. (1988). Stages of word recognition in early reading development. *Scandinavian Journal of Educational Research, 32,* 163–182.

Holloway, R.L., & La Coste-Larey Mondie, M.C. (1982). Brain endocasts in pongoids and hominids: Some preliminary findings on the palaeontology of cerebral dominance. *American Journal of Physical Anthropology, 58,* 101–110.

Holmes, J. (1993). *John Bowlby and attachment theory.* London: Routledge.

Holyoak, K.J., Junn, E.N., & Billman, D.O. (1984). Development of analogical problem-solving skill. *Child Development, 55,* 2024–2055.

Hood, B., & Willatts, F. (1986). Reaching in the dark to an object's remembered position in 5 month old infants. *British Journal of Developmental Psychology, 4,* 57–65.

Hooker, D. (1939). Fetal behavior. *Research Publications of the Association for Research in Nervous and Mental Disease, 19,* 237–243.

Hornik, R., Risenhoover, N., & Gunnar, M. (1987). The effects of maternal positive, neutral, and negative affective communications on infants' responses to new toys. *Child Development, 58,* 937–944.

Horrocks, J.E. (1954). The adolescent. In L. Carmichael (Ed.), *Manual of child psychology* (2nd ed., pp. 697–734). New York: Wiley.

Howe, N., & Ross, H.S. (1990). Socialization, perspective-taking, and the sibling relationship. *Developmental Psychology, 26,* 160–165.

Hughes, M. (1986). *Children and number: Difficulties in learning mathematics.* Oxford, UK: Blackwell.

Hyams, N. (1986). *Language acquisition and the theory of parameters.* Dordrecht, The Netherlands: Reidel.

Ifrah, G. (1985). *From one to zero: A universal history of numbers.* New York: John Wiley & Sons, Inc.

Inagaki, K. (1990). The effects of raising animals on children's biological knowledge. *British Journal of Developmental Psychology, 8,* 119–131.

Ingram, N., & Butterworth, G.E. (1989). The young child's representation of depth in drawing: Process and product. *Journal of Experimental Child Psychology, 47,* 356–379.

Inhelder, B., & Piaget, J. (1955). *De la logique de l'enfant à la logique de l'adolescent.* Paris: Presses Universitaires de France.

Inhelder, B., & Piaget, J. (1958). *The growth of logical thinking from childhood to adolescence.* New York: Basic Books.

Isawa, N. (1992) Postconventional reasoning and moral education in Japan. *Journal of Moral Education, 21,* 3–16.

Itard, J.-M.-G. (1932). *The wild boy of Aveyron* (G. Humphrey & M. Humphrey, Trans.). New York: Century.

James, W. (1890). *The principles of psychology.* New York: Longmans Green.

Jeannerod, M. (1984). The timing of natural prehension movements. *Journal of Motor Behavior, 16,* 235–254.

Johnson, C.N., & Harris, P.L. (1994). Magic: Special but not excluded. *British Journal of Developmental Psychology, 12,* 35–51.

Johnson, M. (1998). The neural basis of cognitive development. In D. Kuhn & R.S. Siegler (Eds.), *Handbook of child psychology: Vol. 2. Cognition, perception, and language* (pp. 1–50, W. Damon, Gen. Ed.). New York: Wiley.

Johnson, M., & Morton, J. (1991). *Biology and cognitive development: The case of face recognition.* Oxford, UK: Blackwell.

Johnston, R.S., Anderson, M., & Holligan, C. (1996). Knowledge of the alphabet and explicit awareness of phonemes in pre-readers—the nature of the relationship. *Reading and Writing, 8,* 217–234.

Jones, S., Martin, R., & Pilbeam, D. (1992). *The Cambridge encyclopaedia of human evolution.* Cambridge, UK: Cambridge University Press.

Josephs, I. (1994). Display rule behavior and understanding in preschool children. *Journal of Nonverbal Behavior, 18,* 301–326.

Joshi, M.S., & MacLean, M. (1994). Indian and English children's understanding of the distinction between real and apparent emotions. *Child Development, 65,* 1372–1384.

Jusczyk, P.W., Cutler, A., & Redanz, N.J. (1993). Infants' preference for the predominant stress patterns of English words. *Child Development, 64,* 675–687.

Kail, R. (1990). *The development of memory in children.* New York: W.H. Freeman.

Kaitz, M., Meschulach-Sarfaty, O., & Auerbach, J. (1988). A re-examination of newborns' ability to imitate facial expressions. *Developmental Psychology, 24,* 3–7.

Kanner, A.D., Feldman, S.S., Weinberg, D.A., & Ford, M.E. (1987). Uplifts, hassles, and adaptational outcomes in early adolescence. *Journal of Early Adolescence, 7,* 371–394.

Karmiloff-Smith, A. (1979). *A functional approach to child language: A study of determiners and reference.* Cambridge, UK: Cambridge University Press.

Karmiloff-Smith, A. (1992). *Beyond modularity: A developmental perspective on cognitive science.* Cambridge, MA: MIT Press.

Kellogg, R. (1970). *Analyzing children's art.* Mountain View, CA: Mayfield Publishing Company.

Kimura, Y., & Bryant, P.E. (1983). Reading and writing in English and Japanese. *British Journal of Developmental Psychology, 1,* 129–144.

Klahr, D. (1995). Solving problems with ambiguous subgoal ordering: Preschoolers' performance. *Child Development, 56,* 940–952.

Klahr, D., & Robinson, M. (1981). Formal assessment of planning problem solving and planning problems in children. *Cognitive Psychology, 13,* 113–228.

Klahr, D., & Wallace, J.G. (1976). *Cognitive development: An information-processing view.* Hillsdale, NJ: Lawrence Erlbaum Associates Inc.

Klaus, M.H., & Kennell, J.H. (1976). *Parent–infant bonding.* St Louis, MI: Mosby.

Koffka, K. (1935). *Principles of Gestalt psychology.* New York: Harcourt Brace.

Kohlberg, L. (1966). A cognitive developmental analysis of children's sex role concepts and attitudes. In E. Maccoby (Ed.), *The development of sex differences.* Stanford, CA: Stanford University Press.

Kohlberg, L. (1982). Moral development. In J.M. Broughton & D.J. Freeman-Moir (Eds.), *The cognitive developmental psychology of James Mark Baldwin.* Norwood, NJ: Ablex.

Kozulin, A. (1990). *Vygotsky's psychology.* Hemel Hempstead, UK: Harvester.

Kreitler, S., & Kreitler, H. (1987). Conceptions and processes of planning: The developmental perspective. In S.L. Friedman, E.K. Scholnick, & R.R. Cocking (Eds.), *Blueprints for thinking: The role of planning in cognitive development.* New York: Cambridge University Press.

Kugiumutzakis, G. (1999). Genesis and development of early infant mimesis to facial and vocal models. In J. Nadel & G.E. Butterworth (Eds.), *Imitation in infancy* (pp. 36–60). Cambridge, UK: Cambridge University Press.

Kuhl, P., & Meltzoff, A.N. (1982). The bimodal perception of speech in infancy. *Science, 218,* 1138–1141.

Kuhl, P.K., & Miller, J.D. (1978). Speech perception by the chinchilla: Identification functions for synthetic VOT stimuli. *Journal of the Acoustical Society of America, 63,* 905–917.

Kuhl, P.K., Williams, K.A., Laard, F., Stevens, K.N., & Lindblom, B. (1992). Linguistic experience alters phonetic perception in infants by 6 months. *Science, 255*, 606–608.

Kunzig, R. (1998). Climbing through the brain. *Discover Magazine*, August 1998.

Landau, B., & Gleitman, L.R. (1985). *Language and experience: Evidence from the blind child.* Cambridge, MA: Harvard University Press.

Laursen, B. (1996). Closeness and conflict in adolescent peer relationships: Interdependence with friends and romantic partners. In W.M. Bukowski, A.F. Newcomb, & W.W. Hartup (Eds.), *The company they keep: Friendship in childhood and adolescence.* Cambridge, UK: Cambridge University Press.

Leakey, M.D. (1979). Footprints in the ashes of time. *National Geographic, 155*, 446–457.

Leakey, M.D. (1987). *Laetoli: A Pliocene site in Northern Tanzania.* Oxford, UK: Clarendon Press.

Leslie, A.A. (1988). Some implications of pretence for mechanisms underlying the child's theory of mind. In J.W. Astington, P.L. Harris, & D.R. Olson (Eds.), *Developing theories of mind.* Cambridge, UK: Cambridge University Press.

Leslie, A.M. (1991). The theory of mind impairment in autism: Evidence for a modular mechanism of development? In A. Whiten (Ed.), *Natural theories of mind.* Oxford, UK: Blackwell.

Leung, E.H.L., & Rheingold, H. (1981). Development of pointing as a social gesture. *Developmental Psychology, 17*, 215–220.

Lewis, C., Scully, D., & Condor, S. (1992). Sex stereotyping in infants: A re-examination. *Journal of Reproductive and Infant Psychology, 10*, 53–63.

Leybaert, J., & Alegria, J. (1995). Spelling development in deaf and hearing children: Evidence for use of morpho-phonological regularities in French. *Reading and Writing, 7*, 89–109.

Linnell, M., & Fluck, M. (2001). The effects of maternal support for counting and cardinal understanding in preschool children. *Social Development, 10*, 202–220.

Lloyd, B., & Duveen, G. (1990). A semiotic analysis of the development of the social representation of gender. In G. Duveen & B. Lloyd (Eds.), *Social representation and the development of knowledge.* Cambridge, UK: Cambridge University Press.

Locke, J.L. (1983). *Phonological acquisition and change.* New York: Academic Press.

Locke, J.L. (1993). *The child's path to spoken language.* Cambridge, MA: Harvard University Press.

Lorenz, C. (1961). *King Solomon's ring.* London. Methuen.

Lucariello, J. (1987). Concept formation and its relation to word learning and use in the second year. *Journal of Child Language, 14*, 309–332.

Lundberg, I., Frost, J., & Petersen, O.P. (1988). Effects of an extensive program for stimulating phonological awareness in preschool children. *Reading Research Quarterly, 23*, 263–284.

Lundberg, I., Olofsson, A., & Wall, S. (1980). Reading and spelling skills in the first school years predicted from phonemic awareness skills in kindergarten. *Scandinavian Journal of Psychology, 21*, 159–173.

Luquet, G.H. (1927). *Le dessin enfantin.* Paris: Delachaux et Niestle.

Luria, A.R. (1959). The directive function of speech development and dissolution. Part I: Development of the directive function of speech in early childhood. *Word, 15*, 341–352.

Maccoby, E.E. (1990a). Gender and relationships: A developmental account. *American Psychologist, 45*, 513–520.

Maccoby, E.E. (1990b). The effect of gender identity and gender constancy in sex-differentiated development. In D. Schroder (Ed.), *The legacy of Lawrence Kohlberg: New directions for child development* (pp. 5–20). San Francisco: Jossey-Bass.

MacFarlane, A. (1975). Olfaction in the development of social preferences in the human neonate. In *Parent infant interaction* (CIBA Foundation Symposium 33). Amsterdam: Elsevier.

Mandler, G., & Shebo, B.J. (1982). Subitizing: An analysis of its component processes. *Journal of Experimental Psychology: General, 111*, 1–22.

Mans, L., Cicchetti, D., & Sroufe, L.A. (1978). Mirror reactions of Down's syndrome infants and toddlers: Cognitive underpinnings of self-recognition. *Child Development, 49*, 1247–1250.

Maratos, O. (1998). Neonatal, early and late imitation: Same order phenomena? In F. Simion & G. Butterworth (Eds.), *The development of sensory, motor and cognitive capacities in early infancy* (pp. 145–161). Hove, UK: Psychology Press.

Marcus, G.F., Pinker, S., Ullman, M., Hollander, M., Rosen, T.J., & Xu, F. (1992). Overregularization in language acquisition. *Monographs of the Society for Research in Child Development, 57*(4, Serial No. 228). Chicago: University of Chicago Press.

Marini, Z.A. (1992). Synchrony and asynchrony in the development of children's scientific reasoning. In R. Case (Ed.), *The mind's staircase: Exploring the conceptual underpinnings of children's thought and knowledge.* Hillsdale, NJ: Lawrence Erlbaum Associates Inc.

Marschark, M., & Harris, M. (1996). Success and failure in learning to read: The special (?) case of deaf children. In C. Cornoldi & J. Oakhill (Eds.), *Reading comprehension difficulties: Processes and intervention* (pp. 279–300). Hillsdale, NJ: Lawrence Erlbaum Associates Inc.

Marsh, G., Friedman, M.P., Welch, V., & Desberg, P. (1980). A cognitive-developmental approach to reading acquisition. In G.E. MacKinnon & T.G. Wailer (Eds.), *Reading research: Advances in theory and practice, Vol. 3.* New York: Academic Press.

Masur, E.F. (1982). Mothers' responses to infants' object-related gestures: Influences on lexical development. *Journal of Child Language, 9,* 23–30.

Matthews, J.S. (1990). *The first drawing.* Poster presented at the fourth European Conference on Developmental Psychology, University of Stirling, UK.

Mayer, R.E. (1992). *Thinking, problem solving, cognition* (2nd ed.). New York: Freeman.

Mayer, R.E., Sims, V., & Tajika, H. (1995). A comparison of how textbooks teach mathematical problem solving in Japan and the United States. *American Educational Research Journal, 32(2),* 443–460.

McClelland, J.L., & Jenkins, E. (1991). Nature, nurture and connectionism: Implications for connectionist models of development. In K. van Lehn (Ed.), *Architectures for intelligence—the 22nd Carnegie Symposium on Cognition.* Hillsdale, NJ: Lawrence Erlbaum Associates Inc.

McDougall, S., & Hulme, C. (1994). Short-term memory, speech rate and phonological awareness as predictors of learning to read. In C. Hulme & M. Snowling (Eds.), *Reading development and dyslexia.* London: Whurr Publishers.

McDougall, W. (1931). *Psychopathologie funktioneller Stoerungen* [Psychopathology of functional disturbances]. Leipzig, Germany: Barth.

McGarrigle, J.A., & Donaldson, M. (1974). Conservation accidents. *Cognition: International Journal of Cognitive Psychology, 3,* 341–350.

McGraw, M.B. (1940). Neuromuscular development of the human infant as exemplified in the achievement of erect locomotion. *Journal of Pediatrics, 17,* 750.

McGraw, M.B. (1941). Development of neuromuscular mechanisms as reflected in the crawling and creeping behavior of the human infant. *Journal of Genetic Psychology, 58,* 86.

McGraw, M.B. (1943). *The neuromuscular maturation of the human infant.* New York: Hofner.

McNeill, D. (1966). *The acquisition of language: The study of developmental linguistics.* New York: Harper & Row.

McShane, J. (1979). The development of naming. *Linguistics, 13,* 155–161.

Meck, W.H., & Church, R.M. (1983). A mode control model of counting and timing processes. *Journal of Experimental Psychology: Animal Behavior Processes, 9,* 320–334.

Mehler, J., & Dupoux, E. (1994). *What infants know.* Oxford, UK: Blackwell.

Mehler, J., Jusczyk, P.W., Dehaene-Lambertz, G., Dupoux, E., & Nazzi, T. (1994). Coping with linguistic diversity: The infant's viewpoint. In J.L. Morgan & K. Demuth (Eds.), *Signal to syntax: Bootstrapping from speech to grammar in early acquisition* (pp. 101–116). Mahwah, NJ: Lawrence Erlbaum Associates Inc.

Meltzoff, A.N., & Borton, R.W. (1979). Intermodal matching by human neonates. *Nature, 282,* 403–404.

Meltzoff, A.N., & Moore, M.K. (1977). Imitation of facial and manual gestures by human neonates. *Science, 198,* 75–78.

Meltzoff, A.N., & Moore, M.K. (1994). Imitation, memory, and the representation of persons. *Infant Behaviour and Development, 17,* 83–99.

Meltzoff, A.N., & Moore, M.K. (1997). Explaining facial imitation: A theoretical model. *Early Development and Parenting, 6,* 179–192.

Meltzoff, A.N., & Moore, M.K. (1999). Persons and representation: Why infant imitation is important for theories of human development. In J. Nadel & G.E. Butterworth (Eds.), *Imitation in infancy* (pp. 9–35). Cambridge, UK: Cambridge University Press.

Merrills, J.D., Underwood, G., & Wood, D.J. (1994). The word recognition skills of profoundly, prelingually deaf children. *British Journal of Psychology, 12,* 365–384.

Michel, G.F., & Moore, C.L. (1995). *Developmental psychobiology: An interdisciplinary science.* Cambridge, MA: MIT Press.

Michotte, A. (1963). *The perception of causality.* London: Methuen.

Millar, S. (1975). Visual experience or translation rules? Drawing the human figure by blind and sighted children. *Perception, 43,* 63–71.

Millar, S. (1997). *Reading by touch*. Florence, KY: Taylor & Francis/Routledge.

Miller, J., & Eimas, P. (1983). Studies on the categorisation of speech by infants. *Cognition, 13*, 135–165.

Miller, J.G., & Bersoff, D.M. (1995). Development in the context of everyday family relationships: Culture, interpersonal morality, and adaptation. In M. Killen & D. Hart, (Eds.), *Morality in everyday life: Developmental perspectives* (pp. 259–282). New York: Cambridge University Press.

Mills, A.E. (1987). The development of phonology in the blind child. In B. Dodd & B. Campbell (Eds.), *Hearing by eye: The psychology of lip reading*. Hillsdale, NJ: Lawrence Erlbaum Associates Inc.

Miura, I.T., Okamoto, Y., Kim, C.C., Change, C.-M., Steere, M., & Fayol, M. (1994). Comparisons of children's cognitive representations of number: China, France, Japan, Korea, Sweden and the United States. *International Journal of Behavioral Development, 17*, 401–411.

Miyake, K., Chen, S.-J., & Campos, J.J. (1985). Infant temperament, mother's mode of interaction and attachment in Japan: An interim report. In I. Bretherton & E. Waters (Eds.), Growing points of attachment theory and research. *Monographs of the Society for Research in Child Development, 50*, 276–297.

Mizukami, K., Kobayashi, N., Ishii, T., & Iwaka, H. (1990). First selective attachment begins in early infancy: A study using telethermography. *Infant Behavior and Development, 13*, 257–271.

Moore, C., & Frye, D. (1986). The effect of experimenter's intention on the child's understanding of conservation. *Cognition, 22*, 283–298.

Morss, J.R. (1990). *The biologising of childhood: Developmental psychology and the Darwinian myth*. Hillsdale, NJ: Lawrence Erlbaum Associates Inc.

Moshman, D. (1995). The construction of moral rationality. *Human Development, 38*, 53–64.

Moshman, D. (1998). Cognitive development beyond childhood. In D. Kuhn & R.S. Siegler (Eds.), *Handbook of child psychology: Vol. 2. Cognition, perception, and language* (W. Damon, Gen. Ed.). New York: Wiley.

Muir, D. (1999). Theories and methods in developmental psychology. In A. Slater & D. Muir (Eds.), *The Blackwell reader in developmental psychology* (pp. 3–16). Oxford, UK: Blackwell.

Muir, D., & Field, J. (1979). Newborn infants orient to sounds. *Child Development, 50*, 431–436.

Munakata, Y. (1998). Infant perseveration and implications for object permanence theories: A PDP model of the AB task. *Developmental Science, 1*, 161–184.

Nathanielsz, P.W. (1992). *Life before birth: The challenges of fetal development*. New York: Freeman.

Nelson, K. (1973). Structure and strategy in learning to talk. *Monographs of the Society for Research in Child Development, 38*.

Nelson, K. (1977). Facilitating children's syntax acquisition. *Developmental Psychology, 13*, 101–107.

Nelson, K. (1987). What's in a name? Reply to Seidenberg and Petitto. *Journal of Experimental Psychology (General), 116*, 293–296.

Nelson, K., & Lucariello, J. (1985). The development of meaning in first words. In M. Barrett (Ed.), *Children's single-word speech*. Chichester, UK: John Wiley.

Nelson, K.E., & Bonvillian, J.D. (1978). Early language development: Conceptual growth and related processes between 2 and 4.5 years. In K.E. Nelson (Ed.), *Children's language, Vol. 1.* New York: Gardner.

Nunes, T., & Bryant, P. (1991). Correspondencia: um esquema quantitativo basico [One-to-one correspondence as a basic quantitative scheme]. *Psicologia: Teoria e Pesquisa, 7*, 273–284.

Nunes, T., & Bryant, P. (1996). *Children doing mathematics*. Oxford, UK: Blackwell.

Oakhill, J., & Yuill, N. (1996). Higher order factors in comprehension disability: Processes and remediation. In C. Cornoldi & J. Oakhill (Eds.), *Reading comprehension difficulties: Processes and intervention*. Hillsdale, NJ: Lawrence Erlbaum Associates Inc.

O'Connell, B., & Bretherton, I. (1984). Toddlers' play alone and with mother: The role of maternal guidance. In I. Bretherton (Ed.), *Symbolic play: The development of social understanding*. London: Academic Press.

Oliner, S.P., & Oliner, P.M. (1988). *The altruistic personality: Rescuers of Jews in Nazi Europe*. New York: Free Press.

Oller, D.K. (1980). The emergence of speech sounds in infancy. In G.H. Yeni-Komshian, J.F. Kavanagh, & C.A. Ferguson (Eds.), *Child phonology: Vol. 1. Production*. New York: Academic Press.

Oller, D.K., & Eilers, R.E. (1988). The role of audition in infant babbling. *Child Development, 59*, 441–449.

Olweus, D. (1993). *Bullying at school: What we know and what we can do*. Oxford, UK: Blackwell.

Overton, W.F. (1998). Developmental psychology: Philosophy, concepts, and methodology. In R.M. Lerner (Ed.), *Handbook of child psychology:Vol. 1 Theoretical models of human development* (pp. 107–188, W. Damon, Gen. Ed.). New York: Wiley.

Papousek, H., & Papousek, M. (1989). Forms and functions of vocal matching in interactions between mothers and their precanonical infants. *First Language, 9,* 137–158.

Park, K.A., & Waters, E. (1989). Security of attachment and preschool friendships. *Child Development, 60,* 1076–1081.

Parker, J., & Gottman, J.M. (1989). Social and emotional development in relational context: Friendship interaction from early childhood to adolescence. In T.J. Berndt & G.W. Ladd (Eds.), *Peer relationships in child development* (pp. 95–131). New York: Wiley.

Perner, J. (1991). *Understanding the representational mind.* Cambridge, MA: MIT Press.

Perry, D.G., & Bussey, K. (1979). The social learning theory of sex differences: Imitation is alive and well. *Journal of Personality and Social Psychology, 37,* 1699–1712.

Perry, D.G., Kusel, S.J., & Perry, L.C. (1988). Victims of peer aggression. *Developmental Psychology, 24,* 807–814.

Perry, D.G., Perry, L., & Kennedy, E. (1992). Conflict and the development of antisocial behaviour. In C. Shantz & W.W. Hartup (Eds.), *Conflict in child and adolescent development.* New York: Cambridge University Press.

Perry, M., Van der Stoep, S.W., & Yu, S.L. (1993). Asking questions in first grade mathematics classes: Potential influences on mathematical thought. *Journal of Educational Psychology, 85,* 31–40.

Peterson, C.C., & Siegal, M. (1998). Changing focus on the representational mind: Deaf, autistic and normal children's concepts of false photos, false drawings and false beliefs. *British Journal of Developmental Psychology, 16,* 301–320.

Peterson, C.C., & Siegal, M. (2000). Insights into theory of mind from deafness and autism. *Mind and Language, 15,* 123–145

Piaget, J. (1926). *Judgment and reasoning in the child.* London: Kegan Paul. (Original work published 1924)

Piaget, J. (1926). *The language and thought of the child.* London: Kegan Paul. (Original work published 1923)

Piaget, J. (1932). *The moral judgment of the child.* New York: Harcourt Brace.

Piaget, J. (1952). *The origins of intelligence in children.* New York: Harcourt Brace. (Original work published in French 1936)

Piaget, J. (1954). *The construction of reality in the child.* New York: Basic Books. (Original work published in French 1937)

Piaget, J. (1962). *Play dreams and imitation in childhood.* New York: Norton. (Original work published 1945)

Piaget, J. (1971). *Biology and knowledge.* Edinburgh, UK: Edinburgh University Press.

Piaget, J. (1972). *Judgment and reasoning in the child.* Totowa, NJ: Littlefield Adams. (Original work published 1924)

Piaget, J. (1973). *The child's conception of the world.* London: Paladin Books. (Original work published 1929)

Piaget, J. (1976). *The grasp of consciousness.* Cambridge, MA: MIT Press.

Piaget, J., & Inhelder, B. (1956). *The child's conception of space.* London: Routledge & Kegan Paul.

Piaget, J., Inhelder, B., & Szeminska, A. (1960). *The child's conception of geometry.* London: Routledge & Kegan Paul. (Original work published in French 1948)

Piaget, J., & Szeminska, A. (1952). *The child's conception of number.* London: Routledge & Kegan Paul. (Original work published in French 1941)

Pike, A., & Plomin, R. (1999). Genetics and development. In D. Messer & S. Millar (Eds.), *Exploring developmental psychology* (pp. 3–23). London: Arnold.

Pinker, S. (1984). *Language learnability and language development.* Cambridge, MA: Harvard University Press.

Pinker, S. (1989). *Learnability and cognition: The acquisition of argument structure.* Cambridge, MA: MIT Press.

Pinker, S., Lebeaux, D.S., & Frost, L.A. (1987). Productivity and constraints in the acquisition of the passive. *Cognition, 26,* 195–267.

Plomin, R., Corley, R., De Fries, J.C., & Faulkner, D.W. (1990). Individual differences in television in early childhood: Nature as well as nurture. *Psychological Science, 1,* 31–37.

Plunkett, K., & Marchman, V. (1993). From rote learning to system building: Acquiring verb morphology in children and connectionist nets. *Cognition, 48,* 21–69.

Povinelli, D.J. (1995). The unduplicated self. In P. Rochat (Ed.), *The self in infancy: Theory and research* (pp. 161–192). Amsterdam, The

Netherlands: North-Holland/Elsevier Science Publishers.

Povinelli, D.J., Reaux, J.E., Bierschwale, D.T., Allain, A.D., & Simon, B.B. (1997). Exploitation of pointing as a referential gesture in young children, but not adolescent chimpanzees. *Cognitive Development, 12*, 327–365.

Premack, D. (1986). *Gavagai! or the future history of the animal language controversy.* Cambridge, MA: MIT Press.

Premack, D., & Woodruff, G. (1978). Does the chimpanzee have a theory of mind? *Behavioral and Brain Sciences, 1*, 515–526.

Previc, F.H. (1994). Assessing the legacy of the GBG model. *Brain and Cognition, 26*, 174–180.

Preyer, W. (1888). *The mind of the child* (Vols. 1 & 2). New York: Appleton. (Original work published 1882)

Pring, L. (1994). Touch and go—learning to read braille. *Reading Research Quarterly, 29*, 67–74.

Purves, D. (1994). *Neural activity and the growth of the brain.* Cambridge, UK: Cambridge University Press.

Rack, J.P., Snowling, M.J., & Olson, R. (1992). The nonword reading deficit in developmental dyslexia: A review. *Reading Research Quarterly, 27*, 29–53.

Rakic, P. (1987). Intrinsic and extrinsic determinants of neocortical parcellation: A radial unit model. In P. Rakic & W. Singer (Eds.), *Neurobiology of neocortex.* Chichester, UK: John Wiley & Sons.

Rakic, P. (1995). Corticogenesis in human and nonhuman primates. In M.S. Gazzaniga (Ed.), *The cognitive neurosciences* (pp. 127–145). Cambridge, MA: MIT Press.

Ramsay, D.S. (1980). Onset of unimanual handedness in infants. *Infant Behaviour and Development, 2*, 69–76.

Reissland, N. (1988). Neonatal imitation in the first hour of life—observations in rural Nepal. *Developmental Psychology, 24*, 464–469.

Rheingold, H.L., & Cook, K.V. (1975). The contents of boys' and girls' rooms as an index of parents' behaviour. *Child Development, 46*, 459–463.

Richards, D., Frentzen, B., Gerhardt, K., McCann, M., & Abrams, R. (1992). Sound levels in the human uterus. *Obstetrics and Gynaecology, 80*, 186–190.

Riley, M., Greeno, J.G., & Heller, J.I. (1983). Development of children's problem solving ability in arithmetic. In H. Ginsburg (Ed.), *The development of mathematical thinking.* New York: Academic Press.

Rogoff, B., & Waddell K.J. (1982). Memory for information organized in a scene by children from two cultures. *Child Development, 53*, 1224–1228.

Ronqvist, L., & Van Hoften, C. (1994). Neonatal finger and arm movement as determined by a social and an object context. *Early Development and Parenting, 3*, 81–94.

Rosenberg, K., & Trevathan, W. (1996). Bipedalism and human birth: The obstetrical dilemma revisited. *Evolutionary Anthropology, 5*.

Rousseau, J.-J. (1974). *Emile.* London: Dent. (Original work publishd 1762)

Rubel, E.W. (1985). Auditory system development. In G. Gottlieb & N.A. Krasnegor (Eds.), *Measurement of audition and vision in the first year of postnatal life* (pp. 53–90). Norwood, NJ: Ablex.

Rubin, K.H., Bukowski, W., & Parker, J.G. (1998). Peer interactions, relationships, and groups. In N. Eisenberg (Ed.), *Handbook of child psychology Vol. 3: Social, emotional, and personality development* (pp. 619–700, W. Damon, Gen. Ed.). New York: Wiley.

Rubin, K.H., Lynch, D., Coplan, R., Rose-Krasnor, L., & Booth, C.L. (1994). "Birds of a feather…": Behavioral concordances and preferential personal attraction in children. *Child Development, 65*, 1778–1785.

Ruffman, T., Perner, J., Naito, M., Parkin, L., & Clements, W.A. (1998). Older (but not younger) siblings facilitate false belief understanding. *Developmental Psychology, 34*, 161–174

Rumelhart, D.E., & McClelland, J.L. (1986). On learning the past tense of English verbs. In D.E. Rumelhart & J.L. McClelland (Eds.), *Parallel distributed processing: Exploring the microstructure of cognition: Vol. 1. Foundations.* Cambridge, MA: MIT Press.

Russell, J. (1978). *The acquisition of knowledge.* London: Macmillan.

Russell, J., Mauthner, N., Sharpe, S., & Tidswell, T. (1991). The "windows task" as a measure of strategic deception in preschoolers and autistic subjects. *British Journal of Developmental Psychology, 9*, 331–349.

Rutter, M., & Quinton, B. (1984). Parental psychiatric disorder: Effects on children. *Psychological Medicine, 40*, 853–880.

Rutter, M., & Rutter, M. (1992). *Developing minds: Challenge and continuity across the lifespan.* Harmondsworth, UK: Penguin.

Saarni, C. (1984). An observational study of children's attempts to monitor their expressive behavior. *Child Development, 55*, 1504–1513.

Saarni, C., Mumme, D.L., & Campos, J.L. (1998). Emotional development: Action, communication and understanding. In N. Eisenberg (Ed.), *Handbook of child psychology: Vol. 3. Social, emotional, and personality development* (pp. 237–309, W. Damon, Gen. Ed.). New York: Wiley.

Sakamoto, T., & Makita, K. (1973). Japan. In J. Downing (Ed.), *Comparative reading*. New York: Macmillan.

Savage-Rumbaugh, E.S. (1986). *Ape language: From conditioned responses to symbols*. New York: Columbia University Press.

Savage-Rumbaugh, E.S. (1987). Communication, symbolic communication and language: Reply to Seidenberg and Petitto. *Journal of Experimental Psychology (General), 116*, 288–292.

Savage-Rumbaugh, E.S., & Lewin, R. (1994). *Kanzi: The ape at the brink of the human mind*. New York: John Wiley & Sons Inc.

Savage-Rumbaugh, E.S., McDonald, K., Sevcik, R.A., Hopkins, W.D., & Rupert, E. (1986). Spontaneous symbol acquisition and communicative use by pygmy chimpanzees (*Pan paniscus*). *Journal of Experimental Psychology (General), 115*, 211–235.

Savage-Rumbaugh, E.S., Murphy, J., Sevcik, R.A., Brakke, K.E., Williams, S.L., & Rumbaugh, D.M. (1993). Language comprehension in ape and child. *Monographs of the Society for Research in Child Development, 58*(3 & 4, Serial No. 233).

Savage-Rumbaugh, E.S., & Rumbaugh, D.M. (1993). The emergence of language. In K.R. Gibson & T. Ingold (Eds.), *Tools, language, and cognition in human evolution*. Cambridge, UK: Cambridge University Press.

Saxe, G.B. (1981). Body parts as numerals: A developmental analysis of numeration among the Oksapmin in Papua New Guinea. *Child Development, 52*, 306–316.

Saxen, L., & Rapola, J. (1969). *Congenital defects*. New York: Holt, Rinehart & Winston.

Saxton, M. (2000). Negative evidence and negative feedback. *First Language, 20*, 221–251.

Saxton, M., Kulcsar, B., Marshall, G., & Rupra, M. (1988). Longer-term effects of corrective input: An experimental approach. *Journal of Child Language, 25*, 701–721.

Schaffer, R. (1984). *The child's entry into the social world*. London: Academic Press.

Schaie, K.W. (1990). Developmental design revisited. In H.W. Reese & S.H. Cohen (Eds.), *Life span developmental psychology: Methodological issues*. Hillsdale, NJ: Lawrence Erlbaum Associates Inc.

Schiff, W. (1986). *Perception: An applied approach*. Acton, MA: Copley.

Schliemann, A.L., & Nunes, T. (1990). A situated schema of proportionality. *British Journal of Developmental Psychology, 8*, 259–268.

Scholfield, P.J. (1994). Writing and spelling: The view from linguistics. In G.D.A. Brown & N.C. Ellis (Eds.), *Handbook of spelling*. Chichester, UK: Wiley.

Seidenberg, M.S., & Petitto, L. (1987). Communication, symbolic communication and language: Comment on Savage-Rumbaugh et al. *Journal of Experimental Psychology (General), 116*, 279–287.

Selfe, L. (1983). *Normal and anomalous representational drawing ability in children*. London: Academic Press.

Selfe, L. (1995). Nadia reconsidered. In C. Golomb (Ed.), *The development of artistically gifted children: Selected case studies* (pp. 197–236). Hillsdale, NJ: Lawrence Erlbaum Associates Inc.

Selman, R.L., & Schutz, L.H. (1990). *Making a friend in youth: Developmental theory and pair therapy* Chicago: University of Chicago Press.

Seymour, P.K., & Elder, L. (1986). Beginning reading without phonology. *Cognitive Neuropsychology, 3*, 1–36.

Shaklee, H., Holt, P., Elek, S., & Hall, L. (1988). Covariation judgement: Improving rule use among children, adolescents, and adults. *Child Development, 59*, 755–768.

Shatz, K. (1992). Dividing up the neocortex. *Science, 258*, 237–238.

Shweder, R.A. (1990). Cultural psychology: What is it? In J.W. Stigler, R.A. Shweder, & G. Herdt (Eds.), *Cultural psychology* (pp. 1–45). Cambridge, UK: Cambridge University Press.

Siegal, M. (1988). Children's knowledge of contagion and communcation in causes of illness. *Child Development, 59*, 1353–1359.

Siegal, M. (1997). *Knowing children: Experiments in conversation and cognition* (2nd ed.). Hove, UK: Psychology Press.

Siegler, R.S. (1976). Three aspects of cognitive development. *Cognitive Psychology, 8*, 481–520.

Siegler, R.S. (1981). Developmental sequences within and between concepts. *Monographs of the Society for Research in Child Development, 46* (Whole No. 2).

Siegler, R.S. (1992). The other Alfred Binet. *Developmental Psychology, 28*, 179–190.

Siegler, R.S. (1995). How does change occur: A microgenetic study of number conservation. *Cognitive Psychology, 28*, 225–273.

Siegler, R.S. (1996). *Emerging minds: The process of change in children's thinking*. Oxford, UK: Oxford University Press.

Siegler, R.S. (1998). *Children's thinking* (3rd ed.). Upper Saddle River, NJ: Prentice-Hall.

Sigman, M., & Ungerer, J.A. (1984). Attachment behaviour in autistic children. *Journal of Autism and Developmental Disorders, 14*, 231–244.

Silk, A.M.J., & Thomas, G.V. (1986). Development and differentiation in children's figure drawings. *British Journal of Psychology, 77*, 399–410.

Simion, F., Valenza, E., & Umiltà, C. (1997). Mechanisms underlying face preference at birth. In F. Simion & G. Butterworth (Eds.), *The development of sensory, motor and cognitive capacities in early infancy* (pp. 87–101). Hove, UK: Psychology Press.

Sinclair, A. (1988). La notation numerique chez l'enfant. In H. Sinclair (Ed.), *La production de notations chez le jeune enfant: Langage, nombre, rhymes et melodies*. Paris: Presses Universitaires de France.

Sinclair, D. (1978). *Human growth after birth* (3rd ed.). Oxford, UK: Oxford University Press.

Singh, J.A.L., & Zingg, R.M. (1939). *Wolf-children and feral man*. New York: Harper & Brothers Publishers.

Slade, A. (1987). A longitudinal study of maternal involvement and symbolic play during the toddler period. *Child Development, 58*, 367–375.

Slater, A. (1985). Visual memory and perception in early infancy. In A. Slater & G. Bremner (Eds.), *Infant development*. Hove, UK: Psychology Press.

Smith, L. (1987). A constructivist interpretation of formal operations. *Human Development, 30*, 341–354.

Smith, L.B. (1999). Not "either", not "or", not "both". *Developmental Science, 2*, 162–163.

Smith, P., & Lloyd, B. (1978). Maternal behaviour and perceived sex of infant: Revisited. *Child Development, 49*, 1263–1265.

Snow, C.E. (1977). Mothers' speech research: From input to interaction. In C.E. Snow & C.A. Ferguson (Eds.), *Talking to children: Language input and acquisition*. Cambridge, UK: Cambridge University Press.

Snow, C.E. (1989). Understanding social interaction and language acquisition: Sentences are not enough. In M.H. Bornstein & J.S. Bruner (Eds.), *Interaction in human development*. Hillsdale, NJ: Lawrence Erlbaum Associates Inc.

Snowling, M.J. (2000). *Dyslexia* (2nd ed) Oxford, UK: Blackwell.

Sophian, C. (1998). A developmental perspective in children's counting. In C. Donlan (Ed.), *The development of mathematical skills*. Hove, UK: Psychology Press.

Spelke, E., & Cortelyou, A. (1981). Perceptual aspects of social knowing: Looking and listening in infancy. In M.E. Lamb & L.R. Sherrod (Eds.), *Infant social cognition*. Hillsdale, NJ: Lawrence Erlbaum Associates Inc.

Spelke, E., & Owsley, C.J. (1979). Intermodal exploration and knowledge in infancy. *Infant Behaviour and Development, 2*, 13–24.

Spelke, E., Vishton, P., & Von Hofsten, C. (1995). Object perception, object-directed action, and physical knowledge in infancy. In M.S. Gazzaniga (Ed.), *The cognitive neurosciences* (pp. 165–179). Cambridge, MA: MIT Press.

Spelke, E.S. (1999). Innateness, learning and the development of object representation. *Developmental Science, 2*, 145–148.

Spencer, H. (1886). *A system of synthetic philosophy: Vol. 1. First principles* (4th ed.). New York: Appleton.

Stackhouse, J. (2000). Barriers to literacy development in children with speech and language difficulties. In D.V.M. Bishop & L.B. Leonard (Eds.), *Speech and language impairments in children: Causes, characteristics, intervention, and outcome*. Hove, UK: Psychology Press.

Stark, R.W. (1980). Stages of speech development in the first year of life. In G.H. Yeni-Komshian, J.F. Kavanagh, & C.A. Ferguson (Eds.), *Child phonology: Vol. 1. Production*. New York: Academic Press.

Starkey, P., & Cooper, R.G. (1995). The development of subitizing in young children. *British Journal of Developmental Psychology, 13*, 399–420.

Starkey, P., Spelke, E., & Gelman, R. (1983). Detection of intermodal numerical correspondences by human infants. *Science, 222*, 179–181.

Steiner, J. (1979). Human facial expression in response to taste and smell stimulation. In H. Reese & L.P. Lipsitt (Eds.), *Advances in child development and behaviour* (Vol. 13, pp. 257–295). New York: Academic Press.

Stern, D. (1985). *The interpersonal world of the infant*. New York: Basic Books.

Stevenson, H.W., Lee, S., Chen, C., Stigler, J.W., Hsu, C.C., & Kitamura, S. (1990). Contexts of achievement: A study of American, Chinese, and Japanese children. *Monographs of the Society for Research in Child Development, 55*, 12.

Stuart, M., & Coltheart, M. (1988). Does reading develop in a sequence of stages? *Cognition, 30,* 139–181.

Stuart, M., & Masterson, J. (1992). Patterns of reading and spelling in 10-year-old children related to pre-reading phonological abilities. *Journal of Experimental Child Psychology, 54*(2), 168–187.

Subbotsky, E. (1994). Early rationality and magical thinking in preschoolers: Space and time. *British Journal of Developmental Psychology, 12,* 97–108.

Super, C.M. (1976). Environmental effects on motor development: A case of African infant precocity. *Developmental Medicine and Child Neurology, 18,* 561–567.

Surber, C.F., & Gzesh, S.M. (1984). Reversible operations in the balance scale task. *Journal of Experimental Child Psychology, 38,* 254–274.

Tanner, J.M. (1978). *Foetus into man.* London: Open Books.

Tardif, T. (1996). Nouns are not always learned before verbs: Evidence from Mandarin speakers' early vocabularies. *Developmental Psychology, 32,* 492–504.

Teasley, S.D., & Parker, J.G. (1995). *The effects of gender, friendship and popularity on the targets and topics of preadolescents' gossip.* Paper presented at the biennial meeting of the Society for Research in Child Development, Indianapolis, IN.

Terrace, H.S. (1979). *Nim.* New York: Alfred A. Knopf.

Terrace, H.S. (1985). In the beginning was the "name". *American Psychologist, 40,* 1011–1028.

Thelen, E. (1984). Learning to walk: Ecological demands and phylogenetic constraints. In L.P Lipsitt & C.K. Rovee-Collier (Eds.), *Advances in infancy research, Vol. 3.* Norwood, NJ: Ablex.

Thelen, E. (1989). Self organization in developmental processes. In M. Gunnar & E. Thelen (Eds.), *Systems and development: The Minnesota symposia in child psychology.* Hillsdale, NJ: Lawrence Erlbaum Associates Inc.

Thelen, E., & Smith, L.B. (1994). *A dynamic systems approach to the development of cognition and action.* Cambridge, MA: MIT Press.

Thines, G., Costall, A., & Butterworth, G.E. (1990). *Michotte's experimental phenomenology of perception.* Hillsdale, NJ: Lawrence Erlbaum Associates Inc.

Thomas, G.V. (1995). The role of drawing strategies and skills. In C. Lange-Kuttner & G.V. Thomas, (Eds.), *Drawing and looking.* Hemel Hempstead, UK: Harvester.

Thomas, G.V., & Silk, A.M.J. (1990). *An introduction to the psychology of children's drawings.* Hemel Hempstead, UK: Harvester Wheatsheaf.

Thomas, G.V., & Tsalimi, A. (1988). Effects of order of drawing head and trunk on their relative sizes in children's human figure drawings. *British Journal of Developmental Psychology, 6,* 191–203.

Thorkildsen, T.A. (1989). Justice in the classroom: The student's view. *Child Development, 60,* 323–334.

Thorstad, G. (1991). The effect of orthography on the acquisition of literacy skills. *British Journal of Psychology, 82,* 527–537.

Tizard, B., & Hodges, J. (1978). The effect of early institutional rearing on the development of 8 year old children. *Journal of Child Psychology and Psychiatry, 16,* 61–73.

Todo, S., Fogel, A., & Kawai, M. (1990). Maternal speech to three-month-old infants in the United States and Japan. *Journal of Child Language, 17,* 279–294.

Towse, J.N., & Saxton, M. (1998). Mathematics across national boundaries: Cultural and linguistic perspectives on numerical competence. In C. Donlan (Ed.), *The development of mathematical skills* (pp. 129–150). Hove, UK: Psychology Press.

Trehub, S.E. (1976). The discrimination of foreign speech contrasts by infants and adults. *Speech Development, 13,* 466–472.

Trevarthen, C., Kokkinaki, T., & Fiamenghi, G.A., Jr. (1999). What infants' imitations communicate with mothers, fathers and peers. In J. Nadel & G.E. Butterworth (Eds.), *Imitation in infancy* (pp. 127–185). Cambridge, UK: Cambridge University Press.

Turiel, E. (1993). *The development of social knowledge: Morality and convention.* Cambridge, UK: Cambridge University Press.

Turiel, E. (1998). The development of morality. In N. Eisenberg (Ed.), *Handbook of child psychology: Vol. 3. Social, emotional, and personality development* (pp. 863–932, W. Damon, Gen. Ed.). New York: Wiley.

Turner, P. J. (1991). Relations between attachment, gender and behaviour with peers in pre-school. *Child Development, 62,* 1475–1488.

Valsiner, J. (1988). *Developmental psychology in the Soviet Union.* Brighton, UK: Harvester.

van Geert, P. (1991). A dynamic systems model of cognitive and language growth. *Psychological Review, 98,* 3–53.

van Geert, P. (1993). A dynamic systems model of cognitive growth: Competition and support under limited resource conditions. In L.B. Smith & E. Thelen (Eds.), *A dynamic systems approach to development: Applications*. Cambridge, MA: MIT Press.

van Geert, P. (1998). We almost had a great future behind us: The contribution of non-linear dynamics to developmental science in the making. *Developmental Science, 1*, 143–159.

van Ijzendoorn, M.H. (1995a). Of the way we are: On temperament, attachment, and the transmission gap. A rejoinder to Fox. *Psychological Bulletin, 113*, 411–415.

van Ijzendoorn, M.H. (1995b). The association between adult attachment representations and infant attachment, parental responsiveness and clinical status. A meta-analysis on the predictive validity of the Adult Attachment Interview. *Psychological Bulletin, 113*, 404–410.

van Lieshout, C.F M., & Doise, W. (1998). Social development. In A. Demtriou, W. Doise, & C. van Lieshout (Eds.), *Life-span developmental psychology*. New York: John Wiley & Sons.

Vihman, M.M. (1992). Early syllables and the construction of phonology. In C.A. Ferguson, L. Menn, & C. Stoel-Gammon (Eds.), *Phonological development: Models, research, implications*. Timonium, MD: New York Press.

Vinter, A. (1986). The role of movement in eliciting early imitation. *Child Development, 57*, 66–71.

Von Hofsten, C. (1980). Predictive reaching for moving objects by human infants. *Journal of Experimental Child Psychology, 30*, 369–382.

Von Hofsten, C. (1983). Foundations for perceptual development. In L.P. Lipsitt & C.K. Rovee-Collier (Eds.), *Advances in infancy research, Vol. 2*. Norwood, NJ: Ablex.

Von Hofsten, C., Feng, Q., & Spelke, E.S. (2000). Object representation and predictive action in infancy. *Developmental Science, 3*, 193–205.

Vygotsky, L.S. (1962). *Thought and language*. Boston: MIT Press.

Vygotsky, L.S. (1971). *The psychology of art*. Boston: MIT Press.

Vygotsky, L.S. (1976). Play and its role in the mental development of the child. In J.S. Bruner, A. Jolly, & K. Sylva (Eds.), *Play*. Harmondsworth, UK: Penguin. (Original work published 1933)

Vygotsky, L.S. (1987). Thinking and speech. In N. Minick (Trans.), *The collected works of L.S. Vygotsky: Vol. 1. Problems of general psychology*. New York: Plenum Press. (Original work published 1934)

Vygotsky, L.S. (1988). The genesis of higher mental functions. In J.V. Wertsch (Ed.), *The concept of activity in Soviet psychology* (pp. 144–188). New York: Sharpe. (Original work published 1981)

Waddington, C.H. (1957). *The strategy of the genes*. London: Allen & Unwin.

Walker, L.J., de Vries, B., & Trevethen, S.D. (1987). Moral stages and moral orientations in real-life and hypothetical dilemmas. *Child Development, 58*, 842–858.

Wallman, J. (1979). A minimal visual restriction experiment: Preventing chicks from seeing their feet affects later responses to mealworms. *Developmental Psychobiology, 12*, 391–397.

Waters, G.S., & Doehring, D.G. (1990). Reading acquisition in congenitally deaf children who communicate orally: Insights from an analysis of component reading, language and memory skills. In T.H. Carr & B.A. Levy (Eds.), *Reading and its development* (pp. 323–373). San Diego: Academic Press.

Watson, J.B. (1919). *Psychology from the standpoint of a behaviorist*. Philadelphia: J.B. Lippincott.

Watson, J.B. (1930). *Behaviourism*. New York: W.W. Norton.

Watson, J.B., & Rayner, R. (1920). Conditioned emotional reactions. *Journal of Experimental Psychology, 3*, 1–14.

Watson, M.W., & Fischer, K.M. (1977). A developmental sequence of agent use in late infancy. *Child Development, 43*, 826–836.

Wellman, H.M., Cross, D., & Bartsch, K. (1986). Infant search and object permanence: A meta analysis of the A not B error. *Monographs of the Society for Research in Child Development, 51*, v–50.

Wellman, H.M., & Gelman, S.A. (1998). Knowledge acquisition in foundational domains. In D. Kuhn & R.S. Siegler (Eds.), *Handbook of child psychology: Vol. 2. Cognition, perception, and language* (pp. 523–557, W. Damon, Gen. Ed.). New York: Wiley.

Werker, J.F., Gilbert, J.H.V., Humphreys, G.W., & Tees, R.C. (1981). Developmental aspects of cross-language speech perception. *Child Development, 52*, 349–355.

Werker, J.F., & Tees, R.C. (1984). Cross-language speech perception: Evidence for perceptual reorganization during the first year of life. *Infant Behavior and Development, 7*, 49–63.

Wertheimer, M. (1961). Psychomotor coordination of auditory and visual space at birth. *Science, 134*, 1692.

Wertsch, J.V. (1991). *Voices of the mind: A sociocultural approach to mediated action.* Cambridge, MA: Harvard University Press.

Whalen, D.H., Levitt, A.G., & Wang, Q. (1991). Intonational differences between the reduplicative babbling of French- and English-learning infants. *Journal of Child Language, 18,* 501–516.

White, B.L., Castle, P., & Held, R. (1964). Observations on the development of visually directed reaching. *Child Development, 35,* 349–364.

Will, J.A., Self, P.A., & Datan, N. (1976). Maternal behaviour and perceived sex of infant. *American Journal of Orthopsychiatry, 46,* 135–139.

Willatts, P. (1985). Development of problem-solving in infancy. In A. Slater & G. Bremner (Eds.), *Infant development.* Hove, UK: Psychology Press.

Willatts, P. (1990). Development of problem-solving strategies in infancy. In D.F. Bjorklund (Ed.), *Children's strategies: Contemporary views of cognitive development.* Hillsdale, NJ: Lawrence Erlbaum Associates Inc.

Wilson, B., & Ligtvoet, J. (1992). Across time and cultures: Stylistic changes in the drawings of Dutch children. In D. Thistlewood (Ed.), *Drawing research and development.* London: Longman.

Wilson, B., & Wilson, M. (1984). An iconoclastic view of the imagery sources in the drawings of young people. *Art Education, 30,* 5–11.

Wimmer, H., & Hummer, P. (1990). How German first graders read and spell: Doubts on the importance of the logographic stage. *Applied Psycholinguistics, 11,* 349–368.

Wimmer, H., Landerl, K., & Frith, U. (1999). Learning to read German. In M. Harris & G. Hatano (Eds.), *Learning to read and write: A cross-linguistic perspective* (pp. 34–50). Cambridge, UK: Cambridge University Press.

Wimmer, H., Landerl, K., Linortner, R., & Hummer, P. (1991). The relationship of phonemic awareness to reading acquisition: More consequence than precondition but still important. *Cognition, 40,* 219–249.

Wimmer, H., Landerl, K., & Schneider, W. (1994). The role of rhyme awareness in learning to read a regular orthography. *British Journal of Developmental Psychology, 12,* 429–484.

Wimmer, H., & Perner, J. (1983). Beliefs about beliefs: Representation and constraining functions of wrong beliefs in young children's understanding of deception. *Cognition, 13,* 103–128.

Winnicot, D. (1971). *Playing and reality.* New York: Basic Books.

Wolke, D., & Meyer, R. (1999). Cognitive status, language attainment, and prereading skills of 6-year-old very preterm children and their peers: The Bavarian Longitudinal Study. *Developmental Medicine and Child Neurology, 41,* 94–109.

Woods, S.S., Resnick, L.B., & Groen, G.J. (1975). An experimental test of five process models for subtraction. *Journal of Educational Psychology, 67,* 17–21.

Woolley, J.D., & Phelps, K.E. (1994). Young children's practical reasoning about imagination. *British Journal of Developmental Psychology, 12,* 53–67.

Woolley, J.D., & Wellman, H.M. (1993). Origin and truth: Young children's understanding of imaginary mental representations. *Child Development, 64,* 1–17.

Wordsworth, W. (1807). Ode: Intimations of immortality. In *Poems in two volumes.*

Wynn, K. (1992a). The origins of numerical knowledge. *Mind and Language, 7,* 315–332.

Wynn, K. (1992b). Addition and subtraction by human infants. *Nature, 358,* 749–750.

Yarrow, L.J., Rubenstein, J.L., & Pedersen, F.A. (1975). *Infant and environment: Early cognitive and motivational development.* New York: Wiley.

Zaitchik, D. (1990). When representations conflict with reality: The preschooler's problem with false beliefs and "false" photographs. *Cognition, 35,* 41–68.

Zelaso, N.A., Zelaso, P.R., Cohen, K., & Zelaso, P.D. (1993). Specificity of practice effects on elementary neuro-motor patterns. *Developmental Psychology, 29,* 686–691.

Zelaso, P.R. (1984). Learning to walk: Recognition of higher order influences? In L.P. Lipsitt & C.K. Rovee-Collier (Eds.), *Advances in infancy research, Vol. 3.* Norwood, NJ: Ablex.

Zelaso, P.R., Zelaso, N.A., & Kolb, S. (1972). Walking in the newborn. *Science, 177,* 1058–1059.

Glossary

Accommodation: The modification of a previous scheme, or creation of a new one, when required.

Active intermodal matching hypothesis (AIM): Hypothesis relating to the matching information from different senses to a single perception.

Alphabetic strategy: Reading by recognition of individual letters.

Animism: The attribution of feelings to non-living things.

Apgar scale: Used to assess the basic physical condition of the newborn child immediately after birth.

Appearance question: A question concerning what something appears to be.

Assimilation: Process by which new information is "taken in" and incorporated into existing schemas.

Attachment: The forming of a close emotional bond, particularly between mother and baby.

Autism: Childhood autism is a rare developmental disorder, often manifest before the second year of life, which involves a profound failure in social, linguistic, and imaginative development.

Babbling: The meaningless vocalising of babies; includes speech-like vowel and consonant sounds.

Backpropagation: In a c-net, one method of altering the connections between nodes during the learning process. Achieved by adjusting the weights of connections backwards after each trial.

Behaviourism: An approach in psychology, defining it as the study of behaviour, and focusing objectively on observable actions. Reference to internal mental activity is rejected.

Binet–Simon scale: The first intelligence test developed by Alfred Binet, which contained a series of tasks of increasing difficulty. Performance on the scale could be compared with age norms to determine mental age.

Brazleton scale: Used to assess the neonatal neurological condition.

Broca's area: The region of the cerebral cortex concerned with speech production. Named after Paul Broca.

C-net: Abbreviation of connectionist network.

Cardinality: When counting the final number reached is the total.

CDI: Communicative development inventories, developed by MacArthur, and comprising the infant and toddler scales.

Choice algorithm: Early strategy for simple subtraction involving counting the number of steps between the two numbers, either up or down.

Classification: Understanding the hierarchical sequence of objects by grouping them in classes and subclasses.

Clinical methods: A research method in which questions are tailored to the individual, with each question depending on the answer to the previous one. Often used to assess mentally ill patients.

Cohort: A statistical term for a group of people with something in common, usually having been born in the same year, in which case their development can be said to have occurred under similar social and historical conditions, with shared experiences.

Competition model: Bates and MacWhinney's explanation of language development as originating from general cognitive mechanisms rather than from social interaction.

Concrete operational stage: Piaget's third developmental stage in which children begin to use logical rules to solve problems. They can deal with more than one salient feature of a problem at a time and are no longer dominated by appearance. However, they are not yet able to deal with abstract problems. This stage lasts from the ages of six or seven to eleven or twelve.

Concurrent vocalisation: Repetition of a syllable at the same time as reading.

Connectionist models: Models of learning implemented on a computer in which there are many inter-connected nodes.

Conservation tasks: Tests designed to see whether the child understands that some properties of an object or substance remain fundamentally the same even when there are external changes in shape or arrangement.

Conspec mechanism: Information about the structure of faces that babies possess at birth.

Context-bound words: Mid-1980s view that first words are only produced in one specific situation or context.

Contextually flexible words: More recent view that first words are used in more than one behavioural context.

Conventional level: The second level of moral development, where the intentions of the actor define the moral position, and social rules are taken into account.

Counting all strategy: Early strategy for simple addition involving the counting of all the items in both sets.

Counting on strategy: Early strategy for simple addition involving counting the second set by starting from the total of the first set.

Cross-sectional studies: A research design in which children of various ages are studied at the same time.

Developmental dyslexia: A syndrome causing problems with learning to read and spell, despite normal intelligence. Also known as word blindness.

Egocentrism: To consider the world entirely from one's own point of view.

Embryonic stage: The second stage of embryonic development, from two to seven weeks, during which the major organs and limbs are formed.

Enactive representation: Acting out how to do things.

Epigenetic landscape: Waddington's metaphor for the development process by which new forms emerge through the interactions of the preceding form and its environment.

Equifinality: The principle that variations in development route and speed nevertheless result in the same end.

Equilibration: Using the processes of accommodation and assimilation to produce a state of equilibrium between existing schemas and new experiences.

Ethology: The study of behaviour of animals in their normal environment.

Expressive style: Style of early language development—more action words and people's names in early vocabulary.

False belief task: A test to see whether a child will act on a knowingly incorrect belief, or be aware that a second person who is not in possession of a certain piece of information may act "incorrectly".

Foetal alcohol syndrome: A pattern of physical and mental abnormalities found in babies whose mothers were heavy drinkers during pregnancy.

Foetal stage: The third stage of embryonic development, from eight weeks to birth, encompassing the remainder of prenatal development.

Formal operational stage: The final stage in Piaget's theory, from 11 or 12 onwards, in which the child becomes able to consider all possible combinations in relation to the whole problem and to reason about an entirely hypothetical situation.

Fortuitous realism: Once a drawing is complete, the child decides the subject it depicts.

Gender identity: The first step in self concept development, in which the child labels him- or herself correctly, and starts to categorise others accurately as male or female.

Genetic epistemology: The critical study of the validity, methods, and scope of genetics.

Genotype: The pattern of genes that an individual possesses.

Germinal stage: The first stage of embryonic development, from conception to implantation in the wall of the uterus at about two weeks.

Grapheme: Symbols such as letters that serve to distinguish words; usually represent phonemes.

Habituation: An automatic process in which attention to novelty decreases with repeated exposure.

Habituation method: Method used to assess abilities of infants in which a stimulus is presented repeatedly until the infant's attention decreases significantly. Then a novel stimulus is presented and the increase in attention is measured.

Hierarchical integration: The use of memory to deal with three objects at a time, one in each hand, and one "stored" elsewhere.

Iconic knowledge: Visualising how to do things.

Intellectual realism: The symbolic representation of an object in a drawing.

Intelligence quotient (IQ): The ratio of mental age, defined by an intelligence test, to chronological age, with a score of 100 representing "average IQ".

Intelligence tests: Measures of intellectual ability, such as the IQ, Binet–Simon, or Stanford–Binet tests.

Irregular words: Words that contain at least one grapheme that does not follow the standard pronunciation.

Joint attention: An aspect of early communication—a mother and her child both looking at the same object.

Linear dynamics: Smooth interactions with the environment.

Logographic strategy: Reading by recognition of whole words.

Longitudinal studies: A research design in which data are gathered from the same individuals over a period of time.

Maturation: A sequence of physical growth characteristics, strongly influenced by genetic inheritance, that unfold as individuals grow older; common to all members of a species.

Mean length of utterance: The MLU is a measurement in morphemes of the average length of utterance.

Metacognition: Our ability to think about our own thought processes; the knowledge of what and how we know.

Morphology: The form and structure of words in a language, especially the consistent patterns that may be observed and classified.

Non-linear dynamics: Sudden change in a discontinuous step or U-shaped pattern.

Numeration: Understanding the sequence of numbering.

Object permanence: The understanding that objects have substance, maintain their identities when they change location, and ordinarily continue to exist when out of sight.

Objective: Public knowledge; true.

Observation: A naturalistic method of data collection, using diary records and observation in the natural environment, or standardised conditions in a laboratory.

One-to-one correspondence: Counting each object only once.

Ontogeny: The development of an individual organism during its lifetime.

Orthographic regularity: A consistent relationship between the sounds of a language and the method of writing them down.

Orthographic strategy: Reading by recognition of groups of letters, or orthographic units.

Orthography: The system of writing.

Overregularisation errors: The tendency to apply grammatical rules in situations that should be exceptions to those rules.

Phenotype: The set of an individual's observable characteristics.

Phonemes: The smallest sound categories in speech in any given language that serve to distinguish one word from another.

Phonemic awareness: The ability to detect and manipulate phonemes within words.

Phonology: The sound system of language.

Phylogeny: The evolutionary history of a species.

Place holder: The use of zero to mark the column value, even though the column is empty.

Place value: The convention of each column in numbers representing certain values, i.e. units, tens, hundreds, etc.

Postconventional level: The third, adult, level of moral development, where moral principles define the goodness or otherwise of actions.

Preconventional level: The first level of moral development, where first the outcome defines whether an action was good or bad, and second the action is considered good if the child's needs have been met.

Preformationism: The now discredited theory of development that all essential properties of an individual are preset at birth.

Preoperational stage: Piaget's second stage of cognitive development involving internalisation of forms of actions that the infant has already mastered. The key feature of this stage, which lasts from two to six or seven years, is that the child is able to focus only on one salient feature of a problem at a time and is dominated by the immediate appearance of things.

Prosocial behaviour: Altruistic behaviours such as sharing, helping, caregiving, and showing compassion.

Qualititative changes: Distinctions based on how degrees of change are expressed.

Reality question: A question concerning what something really is.

Recapitulationism: The now discredited theory of development claiming that, during the embryonic period, an organism passes through the adult forms of species from which it has evolved.

Reference: Human infants are unique in their understanding that pointing refers to an object, which occurs for the first time at around a year old.

Referential style: Style of early language development—more object names in early vocabulary.

Regular words: Words that follow the standard pro-nunciation.

Reputational salience: Aspects of behaviour or belief (such as academic achievement, religion, or sexual behaviour) that contribute to a person's reputation and standing within a peer group.

Retrieval of number facts: Counting by recalling the results of previous additions.

Reversibility: The child has an understanding that actions can be reversed.

Sensorimotor stage: Piaget's first stage in the process of adaptation, from birth to about two years, in which infants co-ordinate sensory perceptions and motor abilities to acquire knowledge of the world.

Seriation: Understanding spatial and temporal sequences.

Social cognition: The focus on children's understanding of social relationships.

Social learning theory: The view that behaviour can be explained in terms of both direct and indirect reinforcement.

Social referencing: The gauging of others' emotional reactions before deciding one's own reaction.

Stable order: Counting using the standard number sequence.

Stanford–Binet test: The best-known US intelligence test. A revision of the Binet–Simon scale.

Strabismus: Another name for squint; caused by paralysis of an eye muscle.

Strange situation test: Used in attachment studies. The child is observed first with the mother, next with a stranger, then alone, and finally when reunited with stranger and mother.

Subitise: To perceive the number of a group of items at a glance and without counting.

Subjective: Private or personal knowledge.

Syllabic awareness: The ability to analyse the sounds within words.

Syllogistic reasoning: The inference of a logical conclusion from two premises.

Symbolic knowledge: Knowledge that is represented using symbols such as speech, writing, or mathematics.

Symbolic play: Piaget believed that symbolic play, where one object stands for another, serves as a rehearsal for real life in the imagination; he developed a three-stage theory of symbolic play.

Syntax: The grammatical arrangement of words or morphemes in the sentences of a language.

Texture gradients: The different gradings of the patterns of surface texture preserved in the image that falls on the retina, indicating relative distances of objects from the observer.

Theory of mind: The ability to think about other people's mental states and form theories of how they think.

Tonic neck reflex (TNR): A baby's first postural reflex, in which the arm and leg extend on the side to which the head is turned, with the arm and leg on the other side being flexed; evident at 28 weeks after conception up to eight months after birth.

Transformational change: Change in form or ability.

Transitive inference: Understanding the relation between objects.

Variational change: The degree that a change varies from the assumed standard.

Visual realism: Depicting 3D reality in a 2D drawing.

Visually elicited reaching: An infant's preprogrammed reaching towards an interesting object.

Wernicke's area: The region of the cerebral cortex concerned with speech comprehension. Named after Carl Wernicke.

Zone of proximal development (ZPD): The gap between capacities that are being developed and those that are not as yet functioning fully.

Author index

Subject index

Entries in **bold** indicate key term definitions

Acknowledgement

The photographs on pages x, 52, 56, 67, 139, 156, 159, 217 and the illustrations on page 204, are reproduced with the kind permission of Margaret Harris.